studies in jazz

Institute of Jazz Studies, Rutgers University
General Editors: *Dan Morgenstern & Edward Berger*

1. BENNY CARTER: A Life in American Music, *by Morroe Berger, Edward Berger, and James Patrick*
2. ART TATUM: A Guide to His Recorded Music, *by Arnold Laubich and Ray Spencer*
3. ERROLL GARNER: The Most Happy Piano, *by James M. Doran*
4. JAMES P. JOHNSON: A Case of Mistaken Identity, *by Scott E. Brown;* Discography, *by Robert Hilbert*
5. PEE WEE ERWIN: This Horn for Hire, *by Warren W. Vaché, Sr.*
6. BENNY GOODMAN: Listen to His Legacy, *by D. Russell Connor*
7. ELLINGTONIA: The Recorded Music of Duke Ellington and His Sidemen, *by W. E. Timner*
8. THE GLENN MILLER ARMY AIR FORCE BAND: Sustineo Alas / I Sustain the Wings, *by Edward F. Polic*
9. SWING LEGACY, *by Chip Deffaa*

Swing Legacy

Studies in Jazz No. 9

Metuchen, N.J., & London, 1989

The Scarecrow Press and the Institute

Swing Legacy

By Chip Deffaa

Foreword by

George T. Simon

of Jazz Studies, Rutgers University

Library of Congress Cataloging-in-Publication Data

Deffaa, Chip, 1951-
Swing legacy.

(Studies in jazz ; no. 9)
Includes bibliographical references.
1. Jazz music. I. Rutgers University. Institute of Jazz Studies. II. Title. III. Series.
ML3506.D43 1989 781.65'4 89-70029
ISBN 0-8108-2282-2

Manufactured in the United States of America

To B.W.

Contents

FOREWORD, by George T. Simon *ix*

EDITOR'S PREFACE, by Dan Morgenstern *xi*

INTRODUCTION: The Swing Tradition *3*

ARTIE SHAW: Back with the Big Band at 75 *17*

CHRIS GRIFFIN: Trumpeting in the Benny Goodman Band *39*

BUCK CLAYTON: From China to Basie, and Beyond *51*

JOHNNY BLOWERS: Experience Counts *71*

MAXINE SULLIVAN: More than "Loch Lomond" *83*

JOHN WILLIAMS, JR.: Still Counting His Blessings *103*

MAURICE PURTILL: "'Nostalgia' is a very dirty word . . ." *118*

LEE CASTLE (part one): A Trumpeter for St. Anthony *129*

LEE CASTLE (part two): "The Third Dorsey" *149*

PANAMA FRANCIS:
From Swing to Rock 'n' Roll, and Back *175*

STEPHANE GRAPPELLI: Parisian Swing *201*

MEL TORME: "I Wanted to be a Big Band Leader . . ." *210*

HAROLD ASHBY: Remembering Duke and Ben *231*

REMEMBERING COUNT BASIE *243*

THAD JONES:
Straight-Ahead with the Count Basie Orchestra *247*

THE BASIE BAND AFTER BASIE *260*

FRANK FOSTER: Back Home with the Basie Band *267*

MERCER ELLINGTON:
Pop Left Him Harry, Cootie,
and a Few Scraps of Paper *288*

WARREN VACHE JR.: A Hot Cornet for Today *319*

SCOTT HAMILTON: Expanding the Tradition *327*

WOODY HERMAN: 50 Years of Leading the Herd *334*

BIBLIOGRAPHY *363*

ACKNOWLEDGMENTS *367*

INDEX *368*

GEORGE • T. • SIMON

Foreword

You know what gets to me about Chip Deffaa and this book? It reminds me of me. How? Well, it projects the same sort of wonderfully joyous, almost naive intensity about the music and the men and the women who were making it that so many of us young jazz writers used to feel and express long before Chip was even born.

Of course the times were different then—very different when it came to expressing yourself through your pen or typewriter. Maybe we allowed our passions greater rein. If you liked something a lot, you just went ahead and said so, period. You seldom worried whether somebody called you naive (which many times you might have been), or might complain because, instead of espousing some sort of cause, your primary aim was to share with your readers your appreciation of the music that meant so much to you and also to encourage those musicians whose work you admired. (Lord knows, we weren't in it for the money. Believe it or not, I was raking in a cool twenty-five dollars a *month* when I first started writing a half century ago.)

Chip is a literary and spiritual throwback (thank goodness, not a financial one) to those days. Throughout much of the book, he projects the same sort of joyous naiveté and respect for the music and musicians he's writing about—much of it overflowing with enthusiasm—that permeated many of our literary efforts. One reason that he comes across like that is because he is a very good listener—a trait not always apparent among some of those currently covering the jazz scene. Not that Chip has remained entirely passive. You'll find him making some rather subjective observations about what his subjects have been talking about, sometimes disagreeing with them, but still retaining his respect for them and what they have been trying to do.

For the most part, though, Chip lets the musicians and singers do their own things, talking about their careers and how they feel about their music and that of others, sharing some of their own joys and frustrations, and all the time leading you directly into the inside of the world of swing.

Part of it is a world that I inhabited forty and even fifty years ago when the bands Chip writes about—Shaw, Goodman, Basie, Miller,

Woody, the Duke, and the Dorseys — were swinging away. Some of his subjects' insights are quite revealing, especially those coming from some of the sidemen rather than from the leaders. And theirs and Chip's observations aren't all rosy either. Some are real downers, like Thad Jones' perceptive "The Society was very permissive in that area — against blacks, that is." But equally indicative of the tone of the book is what another former Basie sideman, Frank Foster, had to say about sidemen in general. Many of them were forced to endure some hard times — social, financial, and of course racial. But motivating so many of them was simply, as Frank points out, "working for the love of the music and the love of the sound of the big bands."

Chip certainly shares both those loves — with his interviewees and with his readers. What he has been able to create is a clearer insight and "insound" of not just the music itself, but also of the spirit of the music and its makers, and, in fact, the spirit of the times as well. But still, I must caution those of you who shared those times — long ago but never-to-be forgotten — to keep them in proper perspective. As one sage once warned us: "It's great to look back. But don't stare!"

George T. Simon
Author of *The Big Bands*

DAN • MORGENSTERN

Editor's Preface

With Chip Deffaa's *Swing Legacy,* the "Studies in Jazz" series departs somewhat from its established format of monographs. But in a very real sense this book also deals with a single subject: the survival of that branch of jazz once known as swing. (The rather more vague term "mainstream" is today's common usage.)

Because Deffaa lets the musicians speak for themselves (he is an excellent interviewer) his book makes a genuine contribution to the growing field of jazz oral history. Much ground is covered here—more than just the "Swing Era." And it is to Deffaa's credit that he chose to interview not just the famous but also the less well known.

Sadly, the timeliness of his efforts is illuminated by the fact that three of his chosen subjects—Maxine Sullivan, Woody Herman and Thad Jones—did not live to see the book published. While he is among the youngest of the new crop of jazz writers, Deffaa is also the one who has most deeply immersed himself in the music's past. His youth gives him a fresh perspective. I'm sure that much of the openness of his subjects derives from the marked difference in age between interviewee and interviewer, and equally sure that they were impressed and delighted by how much this young man already knew about them and the soil in which they grew.

There are many important and informative nuggets to be gleaned from this book, and we are most pleased to add it to our list.

Dan Morgenstern
Director
Institute of Jazz Studies
Rutgers University

Swing Legacy

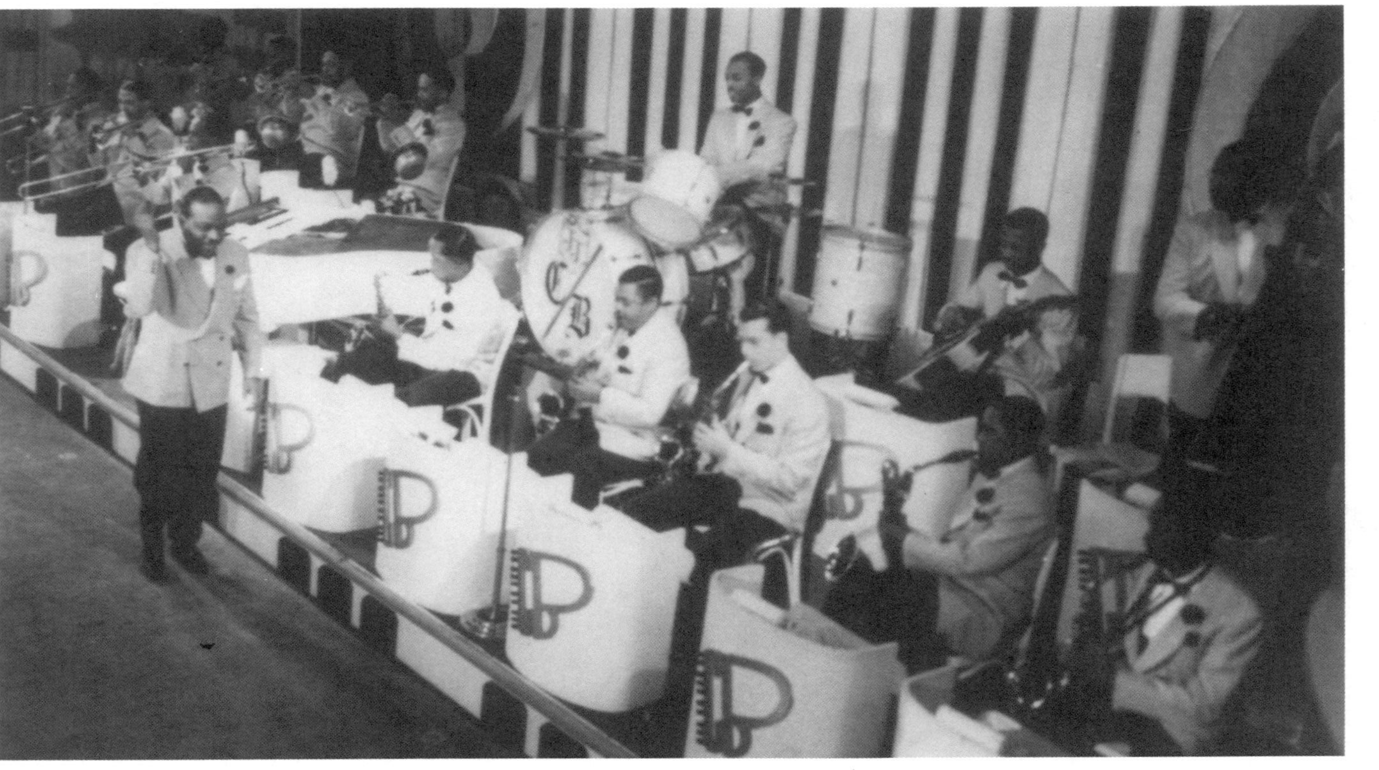

One definition of swing: The Count Basie Band (1941). (Frank Driggs collection)

INTRODUCTION

The Swing Tradition

In the Swing Era (1935-45), jazz and pop music converged to a degree that had never happened before, and certainly has never happened again since. Jazzmen such as Benny Goodman, Count Basie, Artie Shaw, the Dorsey brothers, Duke Ellington, and Woody Herman found their music enjoying tremendous popularity.

Big bands proliferated throughout the nation. And even the more commercially-oriented dance bands usually carried their share of "hot" arrangements, their featured jazz soloists. Such bands may have been offering only diluted versions of the music created by jazz innovators, but the fact remains: jazz was exerting a general influence upon popular music as it never has since.

The term "swing music" was an umbrella that covered both pure jazz of the period (such as Count Basie's "Jumpin' at the Woodside") and jazz-inflected dance music (such as Tommy Dorsey's recording of "The Dipsy Doodle").

The right musicians, of course, could make just about anything swing. In 1937, one radio station cut Maxine Sullivan off the air for her supposed sacrilege of swinging the traditional Scottish song, "Loch Lomond." Plenty of bandleaders succeeded in swinging the classics (and thus, incidentally, avoided the inconvenience of having to pay royalties to living composers). For jazz musicians, it was a rather good period. Many found they could make a buck while still playing the way they wanted to.

But by the late 1940s, the Swing Era was history. Big bands folded by the score, and a lot of fine musicians found themselves forced into other fields to earn a living. Singers replaced bands as the primary interest in the world of popular music. And then around 1954-55 rock 'n' roll came up, becoming the dominant genre in pop music. A few Swing Era survivors forged ahead with their big bands or small groups, but for most of them, the going was much, much harder than it once had been.

Swing music had fallen from favor with the general public. And also, for that matter, with many self-defined jazz buffs. For a curious thing had happened to jazz. Bebop had emerged in the mid '40s, becoming *the* new thing in jazz. And for some reason, it wasn't enough for the first bebop devotees to say how great the creators of this new music were; they also found it necessary to dismiss as passé the music and musicians that had come before. Bebop was a real revolution in jazz. And, with the kind of excess that is customary in revolutions, many supporters of the new movement could find no value in the old order. Swing Era jazz greats who did not want to play bebop found themselves rejected by many young jazz buffs.

Louis Armstrong, for example, had exerted a widespread stylistic influence prior to the advent of bebop. All of the great Swing Era trumpeters acknowledged that he was a major influence upon them. In fact, Armstrong's playing had left its mark upon most musicians (not just trumpeters) throughout the era. But by the late 1940s, Dizzy Gillespie was being venerated as the ideal trumpeter—and Armstrong was being scorned by many as old-hat.

Within just a couple of years in the mid '40s—as pianist John Bunch recently recalled—young alto saxophonists went from wanting to sound like Benny Carter to wanting to sound like Charlie Parker. That was a radical stylistic shift. Carter, who had been an important figure in the swing tradition—as a pioneering big band arranger, sax stylist, and bandleader—suddenly found himself sadly unappreciated in the jazz community. He no longer got many votes in the music magazines' readers' polls. He vanished into the studios, as did a lot of gifted Swing Era players. They were no longer being valued by the general public, nor by many of the jazz fans.

By the time I was attending college (1969-73), jazz in general seemed to be dying, being smothered under the relentless onslaught of rock. Jazz clubs were closing left and right in the late 1960s and early 1970s. And as for swing music—forget it! It was an older tradition. And in American culture, old was being equated with worthless.

But in the mid '70s, jazz began a resurgence, which has continued more or less to this day—gaining momentum, dramatically, in just the last couple of years. Part of that resurgence has been a renewed interest in looking back, and in reclaiming all of our musical heritage.

When bebop came up in the '40s, true believers were expected to renounce admiration for what had gone before. But with the passing of years, the prevailing thinking has changed.

Today, a young jazz devotee is apt to see no conflict between appreciating the gifts of a contemporary jazz artist and those of an older player still working in, say, the swing tradition. (Or, for that matter, a *younger* player choosing to work in the swing tradition.) When Wynton Marsalis, the biggest name among the new generation of jazzmen, makes a point of expressing his admiration for Louis Armstrong, as he often does, we're reminded of the sea change that has taken place. It's OK to praise Armstrong again. And all of the others in that vein.

I saw the first signs of interest in reclaiming the past in the early '70s. I was a sophomore at Princeton in 1970-71, when Benny Carter was invited to serve as a visiting professor of music there. He had been out of the public eye for years. (Leonard Feather had noted in *The Encyclopedia of Jazz*, 1960, that Carter—despite his obvious gifts—was working "without large scale acclaim or economic success.") Carter gave a concert on campus that spring, playing both alto sax and trumpet—and he wowed the students.

Benny Carter and his Orchestra, Savoy Ballroom, New York, 1939 or '40. (Institute of Jazz Studies)

His musical thinking seemed so organically whole. He had never really changed his basic style. He had borrowed lightly from so-called modernists, but he had essentially stayed true to his own way of playing rather than trying to follow every changing trend in music. He swung beautifully, with the same glistening tone he always had.

In the next few years, I watched Carter re-emerge to become a frequent guest star at major jazz festivals. The general refurbishing of his reputation, which occurred in the 1970s, appeared a harbinger of things to come. Nowadays in the *Down Beat* International Critics' Poll, Carter routinely places among the top five on alto sax, getting about the same number of votes as the radically-modern stylist Ornette Coleman. He is not just appreciated, he is venerated, by many younger musicians. Today, we see younger musicians commonly showing respect for older players—a marked change from the "Young Turks versus Old-Timers" scene that prevailed when modern jazz developed. Carter is once again receiving the recognition that should have been his *throughout* the years. He's lived long enough to go from being considered old-fashioned to being considered timeless, a gifted player within a worthy—if older—tradition in jazz.

Many of the older sidemen—The Swing Era survivors who took refuge in anonymous studio work or who were forced to leave music altogether for awhile—have found a renewed interest in them. There are far more jazz festivals these days than in the early 1970s. And the older players are getting more opportunities to express themselves before appreciative audiences.

Beginning in the mid '70s, more concerts were devoted to recreating jazz of the past. Today, pianist John Lewis, whose membership in the Modern Jazz Quartet gives him impeccable credentials as a "modernist," leads the American Jazz Orchestra, which plays original arrangements of the big bands of Duke Ellington, Jimmie Lunceford, Benny Goodman, Count Basie, and others, as well as some new compositions. And young people—not just nostalgia-oriented old-timers—are listening intently to the music, treating it as something of lasting value.

* * *

The late '70s saw the emergence of Scott Hamilton, the finest new tenor saxist to appear in quite a while, and an international favorite today. His gods were Swing Era giants such as Coleman Hawkins and Ben Webster, rather than modernists such as Sonny Rollins or Archie Shepp. Warren Vache Jr. came up about the same time, the first major Louis Armstrong-inspired trumpeter in years (although he's borrowed from beboppers as well). He too has enjoyed great acceptance from jazz critics and fans alike. Today, New York boasts a variety of younger trumpeters (including Randy Sandke, Jordan Sandke, Peter Ecklund, John Marshall) who can play effectively in both an Armstrong-inspired and a more modern style.

Ruby Braff was the only major Armstrong-inspired trumpeter to emerge in the 1950s. In 1960, Leonard Feather noted in *The Encyclopedia of Jazz* that Braff "reported that he had been almost continuously out of work for five years. Possibly because he is a younger musician playing in a basically older style, it has been extremely difficult for him to find work in night clubs." For much of his career, Braff paid dearly for playing in an Armstrong-ish vein when everybody else was following the boppers. But today, at age 60, Braff enjoys great respect, playing the same way he always has. He works steadily in the U.S. and abroad.

Jazz fans are all familiar with the Widespread Jazz Orchestra. That band, initially called the Widespread Depression Orchestra, seemed a fluke when it first broke through in the 1970s—young musicians dedicated to Swing Era sounds. But the band has survived, and it has helped accustom people to the idea of bands reaching back in time for their musical identity. In recent years, Vince Giordano's Nighthawks Orchestra has enjoyed considerable success in New York playing big band charts of the late '20s and '30s, as well as, to a lesser extent, the '40s.

I've gotten a kick out of going into Manhattan's trendy Cat Club and seeing the crowd of people—young as well as old—dancing to 29-year-old Loren Schoenberg's big band. Schoenberg plays undiluted swing—including many brand new arrangements by the legendary Buck Clayton, written especially for this band. Not too many years ago, Clayton, who had been a star trumpet soloist and an arranger on Count Basie's original band, was working a day job, wholly outside of music.

In May, 1985, the New York Swing Dance Society began presenting big bands twice a month at the Cat Club, which was primarily a rock venue. So many people turned out to Lindy Hop that in early 1988, the big band dances became a weekly event.

The point is not that swing is about to overtake other musical genres in popularity—that's hardly the case—but that today's scene is marked by a healthy diversity. It has become acceptable for people to have eclectic tastes, to appreciate music from a variety of styles. And that includes embracing older styles.

The *Wall Street Journal* noted on May 27, 1986: "A decade ago hardly a handful of stations played big bands; now as many as 1,000 do." The *Journal* chalked that up to the greying of America, to older listeners returning to the music of their youth. But younger listeners are checking out those programs as well. Some of the baby-boomers who

Lindy Hopping at the Cat Club, 1988 (Frankie Manning and Judy Pritchett). The club's popular big band dances have got to be the most thoroughly integrated—in terms of age, race, and social status—scene in current New York nightlife. (Photo courtesy Rebecca Reitz)

grew up listening to commercial rock 'n' roll are now exploring more sophisticated sounds.

What is one to make of the fact that in May of 1986, the Glenn Miller Orchestra – more than four decades after Miller himself vanished over the English Channel – was voted one of the nation's five most popular bands, outranking most rock bands, in a poll run by *People* magazine? That poll cannot be taken at face-value. But it cannot be dismissed as meaningless, either.

Bud Katzel, Vice President of GRP Records, told me in July of 1987 that their Glenn Miller Orchestra CD, "In the Digital Mood," had – to the company's great surprise – become their biggest-selling CD, dramatically outselling recordings by such contemporary jazz stars as Billy Cobham and Chick Corea. According to Katzel, sales of "In the Digital Mood" had now exceeded 150,000 units. He added that their recent Duke Ellington Band CD follow-up seemed to be repeating the same sales pattern. An Ellington Band video was being hurried out.

Tom Wachunas, assistant manager at J & R Music World, a major Manhattan record store, commented around the same time: "Jazz in general is experiencing an upswing right now, including its older formats, swing and big band. The buyers are not just older people in their

50s and 60s; we're seeing a good chunk who are younger, in their 30s." His boss, Jimmy Eigo, noted, "There are so many big band albums out now, it's amazing. Doc Severinsen's two records have done really well, and Louis Bellson's just put out a big band album." But could big bands be coming back? He's justifiably skeptical. "They've been saying *that* since the 1940s."

Big band booker Thomas Cassidy of Woodstock, Illinois, said in 1987 that his agency had seen a continuing increase in business throughout the 1970s, with business then holding steady throughout the 1980s. He remarked: "There's an entire Yuppie generation that grew up with the Beatles and the Rolling Stones, that's turning to jazz and big bands because they appreciate the quality of the music. They might see a band at Ravinia or Wolf Trap or at a convention and get hooked. And 50 percent of our bookings these days are at high schools and colleges. When I started in this business 25 years ago, schools weren't booking big bands."

The Glenn Miller Orchestra, still working 50 weeks a year in the 1980s. (Courtesy Glenn Miller Productions)

Rival band booker Jackie Green, head of the Willard Alexander agency, said in 1987 that he had noted "a 17 percent increase in bookings, nationwide, this year over last year, and last year was eight or nine percent over the year before." Green suggested that compact discs, which were bringing the richness of big band sounds to listeners with never-before-heard fidelity, were creating new fans. But the precarious economic conditions of the big band business were underscored by the fact that in 1988 Green's agency went bankrupt.

* * *

Today, as a jazz critic for the *New York Post* and contributor to a number of music publications, I listen to a wide variety of music each week. But I still retain a special fondness for the sound of a swingin' big band.

I enjoy different genres, and I like being challenged by new things. But for me, a band swinging joyously and simply is still hard to beat.

I never dreamed, when I first began checking out the Swing Era 78s in the basement as a boy in the early 1960s, that I'd someday get to know musicians on those records. Much less that preserving their recollections, in articles for jazz publications, would become an important part of my life.

At age nine, out of simple curiosity, I put a Woody Herman 78 on the Capehart phonograph: "Blues in the Night." I found it rather hard to resist. There was another recording of "Blues in the Night" down there as well, by one Jimmie Lunceford and *his* Orchestra, and still another one by Bing Crosby, which got me started on the path of comparing how different artists interpreted the same material. There were sides, too, by Jimmy and Tommy Dorsey, Benny Goodman, Claude Thornhill, Glenn Miller, Duke Ellington, Freddy Martin, Teddy Wilson, Louis Armstrong, and others. Marvelous stuff, and so different from the pop music that played on the jukebox at the YMCA.

As I got older, I read whatever I could find about the music. I bought albums featuring other Swing Era greats such as Artie Shaw, Count Basie, Maxine Sullivan, Bunny Berigan, Billie Holiday, Chick Webb, Jimmie Lunceford, and Ray McKinley.

I checked out, too, the few remaining big bands that had managed to survive—such as Count Basie's, Duke Ellington's, Stan Kenton's, and Lionel Hampton's, as well as the so-called "ghost bands" bearing the names of departed leaders such as Glenn Miller, Tommy and Jimmy Dorsey, and the bands assembled for specific engagements by semi-retired bandleaders of old such as Bob Crosby, Tex Beneke, and Benny Goodman.

In time, my interests broadened. Eventually, as a jazz fan (and later, a jazz writer), I would explore all genres in jazz, from the earliest recorded sides to bebop and beyond. But I would always retain a special affection for swing music. That had served as my port of entry into the larger world of jazz.

* * *

By the time I was in high school, I'd met a few other kids with some interest in jazz. But most seemed to believe that music "progresses" in a straightforward fashion, that each year it inevitably keeps getting better, the way pole vaulters keep vaulting higher. Modern styles of jazz were presumed naturally superior to older styles.

I wasn't sure it worked that way. I wondered if changes in musical fashions weren't somewhat like changes in clothing fashions. Short dresses, for example, might be out of favor for a spell and then return.

I could listen to a Louis Armstrong classic like his 1936 recording of "Swing That Music" and be absolutely knocked out by his soaring, ecstatic trumpet work. I thought his final four trumpet choruses on that record were about the greatest thing I had ever heard. That performance was perfect.

I was surprised, though, at how hard it was to get others to share in my enthusiasm. One high school friend played me Maynard Ferguson's latest recordings, trying to "prove" to me that Ferguson was a "better" trumpeter than the "old-fashioned" Armstrong (and the Armstrong-influenced trumpeters that I liked, such as Bunny Berigan, Yank Lawson, Harry James, Billy Butterfield, and Lee Castle) because Ferguson routinely played notes *higher* than Armstrong and his followers had ever played. Never mind whether Ferguson's notes were as pleasing to the ear. His notes *were* higher.

I could relish even a minor Armstrong recording like "I'll Get Mine Bye and Bye" (1941), digging the beautiful simplicity of the work of Armstrong and his colleagues. Bassist John Williams Jr. didn't play many notes on that record, but they seemed the right notes; they were memorable, and they set Armstrong up effectively. My friend could counter that a *modern* bass player and a *modern* trumpet player would probably play twice as many notes in the same amount of space. True enough. The beboppers *were* using shorter notes, and more of them, in their solos. But is complexity always better than simplicity?

I could listen to clarinetist Artie Shaw or to singer Maxine Sullivan, and hear such natural grace in their work. (And when I was 15, both Shaw and Sullivan had long been retired—presumably permanently—from music.) They were two completely different stylists, but they both treated melody as an ally, rather than as an enemy to be vanquished. They could both do so much with only the subtlest of deviations from the melody.

To some of my friends, adhering that closely to the melody was in itself considered "old-fashioned." Contemporary jazzmen played "freer."

To me, that simply meant we had come into a period in which lyricism was no longer valued as highly by most people as it once had been. But I could hardly consider the graceful phrasing of an Artie Shaw or a Maxine Sullivan to be obsolete. I could accept that fashions in music, like fashions in clothing or hairstyles, change. But I believed that artistry remains artistry. And that eventually, their contributions might be more highly valued once again.

It's good to see that some of that has occurred now.

* * *

In this book, you'll meet 18 people—leaders and sidemen alike—who have contributed to the long swing tradition. Collectively, they have much to tell about the history of the music. But you'll find more than just reminiscences of bygone days here. Virtually all of these artists have been actively working in the 1980s.

There's the forceful and outspoken Artie Shaw, who has returned to the field after nearly three decades away from music. A perfectionist by nature, Shaw knows well the challenges of trying to maintain a first-rate big band in today's rock-dominated world.

And there's the late Maxine Sullivan (who, like Shaw, had left music entirely for some years). In her 70s, she was still working a heavy international schedule and recording frequently. In fact, she was recording more actively in her last years than in the "heyday" of her youth. And in her very last year, she was nominated once again for a Grammy Award.

There's the venerable Buck Clayton, who helped bring American swing to China before starring with Count Basie in the '30s and going on to become one of the real giants of jazz on his own. His recently formed big band has been garnering unanimous raves in New York.

Chris Griffin, Johnny Blowers, and Moe Purtill recall the famed bands of Benny Goodman, Bunny Berigan, and Glenn Miller, respectively.

John Williams, Jr., who worked with Armstrong, Coleman Hawkins, Billie Holiday, and others in the Swing Era, is among those who took a day job after musical preferences shifted in the '50s. And he's re-emerged in the '70s and '80s, touring with the Harlem Blues and Jazz Band (composed of fellow Swing Era survivors), and other groups.

Impassioned (and somewhat embittered) Panama Francis, who leads the exuberant Savoy Sultans today, went from the big band swing of Lucky Millinder and Cab Calloway to become—not so happily—*the* rock 'n' roll drummer in New York in the '50s, before returning to his musical roots.

Swing, of course, was an international phenomenon. Stephane Grappelli and his late partner, Django Reinhardt, were the first two Europeans to swing with the best of the American jazzmen. Today, at age 80, Grappelli continues to win critics' polls as the world's foremost jazz violinist.

Mel Torme—one of the great jazz-influenced singers of our time—came to fame as the big band era was fading. A devoted big band buff, he offers his recollections of that era.

Former Ellingtonian Harold Ashby, called by England's *Jazz Journal International* "the revelation" of the 1985 Nice Jazz Festival, is one of a number of gifted jazzmen who may be better appreciated abroad than in the U.S. He's deserving of a "rediscovery" in this country.

Here, too, are Scott Hamilton and Warren Vache Jr., whose contemporary extensions of Swing Era playing have won many admirers.

Lee Castle's pure-toned horn graced the big bands of Benny Goodman, Artie Shaw, Jack Teagarden, and others. He's probably best known, however, for his association with Tommy and Jimmy Dorsey, and his recollections of them are a valuable addition to the literature on the Swing Era. Sometimes called "the third Dorsey," Castle has now held the title of leader of the Jimmy Dorsey Orchestra for 31 years, longer, actually, than Jimmy himself did. His musicians still play from many of the same charts used by both Dorsey brothers. Castle is a *conservator* of a musical heritage, keeping alive a particular body of music and a way of playing that music. That's one way of maintaining the swing tradition.

On the other hand, you have someone like Woody Herman, who was always restlessly creative. He preferred being an innovator, rather than a conservator. He outlasted his peers, becoming in the 1980s the last of the original Swing Era bandleaders still playing his instrument and still touring with his band on a full-time basis.

He never stood still. He was among the first to incorporate bebop licks into his big band music. By the 1980s, his band was playing occasional numbers with a rock, reggae, or a funk feel, as well as many others, of course, with more of a traditional swing feel. He resisted being pigeonholed into any one category. He was always open to all new developments.

My own belief is that we need both the conservators and the innovators. We need people dedicated to preserving the best of the past, and we need people eager to expand upon our heritage.

Trying to strike an ideal balance between both goals is Frank Foster, who's recently assumed the leadership of what many consider to be the epitome of the swingin' big band: Count Basie's. (The band was voted the number one jazz orchestra in the world in both the

Down Beat critics' and readers' polls in the year that I interviewed Foster, 1986.) A gifted modern tenor saxist and arranger, Foster bears a heavy responsibility. He must keep the Basie Band sounding enough like the traditional Basie Band so that it does not lose its followers. But he must also keep enlarging the band's repertoire, to maintain the musicians' enthusiasm, and the band's reputation as the greatest of the large jazz ensembles. It's a tough challenge, but one that Foster seems well-equipped to take on.

Here, too, is Thad Jones, the late modern cornetist and arranger, who led the Basie Band for a bit more than a year in 1985-86, before he became ill and was succeeded by Foster. Both men would merit inclusion if they had done nothing else in their careers but serve as leaders of the Basie Band. For no band can match the Basie Band in terms of discipline, dynamics, nuances—dig the way the brass will shake or choke certain notes—and the projection of relaxed power.

The Basie Band works constantly, and yet its financial health remains precarious. I have a hunch people won't fully appreciate the greatness of it until the day comes when it no longer exists. *Then* everyone in jazz will be saying: "That was some band, wasn't it?" Why isn't a band like that receiving government and/or corporate financial support, the way leading symphony orchestras are? In its field, it is the equivalent of the best of our symphony orchestras. And it would be a major loss if it were to go under, or to have to lower its high musical standards.

No book on this music would be complete, of course, without mention of Duke Ellington's legacy. Mercer Ellington has not had an easy time in trying to preserve, and authentically present, the wealth of music that his famous father created. For the Duke—one of the real geniuses in the world of jazz—did the work of several men: composing both brief and extended works of music (he is among the all-time greatest of American composers), maintaining what for decades was America's pre-eminent jazz orchestra, and overseeing recording, theater, and film projects. Mercer has been hard-pressed, trying to lead the band (always measured against the high standards his father set), document his father's music, and get Ellington shows staged on Broadway and elsewhere—a most formidable set of tasks.

The chapters that follow are of varying lengths. It should not be inferred that those musicians given more pages are more important than others. Some musicians are given extra space here simply because their stories have never before appeared in any books. And a prime goal of any good jazz writer is to add to our body of knowledge.

The interviews were conducted over the past six years. (Many were conducted in 1985 and '86, after the death of one elderly musician I had admired spurred me to interview others while the opportunity to do so still existed.) Shorter versions of most of the profiles originally appeared in the *Mississippi Rag*. Thad Jones and Scott Hamilton were written about for *Down Beat*; Panama Francis and Johnny Blowers for *Modern Drummer*; Stephane Grappelli for *Jazz Times*; Woody Herman and the Basie Band for *Coda*; "Remembering Count Basie" for *New Jersey Monthly*. Each chapter is written in the present tense, reflecting conditions at the time it was written. (Dates of the interviews are given at the end of each chapter.) Profiles of additional veteran musicians will be published by the University of Illinois Press in a companion volume, *Voices of the Jazz Age*.

Swing is not, by a long shot, America's preferred music today. It may never again reach anything like that status. But it has certainly provided its durability. It is part of our common heritage.

Here, then, are 18 artists who have contributed over the years—and in most cases still are contributing—to keeping the music swinging.

Chip Deffaa
Jazz critic, *The New York Post*
December 1988

Artie Shaw. (Chip Deffaa collection)

ARTIE • SHAW

Back with the Big Band at 75

"We're still fighting the battle of getting an audience out there aside from that for Cyndi Lauper, Prince and Madonna," declares Artie Shaw, 75. "If we get enough of an audience to support ourselves—I'm not looking to get rich, I'm looking to have a band out there that can play music I like. If it does, I'll make a living—so will the men—and that's the best of all possible worlds.

"People tell me they enjoy my band," he adds. "I say, 'Nobody enjoys it more than I do.' If I didn't enjoy it, I wouldn't be here. . . I've walked a number of times."

Indeed Shaw has. He was near the peak of his tremendous popularity as a big band leader when, about 11 o'clock on the night of November 15th, 1939, he simply walked off the bandstand at the Hotel Pennsylvania—away from the screaming fans, away from his 15 hand-picked musicians. Never mind that in some weeks he had been netting as much as $30,000. Shaw wanted out. He went to Mexico to unwind and one of the all-time great swing bands came to a premature end.

But the next year, Shaw was back again, with an all-new big band, featuring trumpeter Billy Butterfield, trombonist Jack Jenney, pianist/harpsichordist Johnny Guarnieri, and a string section.

After the war, Shaw bounced back with still another impressive unit—this time without strings, but with the potent trumpet of Roy Eldridge and the modern piano work of Dodo Marmarosa.

In all, Artie Shaw figures he led no less than nine different bands between 1936, when he made his debut as a leader, and 1954, when he took what he thought would be the final walk away from the music business. After finishing a small-group engagement at the Embers on 52nd Street, Shaw announced he was setting aside the clarinet forever. He turned to other pursuits, including writing and painting.

He never did pick up the clarinet again. To regain his old prowess on the instrument would require too much work, he told interviewers. For a man who had previously been unsurpassed as a clarinetist, to play at anything below his former level would be unthinkable.

And yet in late 1983, Shaw came back still again, supervising a

Artie Shaw. (Courtesy Artie Shaw).

superb new big band, which has been touring the country, off-and-on, ever since then. Shaw rehearses the band and selects the repertoire. Clarinetist Dick Johnson plays Shaw's parts and, on most engagements, fronts the band. Periodically, Shaw himself appears with the band, conducting it and introducing the numbers.

Shaw's band plays the best of his old arrangements, plus a good deal of new material. Shaw agreed to re-enter the big band field, he says, only after making it clear to the booking agency that he was *not* going to be nostalgia oriented.

"The only way it could work on my terms was if I were allowed to do what I want to do, rather than *only* what the audience wants," Shaw states. "I don't mind giving the audience some of it, what they want. But I'm going to do it a different way. This is '85, I'm not going to do what we did in '38. I can't do that. I've grown. And what I did in '38 was a step in my evolution as a person.

"So OK. We tried it. It seemed to work. The question was: Is there enough of an audience out there to support a band like this? These men have to get salaries. They don't make as much as a good plumber, as it is right now. They do it because they love what they're doing. And I love it because I love what I'm doing. But if we're not allowed to love it, and we've got to do what we don't love—no point, then I'm gone again!

"Dick fronts it when I'm not there. But it's my band. Period. Whatever we play is acceptable to me or we don't play it. I'm an editor. I'm a policy maker. If they come up with an arrangement I don't like, we don't play it. If I do think it's communicable, we play it. And by that I mean, I'm talking about a broad range.

"We have pieces like 'I Let a Song Go Out of My Heart.' It's a very difficult arrangement for an audience to hear. When I announce, 'I Let a Song Go Out of My Heart,' the audience starts to say 'Oh . . .' I say, 'No, don't think you're going to hear what you expect. This isn't going to be Johnny Hodges. This is a different thing, a different set of sensibilities, modern—it's 1989 time.' So I say, 'If you don't like it now, stick around for 30 years and you'll like it.' So they laugh and they accept it.

"Dick wrote a piece which we're calling 'Beacon Hill Lavender.' It's a nice piece. Parts of it are very easily comprehended. Other parts you have to hear a bit. But if you put it on a record, they'll hear it," Shaw says.

The band plays the celebrated original arrangements of numbers such as "Begin the Beguine," "The Carioca," "Nightmare," "Star Dust," "Moonglow," and "Softly, as in a Morning Sunrise." Those were hit records. But Shaw also has the band playing some superior arrangements from the old days (such as "The Glider" and "Summertime") which, for one reason or another, were *not* commercial successes when first recorded. "We have most of the old arrangements," Shaw says. "Boston University has the collection now. And Dick has reconstructed a few that have fallen by the wayside." Shaw believes in the timeless validity of those arrangements. And yet, Shaw states, the band is not trying to *re-create* the way those numbers were originally performed.

"We play the same written notes. The notes! But they're not the *music*," Shaw says. "We're playing those notes differently. We're playing them in today's terms. The chart is played differently. If you hear 'Softly as in a Morning Sunrise,' God, it's a whole different thing from what that '38 band did! But it's the same written notes.

"This band plays differently. They play harder. They play with a kind of raw quality. They no longer try to play pretty. Johnny Hodges played alto in a kind of lyrical way. Today an alto kind of honks at you. 'Wake up and listen to what I'm saying,' it says. Well, that's what the band plays like. That's what I mean by modern sensibilities.

"It's the same thing as somebody in Mozart's day playing the clarinet concerto and somebody today playing it. The techniques have changed. You play it differently. That doesn't mean you play a different concerto. You just interpret it differently. So we're playing the same notes. If you hear Dick play my 'Concerto for Clarinet,' he's playing the notes. But it's not me; it's a different sound, and the band is swinging its head off. So all I can say is it's a different feeling. This is today, that was then," Shaw declares.

Does he want Dick Johnson to try to sound like him, as much as possible?

"Hell, no!" Shaw responds. "In certain pieces like 'Star Dust,' the solo I played, as Whitney Balliett has said to me, became a classic. OK, so Dick plays the same notes, but he sure doesn't play 'em like I do. If I were to try to get him to play 'em like I do, I'd be a very frustrated man. So I've said to him: 'Where you have to play those notes, play them, but other places, go, do your own.' "

On some numbers, Shaw encourages the band to stretch out. "Don't forget, in those days you had to do it in three minutes, fifteen seconds. Now we've got as much time as we need. We open them up and do what we do. Make a jazz band out of it in spots, and then come back to the chart. The framework remains at least recognizable to the audience. And so they hear it.

"The band works as much as the audience will allow. Whatever the bookings can take place. If we can continue, the band continues. Otherwise we'll work a couple of months, take a layoff, and the men will go about their business, and then try to get the same band together and go again. It's been spotty," Shaw concedes. The band has had to take layoffs.

"Whatever I make, I pour into the orchestra. I'm going to be making a lot of money in Valley Forge and Cohasset and in Merrillville, Indiana, and Cleveland, and the St. Louis dates with Tony Bennett and Rosie Clooney and those people; I'll make a hell of a lot of money. I spend it on the band." (He doesn't quite spend *all* of it on the band, some who know him would add; he lives well.)

"I'm very happy with this band," Shaw says. "It's a hell of a bunch of players!"

* * *

The general outline of Shaw's career may well be familiar to many jazz buffs. Born in New York City in 1910, he was in his first traveling band by age 15. In the next few years, he worked his way up through the bands of Johnny Cavallaro, Joe Cantor, Austin Wylie (1927-29), Irving Aaronson (1929-31), and Red Nichols (1931). He worked in leading radio studio orchestras in the early '30s, which he found too commercial for his tastes. He left music for a year—shades of things to come—to run a farm in Pennsylvania (1934). He took his first shot at leading his own band in 1936. (For further information on Shaw's early years, his 1952 autobiography, *The Trouble With Cinderella*, is highly recommended.)

Who were Shaw's earliest musical influences?

"I think probably Trumbauer and Bix, first. And then Louis. And then from Louis, I went off to—you know, all the standard brands. Jimmie Noone, a few guys like that. There weren't too many people," Shaw comments. "People have asked me often, 'Who did you study with?' I said, 'The guy next to me.' Or some record that I liked. And when I got to know more than that, I'd find somebody else who knew more. Until finally it got kind of hard.

"I first heard Trumbauer and Bix on records. Then when they came nearby, when I was living in New Haven, I made a pilgrimage to Bridgeport one night. They were playing, the Goldkette band came there, the Ritz ballroom, and I stood in front of that band open-mouthed.

"Then later I went to Harlem. And when I met Willie Smith, he was a big influence. Then I worked in radio and I worked with some fine musicians who weren't jazz players but I learned a lot about breathing and tone control and discipline in playing," Shaw recalls.

On May 24, 1936, Shaw was one of a long line of musicians taking part in what was billed as "New York's First Swing Concert," presented by the Onyx Club at Broadway's Imperial Theater. As far as the public was concerned, Shaw was an unknown at the time. His radio work was anonymous, and he had not received recognition as a dance band sideman. The major attractions at this concert included Louis Armstrong and his Orchestra, the Casa Loma Band, Bob Crosby and his Orchestra, Red Nichols and his Five Pennies, Tommy Dorsey and his Clambake Seven, Bunny Berigan and his Swing Gang, and Stuff Smith and his Onyx Club Band.

Shaw, accompanied by only a rhythm section and a string quartet, offered an original piece entitled "Interlude in B Flat." Shaw proved to be the surprise hit of the concert.

Encouraged by the audience's reception, Shaw soon formed his first organized band, consisting of Shaw on clarinet, Lee Castle (then known as Castaldo) and J.D. Wade on trumpets, Mike Michaels on trombone, Tony Pastor on tenor sax, Joe Lipman on piano, Gene Stultz on guitar, Ben Ginsberg on bass, Sammy Weiss on drums and—once again—a string quartet (two violins, a viola, and a cello). Why did he adopt such an unconventional instrumentation?

Artie Shaw. (Chip Deffaa collection)

"I was trying to do something that wouldn't bore me to death. It's that simple. I mean, if I'm bored, I quit," Shaw says. "I thought a string quartet was a very useful appendage. So I had that and a little jazzband. I couldn't afford what I wanted, which I finally did in 1940, with a big string section *and* a big dance band. I wanted that from the start, but how can you afford it? Life is a series of compromises. Every breath is a compromise."

The hip New York audience at the May 24th swing concert may have accepted the then-novel combination of strings and swing. But the general public in 1936 did not.

"We found we couldn't get booked," Shaw notes. "I couldn't stay alive with the band. The audience's demands and sensibilities at that time wouldn't accept what I was doing. Nobody would accept the idea of a jazz band built around a string quartet. And it was very difficult to get arrangers. I had to do most of the arranging myself. Nobody was writing for string quartets and small jazzbands."

Shaw continued with the string quartet band into 1937. But by late April of that year, he had reorganized along more conventional Swing Era lines (three trumpets, three trombones, four saxes, piano, bass, guitar, and drums, in addition to Shaw on clarinet). The billing now was: "Art Shaw and his New Music." ("Art" did not give way to "Artie" until the summer of '38.)

At first, bookings were slow for this second band, too. Shaw was living hand-to-mouth. The band traveled in a used bus that Shaw had purchased from Tommy Dorsey. The words "Tommy Dorsey and his Orchestra" were still emblazoned on the sides; Shaw could not afford to have the bus repainted.

From March until October of 1938, Billie Holiday sang with the band. Shaw comments simply: "Billie was the best singer I could find, so I hired her. She was out there looking for work. And I paid her what every man in the band got, $60 a week. That's all we could get. It was not much money. And sometimes I didn't make the $60 myself. I had to borrow money to stay alive, to keep that band going. It was very difficult."

In the summer of '38, the Artie Shaw Orchestra broke through big, with hits such as "Begin the Beguine," "Back Bay Shuffle," "Any Old Time," and "Indian Love Call"—all recorded on July 24, 1938. Vocalist Helen Forrest scored with numbers such as "A Room with A View" (December 19, 1938), "Deep Purple" (March 12, 1939), and "All the Things You Are" (October 26, 1939). Soon fans knew the names of key Shaw sideman such as saxists Tony Pastor and Georgie Auld and drummer Cliff Leeman, who was succeeded by 18-year-old Buddy Rich. And of course there was Shaw himself, who seemed capable of doing anything he wanted, flawlessly, on the clarinet. The long, clear, graceful lines of his solos were models of perfection. The band as a whole produced a tight, vibrant ensemble sound.

Shaw's band overtook Benny Goodman's, to become the number one swing band in the 1939 *Down Beat* poll. (Shaw's band did *not*, however, win the *Metronome* poll. Former *Metronome* editor George T. Simon recalls that the magazine received many ballots for Shaw which a handwriting expert determined had all been filled in by the same individual, as well as many typed ballots for Shaw which appeared to have been typed on the same typewriter; the magazine discarded them, and Goodman emerged as the winner.) Shaw, fans said, had dethroned "the King of Swing."

But Shaw bristles at the suggestion that he may have modeled his band on Goodman's.

"I didn't have that much regard for Benny Goodman," he states. "Why would I model myself on him? Tommy Dorsey had the same instrumentation. Did he model himself on Benny? He was there ahead of him. And the Casa Loma Band was ahead of that. People keep talking about Goodman! The Casa Loma Band was the first band to break through. They didn't hide behind the palms, and the musicians themselves made the band. Nobody ever knew the names of a musician in

Artie Shaw and his Orchestra. (Chip Deffaa collection)

Meyer Davis' Band. With the Casa Loma Band, they began to say: 'Oh, here's Pee Wee [Hunt], there's Grady Watts. . .' They began to know people; that was what it was about. So you could say: Did Benny Goodman model his band after the Casa Loma? Or after Fletcher Henderson?" There's a feisty, combatative streak in Shaw that surfaces periodically, and it's surfacing strongly now.

"I modeled my band after the fact that I needed three trumpets and I needed three trombones, and four reeds (not five, as we now have) and a rhythm section," Shaw insists. Case closed.

It was inevitable, however, that Shaw would be compared to Goodman, whether or not he was trying to model his outfit on Goodman's. After all, two superlative clarinetists were leading rival swing bands, with Goodman being promoted as "the King of Swing" and Shaw as "the King of the Clarinet." How could you not compare them? The most ardent fans of both band leaders saw themselves in rival camps. You were either a Goodman man or a Shaw man; you could not be both.

Without in any way minimizing Goodman's tremendous achievements, Shaw ultimately proved the more *creative* band leader. Goodman did his particular thing superbly! But he seemed to settle down, early in the '40s. He no longer was pushing too hard to try new things; he was content to continue presenting the same type of material. Shaw seemed more eager to experiment, to take risks.

Even Shaw's theme song, the moody, dramatic "Nightmare," was unlike any other band leader's. Shaw was always determined to set himself apart from the pack.

"I thought, if everybody's going to be playing a popular song [as a theme], I might as well have something that comes on a little startling. And so, when people said, 'What do you want to call it,' 'Nightmare' seemed as good a title as any," Shaw says.

"When we finally recorded it, I remember that we had to do a three minute and fifteen second record, and all that I had written was the opening and closing. So I had a stop watch on my wrist and I started playing, and building and building a composition. And finally it was time to quit—so I gave them a notation signal and we came to the end. That's the record. In the middle is all improvisation. But I made a kind of composition out of it, building up, up, up, up. And Dick plays it note for note, more or less, today."

Shaw expressed his individuality, too, by playing more *quality* songs—show tunes and evergreens—and fewer current pop songs than the other band leaders.

"The first thing I had to decide was: What do I want to do with this band that no one else has done? The best American songwriters were writing for theater. So I got a lot of those tunes (although there were several outcroppings, like 'Rose Room,' 'Moonglow,' 'I Cover the Waterfront'—some movie tunes). There were composers like Cole Porter, Jerome Kern, Gershwin, Dick Rodgers, Vincent Youmans out there. Why ignore those tunes? Why play 'Avalon' and 'Ida' and 'Jazz Me Blues' over and over? That was the jazz repertoire. I decided, let's get some good American music. I figured if I'd put my time and my energies in, on making arrangements of those things, I'd have a chance of making a classic.

"I thought that these songs would last awhile. You take a popular song, its life was three months. Why spend your time on a tune which is going to disappear in three months? So if you take 'Summertime,' you put an arrangement on that—you can play it for 50 years." Shaw had to fight to record some of the quality songs he believed in. He notes, for example, that RCA Victor didn't want him to record Cole Porter's "Begin the Beguine." It had been introduced in a Broadway flop called "Jubilee" and was considered dead when Shaw insisted in recording it

Artie Shaw and Lana Turner. (Chip Deffaa collection)

in mid '38.

Shaw's only regret, he says, is that he wasted even a portion of his energy on trivial pop songs that he didn't believe in. "I regret having made, 'You're a Sweet Little Headache.' I was talked into it. A lot of those. They weren't good tunes. We did the best we could with them but, you know, I owed a debt to somebody. I allowed myself to be influenced by those considerations. Today I wouldn't for a million dollars. If you're an artist, you've got to be ruthless about what you do."

In '37 and '38, Shaw notes, "I was doing arrangements, kind of prototype, pilot arrangements for other arrangers so they could hear what I wanted to do." But when the band finally broke through big, in the spring of '38, he found he had little time in his schedule for arranging. He left the arranging to others, among the most important of whom were Jerry Gray and Lennie Hayton.

"My band didn't have a quote, *style*. I didn't have, for example, that thing that Glenn Miller had—that one thing, that monotonous sound. (We used it sometimes—the end of 'Any Old Time,' which I wrote and arranged for Billie, for example, had the clarinet over the saxophones. But that wasn't a thing that we foisted on every tune.)" Shaw wanted his arrangers to look for the best way of presenting each individual tune.

"A band leader, if he's going to be any good, is really kind of an editor. He dictates a policy, and the band plays within that policy. Now if it's a broad policy, there's more variety. If it's a narrow, rigid policy like Glenn Miller had, they do one thing, over and over . . . [Miller played some] nice little tunes, but they're very rigid. Nothing, nobody ever makes a mistake," Shaw says. "One of the marks of a band that's trying is that they make a mistake occasionally. You hear some rough edges.

"Like a great painter, he doesn't make everything look like Norman Rockwell, where it's a perfectly framed picture. There's always a little something askew. Look at Degas. There's a portrait—'Woman with Flowers' I think is the name of it—half the picture or three quarters of the picture is flowers. And you see the woman off on one side. That was very astounding in its time. Because a portrait was—there's a head-on thing. Well, a lot of musicians play like that: head-on. Now and then, it's nice to take a thing from a side point of view.

"As I tell my audiences: Jazz is the ability to take a tune and see what's under it and around it and in it, and explore it. And deal with the potentialities in the tune that the composer himself might not have known."

* * *

Throughout his career, Shaw pushed himself to his limits. He developed recurring migraines, and other problems. (He kept large bottles of Emprin with codeine in his clarinet case for the headaches.) On September 16, 1938, he collapsed for the first time, during a battle of the bands with Tommy Dorsey at the 105th Armoury in New York. In April of of 1939, suffering from a strep throat, he collapsed again at the Palomar Ballroom in Los Angeles.

He developed *agranulocytopenia*, a blood disorder that is usually fatal, and he came close to dying himself. For a month, Tony Pastor fronted the band, and arranger Jerry Gray conducted for the band's Sunday night CBS radio show. Shaw returned to work as soon as he was able to do so.

In 1938 and '39, Shaw was one of the nation's preeminent pop idols ("the Madonna of my day," he quips). But he remained wary of the mass adulation. American pop culture puts heroes on pedestals quickly, and just as quickly replaces them with new heroes. Shaw saw the screaming, gaping, jitterbugging teenage fans. Their reactions often seemed to him moronic. Were they all capable of determining which music was the best? How much of their enthusiasm was due to a genuine appreciation of the music? How much was due to a bandwagon effect, a kind of mass hysteria in which American youth periodically get caught up?

Shaw had his own standards of perfection. He tried not to let public clamor control the direction his music took.

Shaw says he realized very early that the better his band got, the less the public would be able to appreciate it (a principle, he adds, that great artists such as Cezanne, Van Gogh, Blake were all aware of). "It's a total inverse ratio," Shaw says. "The better you get, the less people understand you. . . Finally you get so that you're talking to yourself."

When Shaw walked out on the music business in November of 1939, he had no expectation of ever leading a band again. His lawyer and manager told him he was crazy. He was turning his back on a profession that would make him a millionaire.

He didn't care, he told them. He had become sick of the whole scene. He didn't need to be gaped at by hero-worshipping, hysterical youths. And he had driven himself so hard, he had put his health in jeopardy.

Shaw rested in Mexico. The band continued for a few months without him, under the direction of saxophonist Georgie Auld. Without Shaw, however, it didn't draw the crowds.

By the following March, Artie Shaw was back in the recording studio again. He had *not* put together a permanent band; he was still insisting he'd never lead a big band again. But he was obligated to make a few more records under the terms of his old contract with RCA Victor. So he had assembled a large studio orchestra, including strings and woodwinds, simply to make the records required under the contract. Shaw hired William Grant Still, the noted black classical composer, to work with him in arranging a tune he had discovered while in Mexico: "Frenesi."

Shaw's 1940 recording of "Frenesi," made with the studio orchestra, proved to be one of the biggest hits of his career. It was almost as if Shaw couldn't escape commercial success. His former bookers pleaded with him to take out a big band again.

Meanwhile, Shaw found himself strapped for cash. He had spent his great earnings of 1938-39. He returned to band leading in 1940, he admits, primarily to meet his financial needs. Hits such as "Temptation" (September 7, 1940), "Star Dust" (October 7, 1940), "Moonglow" (January 23, 1941), and others soon followed. Shaw and his band were featured in the 1940 Paramount motion picture, "Second Chorus" (with Fred Astaire and Burgess Meredith). From July 1, 1940 through March 11, 1941, they also played on the popular Burns and Allen radio show.

Shaw used nine strings with his band in late 1940 and early '41.

Hollywood tapped Shaw to appear in two full-length films, Dancing Co-Ed *(1939) and* Second Chorus *(1940), plus several shorts.* (Chip Deffaa collection)

Shaw's 1941 band included a 15-piece string section. (Chip Deffaa collection)

On ballads, the band got a lush, romantic sound. Many jazz fans particularly enjoyed Shaw's unusual new small group (his band-within-the band), "the Gramercy Five," which included Johnny Guarnieri on harpsichord. (Who else but Shaw would feature a jazz harpsichord?) And the ever-lyrical trumpeter Billy Butterfield created solos of great beauty.

Shaw recalls that one night in 1940, shortly after Butterfield joined his band, "Billy was playing 'Star Dust' and he went for that E flat, and he splattered the note all over the wall. Pow! A mistake like you couldn't believe. I just signaled, it's OK. So he finished the solo and he came up to me after the set and said, 'Gee, Artie, I'm sorry.' I said, 'Don't be sorry. If you didn't do that once in a while, I'd know you weren't trying.' He said nobody had ever told him that before; he thought that was kind of liberating," Shaw says. It was something Shaw truly believed: the musicians—and the bands—that never made mistakes simply were not trying hard enough.

Shaw used the not-yet-famous Lena Horne as a vocalist for a June 26, 1941 studio date he organized, which also included Benny Carter on alto sax, J.C. Higginbotham on trombone, Jimmy Shirley on guitar, and Red Allen on trumpet. The musicians he selected, except for the string players, were all black—an unusual undertaking in 1941. They recorded such numbers as "Love Me a Little" and "Don't Take Your Love From Me."

He formed his next big band later in '41, featuring trumpeter Oran "Hot Lips" Page, and no less than 15 strings—32 musicians in total. This band recorded such numbers as "Blues in the Night" (September 2, 1941), "Beyond the Blue Horizon" (September 3, 1941), and "St. James Infirmary" (November 12, 1941).

During World War Two, Shaw led a Navy Band—a full-time entertainment unit which included Dave Tough on drums, Claude Thornhill (initially) on piano, and Sam Donahue on tenor sax. The band won an *Esquire Magazine* poll as the favorite band of the armed services. Donahue took over the band after Shaw's medical discharge from the Navy on February 23, 1944.

Shaw began rehearsing a new big band (without strings) in September of 1944. Ray Conniff and Eddie Sauter were among the arrangers for this brassy, forward-looking 18-piece outfit. This band recorded such numbers as "Ac-Cent-Tchu-Ate the Positive" (with Imogene Lynn on vocal, November 23, 1944), "'S Wonderful" (January 9, 1945), and "Summertime" (April 17, 1945). Band members Roy Eldridge (trumpet), Dodo Marmarosa (piano), Lou Fromm (drums), Morris Rayman (bass), and Barney Kessel (guitar) joined Shaw for "Gramercy Five" numbers, such as "Scuttlebut" and 'Mysterioso" (both recorded on July 31, 1945). By this time, Shaw's temperament was well known. A hapless RCA engineer left a note for his superiors, for example, that one of the numbers Shaw had cut at a 1945 recording session was longer than the company liked, but Shaw would have walked if prevented from doing it his way.

By 1946, Shaw was recording for the recently-formed Musicraft label, using as many as 24 strings. The vocalists he used included Kitty Kallen, Teddy Walters, and a singing group called the Mel-Tones. The group's 21-year-old lead vocalist, who had never sung solo on record before Shaw gave him his first chance, was Mel Torme. Shaw's 1946 orchestras were strictly studio ensembles, but a few years later, Shaw was once again performing "live" with a new band.

And so it went throughout Shaw's career. He repeatedly disbanded and re-organized bands, usually returning to music when he needed money. He drew upon the best available musicians; Hank Jones, Don Fagerquist, Zoot Sims, Al Cohn, Tal Farlow, Kai Winding, Mel Lewis, Don Lamond, and Gerry Mulligan all worked with Shaw at one time or another.

Shaw's eight wives have included such celebrities as Lana Turner,

Ava Gardner, and Evelyn Keyes. His marriages were big news in their day. But he prefers not to talk about them now.

After setting aside his clarinet, Shaw tried his hand at running a dairy farm in upstate New York for about a year. He lived in Spain from 1956-60, then returned to the U.S., where he did some film and theater producing. He wrote a novel, *I Love You, I Hate You, Drop Dead!*, which was published in 1965, and he is currently at work on another novel. But in none of his other activities has he made anywhere near the impact he made in the late '30s and early '40s in American popular music.

* * *

When Shaw looks back, is there any one band of his that he was proudest of, or most pleased with?

"No. They were all as good as they could be, of their kind," he says simply. "I would just get restless. People say: Why do you keep changing? Well, why does Beethoven write piano sonatas and symphonies

Shaw's potent 1945 edition of the Gramercy Five: Dodo Marmarosa, piano; the masterful Roy Eldridge, trumpet; Shaw, clarinet; Barney Kessel, guitar; Morris Rayman, bass; drummer Lou Fromm not in picture. (Chip Deffaa collection)

and string quartets?

"I mean, I don't know of any single composer worth talking about, or a musician worth talking about, who did only one thing. It'd be pretty dull. So I kept changing bands. Because different kinds of things would occur to me to do. And I'd need a different kind of instrumentation. It's like a painter. He's not going to paint blue all his life. Picasso painted a lot of different kinds of styles. Why? Because you're growing and you're changing."

Which of the other big bands did Shaw like the most or respect the most?

"Not too many. Not too many," Shaw answers. "I liked Ellington when he was *good*, when he was real good. But he never had really much of an influence, musically, on bands. . . I'm talking about an overall influence. Basie had an influence. I had an influence. Benny had an influence. Even Tommy had an influence, at his best. Because Tommy was a fine musician and he insisted on perfection in that band. And they gave him that. Very close to it. (The only thing is, he got into singers. When you get into singers, you're in the entertainment business.)"

Does Shaw ever wish that he had not stopped playing the clarinet? Has he ever wanted to take it up again?

"No, I don't want to. It's too tough, it's too tough," he declares. "It would have killed me. I'd be dead, now. I mean, my drive to hit perfection—not the best, but the best I could be—it was too, too stressful. So, people ask me if I miss it, the answer is: 'Yeah, if I cut off a gangrenous arm, I'll miss it, but I'd rather be alive with one arm.'"

How much did he practice in the old days? "Oh, Jesus. All the time. I had that horn in my mouth about eight, nine hours a day. That's too long. And there's no time for anything else; I've got a very avidly curious mind about a lot of other things. The music is one thing. Painting is another. Literature is another. So is life. So is whatever. There's too many other things."

How does Shaw view the musicians he's getting today? Are they as good as those he got during the big band era?

"Oh, technically, they're far more proficient. They can read better, they can play more things on their horn," he says. "The biggest problem you have is to get them to come down to an audience's comprehension level. Because sometimes they seem to be so steamed up, so gung ho, that they'll play a handful of notes at such rapid machine-gun fire that the audience can't even hear what they're doing. . . So my biggest problem is to get them to play with a little more selectivity, a little more discrimination. Fewer notes, more meaningful—and then throw in a cascade every once in a while. Then it becomes interesting.

"Last night Dick played some solos with much fewer notes. And I said, 'Man, that's the way to go!' Because you know, everybody playing a handful of notes, it's like saying, 'Look how fast my fingers can move.' It's very important to say, 'Look how good my head is, and how good my ear is.' Pops Whiteman, who wasn't a great musician but knew a good one when he heard one, once said, 'Bix can play more with three notes than most guys do in a chorus.' That's a good line; it says a lot. It's very important to pick your notes. Not to see how many of them you can play. That's something I'm trying to teach these guys."

* * *

Outside of the Blue Note in Greenwich Village, billed as "the World's Finest Jazz Club and Restaurant," signs proclaim: "First New York Club Appearance in 30 Years! In Person, the Legendary ARTIE SHAW and his Orchestra, Featuring Dick Johnson." It's opening night: August 13, 1985.

Inside the packed club, Shaw tells the audience they'll be hearing tunes from the libraries of about nine different bands he's led over the years: "—and all of it is jazz, despite what some critics say!"

The band leaps into "The Carioca." It's the original chart. And yet it's being played a bit crisper, brighter than on the '39 recording; the attack of the brass is sharper. There's a great ensemble ride-out, with Dick Johnson's clarinet rising smoothly above the rest.

It's apparent quite early in the evening that this is a magnificent band. Precise, well-routined—you think of what one of the young musicians told you before the set began, of the endless rehearsals Shaw ran before letting the band appear in public—but also with tremendous elan. And it's working with an outstanding library.

The program mixes the old and the new. "Softly as in a Morning Sunrise" begins the way you remember it from the record, then unfolds into something contemporary. Johnson and electric guitar player Joe Cohn (whose father, saxist Al Cohn, played with Shaw in 1949) trade fours, and Shaw signals them to keep going.

A septet within the band ("the Trafalgar Seven") offers "Beacon Hill Lavender," a new B flat minor blues composed by Johnson. The full band plays a strikingly modern *Porgy and Bess* suite (not all of which is easily taken in on first hearing). But they also offer Eddie Sauter's 40-year-old arrangement of "Summertime." ("Talk about validity!" Shaw says of the chart. "This will be just as good 100 years from now.') Is the performance as good as on the original recording? In this case, it is better. The tempo is a bit slower than on the record, more in keeping with the mood of the piece, and the piano is given more room to develop the theme. The brass articulates more precisely. It is the original arrangement—but actually more fully realized than on the original recording, more emotionally expressive.

"Star Dust" is a real test for the band, because Billy Butterfield's original solo on this number was such a memorable one. The safest approach might be for the current trumpeter to simply imitate Butterfield's original solo. But trumpeter Lou Colombo (one of the band's major assets) does not go that route. He makes his own statement, in his own style. It is a work of great beauty. And, especially important, it *fits*. The performance of the number tonight is breathtaking.

Not all of the soloists, however, can pull it off as effectively as Colombo. Big band music has changed greatly since the late '30s. If a trumpeter inserts a solo with influences of Dizzy Gillespie and his post-war followers into a 1938 chart, it will often stick out awkwardly. And most of today's trumpeters have been influenced by the beboppers.

There are moments tonight when that problem occurs, when the performance of an old arrangement lacks the cohesiveness of the original

recording because a trumpet or trombone soloist is not offering something in the same style as the rest of the chart.

It was easier, in a sense, to perform this music right when it was first created, when the soloists and arrangers all came from a common milieu, when they all naturally thought along similar musical lines. If today's Artie Shaw Orchestra has a problem, it is that some of the solos are played in too modern a fashion for the older charts; they do not seem integral to the music.

Other bands attack the problem differently. Woody Herman manages to avoid a clash of styles by discarding most of his old charts. He concentrates on newer numbers for his young players, and if he plays an older number, it's usually an updated version of the original chart. His players solo freely. A concert by Herman sounds contemporary throughout. The price paid for Herman's approach, of course, is that you lose good older arrangements that remain well worth hearing.

Vince Giordano, leader of the Nighthawks Orchestra (a big band dedicated to accurately reviving the music of the 1920s and '30s) uses vintage charts and note-for-note transcriptions of old records. He avoids stylistic clashes by having his soloists re-create, as near as possible, the solos performed on original recordings. Thus both solos and ensemble passages have the same vintage feel. The price paid for *that* approach is that you lose the opportunity for the soloist to surprise the audience. And re-created solos often cannot fully capture the *spirit* with which their creators imbued them.

By using older charts but allowing his soloists freedom to improvise as they please, Shaw is gambling. When everything works (as in "Star Dust'), the results can be awe-inspiring. If it's not quite working in some other cases, Shaw can try to counsel the soloists (or perhaps try to find other soloists more at home in the swing tradition). His charts are superb. Giving soloists freedom, it seems to me, is needed if the music is to remain alive.

Improvisation is at the very heart of jazz. (Shaw says it's like jumping off a cliff in the darkness and not knowing for sure if you'll be able to catch a branch or something to save yourself.) Shaw's musicians are playing the arrangements—both old and new—with great zest. If they were not given the freedom to express themselves in the solo spots, you wouldn't find that same zest in the band. The current Glenn Miller Orchestra, for example, allows its members comparatively little freedom of self-expression, and the band as a whole sounds mechanical and uninspired.

There is life and color in the Artie Shaw Orchestra, as well as, of course, technical prowess. And the phrasing of the band's most important soloist, Dick Johnson, seems consistently on target.

For my tastes, the Artie Shaw Orchestra (despite the occasional problems of soloists not meshing stylistically with the arrangements) is as satisfying to listen to, overall, as any big band touring the country today. And no other big band can do so many different things quite so well.

There are bands concentrating on modern jazz that surpass the Shaw Orchestra as *jazz orchestras* per se. But none of those bands can do as fine a job as Shaw's on the ballads.

And bands that concentrate on "sweet" music (such as "society" bands) typically can't offer much in terms of jazz.

Unlike some of the "ghost" bands working today, Shaw's band does offer some contemporary jazz originals, such as "Beacon Hill Lavender" and "Gradations." (Shaw says, and he's probably correct: "If we got much more radical, we'd play ourselves out of business.") And yet, unlike strictly contemporary bands, Shaw's band can turn around and romp brightly and effectively through a simple, early swing arrangement of "Rose Room." (How few bands can do this kind of simple, catchy swinging anymore!) And *then* go on to perform a romantic number like "Dancing in the Dark" or "Star Dust" to virtual

Dick Johnson with Artie Shaw. (Courtesy Thomas Cassidy)

perfection. Soloists come in with pinpoint accuracy; ensembles are rendered with both precision and feeling. For sheer beauty, the performances would be hard to beat. Shaw has an outstanding library of music, and his musicians are playing that music far more effectively than the musicians in the Glenn Miller Band or the Tommy Dorsey Band are playing theirs.

That this outstanding big band had to take a two-month layoff this past summer, though, says something.

"It's very tough out there," Shaw acknowledges. "Because the state of the art is: Run to the party, Prince is going to be there. Run to the party, Madonna is going to sing, 'I'm a Material Girl.' And run to the next party and you're going to hear, oh boy, that great thing called 'Girls Just Want to Have Fun.' That's what it's about."

Shaw is proud that his band is offering new compositions. And he is equally proud that his band is offering "Begin the Beguine," "The Carioca," "Summertime" and the rest, *in the original arrangements.* For Shaw believes passionately in the validity of this orchestrated jazz.

It may be necessary, Shaw believes, for our culture to subsidize quality big bands, the way it subsidizes symphony orchestras and ballet and opera companies. "This is a kind of American classical music that is worthy of being preserved and being cherished," he says. "No performer that I know of has been pointing that out, except me."

1985

CHRIS • GRIFFIN

Trumpeting in the Benny Goodman Band

In the late 1930s, Benny Goodman's Band won poll after poll as the nation's number one swing aggregation. Goodman's famed trumpet section, riffing with ease through the arrangements of Fletcher Henderson, Jimmy Mundy and others, was composed of Harry James, Ziggy Elman, and Gordon "Chris" Griffin.

There was no better trumpet section to be found. On the powerhouse numbers, the trumpets could hit hard—really dig into the material. They were strong, yet flexible. And when romantic ballads called for a gentler approach, they softened their touch, always with great intonation.

Though James and Elman are both gone now, Griffin is still very much a part of the musical scene. By temperament, Griffin was never much inclined towards the bravura displays that were hallmarks of both James and Elman. If Griffin didn't get to solo all that much with Goodman, he never seemed to mind. He may not have received the adulation from swing fans that James and Elman received, but he knew—and his musician peers knew—the value of the contribution he was making to the Goodman Band. Griffin was an ideal big band section member.

Griffin recalls of that celebrated trumpet section: "We switched, alternated, in playing lead. Benny never knew who was playing lead . . . . And we never got the [sheet] music out, ever, except for the two or three numbers we'd been given last. We sat on the books [the arrangements]. Then when Harry left to form his own band, a new trumpet player, who shall remain nameless, came in. He made a mistake in reading an arrangement. It threw Ziggy and me—we both dove for our books."

Griffin's tenure in the Goodman Band was the highlight of his career. He played in the band for four years (1936-40), when the band

Chris Griffin. (Courtesy Chris Griffin)

was at its peak. After leaving Goodman, Griffin never lacked for work. He found financial security—if not always creative satisfaction—freelancing in the recording and broadcasting industry. At one time or another, he worked with most of the big names, from Tommy and Jimmy Dorsey to Ella Fitzgerald and Frank Sinatra. There was TV work with the likes of Jackie Gleason, Milton Berle, Garry Moore, and Ed Sullivan. Music increasingly became simply a job for Griffin—something one did to pay the kids' college bills, without concern for what one was assigned to play. It wasn't at all like that in the earlier years, Griffin recalls. Then, music was something special and alive.

Griffin and the music that became known as swing grew up together. It has often been suggested that the Swing Era was "born" with the tremendous success of the Benny Goodman Band at the Palomar Ballroom in late 1935. There is truth in that notion. But pioneering bandleaders and arrangers—men like Fletcher Henderson, Don Redman, and Benny Carter—had been working out the details of how one made a big band swing since the mid-1920s.

Griffin was born October 31, 1915 in Binghamton, New York. When he was 10, his family moved to White Plains, New York. He started on the trumpet when he was 12 (he had already taken a few years of piano lessons by then), and he was soon playing in bands at school and church dances.

In 1927-'28-'29, when other kids his age were more interested in playing ball, Chris Griffin was turning his radio dial to find the pioneering big swing bands, which broadcast from distant clubs and dance halls, places he had no hope of ever visiting in person.

"I started listening to the radio a lot at age 12 or so. I'd listen to Don Redman, Claude Hopkins at night. I'd lie on the floor with my ear towards the speaker and wish I was there with them," Griffin recalls.

At age 15, Griffin joined the New York musicians' union to play in a band at a ten-cents-a-dance taxi dance hall next door to New York's renowned Palace Theater. At the Palace Theater, he could see some of the great bands he had previously enjoyed only on radio and records. He remembers seeing Paul Whiteman, Duke Ellington, and Jean Goldkette "live" in New York in this period, as well as presentation bands—far removed from jazz, but enjoyable to him none-the-less—such as Fred Waring and his renowned Pennsylvanians, and Frank and Milt Britton's comedic band. He gained experience working around the New York-New Jersey area for the next three years.

Griffin was 19 when he made his first recording session (September 20, 1935), backing Mildred Bailey on "When Day is Done," and several other sides for Decca. Red Norvo, who was married to Bailey, led the jazz band assembled for the date, which included such players as Chu

Berry on tenor, Artie Bernstein on bass, Dick McDonough on guitar, and a piano player fresh out of Chicago by the name of Teddy Wilson. Such racially mixed jazz groups were unusual in the early '30s.

In the fall of '34, Griffin met trumpeter/arranger Toots Camarata (who would later arrange most of Jimmy Dorsey's big hits). Together, they helped Joe Mooney, a blind pianist, accordionist, singer and composer, organize his first band, which played for six weeks at a club in Hackensack, New Jersey, called the Eldorado. Many top musicians came out to Hackensack to hear Mooney's group.

In the winter of 1934-35, Griffin joined Scott Fisher's Orchestra, which was booked for an engagement at the Tic Toc Club atop the Park Central Hotel. Performing in the adjacent Coconut Grove was Charlie Barnet's Band. After finishing with Fisher, Griffin would head over to sit in with Barnet. When Fisher's engagement ended, Griffin joined Barnet's Band. His fellow trumpeters in the band included Toots Camarata and Eddie Sauter (who also arranged). Red Norvo, Griffin recalls, acted as a kind of sub-leader in the band.

Barnet was far from famous then, but he had a strong, swinging band, featuring his own virile tenor and some advanced charts for 1934. Barnet's was the first white band to play the Savoy Ballroom and the Apollo Theater in Harlem, according to Griffin. Barnet's Band was playing the Apollo, Griffin recalls, while Jimmie Lunceford's Band was playing at the neighboring Harlem Opera House. Band members fraternized, and Griffin struck up lasting friendships with Lunceford's drummer, Jimmy Crawford, and his arranger and trumpeter, Sy Oliver, who would later have so much to do with creating the sound of the Tommy Dorsey Band of the '40s. The Barnet Band headed on tour, finally landing at the Roosevelt Hotel in New Orleans for six weeks.

Meanwhile, on August 21, 1935—the date some consider the birth date of the Swing Era—Benny Goodman's Band opened at the Palomar Ballroom in Los Angeles. The band hadn't enjoyed much success to this point. In fact, it had just concluded a cross-country tour so disastrous that Goodman assumed he would have to give up the band.

At the Palomar, Goodman pulled no punches. He figured if the band was going to go out, it might as well go out swinging. He was as surprised as anyone at the enthusiastic reaction of the young people who packed the Palomar when the band dug into Fletcher Henderson's arrangements of "King Porter Stomp," "Blue Skies," and "Sometimes I'm Happy." Goodman's triumph at the Palomar secured him a line of bookings. More than that, it virtually launched the Swing Era. Other leaders tried to emulate his band, and they tried to steal his players.

In the fall of 1935, Griffin joined Joe Haymes' Band. Haymes kept forming bands which other musicians would hire away. Tommy Dorsey, for example, had just hired virtually all of Haymes' musicians, to form his first big band of his own, in September of '35. Griffin did not stay too long with Haymes—just long enough to fall in love with, and marry, Haymes' female vocalist, Helen O'Brian, to whom he is still married.

Griffin next landed a coveted spot in the CBS radio house orchestra, replacing Bunny Berigan, who had left to form his own group.

Jazz aficionado/record producer John Hammond, who was the number one booster of the Benny Goodman Band from its inception in 1934, heard Griffin one night in the spring of 1936 and asked: "Do you think you're ready to join the Benny Goodman Band?"

Griffin recalls: "It was like asking a rookie if he wanted to play with the Yankees! We all loved that band. It was *the* band at the time."

At the time, Griffin was making $110 a week at CBS—when $30 or $35 a week was a good wage. "I told Benny I'd like $125 a week. Benny said: 'How about $100?' 'I've *been* making $110,' I told him. 'Yes,' Benny said, '—but you weren't playing with the Benny Goodman

Benny Goodman Orchestra, summer of 1936. Chris Griffin is at far right. (Institute of Jazz Studies).

Band.' " Griffin joined on Goodman's terms. Goodman, Griffin would learn, had a general reputation for being tight with a buck.

The other trumpet players in the Goodman Band, when Griffin joined in the Spring of '36, he recalls, were Pee Wee Erwin (who was to become a lifelong friend) and Nate Kazebier. Goodman was making changes in personnel. Trumpeters Zeke Zarchy, Manny Klein, and Irving Goodman (brother of Benny) all worked for Goodman at least briefly in the next few months. By year's end, Goodman had hired Ziggy Elman and Harry James. The trumpet section of James, Elman, and Griffin remained intact throughout 1937 and '38. The personnel of the whole band remained rather stable in that period—almost unquestionably the peak period of the Goodman Band—before Goodman's stars began leaving the band.

After Griffin joined the band, they headed west on one-nighters. In California, the band appeared (along with Jack Benny, Burns and Allen, and others) in *The Big Broadcast of 1937* (which was actually filmed in 1936). After some road work, they hit New York, opening at the Madhattan Room of the Hotel Pennsylvania for a lengthy stay. And then came the Paramount, where the band had the kids jitterbugging in the aisles.

There were a raft of classic Goodman sides in this period: "Sing, Sing, Sing" and "Bugle Call Rag" (both July 6, 1937), "Changes" (July 7, 1937), "Sugarfoot Stomp" (September 6, 1937), "Roll 'Em" (February 15, 1938), "Don't Be That Way" (February 16, 1938), "One O'Clock Jump" (February 16, 1938), and "I Let a Song Go Out of My Heart" (April 22, 1938).

In *Hollywood Hotel*, a 1937 Busby Berkeley musical, the Goodman Band wailed "Sing Sing Sing" (among other numbers). It was a dramatic performance, as satisfying to watch as to listen to, thanks to some imaginative lighting, editing, and camera work—one of the few times Hollywood has shown how a big band can be photographed effectively.

Louis Prima got composer credits on "Sing Sing Sing." Although he created the original melody, members of the Goodman Band worked out, during live performances, the extended routine which the public remembers. Griffin recalls: "A couple riffs were mine, some were Pee Wee's, some were Harry James.' It was a head arrangement, after the beginning part. It was written out later."

Griffin took comparatively few solos in the Goodman Band, though he was featured on "Boy Meets Horn," composed by Duke Ellington. And on the recording of the Carnegie Hall Concert, Griffin's horn takes the brief but electric solo on "The Blue Room." Harry James and Ziggy Elman had far more featured spots. Griffin comments simply: "They were very sensational players. I was a more quiet type player."

He greatly enjoyed playing alongside James and Elman, he says. He recalls with justifiable pride: "Duke Ellington said it was the greatest trumpet section there'd ever been."

Swing fans were puzzled by the fact that the Goodman trumpeters took turns in leading. (Most bands had a lead trumpeter, a featured hot soloist, and a third trumpeter who simply followed what the lead trumpeter was playing.) Harry James, writing in *Metronome* magazine in June, 1938, explained:

> We just get the first parts in rotation. If an arrangement comes in and it's Ziggy's turn to get the lead, he takes it; if it's Chris's turn, he takes it, and if it's my turn, it's handed over to me. . .
>
> The funny part is, though, that most people can't tell just by listening which one of us is playing lead. And it seems funny that we should have such similar tones and style when we play so differently. Chris has a one-third top, two-thirds bottom embouchure, Ziggy's is two-thirds top and one third bottom and dangerously close to his ear, while mine's a slightly off-center, half-and-half, puffed-out-cheek affair.[1]

Griffin is proud that he, James, and Elman had such good rapport that Goodman could not tell who was leading the section. "The second and third trumpets would simply play up to whoever had the first part," says Griffin, "and we blended very well. We played together so much that it became second nature to think as one.

"These days it seems that everybody wants to play lead; but the harmony parts, the underneath parts, are just as important. A bandleader has to get this idea across. To get the best sound you have to have good sections. You can have a band with great individual players, but if the members of each section don't gel, they won't produce as good a sound as a band made up of lesser players who play as a team."

Griffin says that the endless repetition of material during rehearsals and performances made the numbers sound almost effortless, as if they were being improvised; he also says it gave the players a feeling of unity.

"The training I got with Benny Goodman was excellent—the best," says Griffin. "He was a hard taskmaster and, at first, I thought maybe too hard. His way of rehearsing a band was like nobody else's, and it seemed like a lot of extra work at the time; but Benny got results.

"First we'd run the chart down as a group, then the brass and reed sections would rehearse separately. Finally the two sections would rehearse the number together, over and over, without the rhythm section. None of the other leaders I worked with rehearsed a band this way—without the drums, bass, guitar and piano. We had to keep time and make the tune swing by ourselves. Benny's idea was that, in this way, the band would swing better and have a lighter feel. If you didn't depend on the rhythm section to swing, you would swing that much more when the rhythm section finally was brought in.

"It wasn't a complex book. The arrangements were not that tough, actually. All Benny was interested in was that it would swing. He knew simple things go best. The more complex a number is, the harder it is to make it swing. But he was a hard taskmaster with rehearsals. They were too long, sometimes. 'Let's just take the intro again,' he'd say. You'd start at the beginning, waiting for him to cut it off, and play it all the way to the end again. We'd rehearse over and over—especially the part that included his solo."

Griffin recalls clearly the many attempts of rival bandleaders to steal musicians from Goodman. Different ones used different approaches, he says. Artie Shaw, he remembers, "would be lingering in the

A rare shot of Chris Griffin soloing with the Benny Goodman Orchestra, 1939. (Frank Driggs collection)

hallways, sort of like someone selling French postcards. He'd whisper: 'Chris, would you like to join my band?' Tommy Dorsey, on the other hand, would come in with an entourage—a few musicians and [vocalist] Jack Leonard. He would sit down next to Benny Goodman—or within earshot—and say, loud enough for everyone to hear: 'Why don't you guys join a good band?' And Jimmy Dorsey—a beautiful, warm man, quiet, a lot easier to sit around and talk to than Tommy—he'd never try to steal players at all."

The January 16, 1938 Carnegie Hall Concert may have been the high water mark of Goodman's career as an orchestra leader. Gene Krupa left to form his own band early in 1938. Harry James left to form *his* own band early in '39. (Griffin recalls being introduced shortly afterwards to Harry James' new band singer, a skinny young kid that nobody had yet heard of, who said something like: "Gee Mr. Griffin, it's an honor meeting you." The singer was Frank Sinatra.) In 1939, pianist Jess Stacy quit Goodman, declaring that working with Goodman had been too great a strain, that he had never really known where he stood with Goodman. The following year saw the departure of Lionel Hampton to form *his* band, and Ziggy Elman to star in Tommy Dorsey's Band. Although Goodman found excellent musicians to replace every one of the musicians who left his band, the overall effect was never quite the same again. The great Goodman Band of '37-'38 was gone forever. Goodman would try new, musically more complex, directions in the '40s. But his major contribution to American music had now been made.

* * *

"I gave my notice to Benny early in 1940," Griffin recalls. "I went back on staff at CBS for four or five months, before freelancing. I was expecting my second child, I was 24, I wanted to settle down."

Under leaders such as Ray Bloch, Leith Stevens, and Axel Stordahl, Griffin played for many of the top radio programs of the day—from quiz shows to crime shows to variety shows. When Frank Sinatra decided to go "on his own," after singing with Harry James and Tommy Dorsey, it was Griffin who—at Sinatra's request—organized the brass section for the radio orchestra backing him. Griffin worked on Perry Como's show and Kate Smith's show. He recorded with Peggy Lee, Billie Holiday, Dick Haymes, Ella Fitzgerald, Louis Armstrong, and Bing Crosby.

And there were always chances to sit in with name bands. "I would sub for Bunny Berigan when he was with Tommy [Dorsey], between doing an early and a late show on radio. If I had an early radio show that I'd have to repeat three hours later for the West Coast, I could do a 10:00 show in between with Tommy or Jimmy. I miss both the Dorseys."

Griffin recorded with bandleaders such as Artie Shaw, Woody Herman, Tommy and Jimmy Dorsey, and Bob Crosby. All of the bandleaders knew he would be a reliable, solid contributor to a brass section.

Griffin found steady work in television. It was Griffin's horn soaring above the ensemble that viewers heard each week at the opening and close of the "Jackie Gleason Show." Griffin improvised the trumpet obligato, which was then written into the arrangement. Gleason also recorded instrumental albums (on which he would serve as conductor) from time to time. "Jackie Gleason would get, like, four brass sections and a rhythm section in the studio. The most outlandish groups. His name for me embarrassed the hell out of me. When I'd come into the room, he'd say: 'Here's steel-lips now!' "

Griffin played in the "Tonight Show" orchestra when it was conducted by Skitch Henderson. And he played in the orchestra on the "Ed Sullivan Show," from the very first broadcast in 1948 straight through until the last broadcast in 1971.

This was a far cry from the music he had originally wanted to play, he says, but he had six kids, and it supported his family well. He reflects, though: "I lost a hell of a lot of interest in music playing with Ed Sullivan weekly. We played for every kind of act. I was just playing to put my kids through college. I didn't listen to the music we were playing, backing dog acts and so on. It was very commercial. I became a commercialized musician."

From 1966-1970, he and Pee Wee Erwin ran the Erwin-Griffin Music School, with nine studios and thirteen instructors. The late Erwin was a close friend of Griffin's, whose career had followed a similar pattern. Erwin was a featured trumpeter with Benny Goodman and Tommy Dorsey in the '30s, then vanished into the recording and broadcasting studios, re-emerging to play more small group jazz late in life.

The networks dissolved their house bands in the early '70s, Griffin says. "In 1973, I called a friend with a band at Tammiment Resort in the Poconos. In the summer I could play in the band evenings, and play golf every day. For nine years, I was up there."

He's gotten periodic calls to work in big bands. In 1973, for example, he went to England with a Tommy Dorsey-type unit led by trombonist Warren Covington, and featuring Pee Wee Erwin. He's played with Guy Lombardo's Royal Canadians under the direction of Art Mooney. And for a couple of concert dates recently, he played the old Glenn Miller warhorses in a band put together for Tex Beneke.

Griffin also played with Benny Goodman — both on records and in concert appearances — on a number of occasions over the years after he left the Goodman Band in 1940. The last times were in a series of a dozen or more concerts, perhaps five years ago, Griffin says.

"Benny is a very odd person," Griffin comments. "He's hurt an awful lot of people. Not me. But he could be very difficult. He's an enigma, hard to figure out. The last time we worked together, he said something like: 'You're playing your butt off. Never heard you play better.'" In spite of the comment, Goodman never called Griffin to work for him again, Griffin notes.

Griffin says he would never want to fully retire. Today, with his children grown and his responsibilities lessened, he gets more opportunities to play in small-group jazz settings. He'll occasionally play jazz at spots such as Eddie Condon's in New York. He performs regularly in New Jersey with the "Syncopatin' Six," led by bass player Warren Vache Sr. He enjoyed working with Bud Freeman a while back at Waterloo Village in New Jersey. When the opportunity arises, he'll lead his own "Chris Griffin All-Stars," a group which, depending upon the occasion, might include players such as Walt Levinsky and Bobby Levine (reeds), Marty Napoleon or Jane Jarvis (piano), Sonny Igoe (drums), Major Holley (bass), and the like. He's a self-effacing kind of leader, happy to give every other member of the group as much or more solo space as he gives himself.

Griffin's horn is not as strong as it was 40 years ago (any more than Frank Sinatra's voice is as strong as it was 40 years ago), but give him a good old good one, such as "The Tin Roof Blues," to stretch out lazily on, and he'll show that he still has plenty to teach most younger trumpet players. It is evident in his small-group jazz work that he formed his style in the era when Armstrong was the dominant force, and that he hasn't been influenced at all by post-Swing Era stylists. He gets an attractive, burnished sound (sometimes with just a bit of grit in it to make it interesting). He can make much of just a few notes, in the melodious way that Armstrong could (which sometimes seems to be a dying art).

He says: "The sound you get from your horn is more important than playing a lot of notes. Young musicians should listen to lots of good players of all styles, and work on intonation. A lot of today's players are too damn notey. The musicians went beyond the public, using 64th notes throughout.

"Which trumpeters do I enjoy? I can listen to Ruby Braff, Warren Vache I like very much, Pee Wee [Erwin], Bobby Hackett, Yank Lawson (he's unique), Billy Butterfield. Of course Louis Armstrong," Griffin says. And, he adds, he enjoys listening to his son, Paul Griffin, a trumpeter in England who leads a jazz-rock fusion group.

On a wall in the living room of the Dumont, New Jersey home in which he's lived for more than 20 years, Griffin has a plaque from the

National Academy of Recording Arts and Sciences in recognition of his participation in Benny Goodman's history-making 1938 Carnegie Hall Concert. The recording of that concert has been given "hall of fame" status by NARAS. But otherwise, there are no mementoes in sight, no visible cues that Griffin was once part of America's number one swing band.

Plenty of trumpeters would have given their eye teeth to have been in Griffin's position in the late '30s, playing those celebrated Goodman killer-dillers night after night. Certainly, it was a thrill and an honor for Griffin to have been chosen for the Benny Goodman Orchestra in 1936, and to have played in that powerhouse outfit throughout its peak years. But he notes that personally, his tastes in music leaned towards less sensational-type playing.

"I'd rather have been with a more melodic band like Les Brown's than with the Goodman Band," Chris Griffin comments. Which other bands did he like? "Claude Thornhill had a very pretty band. Woody Herman I would've liked back then. Woody's a little too strong and powerful for me now. I always liked the melodic bands."

1983

BUCK • CLAYTON

From China to Basie, and Beyond

If one person knows how to make a big band swing, it's the one-and-only Buck Clayton," declares bandleader Loren Schoenberg, 27, at a 1986 tribute to the renowned trumpeter and arranger at New Jersey's Somerset County College.

Clayton led his own band in the U.S. and China (1933-36) before rising to fame as a trumpeter in Count Basie's original big band (1936-43), and going on to a distinguished career as a major jazz soloist. Now retired from trumpet playing, he concentrates on arranging.

Clayton writes in a classic swing style. You savor his music because you realize there's almost nobody writing like that anymore. There are a good number of arrangers writing swinging charts with the spirit of the modern-day bands of Basie, Woody Herman, or Buddy Rich. But Clayton can write material that would have been well suited for the *original* Basie Band (and he *did* write for that band, from the very beginning). His music can convey the spirit of the late '30s. That was his era. And the musical values he absorbed in growing up, which would have once shaped his trumpet solos, today shape his arrangements for big bands. The simple, buoyant swing he writes is *not* being turned out by younger arrangers today. It's almost as if one had to have grown up in his generation to write it naturally. Schoenberg's band loves playing Clayton's music today. And it's simply a joy to hear.

At the Clayton tribute, the band alternates between brand new compositions by Clayton—such as "Pretty Peepers," with the saxes rising fluidly through circular phrases, and "Smoothie," with four muted trumpets reminding us you don't have to swing hard to slay an audience—and well-remembered oldies such as "Avenue C" and "Down for Double," which Clayton scored for Basie more than four decades earlier. The bandleader tells the audience of Clayton's work on some classic Billie Holiday recordings, and trumpeter Dick Sudhalter

Buck Clayton. (Photo by Nancy Miller Elliott)

rises to evoke Clayton's original, sensitive obligatos. Then Paulie Cohen, former lead trumpeter with the Dorsey Brothers and Basie, comes down in front to re-create an early Clayton tour-de-force, "Fiesta in Blue." Cohen finds all of the drama in the first, plunger-mute chorus, and then wraps things up with brilliant open work—the individual notes hitting the audience smack in the face.

A clearly-moved Clayton tells the audience: "The band sounds beautiful and it knocks me out. For me, it's quite an emotional trip, hearing things I did. . . a few years ago. It's a pleasure hearing Dick Sudhalter play my first recorded solo on 'Why Was I Born,' and hearing Paul Cohen play my solo on 'Fiesta in Blue.' If I knew they were going to play those solos later, I'd have played them better the first time!"

* * *

Wilbur "Buck" Clayton, one of the true greats of jazz, was born November 12, 1911, in Parsons, Kansas. He started out at age six on piano, he tells me during a relaxed afternoon visit to his Jamaica, Queens, New York home. From about age seven on, he worked in a trio with two other boys—one of whom drummed, the other hummed on a tissue-paper-covered comb. They entertained at birthday parties, playing popular songs of the day, such as "Hard-to-Get Gertie."

Clayton was 18 when he switched to trumpet, inspired in part by the man who was *the* premiere trumpet player in nearly everybody's opinion in 1929: Louis Armstrong.

"Louis was one of the main reasons that I switched to trumpet," Clayton recalls. "My father had a church band. And they'd play for marches on Sundays, they'd play in the park on Sunday afternoons, free. He had been trying to get me to get a little cornet anyway, and play in the band with him. And when I heard Louis the first time, I said, 'Oh well, *that's it*. I'm going to get me a trumpet.'"

Clayton's parents supported his interest in becoming a musician, even if they did not share his enthusiasm for hot music. "My mother didn't care too much for jazz. She liked classical music. But she didn't object. And my father, he didn't object either. But he didn't know much about jazz. The only thing he knew about jazz was Fats Waller. He liked Fats Waller. But that's about the only one I ever heard him speak of. My mother didn't care much for jazz, until years later, when I played Carnegie Hall. Then she says, 'Well, if jazz is good enough to go into Carnegie Hall, it must be pretty respectable now.' Because in the early days it wasn't. The only people who liked jazz was prostitutes. And they'd play in these little dives way down in the basement somewhere. And fights and all that. So my mother didn't want that."

With a friend, Clayton bummed a ride to California on a freight train. He stayed a few months, practicing on his trumpet; he was not yet good enough to get work professionally. He returned to Kansas to finish high school (he graduated in 1930), and then set out again—this time "for good"—for California.

He took whatever day jobs he could find in Depression-era Los Angeles: working in garages, washing dishes, and the like. And he sat in on trumpet where he could. His first real, steady gig, he recalls, was playing in a six-piece band in a taxi dance hall.

From there, he moved up to a 14-piece big band, in which he played for about a year. "And that was the first time I'd ever seen an arrangement, you know, when they brought in these pieces of music. Because in the taxi dance hall, we didn't have music; we'd just play. I learned arranging mostly out of curiosity. I couldn't understand how a man could write for saxophones and trombones and everything—and he doesn't play them." Clayton studied with the band's arranger. "And then after I got into it, I liked arranging about the same as I liked playing."

Clayton was the youngest member of the next big band he joined—Earl Dancer's—but with his flair for arranging and his growing prowess as a trumpet soloist, he quickly established himself as a key member of the band. Dancer had been Ethel Waters' husband and manager. But he and Waters had had a falling out, so Dancer had moved from New York to Los Angeles, where he organized a band and opened a nightclub as the band's base. Dancer had plenty of contacts in the film industry,

Buck Clayton's Big Band, early 1930s. (Courtesy Buck Clayton)

and soon his band was working steadily in pictures.

"We made a lot of movies," Clayton recalls. "The very first one I made was called *Broadway Bad*. Another was called *Lady for a Day*. And we did part of the music for *Forty-Second Street*. I used to work in the movies two or three times a week, almost. Sometimes we were just on the soundtrack. But a lot of times we were seen in the movie, too. George Raft was one of my favorite people. Sometimes our acting would be playing on the stand, and the gangsters would come in and all of a sudden the whole place would be shot up. Our acting part would be to be scared and grab our horns and run off. That was about all the acting we ever did."

But Earl Dancer, Clayton notes, was an inveterate gambler. He would take the band's earnings, get into a poker game, and lose everything. Too many times, he was unable to pay his musicians. "The guys in the band didn't want to break it up because it was a good band. But we couldn't go on like this. Because we didn't have any money—we couldn't pay our hotel rent—he'd lose it all the time," Clayton recalls. "So we decided to dump Earl. And they chose me to be the leader of the band because I could write; I had been writing arrangements."

It was 1933. An agent arrived in town from Shanghai, China. He was seeking to book a band for a lavish international casino in Shanghai. He asked Clayton if the band would be interested in working overseas. "We all were very happy to go," Clayton notes. "Nobody was making any money in the states in 1933. There was breadlines, people selling apples. They offered us $100 a week—each—to go over there. And I was making $250, because I was the leader. That was a *lot* of money in that time. (The average salary in the states was around $20 a week at that time.) So we went over and stayed a couple of years. We had a beautiful time over there.

"We played in the international settlement in Shanghai. There were Russians, Americans, French, Japanese, English, everybody was in this settlement. But they had to be rich. And we were in the casino, a beautiful place. There was gambling. In the back there was greyhound racing. And oh, all kind of—everything.

"We played all my arrangements. Some of them were originals, some of them were standards, and some of them were Duke Ellington's. There was another band there from America, too, in a big hotel. They used to come down and listen to us, when we'd play," Clayton recalls. Clayton's band included alto saxist Caughey Roberts, who Clayton would later bring into Count Basie's Band. Teddy Weatherford starred on piano.

"That was a very pleasant two years. I decided to leave China only because I knew there was going to be a war. The Japanese were coming into China and they were holding maneuvers—right in the middle of Shanghai. The nightclubs would stay open all night. Sometimes we'd come out of a club around seven o'clock in the morning, and we'd see these Japanese soldiers, running behind automobiles with their guns, training. The Chinese people were so afraid of the Japanese.

"So I told my guys, we better get ready to get out of here, because it's going to explode pretty soon. And about 10 days after we left, the war broke out. We got out just in time."

* * *

"I arrived back in the U.S. in '36 and re-formed the band. And we played a few dates around Los Angeles and Hollywood.

"But by that time, I wanted to come to New York. Hollywood closes up at 11:00 at night. (It used to, then.) I couldn't convince my guys to come to New York. They said, 'Nah, there's too many musicians out of work.' And too, they liked the way of living in California. Barbecues, outdoors. And they all had nice homes. So I finally said, 'Well, OK, you guys can stay here, but I'm going to split. I'm going to go, myself.'

"I was on my way to join Willie Bryant, here in New York. But I stopped back in Kansas to see my mother. My town's only about an hour and fifteen minutes ride from Kansas City. And when I went to see my mother, well—I had heard about Count Basie and Lester Young and the guys while I was back in California. So I said, 'I'll go listen to them on the way to New York.' And I went to Kansas City and I met Basie. I met everybody, and everybody knew me, because they had heard me broadcast from California. And Basie said, 'Well, you know we're going to New York in about two months and I need a trumpet player'—because Lips Page had just left—'Why don't you go with us?'

"That's how I joined Basie. After I heard them, they sounded so good that I figured Willie Bryant couldn't sound any better than these guys. And they were going to New York. They had some good jobs lined up in New York. Roseland Ballroom was the first one. And some big hotels.

"But first, I played with his band out there, at the Reno Club in Kansas City. I stayed about six weeks or two months."

What was Kansas City like, during Clayton's stay in 1936? "I don't know; It's hard to describe," he answers. "Because there was no money in Kansas City, but everybody seemed to be having a good time. We were making $14 a week. See, I had come from $250 down to $14, just to come with Basie. But everybody had a ball, I think, just playing. We didn't care about much. But it was such a pleasure to play, with Basie and the guys. Everything was cheap. The meals, you could eat for 75 cents. And we knew that there were better things coming later, so we just had a good time.

"And the guys used to meet, to jam. In Kansas City, when we'd get through work, Lester would leave from our club and Jo Jones, practically the whole band. And then guys playing with other bands—when they'd get through work at four in the morning, everybody would meet in this one place where we used to go to jam, then we'd stay up all night until eleven o'clock in the morning. . . You'd sleep till it's time to go to work. And do the same thing day after day. Get up, eat and go to work, and do the same thing."

Some musicians were aware of Count Basie in September of 1936, Clayton notes, but as far as the general public was concerned: "Nobody knew anything about Basie. Nobody." Count Basie's recently organized band (which at that point included but nine musicians) had not yet made any records, had not yet played anywhere except in Kansas City.

"At that time in the band, we had a trumpet player named Tatti Smith, and another fellow was Joe Keyes. Plus myself. Three trumpets, one trombone: George Hunt. The band was only nine pieces. The saxes were: Lester [Young] and Jack Washington. Herschel [Evans]—after I left California, he had joined Lionel Hampton. Then when we got ready to leave Kansas City to go to New York, Basie sent for Herschel to come. And Herschel came, in time for us to leave for New York together. But he didn't play in the Reno. We had Jo Jones [drums], Walter Page [bass], Basie [piano], two saxophones and four brass."

The band had drawn the attention of jazz aficionado John Hammond, who had been instrumental in getting it booked into New York, which was a prerequisite for national success.

"But we had to expand the band now. You know, to play in the Roseland Ballroom, you couldn't go in there with nine men. There was a law that said you had to have so many men. We opened up against Woody Herman. And he had 16, I think. He was on one bandstand, and we were on the other. So we had to hire six more guys. Which put us up to about 15. And later went up to 16. But we had to get some new fellows to add on.

"But that did something, it slowed the band down. Because when it was nine, everything just flowed so evenly. And when you get these other guys and they don't know the music, we had to rehearse a lot. And at first it didn't work out so good. Later, of course, it did—when we got good guys.

"We played Chicago, in the Grand Terrace. These six new guys that we had brought in to augment the band from nine to sixteen, we found some of them couldn't read. And we didn't know it. We thought they were reading until they put some music in front of us in Chicago. And it was for a show. Two shows a night. And some of the music was a little hard, like a dancing team or an acrobatic team, where it wasn't just ordinary music. You had cues and things. And some of these guys couldn't read. So that's when we almost fired the whole six that we had added to the band. And that's when Freddie [Green] came in, Dickie Wells came in, Benny Morton came in—so it was altogether a better band. Much better. . . Caughey Roberts, who had been in my band in China, came to New York with us, played the Roseland, but then they hired Earle Warren instead, because Earle was a better lead saxophone player."

The band Clayton joined in Kansas City was not using written arrangements. "It was all what we called head arrangements. We'd get together and play on something and then memorize it. I was the first one to write for the band, after I joined it. Then I wrote some things. The very first arrangement that I wrote we didn't record; it was called 'Baby Girl.' And then later when we came to New York, we started getting other arrangements from different people."

A couple of the numbers that Basie's big band played in New York were numbers the nine-piece band had been playing as head arrangements back in Kansas City. "There was 'Moten Stomp' [also known as

The Count Basie brass section, 1937. Left to right: Eddie Durham, trombone; Dan Minor, trombone; Buck Clayton, trumpet; Bobby Moore, trumpet; Benny Morton, trombone; Ed Lewis, trumpet. (Institute of Jazz Studies)

"Moten Swing"]. That we had played in Kansas City. And then, you know, when we got to New York, we made a big, nice arrangement on it.

"And 'One O'Clock Jump.' We played it—but it wasn't called 'One O'Clock Jump' originally. It had another name, but we couldn't call it that on the record. The only reason we called it 'One O'Clock Jump' was—We had made the record, and then the guy says, 'Well Basie, what's the name of it?' He says, 'Well, I can't call it what I used to call it; it's kind of a dirty name.' And it was just about one o'clock. He looked at the clock, and he called it 'One O'Clock Jump.'" (The original title, which Clayton avoids mentioning by name, was "Blue Balls.")

When the band hit New York, Clayton recalls: "It clicked right away. Right away. We went to the Apollo Theater and the Savoy Ballroom.

"Because, you see, we didn't come directly to New York. We went on the road first. We left Kansas City on Halloween, October 31, which is the first of November. We didn't open in New York until New Year's. We traveled all down south and up north, around Boston. So when we did get to New York, we were pretty well together."

On January 25, 1937 (according to the Brian Rust discography), Clayton recorded with Teddy Wilson and Billie Holiday. "John Hammond had booked us," Clayton recalls. "We were in New York now. And he wanted me and Lester and Jo Jones, Walter Page to record with Teddy Wilson and Billie Holiday. And he had Benny Goodman on the date, and Freddie Green. I'd never seen Benny at that point—I'd heard him, but I'd never seen him. So that was our first date. Teddy was the leader and Billie was the vocalist—she sang 'Why Was I Born' and some other things. The rest of us were just the sidemen."

The Rust discography indicates that the Basie Band's first recording session occurred on January 21, 1937. Clayton's own recollection, it might be noted, is that the band's first recording session occurred after the Teddy Wilson-Billie Holiday session.

On his records with Basie, Clayton often played muted trumpet. "Not that I wanted to," Clayton states. "Basie always would insist on it—but only on making records. We'd have a recording session in the afternoon. To make the record, Basie would always do like that [Clayton gestures with his hand, which means: *Put a mute in it.* Then we'd go out that same night and play a string of one-nighters, he wouldn't care whether I used that—I could play open if I wanted to. He just thought that on the record, the mute would be better than playing open. That was his idea. I like to play open, to tell you the truth, all the time." Clayton may have preferred playing open, but he soon won recognition as a master in the use of the cup-mute.

Among the numbers Clayton arranged for Basie's Band were "Taps Miller," "It's Sand, Man," "Love Jumped Out," "What's Your Number," and 'Down for Double." Guitarist Freddie Green supplied the initial idea for "Down for Double," which became a solid favorite with the band. "Freddie hummed and asked if I'd make it."

The popular "Red Bank Boogie" was a Clayton original. "I wrote 'Red Bank Boogie' for Basie—it's nearly all piano. He didn't know I was making it at the time.

"It wasn't that many, you know, that I made. Because he had so many other people writing for the band: Jimmy Mundy, Don Redman; oh, he had a lot of guys." Trombonist/arranger Eddie Durham made a major contribution to the Basie book during his year-long stay in the

Count Basie and Buck Clayton. (Institute of Jazz Studies)

band, beginning in July of 1937. After Durham left, Clayton was the main arranger within the band itself. (Basie's arrangers were not generally players in the band.) But Clayton didn't have much time for arranging. Trumpeting came first for him. And besides starring on trumpet with Basie, he frequently made recording dates with others.

Who were his favorite performers in the Basie band? "Lester [Young]. Lester was my favorite, first. And Jo Jones. Herschel [Evans]. Dicky Wells. That's about all." And who was his closest friend within the band? "Freddie Green. I still stay in touch with him. But he's on the road so much."

When Clayton was in Basie's band, was that his favorite band? Did he think it was the best band in the country?

"Uh, yeah," he answers after a pause. "But. . .sometimes I think Duke was always ahead of us. I wouldn't say that now, because Basie's Band has improved so much. But Duke—all of us thought that, even Basie—we all thought that Duke was the tops. But eventually Basie got to be as good, I think; maybe better. When he started getting these good arrangers, like Quincy Jones."

Basie's distinctive piano playing was important to the band's success, Clayton observes.

"Yeah, it was. You know, you could always tell Basie's playing. And Basie used to be a hell of a good piano player. When I first met him, he played fast and. . . Yeah, he was a hell of a good piano player. But—I don't know, as he got older, finally, he just trickled out. But he still had his style, at whatever he did. You know, when he got older, to be around from 75 to 80, all he wanted to do was just enough so the people could know that it was him. And he would ask the arrangers not to put lengthy piano solos in. Just a little bit. So, that's why he finally ended up—that all he had to do was take two fingers at the end. You'd know it was Count Basie. But he'd feature the rest of the band."

Basie's Band of the late '30s and early '40s was loaded with jazz stars: players such as Lester Young, Herschel Evans, Buddy Tate, Jo Jones, Walter Page, Benny Morton, Dickie Wells, Harry "Sweets" Edison, and Buck Clayton. (Jazz writer Richard Sudhalter has commented: "It was really a soloist's band. The 'arrangements' were mostly connective tissue.") There are many who would rate it as Basie's finest outfit. Certainly Basie would never again have so many star soloists.

Occasionally, you'll hear someone suggest that jazz musicians have to indulge heavily in alcohol and/or drugs in order to reach their maximum creativity. Clayton, who has worked with many of the greatest of jazz artists in his career, says he doesn't believe there's any link between playing well and getting high on alcohol and/or drugs. "When I was with Basie, all we did was smoke pot. All of us, everybody used to turn on. But we wouldn't do it to play. I never did like to play [high]—the only time we'd do it was when we had nothing else to do. We didn't look for it to be an inspiration, you see. The best thing we would do sometimes was to drink. We did that. And not to get drunk. But if you're tired, we'd take a couple of drinks; then you might feel a little bit more like playing. Nothing more than this scotch and soda or vodka or something like that. And then if you wanted to do it too much, you'd do it after work's over. Then you could go out and get loaded if you wanted to. But it's not necessary," he reflects.

* * *

In 1943, Clayton was drafted, ending his tenure in the Basie Band. He spent about three years in the army. He played in bands at Camp Shanks (with Sy Oliver) and Camp Kilmer (with Mercer Ellington), both in New Jersey.

He still kept active, on the q.t., in the greater world of jazz, though. "I was arranging for bands outside the army. I made some for Harry James, I made some for Tommy Dorsey, and other people. 'Jackpot' was one arrangement, 'Aces and Faces' was another; I don't remember all of them. I wasn't supposed to do it. I wasn't supposed to record either, but I did. We'd sneak out and make records with different

Clayton and company, on the bandstand at Eddie Condon's Club in New York, early 1950s. Condon is on guitar. (Courtesy Buck Clayton)

people."

After the war, Clayton worked in small groups, occasionally under the leadership of others, such as pianist Joe Bushkin or guitarist Eddie Condon, but mostly as leader of his own "all-stars." He found he preferred the flexibility and freedom of small-group playing to big band playing.

"I joined Eddie Condon, and I got more of a kick because we didn't have to play arrangements, all we did was play solos. And I'd rather just play solos. Because in a big band, you have to wait until your turn comes, and you might have a solo every 15 or 20 minutes. So I just preferred a small group. And I didn't want to go back with Basie, wearing uniforms and catching buses and all that; I didn't have to do that now. I worked in Eddie Condon's Club about a year or two. I replaced Rex Stewart, who had played with Condon a couple of years (replacing Wild Bill Davison). That was Dixieland. I had to learn Dixieland songs. But after I learned 'em, I liked 'em. When I went into the Embers Club with Joe Bushkin, it was a different kind of music. But I liked it all. It was all solos."

Clayton may have been inspired early on by Louis Armstrong, as, indeed, to one degree or another, were virtually all trumpeters of the Swing Era. But he was never an imitator. There's no chance that a listener might mistake one of Clayton's recorded solos for one of Armstrong's (the way a listener might mistake one of, say, Taft Jordan's recorded solos for one of Armstrong's). Clayton found his own brisk, energetic approach.

He comments: "You don't want to keep playing somebody else. At the beginning, if you can have a good inspiration to get started, then you just automatically develop your own style. There's some guys, though, that never get away. I know some guys that started playing like Louis, and all their life, they never could play anything unless they heard Louis play it. And they'd play it just like him. But it wasn't anything original."

By chance, Clayton and trumpeter Bill Coleman developed along rather similar lines. "Bill Coleman and I just happened to play like each other. That doesn't happen often. I remember the first time I ever heard Bill on a record, John Hammond says, 'Buck, I want you to listen to this.' And he pulled out a record. And I listened and I listened. Finally I says, 'John, I don't remember making that.' He says, 'That's not you. That's Bill Coleman.' That's the first time I ever heard him. And he sounded just like me. And later, we made a record together called 'B.C. and B.C.' We just sounded alike. He'd been playing that way all his life."

Who were Clayton's favorite trumpet players (aside from his early inspiration, Armstrong)? "Roy Eldridge. Cootie Williams I liked. Harold Baker. And then there's another fellow named Freddy Webster. And Clifford Brown. That's about all," Clayton replies.

He never became a bebopper, when bebop was the rage. But he was flexible enough to work with Charlie Parker and others in the bebop vein on occasion.

"Yeah, I made some things where Charlie was on the date, Dexter Gordon, Charlie Parker, and myself. Bebop? I liked *some* of it. Some of it I liked; some of it I didn't. I liked the way Charlie Parker played it. But see, the only thing is, there's a million imitators, and they never could do what Charlie did. They tried their best to do what he was doing, but to him it was natural—to them it wasn't. They never could. I never did care much for most of it. But I liked the way he played."

Clayton also found time for freelance recording dates with pop singers such as Peggy Lee, Frankie Laine, Lena Horne, Rosemary Clooney, Patti Paige. Mostly though, his work was in jazz.

* * *

At one time or another, Clayton played alongside most of the big names in jazz of his day, from Coleman Hawkins to Roy Eldridge to Sidney Bechet. From 1949 on, he made repeated trips abroad, and found appreciative and serious audiences in Europe.

He continued as a major jazz soloist into his 50s, recording frequently. His style wore well, and he had many admirers. One 1966 reviewer went so far as to term Clayton the best trumpeter then working in jazz. Indeed, he may have been the best of the Armstrong-inspired trumpeters working at that point. By 1966, Armstrong's own playing was a shadow of what it had once been.

A July 19, 1967 review by jazz critic Patrick Scott of the *Toronto Daily Star* (headlined "That Buck Clayton Horn Fire Comes Out Hotter Than Ever") gives us a feeling for Clayton's status towards the end of his career as a trumpeter.

Scott wrote:

> You can count on the digits of one hand, excluding the thumb, the survivors of the Golden (or Swing) era of jazz who are playing at least as well today as they were 30 years ago, and only one of them is a trumpeter.
>
> And the remarkable thing about Buck Clayton is that he gets better every year, which is even more remarkable when you consider how good he was to start with.
>
> He was in a class, then, with Roy Eldridge and Bill Coleman and Cootie Williams, each of whom has long since lost his powers of consistency, and only a bar or two behind Henry (Red) Allen, who is dead, and Louis Armstrong, who, if only on compassionate

> grounds, should be retired and preserved in Swiss Kriss as a global monument.
>
> And yet here is Clayton. . . playing with at least as much subtlety, at least as much conviction, and at least as much swing as he's ever possessed—plus a good deal more firepower.

Different jazz buffs, of course, would have their own ways of amending Scott's ranking of jazz trumpeters. Some would no doubt want to switch Roy Eldridge and Red Allen in the above listing. Many would add Bunny Berigan and a couple of other trumpeters to that select group on the next rung under the one occupied by Armstrong. But you'd find a consensus would emerge, agreeing that Armstrong was unsurpassed in his day (just as, say, Shakespeare was unsurpassed in his day in literature) and that Clayton was among a handful of exceptionally fine players on the next rung (where you would place, say, Christopher Marlowe in relationship to Shakespeare). The Swing Era was marked by a tremendous outpouring of talent in music (just as Shakespeare's era was marked by an outpouring of talent in literature), so that those just below the top rung were also artists of great gifts. That profusion of talent is the mark of a real golden age in any art form.

* * *

As a trumpeter, Clayton may have been unsurpassed in his idiom in 1967. But the aging process had begun catching up with him. And by 1969, he was forced to give up playing the trumpet. "I had physical

Coleman Hawkins and Buck Clayton. (Courtesy Nancy Miller Elliott)

problems," he recalls simply. "Oh, there were so many things that started getting bad."

Great trumpeting requires more than great imagination and great soul; it requires stamina, and the effective use of many well-maintained muscles. Trumpeters practice regularly. And with age, practice becomes increasingly essential.

Faulty dentistry caused serious problems for Clayton as a trumpeter. He had had a bridge placed in his mouth. And as he pressed the horn against his lips to play, the bridgework cut into the inside of his lips. He tried to ignore the problem, tried to mask the pain he felt while playing, but the problem only got worse. Eventually, he had to have the inside of his mouth sewed up. "I had 32 stitches," he recalls. He was still unable to play comfortably. "And there were other problems, health problems. And I just—sorry, but I just gave it up."

At age 58, Clayton tried to find another line of work. But what do you do after you've earned your living as a major jazz star? He could not find anything that could pay him the kind of money he had been used to making. And the jobs he tried now brought him neither the prestige nor the creative satisfactions he had previously enjoyed.

"I worked in the musicians' union for about a year," he remembers, the tone of his voice making it clear that the labor had been joyless for him. "Then I worked as a salesman. I had to walk up and down all the streets of New York, Park Avenue, Lexington Avenue, selling—I was working for a magazine. I was supposed to get these people to put in advertisements in our magazine. I didn't like that either. Oh no, I didn't like that. And a lot of times I'd go to these offices to talk with the executives, the head of the company. And they knew me from when I was playing music. And they'd say, 'What are you doing selling, what are you doing, doing this?'"

Clayton was also writing arrangements in his spare time, which he did enjoy. He supervised some memorable recording dates, for albums entitled "Buck Clayton Jam Sessions." But the urge to play trumpet again still burned within him.

In 1975, he attended Dick Gibson's annual jazz party in Boulder, Colorado. There trombonist Trummy Young told Clayton that he too had had a bridge that had cut into his lip, but that a dentist had made a custom shield for him which prevented the bridge from cutting him and which had enabled him to continue playing. Young urged Clayton to see his dentist; maybe Clayton could play once again.

It took four visits to the dentist in Boston, but Clayton finally had a shield devised for him. He played his horn at the dentist's office, while the dentist made adjustments, trying to provide as much comfort as possible for him.

He made a valiant effort to come back. But after a seven-year layoff, he no longer had the muscles he needed. He could no longer lead a group for hours with the power and verve he had once exhibited. "At first I'd thought I'd be able to get it back together," he remembers. But eventually he realized that he was not going to be able to regain his former prowess. There had been too long a layoff. And he was now nearly 70.

His final recording session was in 1979, with friends such as Red Richards (piano), Norris Turney (alto sax) and Johnny Williams (bass). "I don't even think about that. . . Everything went wrong on that date. My lip started hurting. And I had a hernia that started bothering me. And I just couldn't play anything." He decided to set aside the horn for good.

"I taught at Hunter College for five years. I liked the people there. But you know, no teacher gets a lot of money. And there was nothing rewarding about teaching school. I had charge of the jazz. And I had to teach little students that had never played with a band, how to play in a section. And I had to teach them little singers how to sing with a band accompaniment, things like that. I didn't like it, I didn't like the

Two living legends pick up lunch in New York: Woody Herman and Buck Clayton. (Photo by Nancy Miller Elliott)

money part. So I left," he recalls.

* * *

"I just decided I better write, arrange music, because I can make much more money arranging than I could teaching school. The only thing about arranging is that there's not many big bands to write for. But anyway, it's better than teaching school. And when you make a record, when you make a good arrangement and you hear it back, it's very rewarding," Clayton says. And that word *rewarding* seems key. Clayton works as an arranger today with great enthusiasm. He may no longer be playing, but he remains an active participant in the world of jazz.

He wrote the charts used by a Basie alumni band which toured Europe a few years back. "We went to Europe, played in five or six different countries, stayed about eight weeks. Sixteen musicians." And he wrote the charts for a smaller band (recalling Basie's original Reno Club band), which performed in an all-star Carnegie Hall tribute to Basie, organized shortly after Basie died in 1984.

Currently, Clayton is writing arrangements for the big bands of Loren Schoenberg, Dick Meldonian and Sonny Igoe, Grover Mitchell, Humphrey Lyttelton, Nat Pierce and Frankie Capp, and Panama Francis—the Savoy Sultans. He is also writing small-group arrangements for the Howard Alden-Dan Barrett Quintet. Sometimes he writes originals. Other times, bandleaders ask him to arrange standards for them.

"I just like to write most of the time. That takes up hours and hours, but I like it. Sometimes, even if I don't have a band to write for, I'll just write for something to do. I really wish that there was more big bands," he comments, adding after a pause: "But there isn't. Not like it used to be.

"In the United States, you know, the big cities had at least five big bands in it. Kansas City would have eight or nine. New York—God knows how many they had. So there were hundreds of big bands when you take in the whole country.

"But when TV came, people wouldn't go out to ballrooms anymore. People found out they could just stay home and enjoy themselves; they wouldn't go out to dances anymore. And the bands just went down. And then the ballrooms disappeared, too. And look at 52nd Street. There's not a club on the street. There used to be one club behind another club for two or three blocks. Now they're all skyscrapers. And outside of New York, in Detroit and those places like that, they're all garages and parking lots. So there's really nowhere for a big band to play.

"A lot of people stay home. It's too bad, though. You think, there

Buck Clayton conducts his hand-picked big band at Parsons College in New York, November 1988. Left to right: Howard Alden, guitar; Mike Migliore, tenor sax; Chuck Wilson, alto sax; Doug Lawrence, tenor sax. Not visible: Joe Temperley, baritone sax; Paul Cohen, Spanky Davis, Randy Sandke, trumpets; Dan Barrett and Joel Helleny, trombones; Marty Napoleon, piano; Eddie Jones, bass; Butch Miles, drums. As Alden aptly puts it: Clayton's writing is so dynamic that simply playing the notes as written guarantees the band will swing. (Photo by Nancy Miller Elliott)

was hundreds of bands.

"And when they had all those hundreds of big bands, you'd get hundreds of stars. Today, there's nothing to look forward to. So there's not that many musicians trying, like there used to be. Everybody was trying to belong to Benny Goodman's Band or Duke Ellington's Band. They worked themselves crazy trying to be that good. Once in a while, now, one will come up. A young one, like Scott Hamilton or Howard Alden. But they're the exceptions."

* * *

Clayton enjoys going to hear those "exceptions"—those younger players who work well in the type of music he prefers. He'll go out to hear players such as Scott Hamilton, Loren Schoenberg, Howard Alden and Dan Barrett (all of whom, incidentally, have recorded Clayton numbers). He was listening to a record of Schoenberg's band playing one of his numbers when I arrived at his house that day. Guitarist Alden, 27, makes a point of telling audiences that Clayton is the quintet's resident arranger, as well as being one of the few people in jazz to whom the oft-used word "legend" is really applicable.

Clayton receives the respect and admiration of younger jazzmen who recognize the timeless validity of his contributions. He is an elder statesman in the community, and is treated as such. It's good to see him at performances, listening to young musicians bring to life the music he continues to create.

1986

* * *

A profile such as this one really only begins to tell the story of a major jazzman such as Clayton. It would take a whole book to do justice to his extraordinarily full life. Happily, such a book is now available. Clayton completed his autobiography not long after this interview took place. *Buck Clayton's Jazz World*, written with the assistance of Nancy Miller Elliott, was published by Oxford University Press in 1987.

That same year, Clayton's new hand-picked big band, playing his arrangements exclusively, made its debut on the New York jazz scene, with a week's engagement at Fat Tuesday's. It received outstanding reviews, and has been making periodic appearances in New York clubs and concert halls since then.

The band was the hit of the 1988 Nice Jazz Festival. Its buoyancy, grace, and elan are well captured in its first album, "A Swinging Dream," released by Stash in 1989.

JOHNNY • BLOWERS

Experience Counts

His teenage students know he's experienced, but it's doubtful that many realize just how experienced drummer Johnny Blowers is. In a career that spans six decades, Blowers has recorded with the small bands of jazz greats such as Sidney Bechet, Bobby Hackett, Eddie Condon, Red Norvo, Yank Lawson and Bob Haggart. And he's also drummed with big bands led by the likes of Bunny Berigan, Ben Bernie, Woody Herman, Jan Savitt, Billy Butterfield, Artie Shaw, and Sy Oliver. He was a staff musician at CBS for five years, at NBC for seven and a half years, and at ABC for two and a half years.

Blowers was on the date when Billie Holiday first recorded her classic "Lover Man," when Ella Fitzgerald did "Try a Little Tenderness," when Louis Armstrong cut "Blueberry Hill" and "La Vie En Rose." Ask Frank Sinatra who Johnny Blowers is. Their association—on recordings, broadcasts and concert dates—spanned 10 years.

Kenny Davern, the great soprano sax and clarinet player, introduced Blowers at a recent concert as the man who has probably played and recorded with more different jazz and pop notables than any other living East coast drummer.

Blowers started drumming before movies could talk. And he was there to make the date when the first stereo jazz album was cut. But when he ripped into his solo on "Caravan" at last year's Kool Jazz Festival—a number he had first played with Bunny Berigan's big band 45 years earlier—he seemed ageless.

* * *

At his home in Westbury, Long Island, Blowers mixes reminiscences of his early days with advice for drummers just starting out. His words are firm, decisive; his southern-inflected speech appropriately rhythmic.

"I never wanted to do anything but music," Blowers says. There were no drumming teachers in Spartanburg, South Carolina, where he was born in 1911, but his father played drums in the pit orchestra of the local theater, accompanying touring vaudeville artists, dramatic companies, and minstrel shows. Blowers watched his father play, and began drumming himself at age eight. In his teens, he began filling in for his father in the orchestra from time to time.

"My father sure wasn't going to teach me, because he said, 'The student never pays any attention to the parent,'" Blowers notes. So Blowers used records to teach himself.

"My dad got Mr. Alexander, who owned the best record shop and piano store, to let me work for him. Mr. Alexander made two calls to my dad saying, 'You're going to have to have a talk with John, because every time we get a new load of records, he's in the back, playing those records and practicing by them. I can't find him—to serve the people.' After the third time, he fired me.

"But I knew everything that Red Nichols and the Five Pennies played. I knew everything the Dorsey Brothers played. . . And you'd find records of Ben Pollack, sure, with Benny Goodman playing clarinet, Jack Teagarden playing trombone. And McKinney's Cotton Pickers and Don Redman—oh, I'm telling you. . . *Boy*! And Duke. There was no Count Basie then. I'm talking about 1927 and '28. I was just a little kid, but boy. . . I knew those records. I could sit down with a set of drums and play right along—I knew every break. And I was getting all the books on drumming that I could," Blowers recalls.

Blowers was about 16 when the theater pit orchestra in Spartanburg came to an end. "Once Al Jolson made *The Jazz Singer* [the first talking picture], that finished the theater down south," he notes. "So they organized a dance band. My Dad used to let me sit in and rehearse some. From there I went to Fort Meyers, Florida, and finished high school. My last two years in high school, I worked in a good dance band. I went to Oglethorpe University in Atlanta, for two years. I found a couple of teachers there, but they weren't the kind of teacher I was looking for because they were not keeping up with the modern

Jolson's great success in The Jazz Singer *(1927) not only eliminated silent movies, it eliminated the pit orchestras that played in countless movie theaters. In Blowers' hometown, the out-of-work musicians formed a danceband.* (Chip Deffaa collection)

thing."

In 1934 and '35, Blowers freelanced in Atlanta, before joining Bob Pope's Orchestra, which toured the south and midwest. Pope's was a good-enough "territory band" for RCA Bluebird to record it. And while drumming with it in '35-36, Blowers got to meet some of the foremost drummers of the times, such as Dave Tough and Gene Krupa, when the bands they were in would hit the south. "I was greatly impressed with Gene Krupa, Dave Tough, Ray McKinley. I could hear them all the time. And Jo Jones with Count Basie. And Sid Catlett. And there was a small band with Zutty Singleton and Roy Eldridge, in a little place called the Three Deuces in Chicago, and I used to hear them on the radio about 1:00 in the morning," Blowers recalls.

* * *

Blowers knew that if he wanted to really make it as a musician, he had to go to New York. He hit the city in '37.

"My mother used to write me, 'How are you doing?' And I'd *say*, 'Oh, I'm doing great. . .' Well, it took me 10 years, after I began to have a bit of success, to eat a bowl of soup again. Because I used to eat three bowls of soup a day when I first got to New York. Morning, noon, and night. . . Oh God, I'm telling you. We found an old German restaurant, over on around Tenth Avenue. For around 15 cents, you got a large bowl of vegetable soup, and the Germans put a big basket, filled with bread, on the table, and plenty of butter," Blowers says.

"I used to go to the dime dance halls. They had a lot of them on Broadway, and I'd buy a dollar's worth of tickets. I'd get up to the band and when they'd take an intermission, I'd say to the drummer, 'You know, I'm new in town and it's really tough. I was wondering if I could sit in.' He'd say, 'No way. The best thing you can do with those tickets is to use them to dance. There's no sitting in.'"

Blowers practiced his drumming. "I was one who always loved to practice," he notes. "I practiced as much as three and a half, four hours a day. Gene Krupa used to practice six to eight hours a day." And he went to the jazz clubs.

Knowing someone who knew someone finally made all the difference, Blowers says. A friend of Blowers from Atlanta, a piano player named Fred DeLand, came up to New York and stayed with Blowers. And the two headed down to Nick's in the Village, a celebrated jazz joint and musicians' hangout.

"Nick's was not much larger than my living room here. And when you get in there, you're stuck in there like sardines. We're at least six deep to the bar. And you ordered your drinks like chain style. The bartender makes you a drink and then they pass it over the heads of the guys, and then you pass your money back. And here's a six piece band over in the corner, and it's very exciting. DeLand said, 'John, I think I know that trombone player. His name is George Brunis,'" Blowers recalls. In those days, a number of the big bands fielded softball teams, which would compete against each other when the bands had dates in the same cities. Brunis had toured with Ted Lewis' band, and for a week in Atlanta, Brunis and DeLand had been on opposing softball teams.

"Brunis looked at him and said, 'Hey! Atlanta, Georgia—*softball*.' And I said, 'Holy Mackerel, you got to introduce me to him,'" Blowers recalls. "I told Brunis, 'I can't get myself arrested. I can't get anyplace to play.' He said, 'Well the guy drumming here'll let anybody sit in, as long as he gets the money.' He introduced me and I sat in. . . And who walked in? Bobby Hackett walked in, Bud Freeman walked in. Charlie Barnet came in to sit down and have a drink, not to play. Jimmy Dorsey came in there. And there was a singer by the name of Red McKenzie who, many years before that had been with Whiteman, and of course he and Condon had had the Mound City Blue Blowers. We finished the set, and McKenzie walked over to me and said, 'What are you doing?' I said, 'Nothing, I'm just living from hand to mouth.' He said, 'Well come down here and sit in, because you're not going to be out of work long. You play those kind of drums, you'll be a busy boy.'"

Six or eight weeks later (in late '37), Blowers recalls, McKenzie invited Blowers to join the new band being formed to play at Nick's. Led by trumpeter Bobby Hackett, it also included George Brunis, Pee Wee Russell on clarinet, Eddie Condon on guitar, and Dave Bowman on piano. With this band, Blowers made his first recordings in New York. And soon afterwards he cut sides with Teddy Wilson.

The Hackett band (with Blowers) made guest shots on the "Saturday Night Swing Session," a major CBS radio show of the era, and also appeared in a 1938 motion picture based on that radio show.

"God, it's amazing. I came to New York in 1937 and what happened to me in my first year, it was like a whirlwind. Gene Krupa was writing for *Metronome*. And he gave me several mentions in there. Guys were asking questions like, 'How do you keep the hi-hat cymbal from moving like that?' And, he said, 'Well, one of the easiest ways — Johnny Blowers down at Nick's just drives an ice pick right in the floor to hold the hi-hat still.' All these things were greatly helpful. I was being written up in *Down Beat*, and in *Metronome*; it's amazing how that carries. At the time we went into Nick's, in December, I didn't know anyone; six months later I knew everyone and they knew me," Blowers notes.

"Around March, 1938, Benny Goodman and Gene Krupa had a disagreement, and Gene left Benny's band to organize his own band. Dave Tough was working with Bunny Berigan. Benny Goodman immediately offered Dave enough money to get him into his band. Well, this left Berigan wide open. And Red McKenzie knew about it and called Bunny. So Bunny came down there one night and listened to us for a couple of sets, without saying anything. And about three days later, McKenzie called me and said, 'Bunny Berigan is going to offer you the job.'"

Blowers states that, except for McKenzie's pushing him, he might never have made the move. He found that he was just a touch frightened about hitting the big time so quickly. Replacing Dave Tough was a dream. But was he ready yet? "I said, 'Red, I can't take the job, because I don't have the confidence. I can't play with that big band.' McKenzie said, 'You can play with that band. You're not just going to hang around here and just stay with a jazz band like this all your whole life.'

"Bunny called. And at that time, we were making $50 a week in

Nick's," Blowers says. And $50 a week was damned good pay during the Depression. McKenzie told Blowers to ask Berigan for $200 a week. "And I said, 'You got to be kidding! From $50 to $200?' He said, 'Well, you got to try.' So we talked on the phone, and Bunny said, 'What kind of money are we talking about?'

"And I was going to say like $100. But McKenzie, he's listening to the phone conversation. I said, 'Well, what about $200 a week?' Bunny said, 'Well I can't pay you $200, but I'll give you $185.' And I said, 'That's plenty!'

"So. . . I went with the band. My first recording date with Bunny was April 21st, 1938, and that's my birthday," Blowers recalls. In addition to recording for RCA Victor, the band recorded much of its library in the form of transcriptions for radio broadcasts.

Berigan was one of the all-time great jazz trumpeters, and he hired a succession of great drummers. In 1937-38, Berigan had George Wettling, Dave Tough, Blowers, and Buddy Rich. "It was a good band. And it was a lot of work, and it was a whole new environment for me. Because that was really a big band. And *strong*. And I practiced during the day. I studied the arrangements. I enjoyed it very much," Blower says.

"I had good time, which is very very important, because without it, you haven't got anything. If the drummer races, that can destroy your feeling. If he slows you up, that's even worse," Blowers notes. And he was accepted as a peer by the other big band jazz drummers.

"We used to practice together. I practiced with Dave Tough and Cozy Cole, and Sid Catlett and Jo Jones. Gene Krupa. You practiced rudiments. And being with them and watching them play, I learned a great deal from all of them. Cozy Cole—he was with Benny Goodman doing the Paramount Theater, and I used to go down to the Paramount and we'd get a chair or a bench and put a pillow on it, and I'd sit on one side and he'd sit on the other and we'd sit there and practice like mad, all between shows. And we all did.

"At that time, drums were being featured a bit more. They were coming out of the background, from being just a time-keeper. But the one record that did more for the drummer in solo work, and which then would show off just how good a drummer you are, was when Krupa made 'Sing Sing Sing' [July 6, 1937]. This took the drummer out from behind the band and put him in the limelight. From then on, every leader was looking around for something good for a drummer to do as a solo in the band. I did 'Caravan' with Bunny Berigan. Ray McKinley did 'Parade of the Milk Bottle Caps.' Dave Tough did some solos. Dave didn't like solos at all—he just detested them—but naturally he had to do them. He did some with Tommy Dorsey and he did some with other small bands that he worked with," Blowers recalls.

"I stayed with Bunny until the situation began to get kind of bad. Unfortunately his problem of drinking got worse, and a lot of things were going on in the band. Bunny was never really a leader. He was delightful. But when you're running an organization, you've got to tend to business. And business was getting out of hand because drinking was getting in the way. And there were a lot of disagreements with

Johnny Blowers—endorsing Slingerland drums—and Bunny Berigan, 1938. (Courtesy Johnny Blowers)

management over finances. I treated it like: 'Look—my guarantee is I'm supposed to get this. . . and I want it.' And there were all little shady deals here and there. So I left," Blowers recalls.

Ben Bernie, "the Old Maestro," was coming out of retirement to form a young swing band. In 1939, with trombonist friend Lou McGarity, Blowers went with Bernie for a year and a half. One of the band's first recordings was a feature for Blowers, "Drummer's Day."

Blowers next played with Jan Savitt's big band for six weeks. "I was going to stay longer, but I didn't want to travel anymore," he recalls. So when Savitt left New York City for a road tour, Blowers stayed behind, accepting an offer to become a CBS staff musician. Blowers had fallen in love, and his fiancee refused to marry him unless he gave up the road. His colleagues in the CBS band included former sidemen from various top big bands, such as Will Bradley, Pee Wee Erwin, Hymie Shertzer, Chris Griffin, Lou McGarity. And Blowers continued to do jazz work in clubs and concerts, and for recording dates.

He also continued to take lessons. One of his best teachers, he recalls, was, "Al Brummel, who was with the Metropolitan Opera—he was a fine drummer. I studied tympany with him. Then I went over to Fred Albright and studied the vibes and xylophone with him, so that I could do the studio work that I was called upon to do. I did work some under Howard Barlow with the Columbia Symphony. They just put it on the schedule; they didn't ask me. I went to the contractor and I said, 'Look, I'm not a symphony drummer. I'm just a plain, ordinary jazz drummer.' He said, 'You're better than that. You can do it.'

"I learned a lot with Freddy Albright, who worked with Toscanini; he did the 'Telephone Hour' from time to time, and did the 'Firestone Hour' as a regular drummer. Lionel Hampton studied vibes and xylophone with him. I think Terry Gibbs studied some with Freddy. Terry Snyder, who was Perry Como's drummer, studied with Fred. And I would consequently get more books, and practice. As a professional, now, I still practice every day,' Blowers notes.

Blowers learned a great deal from his peers. All of his life, he says, his friends have been fellow musicians. And during the swing era, he says, many free hours were spent hanging out with other jazzmen. "Around the corner from me, on 50th Street between Broadway and Seventh, there was a place called the Crown Bar. Pee Wee Russell hung out in there, Miff Mole hung out in there, Red McKenzie. And there was a great place up the street on Seventh Avenue between 51st and 52nd called Charlie's Tavern. And then too, a lot of guys would come by and see me in the afternoon. We'd do some practicing or we'd sit and listen to records or we'd talk, but it was all music, music, constantly.

We'd listen to the 'Milkman's Matinee' all night long on WNEW."

Blowers' next-door neighbor in his apartment building, for a time, was that master of the electric guitar, Les Paul. And often, after finishing their paying gigs, the two would head out late at night, looking for joints where they could sit in for free.

Blowers did radio show after radio show. He had a medical exemption from service, but he played hospital gigs, accompanying Al Jolson and Eddie Cantor as they sang for servicemen. He recorded several V-Discs (recordings made for distribution to members of the armed forces) with Red Norvo's Band, and appeared in a motion picture with that band. "I made V-Discs with Yank Lawson and Billy Butterfield; I was making V-Discs with everybody in the world. I made V-Discs with Lionel Hampton, I made one with Woody Herman. And we were making them all during the night. I made V-Discs at dates that started at 2:00 in the morning. I made V-Discs that started at 8:00 in the morning. All the top musicians in the country—we made these V-Discs," Blowers says.

During the war, vocalists began becoming more prominent. And after the war, big bands began to fade as public attractions. Blowers made many commercial record dates with Dick Haymes, Jo Stafford, Margaret Whiting, and other vocal stars of the period, before the start of rock 'n' roll. He got an occasional chance to play with a big band in New York, such as Woody Herman's, for example, for a 1948 Paramount Theater engagement. And he always made time for the small band jazz he loved, playing everywhere from Town Hall to Eddie Condon's Club and even briefly his own Johnny Blowers' Club in New York. But the steady money was in playing softly behind pop singers, working under maestros such as Axel Stordahl and Nelson Riddle.

Blowers says he didn't mind backing singers, which called for a different kind of drumming than either playing in small jazz bands or in big swing bands. He welcomed any challenge.

The one singer with whom Blowers was most closely associated was Frank Sinatra. Blowers was the drummer on Sinatra's first solo radio show, a short-lived venture entitled "Reflections," which CBS presented, without a sponsor, in 1942.

Over the next ten years, Blowers worked on all of Sinatra's radio programs. Blowers was the first New York musician, he says, to be permitted to remain on the CBS staff and yet do outside commercial radio programs. 'He had some big radio commercials. Vim's vitamins was one. We did another show for Max Factor. We did a cigarette commercial. These were big half-hour shows," Blowers says. And, during this period, Blowers played on Sinatra's recording dates.

"My association with Frank Sinatra was one of the best that I probably will ever have with any human being, other than a relative or something. I don't think I could have had a brother that I could have gotten along with better. He's a perfectionist. And he pulls no punches. If you play, you stay with him. If you can't play, you don't last but about 15 minutes. We had some great times together," Blowers says.

"Like July Fourth and Labor Day, we would go off and do three days at a theater. We would do Atlantic City, or we'd do a big theater in Hartford, Connecticut, and we went down and opened the Casablanca in Miami, Florida. We would do these between the radio shows, and they were great fun. Most of the times we took just the rhythm section, and we would hire the rest of the band there. But we did some dates with Frank just with the rhythm section. I enjoyed working with him very much. In 1952, he left New York to act in *From Here to Eternity* and he received the Academy Award," Blowers recalls. The movie revived interest in Sinatra, and he relocated, more or less permanently, out west. Irving Cottler became his regular drummer.

For several years, Blowers was associated with Eddie Fisher, whose singing career was then booming. Fisher's TV shows were broadcast from New York, which was convenient for Blowers. And Blowers and pianist Ken Lane made some trips with Fisher for concert dates, with augmented orchestras, much as Blowers had done with Sinatra.

There were occasional jazz forays for Blowers. In 1953, he drummed on a Sidney Bechet album; four years later he drummed on "Joe Marsala's Chicago Jazz," which he says was the first jazz album ever recorded in stereo. But most of his time in the '50s was spent in the more lucrative commercial studio work. At one time or another Blowers played all of the top TV shows, including Ed Sullivan's and the "Kraft Music Hall." He drummed on Nat King Cole's Show. He taught drumming to TV host Dave Garroway. And he sat in with many top name big bands on ABC's "Bandstand" (not to be confused with Dick Clark's "American Bandstand"), which was something of a last hurrah on TV for big bands.

* * *

But gradually, the people running the networks changed. Work was being assigned to a new crop of drummers. By the '60s, Blowers was on the outside. He tried, briefly, moving to the coast. It didn't help. Back east, he turned to teaching. And more and more often, in the '70s, to the work he had always enjoyed: playing in clubs and concerts with small jazz bands.

He toured with Sy Oliver in 1970. From 1970-73, he worked in Stephen Sondheim's Broadway musical *Follies*, appearing in an onstage quartet with fellow jazzmen Taft Jordan, Aaron Bell, and Bob

Curtis. In 1976-77, he played with the World's Greatest Jazzband of Yank Lawson and Bob Haggart. He moved into the 1980s by heading to Holland with trumpeter Pee Wee Erwin. He appeared in Richard Sudhalter's "Hard Times, Good Times' retrospective, emceed by Studs Terkel, at Town Hall in New York. And in recent years, he's done many dates with his own "Giants of Jazz," an impermanent aggregation that

Johnny Blowers. (Courtesy Johnny Blowers)

has included, from concert to concert, jazzmen of the caliber of Bucky Pizzarelli, Warren Vache Jr., Clarence Hutchenrider, Kenny Davern, Johnny Mince, and Milt Hinton. And he's drummed with the Harlem Blues and Jazz Band.

Blowers notes that anyone who intends to make a career of being a drummer had better be ready to be flexible. His own career is a testimonial to that. When Blowers started drumming as a boy, network radio did not yet exist, much less television. Every city in America had a theater pit orchestra, which he assumed then would always be there. (For without them, what would the traveling shows do?)

In his career, Blowers has seen the creation and disappearance of job category after job category. Today, one can no more expect to find work as a network staff musician than as a member of a local pit orchestra, playing for touring minstrel and vaudeville shows. Blowers saw the rise and fall of the big bands. He saw jazz grow and decline in general popularity. He saw radio boom and then all but vanish as a source of employment for musicians. He made the switch into television, playing top shows that emanated from New York, and then saw TV leave New York.

Blowers backed singers from Jolson to Sinatra. Today, he spends part of his time teaching youths rock drumming. Blowers advises aspiring drummers to be ready to play every kind of music in their careers, whether it is music they like or don't like. And to expect the industry to keep changing, in ways no one can possibly predict or imagine. He tells them to practice daily, and to find some place to work where they can be seen, whether it's in a marching band, rock band, or jazz band. "Play, play, play, *play*," he urges them. "If you don't know anybody, put your note up on a billboard: 'I'm playing drums. If anyone's interested, let me know.' You've got to get the exposure," he says. "As well as I played when I got to New York in 1937, for God's sakes, if I couldn't get any exposure, I could have stayed that way for the rest of my life."

1984

MAXINE • SULLIVAN

More than "Loch Lomond"

Struggle's, a jazz club in Edgewater, New Jersey, is packed. Two headliners are scheduled for tonight: Maxine Sullivan—the famed "Loch Lomond" girl of the late 1930s, now 73 years old—will be singing; she will be backed by Doc Cheatham—one of the last of the great Swing Era hot trumpeters—and his Quartet.

Cheatham's group opens the set, warming up the crowd for Sullivan. Cheatham offers "Keeping Out of Mischief Now," the notes pure and golden, with occasional, sudden fierce notes bursting through. His feet are firmly planted, his arms bent out from his body like wings, his trumpet raised heavenward. His is a majestic figure, and he has the undivided attention of the patrons crowding the tables.

Standing at the bar, in back of the tables and unnoticed by the patrons, is Maxine Sullivan, waiting to go on. And if you're close enough, you notice something else. She is humming along with the music, as if getting revved up for her performance. Cheatham's pianist, Don Coates, takes a chorus. And at the bar—inaudible (except to those standing right alongside her)—Maxine Sullivan is now singing, low, liltingly, to herself.

Cheatham goes into "Give Me a Kiss to Build a Dream On." Sullivan is not only softly humming and singing now, she is tapping out the beat with one hand on the bar. You sense she can't wait to get onstage.

This chapter incorporates recollections Maxine Sullivan offered for the joint benefit of radio interviewer Doug Hall and the author.

Finally, Cheatham introduces her: "The greatest little lady that I've ever known." He says that back around 1938—when he was with Cab Calloway's band and she had recently broken through to national fame with her recording of "Loch Lomond"—"I was in love with her once. I used to follow her around when she was with John Kirby."

She responds that this is the first that she's ever heard of it. "Better late than never," Cheatham replies. And she ad libs—singing—"This could be the start of something big."

And now she's off. Once she starts singing, there's no stopping her. Nor would anyone want to. Her eyes are alive with joy. She swings easily through "I've Got the World on a String," "One Hundred Years from Today," "Please Don't Talk About Me When I'm Gone," "Cheatin' on Me," and other favorites in her current repertoire. She's a tiny dynamo. She grins broadly, lighting up the room. And when Cheatham takes a number on trumpet—"Muskrat Ramble"—she surprises him by getting a flugelhorn and joining in.

* * *

Maxine Sullivan. (Courtesy Harriet Wasser)

Maxine Sullivan, christened Marietta Williams in 1911, will tell you that she's been singing all of her life. And she can pretty well date her first public performance.

She recalls: "My aunt, who is 90-some-years-old now—her favorite story is the one about when I was three years old, and she had given me a piece to recite in church. She said, 'If you're not talking loud enough, I'll give you a signal.' Well, when it came my turn to appear, I sang 'The Chinese Blues'! And of course, my aunt was going crazy back there, and to me that meant sing louder—and I belted it out. She went back and tried to apologize to the preacher, but he said, 'Don't say anything to her, because she might not do anything again.'

"And then when I was about nine or ten years old, I sang, 'I'm Forever Blowing Bubbles,' at the Carnegie Library in Homestead, Pennsylvania." (Sullivan grew up in Homestead, just outside of Pittsburgh.)

"The family was quite musical, I mean the back porch type. My grandmother on my father's side, she had 10 children, and all the boys played some kind of an instrument. In fact, the youngest one of the family, Harry Williams, he had been in an orchestra that Earl Hines was in. The orchestra was under the direction of a man by the name of Lois Deppe, who was a singer. And they recorded and toured as far back as 1922. But my Uncle Harry got tired of the road, and he didn't like to play the drums anyway, so he started playing the saxophone, and he formed a group called the Red Hot Peppers. I was old enough by then to tag along behind the band. So when he'd play these little gigs, I used to follow around with him.

"And in 1935 and '36, around that time, I began to go out and do little gigs on my own. In fact, in 1936, I had the opportunity to audition at a club in Pittsburgh called the Benjamin Harrison Literary Club.

"It was an after-hours spot, with eight tables. It had been, during prohibition, a chartered club. It stayed open until—I mean, I worked from two o'clock until *unconscious*. But in 1936, of course, the so-called legitimate restaurants and clubs that served liquor closed at two o'clock. So most of the musicians, and the performers, when they got off from work, they'd wind up at the Benjamin Harrison Literary Club. And I'd go to work at eleven o'clock at night, but business didn't really begin to happen until about two o'clock in the morning, when all the guys and gals got off from work, and came up.

"And that's where I met Gladys Mosier, the girl pianist with Ina Ray Hutton's all-girl band. She said, 'If you ever come to New York, look me up.' So I stayed at the Benjamin Harrison Literary Club for a year; I saved my money, and I took a Sunday excursion to New York. I don't know what I expected to do—you know, turn New York on its ears, overnight."

She had told almost no one that she was going to New York. If things didn't work out there, she figured she could catch a train back to Pittsburgh in time to work Monday night, as usual.

When she telephoned Gladys Mosier, she was surprised that it took Mosier a moment to remember who she was.

"Gladys said, 'Well, you know I can't do anything for you overnight—you'll have to stay over until Wednesday.' Well, that was a very big decision for me to make because I had a return stub to get back to Pittsburgh before then, to my job. I decided to stay." Sullivan still has that 1937 return ticket to Pittsburgh.

"Gladys got in touch with Claude Thornhill, who was arranging for Andre Kostelanetz at CBS at the time. I was living at 409 Edgecombe Avenue, around 155th Street, so they came up on Wednesday early. And we auditioned in every gin mill from 155th Street down to 52nd street. Joe Helbock, who was the manager of the Onyx Club, was out on the West Coast trying to get Stuff Smith back. And Carl Kress, the guitar player, who was a friend of Claude's, happened to be at the Onyx. I auditioned on Wednesday and went to work on Friday." Kress made the decision to hire Sullivan, as a relief act, in Helbock's absence.

She was singing on New York's famed Swing Street within a week of her arrival in the city. She didn't realize until years later just how extraordinary that was.

"During the first few weeks, I appeared during intermission with a piano player. In the meantime, Joe Helbock came back. And when he found me singing there, he said he needed a singer like he needed a hole in the head. But by that time, Claude had really gone to work, and he arranged a recording session, and we made a record. And I recorded 'Gone With the Wind' and 'Stop! You're Breaking my Heart.'" Those first two recordings (cut June 4, 1937) were released under Thornhill's name, with Sullivan credited as vocalist. They were issued on two separate '78s; the flip sides had numbers under Thornhill's name, featuring another unknown vocalist, Jimmy Farrell. Sullivan's recording of "Gone With the Wind," the first recording ever made of that tune, did well enough to get her her own record date. And from that moment on, her records were released under her name.

By this time, Sullivan had moved up from singing with the intermission pianist to being featured with the band at the Onyx Club. And she was going over big with the audiences. She remembers Thornhill—who was a great believer in her from the start—sitting outside on the curb, weeping with joy at her success there. Musicians were coming around to hear her. And *The New Yorker* wrote her up, which helped spread her name around.

Her big number back in Pittsburgh, which she was still doing at the Onyx Club, was "Trees." She had taken the stiffly proper lyrics of that song, which bordered on the pretentious, and given them a relaxed swing treatment. (She maintains she *had* to swing "Trees"; there was no way she could have sung it straight.) Thornhill cast about for other material that she could treat in that manner.

For her first recording session under her own name, on August 6, 1937, he picked out two traditional songs for her: "Loch Lomond" and "Annie Laurie." She also recorded two pop songs, "I'm Coming, Virginia," which had been part of her repertoire in Pittsburgh, and would remain in her repertoire a half century later, and "Blue Skies." Thornhill's sidemen for the session included several musicians who were playing at the Onyx Club at the time, including bassist John Kirby, clarinetist Buster Bailey, and drummer O'Neill Spencer, who would become members of Kirby's own band the following year.

"Now 'Loch Lomond'—that was Claude's idea. In 1937, around that time, some of the bands were swinging the classics; Tommy Dorsey

Maxine Sullivan. (Institute of Jazz Studies)

had done 'Song of India' and I guess they were looking for new material. Besides pop material, they were digging up the classics—and then by their being in public domain, they didn't have to worry too much about royalties. In fact, they could claim them as their own." Thornhill could collect royalties for his special arrangements of such public domain tunes.

"Everybody knows 'Loch Lomond'—it's a song that everybody sings in school at one time or other. So the song wasn't new. The idea was to just swing a traditional song. I think one of the things that happened, that maybe sort of shot it up was the fact that the first time I did it on the air, there was a show at the time called the 'Saturday Night Swing Club,' and I sang 'Loch Lomond' on the show and Leo Fitzpatrick, a station manager in Detroit, cut it off the air. He said it was sacrilegious to swing a traditional Scotch song. And the following Saturday, we had a showdown between the two stations, and he had a big orchestra and a choir, Ray Heatherton and Rise Stevens, and I'm on this end with a small group doing my version—it was something else! I ran into Leo Fitzpatrick later on in years, and we talked about this, and the only thing he had to say was, 'Well, it didn't hurt you.'"

Benny Goodman successfully recorded "Loch Lomond" with Martha Tilton on vocal in November. According to Sullivan, Goodman arranger Jimmy Mundy copied Thornhill's arrangement after hearing Sullivan's record on a jukebox.

Ella Logan tried to get a bit of publicity for herself by picketing the Onyx Club, claiming that she had sung "Loch Lomond" before Sullivan. Sullivan's answer was that countless people had sung it, and there was certainly nothing unusual about a Scottish girl singing it. It went without saying that there *was* something unusual about a black girl swinging it.

It was Sullivan's great success swinging this traditional song, she adds, that prompted Chick Webb the next year to have *his* vocalist, Ella Fitzgerald, try swinging "A-Tisket, A-Tasket," which became Fitzgerald's first smash hit.

The tremendous success of "Loch Lomond" made everyone familiar with the name of Maxine Sullivan. She notes, however: "My real name is Marietta Williams. I was calling myself Maxine before I came to New York. But I guess it was Claude's idea to call me Sullivan." He said he didn't want her confused with another jazz singer, Midge Williams.

Not that there was ever much chance of confusing Maxine Sullivan with any other singer. She had an unusually clear, pure voice—she was billed for a while as "the Lass with the Delicate Voice"—and she had her own, straightforward, gently swinging style. And, unlike her jazz contemporaries, she was now being offered a great deal of traditional material to sing, in attempts to duplicate the success of "Loch Lomond." In 1938, for example, she recorded "Dark Eyes" and "It Was a Lover and his Lass." In '39, she did "I Dream of Jeanie with the Light Brown Hair," "Drink to Me Only with Thine Eyes," and "Jackie Boy." In '40, she did "If I Had a Ribbon Bow" and "Who is Sylvia?" Throughout these years, she also recorded quality pop songs (such as "Ill Wind," "Night and Day," "It's Wonderful," "St. Louis Blues," "My Blue Heaven," "When Your Lover Has Gone"), but it was the traditional songs that set her apart, established her identity.

Sullivan took nothing, in terms of style, from Ella Fitzgerald or Billie Holiday (both of whom were younger than she), who today are usually named as the leading jazz singers of the Swing Era; Sullivan had formed her style before she had heard of them. Fitzgerald began singing with Chick Webb in 1935. Sullivan first heard Fitzgerald "live" — and even got her autograph — when the Webb Band played

Maxine Sullivan, singing with the John Kirby Band, NBC studio, New York, 1939. Russell Procope, alto sax; Charlie Shavers, trumpet; Buster Bailey, clarinet; O'Neill Spencer, drums; Billy Kyle, piano (partially hidden). Missing from picture: John Kirby, bass. (Frank Driggs collection)

Pittsburgh, at some point prior to Sullivan's leaving for New York in the spring of '37.

"I still think Ella's, you know, the greatest," Sullivan declares, going on to make it clear that although she enjoyed Fitzgerald's and Holiday's work, neither was an influence on her. "See, Ella and Billie and me were contemporaries, although I was in a different bag altogether. I didn't get a chance to do, to compete in the popular vein, you know. But I listened in earlier days to, oh boy I go back. . . Ethel Waters, Mildred Bailey, Connee Boswell, and Ruth Etting, and all those people, you know." Asked if they were influences on her, she responds: "Oh yeah! Definitely! Yeah." Asked if musicians influenced her too, she adds: "Mainly musicians, yeah. . . . Well, naturally I was, by Louis Armstrong, and mostly bands. I liked Benny Goodman, you know, when he was numero uno. . . ."

And of course, Maxine Sullivan influenced other vocalists, as well. In a September, 1946 *Metronome* interview, for example, Dinah Shore told George Simon that the female vocalist who had most impressed her of late was Peggy Lee. But Simon reported: "Dinah also leans towards Maxine Sullivan, the way she sang on those records, especially 'Nice Work if You Can Get It.' She admits that Maxine had a big influence on her style when she was still back in Nashville." Shore came to New York in '38, and her unaffected, lilting singing style owed much to Sullivan.[1]

Sullivan stood motionless as she sang at the Onyx Club, with a natural kind of dignity. She was good looking, clearly self-confident, and had a winsome smile. Her style was direct and intimate. And yet she could also convey a certain degree of reserve, a friendly you-can-look-but-don't-touch kind of attitude.

Many have commented, over the years, on the warmth, gentleness, and sweetness Sullivan radiates. But old friends have noted there has always been a fundamental strength under that sweetness. Sullivan had to be tough not to get exploited when she first arrived in New York. She never allowed people to push her around. And *that* side of her was acknowledged in a nickname bestowed upon her in early years by fellows who discovered she wasn't about to let anyone take advantage of her: "Hardtack Annie."

Sullivan's public attitude remained cheerful, congenial—in contrast to the embittered moodiness that Billie Holiday could convey. But

[1] And in a 1986 interview in *Cashbox* magazine, Joe Williams commented: "I think that every singer in the world should be forced to sit and listen to Maxine Sullivan." Williams, who started singing professionally the same year that Sullivan broke through to fame, liked the unstrained quality she always got. At Sullivan's funeral in 1987, Williams said she had something to teach all singers: "Keep it simple."

she seemed to keep a certain psychological shield around her. It helped protect her from being worn down by the injustices of life, the way Holiday was. It also may have prevented her from reaching, in her performances, the emotional depths that Holiday could reach. Holiday was repeatedly, in a sense, opening her veins and letting herself bleed before her audiences. She could make you share in a sense of tragedy. Sullivan was more self-contained. She tended—particularly in her early years—to stay closer to the surface of the songs; she tended to keep things lighter, less involved. She did not deal in tragedy, any more than Ella Fitzgerald did.

As Sullivan grew older, her singing gained notably in emotional depth. She became freer in her singing, and more of a blues feeling emerged on certain numbers. But Sullivan never had the emotional depth of Holiday; that simply was not her strong suit as a singer, any more than it was Fitzgerald's.

Sullivan never had another record that equaled the great commercial success of "Loch Lomond," but she turned out a fine series of critically acclaimed sides. When *Metronome* magazine compiled its list of "Best Records of 1937," it headlined, "Tommy Dorsey and Maxine Sullivan Cop Top Honors." Dorsey's band had seven recordings on the list. Sullivan had five; no other vocalist equaled that number.

George T. Simon gave capsule summaries of Sullivan's best recordings: "'Gone With the Wind': Most mellow and bedroomy of all of Maxine's vocals plus beautiful band backing; 'Loch Lomond': Colossal swing of voice and arrangement; 'I'm Coming, Virginia': Ditto, but in a bit sadder vein; 'Blue Skies': Maxine shines in an almost melancholy gladness; 'Nice Work if You Can Get It': A real, slow, beautiful seducer; magnificent backgrounds, as usual."

Those "magnificent backgrounds" were all due to conductor/arranger Claude Thornhill, who had not yet formed his own big band. (When he did, in 1939, he was identified in *Metronome* as "Maxine Sullivan's and Skinnay Ennis' arranger.") Thornhill's sensitive backing contributed much to Sullivan's success. They were a good musical team, but some strain developed and in 1938, they split permanently.

That same year, John Kirby organized the sextet for which he is remembered by jazz buffs today. He had been working for quite some time with clarinetist Buster Bailey at the Onyx Club. "And when Lucky Millinder's Band came off the road, Kirby got Charlie Shavers [trumpet], Russell Procope [alto saxophone], Billy Kyle [piano], and O'Neill Spencer [drums], and formed his group, which was called at the time, 'the Biggest Little Band in America,'" Sullivan recalls. Sullivan's voice and Kirby's subtle, elegant, chamber music type of jazz—Lou Singer provided some of the more memorable arrangements—proved a winning combination, on records and on radio.

Sullivan and Kirby were married in 1938. "And in the meantime, my stock had gone up a little bit. And I was called out to California to appear in a club, and also in a movie called *St. Louis Blues*, which starred Lloyd Nolan and Dorothy Lamour.[2] I sang 'St. Louis Blues,' 'Loch Lomond,' and 'Dark Eyes,' and while I was there, Hoagy Carmichael wrote a little segment—there was a scene where I was sitting on a river bank, and Nat King Cole's group is playing in the background, while I did 'Kinda Lonesome.'

"While I was out there, I did another movie. Louis Armstrong was appearing in a movie, *Going Places*, with Dick Powell and Anita Louise. And so they sort of grabbed me while I was there, to save on the transportation. Johnny Mercer wrote a piece for the movie called 'Mutiny in the Nursery.'

"Then I came back to New York, and Louis and I appeared at the Cotton Club. It was downtown then, on 47th Street. And for our opening of the show, they projected on a paper movie screen a scene from *Going Places*, in which Louis and I are singing 'Jeepers Creepers' to the horse, and he had on his groom outfit, and I had on my maid's uniform—and then we burst through that screen, in those same costumes, every night."

The show, which co-starred Stepin Fetchit along with Armstrong, and also included the comedy team of Stump and Stumpy, Midge Williams, Dan Healy, Princess Vanessa, and Soccares' Orchestra, was the very last presentation of the Cotton Club. It closed June 10, 1940. Sullivan says she's closed better joints than that.

And she had more important projects to take care of. "Kirby and I had a radio show on CBS every Sunday for about two years, called, 'Flow Gently Sweet Rhythm.'" The show was a groundbreaking venture in broadcasting. For here were black performers starring in their own regular network show. Black bands had long been featured in remote broadcasts from clubs or dance halls, but that was not as prestigious as getting a show of one's own.

"While we had the show, in '40 and '41, it was during the ASCAP strike. We were forced to do traditional material, Kirby's arrangements of the classics and my little arrangements of the folk songs, and some tunes that were written on the spur of the moment. That's how BMI came into existence, because they had to keep writing songs. Charlie Shavers had a tendency to interject a few notes from some of the ASCAP tunes into his solos, and the guy upstairs, the manager, he was going

[2] This 1939 film, which occasionally shows up on late-night television, was retitled *The Best of the Blues* after a film biography of W.C. Handy bearing the name *St. Louis Blues* was made in 1958.

Louis Armstrong and Maxine Sullivan. (Frank Driggs collection)

crazy, hoping that Charlie wouldn't go into one of the ASCAP tunes. If he got into it, they would have to turn it off, see. (But Charlie was pretty conscientious about that; he sort of stayed away from it.)

"Kirby's band did very well, but when the war broke out he lost the guys in the band; they went into the service. And that was the end of the Kirby band because it was difficult to replace his men, for the simple reason that it was a very disciplined band, and they were playing tricky arrangements, which weren't on paper. And most of the musicians at the time just were not disciplined to play arrangements in a small group. It was like every other small group was more or less a jam session. So he tried for a couple years. But eventually, the band just fell apart because he didn't have the guys."

Kirby and Sullivan often found their careers taking them apart from each other. "My career had sort of got above his; he hadn't really made it yet," she notes. "And so we sort of separated because I was out on the road doing vaudeville, and he was doing clubs. They tried to make a package out of it, but it didn't go well in vaudeville. It wasn't dynamic enough."

But in the meantime, there were other projects. "*Swingin' the Dream* [1939]—Oh yeah, that was a classical flop. 'Darn that Dream' was the hit song that came from that show. Louis Armstrong played Bottom, I played Titania. And Sonny Payne was in it, too. He was about 11 years old at the time, and years later he wound up being Count Basie's drummer. And it had wall-to-wall actors and musicians. Benny Goodman was on one side with a combination, Eddie Condon on the other side with a combination, and Don Voorhees in the pit. Cast of thousands. We did 13 performances. Well, the Center Theater, which was on 50th Street and I think Sixth Avenue, was a huge theater and swing wasn't everybody's cup of tea, even in 1939. And the theatergoers weren't altogether with it. And it folded."

She toured, and also cut a few records, with Benny Carter's big band. 'We covered 23 states in six weeks, doing one-nighters. That was a trip. When I got back to New York, I kissed the ground; I said I wouldn't do that anymore. And I often wondered how the singers like Ella Fitzgerald, who traveled that route back and forth many years, and Helen Humes, and all the girls that sang with bands, how they could stand the one-nighters, because it was horrible. You hardly got a chance to rest. Sometimes it was hard to get accommodations. You had to sleep on the bus, practically eat on the bus—and *long jumps*. We had a jump from Orlando, Florida, to Baton Rouge, Louisiana."

She and Kirby often saw so little of each other—his band also traveled—that they finally seemed to feel they didn't need each other anymore. They were divorced in 1942. Kirby died a decade later.

She married stride pianist Cliff Jackson. (Interestingly, both Kirby and Jackson had first heard Sullivan singing years before at the Benjamin Harrison Literary Club in Pittsburgh.) Home for them and their daughter Paula, born in 1944, was 818 Ritter Place in the Bronx, where Sullivan still lives today.

Sullivan was in demand at posh night spots. La Reuban Bleu on East 56th Street in Manhattan became a base for her in the late '40s and early '50s. In 1948 and 1953, she played in Great Britain. She sang "Loch Lomond" once, naturally, on the shores of Loch Lomond in Scotland—and was startled to discover how large it was; she had always envisioned a pond. She was also surprised to find that in Great Britain she was better known for her recording of "The Folks Who Live on the Hill," which had evidently received considerable BBC airplay over the years, than for 'Loch Lomond."

A glamorous Maxine Sullivan, in costume for Swingin' the Dream, *1939.* (Frank Driggs collection)

She recorded infrequently in the 1950s. From 1953-57, she periodically played the Village Vanguard in New York. She toured, too, but she realized she was no longer the draw she had once been. And musical trends were changing. Rock 'n' roll had become the thing. And she knew she could not be a star in that scene. Sullivan made one recording, she says, which does not show up in the discographies. Someone got her to cut a rock 'n' roll version of "Loch Lomond," with guitars and bass backing her. She does not know if it was ever released.

In 1957, after celebrating her 20th anniversary in the business at the Vanguard, she announced her retirement. She wanted to give more attention to her daughter, Paula, who was then about to enter junior high school, and she had gotten "tired of singing 'Loch Lomond.'" In vaudeville, she recalls, she sang it four times a day, seven days a week. And no matter where she played, for 20 years, people always expected it. If she wasn't singing "Loch Lomond," she was expected to sing similar, traditional type of material: "Annie Laurie," "As the Tide was Flowing In," or "Raggle-Taggle Gypsies." She was 46 years old.

For the next 10 years, she notes, "I was involved in the community. And then I wound up working for the Board of Education. I worked in several capacities. I started out as a Parent Association president. I increased the membership, and I had a lot of volunteers. They didn't know who I was. I never did any singing at all. I was serious. I wound up being the chairman of the local school board in my district. I served six years on the local school board."

She was more concerned with local children having to endure overcrowded classrooms and deteriorating conditions in the neighborhood than she was in the world of music. Only at the very end of her involvement in the school system did the children find out who she was.

* * *

In 1967, Sullivan agreed to play two weeks at Blues Alley, a new club in Washington, D.C. "I had a very successful engagement, but I still hadn't decided I wanted to get back into the stream, because it was rock time and I didn't know how I would be received. I was saying to myself, 'No way am I going to get involved.'"

But she tested the waters again in '68, when she sang at one of Dick Gibson's Denver, Colorado, jazz parties. "And so while I was out there, I ran into all the guys, like Bob Haggart and Yank Lawson, and Teddy Wilson and Clark Terry, Bob Wilber, Bobby Hackett, and I had quite a successful appearance there. So Dick Gibson decided to form the band—the World's Greatest Jazz Band. They came to New York and opened at the Riverboat. I went down to catch them, and Bobby Hackett happened to be in the audience. He said that he was opening in January of 1969 for eight weeks, and would I go in with him? So I

Maxine Sullivan sings at a 1985 fundraiser for her "House that Jazz Built." (Chip Deffaa collection)

said I would, and that was the re-entry for me. I made an album for Bob Wilber, the Hoagy Carmichael thing, and then at the end of the engagement at the Riverboat, I went into the Down Beat with the World's Greatest Jazz Band. And then when they said they were going to Europe, I couldn't resist the offer."

Since 1969, Sullivan has been a continuing and vital presence on the jazz scene. And she has also recorded with far greater frequency than she had for years prior to her 1957 retirement, although not all of the albums have done her justice. (She also found time to appear in two Broadway shows: *Take a Giant Step*, starring Louis Gossett, and *My Old Friends*, for which she was nominated for a Tony Award in 1979.) She has recorded with Bobby Hackett, Vic Dickenson, the World's Greatest Jazzband of Yank Lawson and Bob Haggart, Bob Wilber, Earl Hines, Doc Cheatham, Keith Ingham, and others. She has become, by far, the favorite vocalist in traditional jazz circles.[3]

[3] Her popularity was reflected in a jazz poll run by George Buck, owner of such record labels as Jazzology, Audiophile, and Progressive. He polled his mail-order customers; more than 4000 responded. The results were released shortly after Sullivan's death in 1987. She placed first among female vocalists, just ahead of Ella Fitzgerald. Mel Torme and Joe Williams were the top two among male vocalists.

"In January, I went to Tokyo with Scott Hamilton and his group. And we did 10 concerts. We were there for about 17 days. We played in Tokyo and other cities, and while we were there we made an album, which I think is going to be very good. I'm pretty sure that it'll be distributed mainly in Japan, but maybe some copies will be sold here in the United States.[4]

"Right now, I'm looking forward to a jazz cruise that I'm going to do for four weeks on the S.S. Norway. And I go out to California each Memorial Day to do the Sacramento Traditional Jazz Society Jubilee, and then I have a special day out there—my own day in December—for the Sacramento Traditional Jazz Jubilee. And I'm going to do the Conneaut Lake thing again—I do that jazz festival every year—and I got a few gigs that I do on weekends, and I do just enough to keep me busy and not tire me out too much. I mean, I can't get involved *too* steadily, because I'm 73 years old, I'll be 74 in May, and I don't want to kill myself."

Sullivan also devotes time and energy to "the House that Jazz Built," which she established in the Bronx in 1975 to preserve and promote jazz. Supported by members' donations and occasional grants, "the House that Jazz Built" serves as a repository for research materials, and as a kind of jazz base in the borough, presenting occasional benefit jam sessions and workshops, and introducing local youths to the wider world of jazz. It's also a reflection of Sullivan's commitment to her community, the Bronx.

That community has not fared well in recent times. The residents, largely black and hispanic, are poor. The many abandoned and decaying buildings remind one of photos taken in Europe after the war.

On a drive through the community one afternoon, heading to her home after an appointment in Manhattan, Sullivan notes quietly: "It's all being torn down." The burned-out shells of buildings are haunting. "We've got more vacant space. I think we're going back to, going to change it back to farms. . . . See the empty buildings?" she says.

"In fact, I worked in the junior high school—and the school's right across the street from where I live—and now, guess what? The school was built for 1600 students and two years ago, they had to move the remaining students into another school, because they only had 65 students. Now they've got special programs in there. The neighborhood! They've torn down a lot of houses. No kids."

Sullivan has stayed. She can't turn things around in the Bronx. But this is her world as much as the world of jazz clubs, festivals, and

[4] The album, entitled "Uptown," was released in the U.S. on Concord Records. It received a 1986 Grammy nomination as best female jazz vocal album, Sullivan's third such nomination since her emergence from retirement.

cruises. "I've been living in the same house for 40 years," she notes. 'The majority of the people that I know, that I was involved with in the school system, don't even know that I'm Maxine Sullivan. Because my name is Marietta Williams. . . . Some of my neighbors call me Maxine, some of 'em call me Mrs. Williams."

* * *

There's no pretense to Maxine Sullivan's work, any more than there is to her personality. She sings simply, directly, landing lightly on the notes. She'll hold onto a word here or a phrase there, subtly putting her mark onto the material. She hasn't got a big voice. But she uses it wisely.

It's the simplicity of her style that is so appealing. She's our senior-most female jazz singer, and she offers a way of singing that was formed in a long-gone era: in the early '30s, before bebop, before even swing hit full stride. She likes to sing the melody straight in the first chorus, improvise a bit in the second chorus. Then an ending, and she's done. There's never any excessive ornamentation. And throughout it all, there's a buoyant, natural swing. Her self-confidence is appealing.

Sullivan's been blessed with quite a lovely sounding voice. The timbre is unusual, and attractive—whether she's singing, or simply offering an ebullient greeting to a fan. "Yeah!" often serves as her reply to people saying hello to her, particularly if she doesn't know, or may have forgotten, their names; for me, that familiar "Yeah!" seems to embody her general affirmation of life.

After some 50 years in the business, Sullivan has mastered her craft. She can speak/sing a line like, "I ought to cross you off my list" (from "Between the Devil and the Deep Blue Sea") and make it sound as if the thought has just hit her. She enunciates precisely, without losing a relaxed feeling.

And she works *with* musicians. She thinks of them as colleagues, not hired hands backing her. Listen, for example, to Sullivan's recording of "Ill Wind" on her latest album ("Great Songs from the Cotton Club by Harold Arlen and Ted Koehler," released by Stash Records, 1984, and nominated for a Grammy Award). She doesn't sing at all during the first two minutes of the five-minute-long recording. Instead the mood builds in a masterful extended solo by Al Klink on tenor sax. Singers with less talent but more ego would never have permitted such an introduction. And Klink weaves in and out, after she finally does come in. "You're only misleadin'—" she sings, and Klink's sax answers her. Beautiful interplay. She's made as effective a recording of this classic torch song as one can hope to hear.

Sullivan, it should be noted, spent many hours in recording that album. Her voice, due to her age, was not as good on some occasions as on others. She was willing to do whatever retakes or overdubs her producers, Bill Rudman and Ken Bloom, thought were needed to get the best possible representations of her art. She appreciated their perfectionism. She asked them, "Where were you guys 40 years ago?" But she also made clear to them what the bottom line was: "Nobody tells me how to phrase," she said flatly. There she was "Hardtack Annie" again. She knew intuitively what worked best.

Sullivan seems to prefer upbeat songs. "We Just Couldn't Say Goodbye," "Between the Devil and the Deep Blue Sea," "Raisin' the Rent," "As Long as I Live," "I'm Gonna Sit Right Down and Write Myself a Letter"—these are all songs that she loves to sing nowadays. And she projects a tremendous elan doing them. You feel good just

Maxine Sullivan, 1986. (Chip Deffaa collection)

being in the same room.

But her voice is also especially well-suited now for the occasional slower, brooding numbers, such as "Ill Wind," that she'll tackle. Or the wistful, bittersweet things such as, "You Gave Me Everything But Love."

A case can be made that Maxine Sullivan has never been a better singer than she is today. Oh, by legitimate standards, of course she had a better voice when she was young. It had an unusually clear, bell-like quality then. Sullivan's voice is darker now, and sometimes trails off at the end of a phrase. But it is, for this listener anyway, a far more interesting voice today. Less "perfect" perhaps. But with greater emotional impact. She could not have done an "Ill Wind" or a "You Gave Me Everything but Love," as movingly back in the '30s. There is a vulnerability in her voice now that wasn't there in her youth.

In addition, Sullivan generally seems to exhibit a greater jazz feeling now than on many of her early recordings. Her overall approach is a bit looser, freer, more relaxed. She swings more, will experiment a bit more, without ever getting far from the melody. And with subtle changes of inflection, she is more apt to occasionally surprise us.

She is also, by and large, singing better songs today. And continuing to expand her repertoire. "In the early days," Sullivan says, "I was sort of locked in with doing more or less swing versions of folk tunes, because 'Loch Lomond' sort of stereotyped me, and I really got stuck there for a while. Although on every record that I did, on one side was a folk standard and on the other side was a pop standard. But I got tired of showing up in places, and all they knew I did was 'Loch Lomond.' So I quit. And when I came back, I felt a little bit freer. I wasn't compelled to stick to the folk material. . . . Although still," she notes, "when I make personal appearances, there's always one person in the audience gonna holler out for 'Loch Lomond.'"

1984

* * *

Maxine Sullivan died April 7, 1987. She had continued performing, even as her strength was fading, virtually up until the end. At a "Highlights in Jazz" tribute to her in New York, just a few weeks before she died, she roused the crowd to great enthusiasm with a medley of "St. Louis Blues" and "Everyday (I Have the Blues)," which had become her surefire concert closer, and which she never got around to recording. She suffered bouts with pneumonia in her last years, and—although it was not made public until her death—she was fighting lung cancer in the final year. She was one plucky trouper. A final reminder of her artistry, "Together: Maxine Sullivan Sings the Music of Jule Styne," was released by Atlantic Records in October, 1987. She had completed that album in January, just three months before she died. It contains some of the most satisfying recordings she ever made.

"She was fabulous," Bucky Pizzarelli was quoted as saying in the U.P.I. obituary. "Anybody who wants to learn to sing should buy a batch of her records. Nobody, male or female, could sing a melody the way she did."

Maxine Sullivan at the 1985 Conneaut Lake, Pa., Jazz Festival. (Chip Deffaa collection)

JOHN · WILLIAMS · JR

Still Counting His Blessings

ass player John Williams Jr., 77, opens his photo album almost shyly, explaining something about his wife having put it together; he would never have gotten around to it. The pictures prompt a stream of memories.

Here's a shot of the Louis Armstrong Orchestra of 1940, taken in Montreal. That night, Williams recalls, was one of the nights that they couldn't get hotel accommodations due to racial discrimination; the whole band wound up sleeping at a house of prostitution. Here's a shot of Williams with Armstrong and a small group at a 1947 Carnegie Hall Concert. "Pops and I sang 'Rockin' Chair' together," he mentions.

Here's Billie Holiday ("just a beautiful person"); Williams made the dates when she recorded "Strange Fruit" and some other memorable sides in the late '30s. Here's Teddy Wilson and Edmond Hall, with whom he played at Cafe Society in the '40s. And Edmond's brother Herb, Doc Cheatham and Williams all relaxing in Denmark where the three musicians toured and recorded in 1979, when all of them were over 70. Older photos of leaders Williams has worked with, including Coleman Hawkins, Lucky Millinder, Benny Carter, and Johnny Hodges.

"All of the leaders I've been with was regular," he says. "You know what I mean, they never stayed off to themselves. Such nice guys. And tops—the giants in their field." He puffs easily on his pipe. "God's been good to me."

* * *

As a boy growing up in Memphis, where he was born, March 13, 1908, Williams started on the violin, which he studied for several years. 'But when I went into Booker T. Washington High School (a colored high school in the south part of Memphis, with about 1200 students), they had a hundred-piece brass band," he remembers. "The principal, Professor Hamilton, was a trombonist, and he would teach you, privately, any instrument that you had and you wanted for the band. My father had wanted me to play the violin, but I didn't care for it too much. So I left my violin in the lavatory in high school, figuring someone would take it—which they did.

"So I went to Professor Hamilton and told him, 'My people, we're not poor, but they're not able to buy me an instrument. . .'" Williams recalls. Hamilton got him a donated, second-hand tuba to play.

"And so my last two and half years in high school, I played the bass horn in this 100-piece band. We would play the May-poles, the May Day parades, Fourth of July celebrations, and picnics, and then the different high schools would have contests between the bands," Williams says.

Booker T. Washington High School had a proud musical heritage. The great clarinetist Buster Bailey had graduated from there, as had trumpeter Johnny Dunn before him, Williams recalls. "They had both gone off to New York, and made a name for themselves."

Manassas High School, in north Memphis, took great pride in its school band as well. "See, at the time when I was in high school, Jimmie Lunceford was the English and athletic teacher at Manassas High. That's where [Jimmy] Crawford and Russell [Bowles] and Mose [Allen] and all of them came from," Williams says, naming members of Jimmie Lunceford's renowned big band, which evolved out of Lunceford's high school band of the mid and late '20s.

"After high school, I played in a pit band in the Palace Theater in Memphis. And T.O.B.A. circuit shows would come in every week.[1] Ethel Waters, she used to come in. The Whitman Sisters, they had a big show. The T.O.B.A. circuit would start in Chicago, go all the way to New Orleans, and circle around to the big cities. If the show came in

[1] T.O.B.A. stood for "Theater Owner's Booking Association," a group of theater owners who booked black touring shows; some performers quipped that the initials stood for "Tough on Black Asses."

and had their own band, we would just play an overture. And then when the show was over, we would play another overture and we were through. If the show didn't have their own band, then we had to play their music.

"So, I stayed there until Billy Pearson's Brownskin Models from Chicago came through. They needed a bass horn then, and so I left home. In Chattanooga, Jimmy Taylor asked me to join his band, staying with him and his wife." Williams stayed in Chattanooga for almost a year. After Graham Jackson's 14-piece Atlanta-based band bested Taylor's eight-piece unit in a "battle of the bands" around 1930, Williams joined Jackson's band.

John Williams. (Courtesy John Williams)

"I used to admire the bass horn player that was with the Coon-Sanders Band [Elmer Krebs]. They used to broadcast every night from the Blackhawk Cafe in Chicago, so we'd hear them on the radio. He was playing melody, and a little jazz on his bass horn, back in that time. Because I was down south, you know, I couldn't hear the bands up here in New York. So you could hear Earl Hines; his broadcasts came from the south side of Chicago. And Coon-Sanders was in the Blackhawk. I hadn't gotten started yet on the bass violin," he notes. He enjoyed the bass player with McKinney's Cotton Pickers, too.

"And then you began to hear records of Louis, and Duke Ellington, Fletcher. Well, everybody was listening to Duke back then. And I listened to [bass violinist] Wellman Braud. And all the bands was changing over from the tuba or Sousaphone to the bass violin. A bass violinist I had met in Chattanooga says, 'Look, I got an old bass laying around the house and nobody's using it. Why don't you take it, and learn how to play it?'" Williams recalls. He took lessons, on-and-off, from the middle of 1930 through most of 1931 with a bass violinist from the Atlanta symphony.

Braud was his initial influence on the bass violin. "Braud had, to me, a big round tone. Always got a good sound out of his instrument. Of course later on, you know, you heard other bass players, like John Kirby, Billy Taylor, and of course Slam [Stewart] came along, and Pops Foster—you know, after he got to New York—you could hear most of these," Williams says.

* * *

For the next few years, Williams worked busily under the leadership of territory band leaders Graham Jackson, Jean Calloway (who was promoted as being a distant cousin of Cab, according to Williams), Billy Fowler, and C.S. Belton.

Belton was called "the Duke Ellington of the South," Williams says. "The band had most every arrangement Duke had ever made. They had a big bus, two valets, a bus driver, a 14-piece band, five uniforms. Every night the money was split up equally among the guys. So I'm a rich man now," Williams recalls with a laugh.

"We came to New York and the owner of the Savoy, Mr. Buchanan, wanted the band. But he didn't pay. See, we had been making $80, $90, $100 a night. And the salary in the Savoy, with the great Chick Webb and Ella Fitzgerald, was only $33.50 a week. So we didn't take the job. This was about '35.

"Now Baron Lee had been working in front of the Mills Blue Rhythm Band. And I guess he'd had a falling-out with Irving Mills. He wanted a band because he had four theater dates lined up with Jack Johnson [the former boxing champion]. And he used our band for them. Lee was a nice tall, dark brown-skinned man. He would make up like a comedian; he had an act that he would do outside of the numbers that the band was featured in.

"I had heard my father talk about Jack Johnson, so to be along with *Jack Johnson*—my head was like this! On stage, he would shadow box, and he would relate different fights that he had had, and how he won the heavy weight world's championship, and strip down to his waist and show: no cauliflower ears, you know, no marks on the body. And he could get in the ring with whoever wanted to get in the ring with him. I think Joe Louis' name had begun to come up in '35, and Johnson'd say: 'He couldn't hit me for three minutes.' It was a show. They had the band, about eight chorus girls, a soubrette, a comedian, and a dancing act or something."

In Philadelphia in the fall of '35, Williams became friends with bass player Al Hall, who got Williams a job in a house band at a plush Philadelphia club. It didn't last long. Providing comedy at the club were Moms Mabley and Detroit Red, whose lines proved too "blue" for the tastes of a judge who visited the club one night. "I was off with a cold the night that the police raided the place," Williams remembers. "The rest of the guys in the band were taken to jail, and the place was closed. Moms Mabley made us lose our job! The salary wasn't much but the tips was great. In front of the band, they had a big statue of a cat with his mouth open and a red light, and customers would throw money in it. There was a fellow that used to come in—they say he was a gangster; I don't know whether that's true or not—he was crazy about 'Yes Sir, That's My Baby.' So whenever he came in, I don't care what we were playing, we would segue right into 'Yes Sir, That's My Baby.' This is $50. And there was a big oil man that used to come in. He liked Julia, one of the singers in the show. And when he came in, he wanted her to sit with him—that's all. That's $100. He liked, 'When My Sugar Walks Down the Street, All the Little Birdies Go Tweet, Tweet, Tweet.'"

Before long, apparently on the recommendation of pianist Billy Kyle, (who had worked with Williams in the raided nightclub), Williams was playing bass in the Mills Blue Rhythm Band, which was now being led by Lucky Millinder. The band included such fine musicians as Charlie Shavers, Harry Edison, Carl "Bama" Warwick, Tab Smith, Danny Barker, O'Neill Spencer, and Billy Kyle. Williams stayed with Lucky Millinder through all of 1937 and into 1938; he was there when the band recorded such numbers as "Blue Rhythm Fantasy" and "Prelude to a Stomp" (both February 11, 1937). This was Williams' first nationally-known band. 'We played all around, mostly theaters and dances. We played the Paramount and the Apollo, Loew's State. We'd go into the Savoy for two or three weeks, sometimes. And then you would make the circuit: Baltimore, Philadelphia, Chicago, some would go to the West Coast. We were on salary then. And broadcasting a lot.

* * *

"When I left Lucky, I went with Benny Carter for a short while in '38. Then John Hammond got a job for Frankie Newton, a wonderful trumpet player and arranger, in the Cafe Society Downtown. We had been meeting at Small's Paradise on Sundays. They had those breakfast dances, after the cabaret closed. The clubs would close at four o'clock and all of the musicians would come back to Small's. It was like a camp meeting, because the guys you didn't see during the week, you'd see them there on Sunday mornings, jamming. Roy [Eldridge], Chu [Berry], everybody would come over. So, Frankie got the band together there and we opened Cafe Society Downtown, with Billie Holiday. Jack Gilford—another wonderful person—was the comic there."

Barney Josephson's Cafe Society Downtown represented something new on the Manhattan nightlife scene. Josephson wanted a first-rate club that would be fully integrated. He had been strongly put off by the attitudes of places like the Cotton Club, where great black musicians, singers, and dancers were presented for the entertainment of whites. Josephson made it known that he wanted blacks and whites to feel equally at home in his club. Both shows and audiences would be

John Williams (with bass at far right) in Lucky Millinder's Band, 1937. (Courtesy John Williams)

racially mixed. And putting a white comedian—Jack Gilford—on the same club bill with a black singer/headliner—Billie Holiday—was highly unusual in '37. Josephson, like Hammond, was a committed liberal when it came to racial matters.

The Cafe Society gig led to Williams making a number of records with Billie Holiday.

"Billie was certainly well known by then," Williams recalls. "By '38, you know, she had made a lot of things with Teddy Wilson. Teddy's responsible for her—well, John Hammond, too. John Hammond was crazy about her. He could have had Ella Fitzgerald but he took Billie instead. He could have had both of them; so I was told. Fletcher and Benny Carter had him come up to Fletcher's house, because they had heard Ella Fitzgerald. And he listened to Ella, but he was so wrapped up in Billie, he just stuck with Billie. Billie was beautiful, a beautiful person. Regular, you know. If Billie Holiday came in here, she wouldn't sit over there, she'd come right here and sit in the middle of us."

In the previous two years, Holiday had sung with the big bands of Count Basie and Artie Shaw. She had suffered racial insults while touring with both bands. And not just in the south, either. During Shaw's extended stay at the Hotel Lincoln in New York, the management had told Shaw that Holiday would not be allowed to use the elevators that hotel guests used; she would have to use a freight elevator instead. They did not want patrons to imagine that their hotel admitted blacks!

Holiday and the musicians were treated with full respect at Cafe Society. And Barney Josephson encouraged Holiday to sing a song that allowed her to express some of her bitterness over racial prejudice in America. Called "Strange Fruit," it dealt with the lynchings of blacks in the south. Their bodies were the "strange fruit" hanging from the poplar trees. It was a powerful statement, made all the more so by Holiday's delivery. It was anything but the sort of light entertainment one usually found in New York nightclubs. But the song went over well at the club. Josephson was all for Holiday singing it. Others close to her advised her to steer clear of it; it was too controversial.

Holiday was then recording for Vocalion (part of the American Record Corporation). Williams says that the company didn't want anything to do with "Strange Fruit." Holiday was eager to get the song on wax, but at the recording session the company balked. They let Holiday and the musicians go home early rather than record that song.

"We got paid for the whole session, as if we had made four numbers. But they wouldn't do 'Strange Fruit,'" Williams recalls.

"Well Billie felt very bad and upset, because she wanted to do it, and they wouldn't record it. She was under contract to them. If they don't want you to record something, you can't record it—not with them. So somehow, she got hold of Milt Gabler, who had this little studio on 52nd street," Williams notes.

Gabler worked it out so that *he* could record "Strange Fruit" and release it on his small, independent label, Commodore. Williams remembers Vocalion as agreeing to print the records for Gabler, promising to make as many copies as Gabler might need.

Also recorded at that same April 20, 1939 session for release on Gabler's recently-created Commodore label were three other classic sides: "Yesterdays," "I Got a Right to Sing the Blues," and "Fine and Mellow." Backing Holiday was Frankie Newton's Band from Cafe Society: Newton (trumpet), Sonny White (piano), Tab Smith (alto, soprano, clarinet), Kenneth Hollon (tenor sax), Stanley Payne (baritone sax), Eddie Dougherty (drums), Jimmy McLin (guitar), and Williams (string bass).

Williams also made the dates when Holiday recorded such sides as "Dream of Life" and "That's All I Ask of You" (both January 20, 1939, with a band including Charlie Shavers and Chu Berry); "Long Gone Blues" and "You're Too Lovely to Last" (both March 21, 1939, with Hot Lips Page); "Them There Eyes," "Some Other Spring," and "Swing Brother Swing" (all July 5, 1939, with Charlie Shavers); "Body and Soul," "Falling in Love Again," and "Ghost of Yesterday" (all February 29, 1940, with Roy Eldridge); "Jim," "I Cover the Waterfront," and "Gloomy Sunday" (all August 7, 1941, with Teddy Wilson); "Mandy is Two," "Until the Real Thing Comes Along" and "It's a Sin to Tell a Lie" (all February 10, 1942, again with Teddy Wilson).

And while based at Cafe Society Downtown, Williams found time for assorted other recording dates. There were sides with Buster Bailey ("Chained to a Dream," "Light Up," December 7, 1938); Harry James ("Home James," with Albert Ammons on piano, and "Jesse," with Pete Johnson on piano, both February 1, 1939); James P. Johnson ("Hungry Blues," March 9, 1939); the Port of Harlem Jazzmen, including Meade Lux Lewis ("Port of Harlem Blues," April 7, 1939) and Sidney Bechet ("Blues for Tommy," June 8, 1939); and Frankie Newton ("Tab's Blues" and "Jitters," both April 12, 1939).

* * *

"We were at Cafe Society Downtown about a year. When they decided to put another band in, I went with Coleman Hawkins, a little band in the Golden Gate here in New York. I stayed with Hawkins until I went with Louis in '39," Williams recalls.

Williams was part of Hawkins' All-Star Octet, which also included

Benny Carter (tenor sax), J.C. Higginbotham (trombone), Danny Polo (clarinet), Gene Rodgers (piano), Lawrence Lucie (guitar), and Walter Johnson (drums) when they recorded "The Sheik of Araby," "Bouncing with Bean," "My Blue Heaven," and "When Day is Done" (all January 3, 1940).

"Coleman was a regular person, you know, he would just hang out with the guys. Nothing stuck up about him. The guys tease me now about eating. I could eat two dinners then. And so would Hawk. I remember in Washington, we went in this cafe between the shows. And we would order two dinners apiece. And the waitress would start setting up for four people. Hawk would say, 'All right, there's only two of us.' She'd say: 'You mean to tell me just the two of you's gonna eat two dinners apiece?'

"One night in the Golden Gate, Chu Berry came in. Guys used to come in that you would know, and they could sit in. They'd play an arrangement, play parts along with whoever it was, the trumpet or the trombone, and take solos, you know. So Chu comes in, walks up on the bandstand, takes his horn out. Standing there, I think it was Joe Guy. Anyway, just after Joe finished his solo, Chu played eight choruses, put his horn back in his case, closed it up and walked out. So Coleman looked around at us and laughed, and said, 'That man is crazy.' Oh, we had a lot of fun."

* * *

"I was with Louis Armstrong, I'd say off-and-on for about five years. It was his big band. Sidney Catlett. Charlie Holmes was in the saxophone section, Prince Robinson, Joe Garland was the tenor player and the baritone; he was the musical director. Rupert Cole was the altoist; he was with Don Redman for years. [J. C.] Higginbotham, [Wilbur] de Paris, George Washington, on trombone. Red Allen was on trumpet. . . . And Red played all he wanted; Louis never held anyone back. Big Sid Catlett on drums, Lawrence Lucie, guitar, Luis Russell, piano . . . and Pops. A 14-piece band, with two singers, and Pops. Sonny Woods was the man singer. They had two different girl singers while I was there. This was around '40, '41, '42.

"Pops liked to play jokes on you. He had a joke he used to put on a new member he had coming into the band. Saxophone, trumpet, whatever it was . . . He would say: — [and now Williams goes into the famous Satchmo rasp] — 'Gates, when you do your solo on this number, you gotta come down front with me.' So he'd be standing, rockin' — there was a little rock he'd do. And just before you'd hit your last note, he'd say, 'Boy, your fly is open!'" Williams laughs at the memory. "We knew what was going to happen but his reaction—the guy'd jump—the people would start laughing. They thought it was an act.

"So Joe Garland figured a way to catch him. At the theaters, Pops' valet used to bring his trumpet case down for him, with handkerchiefs. You know, you always saw him with white handkerchiefs. And Joe said, 'I got an idea. I'm going to buy two boxes of Kleenex, and when his valet brings his case down, I'm going to take all the handkerchiefs out and put the Kleenex in.' And he got a chance to do it. Pops played the first number, and he announced the second number. The band's playing—he's coming in about the last chorus or something. And he comes back to get a handkerchief. It's soft; he picks it up to wipe his face—and he says, 'Goddam—another Pearl Harbor!' We couldn't catch him after that.

"One night Lawrence, Pops, and myself were coming back from a restaurant after the show. I hadn't changed my clothes and although it was warm, you know, when you play you're wet, and then you cool off. We ate and were walking back. I said, 'Gee, I feel chilly, Pops.' And he took his coat off and put it around me. I'll always remember that.

"And when we were leaving on those tours, at the hotel the people'd be standing around. There'd be a man on crutches, or in a wheelchair—a fifty dollar bill:—[Williams pantomimes Armstrong giving a handout, putting money into my fist, then speaks low in remembered Armstrong tones]—'Here, take care of yourself.' No camera looking, you know, no camera. This is *every day*, now. The man had so much compassion for his fellow man. Wonderful. He was a prince. Some man.

"Well, occasionally you'd have some younger guys who'd say, you know, 'Pops is great, but he's old fashioned.' But all of those people that said something like that—Pops still stayed up here, and you didn't hear nothing about them after a while."

Armstrong rarely told Williams how he should play. "You asked him whether he liked what was behind him," Williams recalls. "Of course, most of the music was arranged. So naturally an arranger writes: two here and four here, maybe four the first chorus and two behind this singer, playing, and four the last chorus. A lot of times, say on some of the old numbers that he'd made, we didn't have an arrangement of it. So naturally, guys are playing there over the harmony and stuff. 'Pops, what you want here?' 'Well, play what you want' or, 'When I'm singing, son, play two; after that, do what you want.' Which ones didn't we have arrangements on? Like 'Sweethearts on Parade,' some of those real old things, I guess, 'That's My Home,' 'St. Louis Blues,' things like that. You know, you don't carry every arrangement that was ever made with you." Occasionally, for a couple of bars on older numbers Williams would have to slap the bass ala Pops Foster (one of his predecessors in the Armstrong band), but he never really liked bass-slapping, he says, since that technique sacrificed beauty of tone.

Williams was on hand when Armstrong used a septet (made up of members of his big band) to record such numbers as "Everything's Been Done Before" and "I Cover the Waterfront" (both March 10, 1941), and "Hey Lawdy Mama," "I'll Get Mine Bye and Bye," "Yes Suh!" and "Do You Call that a Buddy?" (all April 11, 1941).

* * *

The swing years were good years for Williams, happily remembered. He never lacked for work, nor for top musicians to work with. But he also recalls clearly the indignities due to racial prejudice that blacks endured. Problems were more apt to crop up touring than in New York.

John Williams. (Chip Deffaa collection)

"You go through a lot of things that the white musician don't. Even in the north, in some places. Montreal, Canada, with Louis in 1940, for instance. Joe Glaser always booked reservations in these cities for us. We were playing in this amusement park at night in Montreal, and when we walked in the hotel, the desk clerk disappeared. After a while the manager came out and said that he was very sorry but they had 'overbooked.' So we had to go stay in a house with ladies of the evening." Williams laughs a small laugh as he remembers it.

"You'd go south and play the big hotels, affairs—you'd have to go in the back door. While you're playing on the stand, they all come up and hug and kiss you; you're great and wonderful. But when you're ready to leave, you have to go back out the back door. One time we were playing somewhere in Tennessee. We were on the train and coming back towards St. Louis. You would hit part of—was it Arkansas or Mississippi?—anyway, you'd just cross the state line, go a little into the other state and then come back in. When you'd cross that state line, you'd have to sit in the back—get up and move in the back coach. This was with a small group, because with the big band, you had your own coach—no problem there.

"With Lucky, we played an affair one time for President Roosevelt. We came out on the capitol grounds—and you couldn't get a hot dog. In Washington, when I was with Lucky, playing a theater downtown, Chuck Richards was the man singer, and he always opened up in a white linen suit. The manager of the theater came back after the first show and said: 'Lucky, I don't care, but tell your singer as long as he's here, don't open again in that white suit!'

"Pennsylvania, I think, was the first state to legalize equal right... But I remember, right outside of Harrisburg we stopped one day. They didn't turn us down, serving us food—but the white people was paying 25 cents for a hot dog and they was charging us 40.

"And then you'd go in some southern states and nobody said nothing, especially if like you were doing something for the city, and the big officials. They would have a place for you in the hotel dining room, a big table set up for you to eat.

"But I remember with Pops, we played Joliet, California, for city officials, this big affair. And when we finished, there was no place to eat. One of the organizers of the affair says, 'Louis, I'm sorry, we should have at least had sandwiches and coffee for you all. The only place open is in the train station.' So Pops got in the bus with us; I think his wife drove the car. Well, when the night crew—I guess it was two waitresses and the manager or something—saw 14 colored people walking in with one white man, they vanished. Louis stood there and after awhile the manager came out. And when he recognized Louis, he said, like, 'Pops! I've been wanting to meet you for years.'

"So Pops said, 'Well Gates, I'm glad to meet you. We're kind of hungry. Can we get something to eat in here?'

"He says, 'Louis, I cannot let you sit down in the dining room. But I tell you what I'm going to do. You and the fellows sit at the counter. I'll serve you.' So he went back in the kitchen with the cook, and they served us. But if it hadn't been for Pops, we wouldn't have been served. He was well-loved."

* * *

In late 1941, Williams joined Teddy Wilson's Band at Cafe Society Uptown (a second club opened by Barney Josephson), where he worked until 1944. (He went back to Armstrong for a tour of two or three weeks during that period, when Wilson took off.) He recorded various sides with Wilson's band, including one session with Lena Horne, at which she recorded "Out of Nowhere" and "Prisoner of Love." The band originally included Benny Morton (trombone), Emmett Berry (trumpet), Jimmy Hamilton (clarinet), J.C. Heard (drums), Wilson (piano), and Williams (bass).

After Wilson went back to Benny Goodman in 1944, Edmond Hall (who had replaced Jimmy Hamilton when Hamilton joined Duke Ellington) took over the band. Louis Armstrong appeared at Carnegie Hall with Hall's band in 1947. A live recording of this concert (which includes Armstrong and Williams singing "Rockin' Chair" together) has been released on Collectors Rarities and other labels. Williams worked with Hall at Cafe Society Uptown until 1948. (Recordings he made with Hall in 1944 have been reissued on a Circle LP, "Rompin' in '44.")

Williams always liked working for Barney Josephson. He turned down opportunities to join name big bands, happy to remain at Josephson's club.

"When I was with Teddy [Wilson], Duke Ellington used to come in the club. He asked me twice to go with him," Williams recalls. "But at that time, I was recording a lot, and Barney Josephson had called us in the office and said, 'As long as I have a place, you can have a job.' So he's got Cafe Society Uptown and Downtown. I had just left Louis. Why would you want to go back on the road? You're here in New York where you're making more money, and you're at home. So you figure a man with two places, you'd always have work. And Barney Josephson's a good man—no prejudice at all.

"You know, though, I think every musician wanted to play with Duke. He was another lovely person. I think one of the greatest compliments I have heard a fellow musician pass to another one was given to Duke. One night at Cafe Society there was Benny Goodman and Earl

Hines and Count Basie and Art Tatum. . . . They always used to come by because they liked Teddy, and once in a while they would all come in together. They're all sitting there, and Big Sidney and myself—we hadn't seen Basie in a long time, so we went to the table. We're sitting there talking—the same musicians' talk about different chords and different musicians. Tatum says, 'Where's the Duke? He's holding us up.' After a while, Duke comes in—and all of them stood up. And Tatum says: 'Now, here's a man that knows all the chords.' *Coming from Tatum!* And Earl Hines say, 'Don't play nothing, 'cause he'll steal it.' But I thought that was a wonderful compliment. Duke just smiled and hugged them and sat down."

* * *

From 1948-'52, Williams played in Tab Smith's house band at the Savoy, which included trumpeter Herman Autrey, pianist Red Richards, and drummer Walter Johnson. (They recorded for the Manor label.) "Music might have been changing outside," Williams recalls, "—but in the Savoy it was still swing. Chick Webb and all that. No rhythm and blues there. It was swing music every night." On the side, William also played on demos made by singing groups and early rock 'n' roll artists. He says the musicians were often cheated in those situations, being paid a small sum for simply doing a demo, which would sometimes then be surreptitiously released as an actual record outside of the U.S.A.

Williams was bassist for Johnny Hodges' small band of the early '50s, and may be heard, for example, on the Verve album, "Used to be Duke," which also features Lawrence Brown, Shorty Baker, Harry Carney, Jimmy Hamilton, John Coltrane, Richard Powell, and Louis Bellson. And he gigged around town as he could, playing at weddings, parties, etc. His preferred music—swing—had clearly had its day.

Following marriage to his wife, Melrose, Williams took a day job in a bank in the mid '50s and became a part-time jazz musician. He did not want to tour. And he could not count on a satisfactory income from the jazz gigs he was getting in the city. He could still take weekend gigs. In 1968, he traveled to France for several weeks with Buddy Tate. While there, noted critic Hughes Panassie wrote that Williams' "punch, the way he was pushing the orchestra, was making a tremendous impression. . . . Musically and visually, John Williams Jr. was giving the impression of Braud—the same Braud I saw in 1933 with Duke Ellington. . . . They, Williams and Braud, have a way of throwing the notes at the audience, as if sending them snapping, to 'whip' the orchestra with a swing, strong and decided."

Williams became more active in music once again when he retired from the bank in '73, playing often with Red Richards, then touring with Bob Greene's "World of Jelly Roll Morton" concert troupe (1978-82), and the Harlem Blues and Jazz Band (1978-present). Since the late '70s, he has made albums with such musicians as Red Richards, Bob Cantwell, Norris Turney, Taft Jordan, Doc Cheatham, and Herb Hall.

In the New York area, he may often be heard today with Bob Cantwell's Saturday Night Stompers. He still gets a glorious full sound from his instrument, and, working in tandem with 84-year-old drummer Freddie Moore, he provides an authoritative rhythmic foundation for that traditional jazz septet.

Looking back on a career that has spanned six decades, Williams is inclined to count his blessings. "I was never in a band where there was any animosity, or this one didn't speak to that one," Williams reflects. "It seems like every group I was with, the guys all acted like buddies. I've been very fortunate."

1985

MAURICE • PURTILL

"'Nostalgia' is a very dirty word..."

"Mid spotlights and celebrities, the Glen Island Casino opens its 1939 season. . . ." The orchestra's theme swells and then fades as announcer Hugh James continues his introduction. "NBC's microphones are present at Glenn Miller's smart opening." The musicians go into "Sunrise Serenade." In homes across the country on the night of May 17th, 1939, radio listeners can imagine the throngs dancing in the glamorous setting to the Glenn Miller Orchestra.

But at his apartment in Fair Lawn, New Jersey, Maurice ("Moe") Purtill recalls: "You could have shot deer in the Glen Island Casino that first night. Nobody was there. Glenn was way over his head in debt. He was counting on the radio exposure to make the band."

Purtill was there. From early '39, before Miller made it big, until late 1942 when Miller joined the army and broke up his band, Purtill was the drummer for the Glenn Miller Band.

The years with Miller were great, Purtill says. But he adds: "I'd have called for the guys in the white coats, if you'd have told me back then that today they would still be playing Miller music." Purtill also drummed for Red Norvo, Raymond Scott, Tommy Dorsey and other well-known leaders.

He insists, before getting into the story of his career, that he really doesn't much care for looking back. "'Nostalgia' is a very dirty word to me," he says.

* * *

Purtill was barely out of Huntington, Long Island, High School, he recalls, when he got his first big job in Red Norvo's septet (1936). "Red's one of the nicest men in the business and one of the tastiest musicians alive. He taught me an awful lot," Purtill says. Purtill continued to drum for Norvo when he formed a big band. "That was one of the best bands I ever worked with. A jazz band. Wasn't commercial at all. Red doesn't have an ounce of commercial blood in him. We played what we loved to play." With Purtill in Norvo's big band was trumpeter Lee Castle (then Castaldo), who today is the leader of the Jimmy Dorsey Orchestra. By early '38, they had both moved on to Tommy Dorsey's Band.

"I roomed with Lee on the road," Purtill recalls. "We had a lot of laughs, but Lee's a hypochondriac. He'd carry more pills with him than a chain of drugstores. I remember returning to our hotel room once, in Washington, DC, in the middle of July—he had the windows closed, the tub filling with hot water, it felt like a steambath—and Lee, in his robe, was saying he had been in a draft and was afraid he was getting pneumonia. Tommy liked him very much."

Tommy Dorsey was riding high then. He had scored with "Song of India" and "Marie" the previous year. Purtill was in the band when Dorsey recorded such numbers as "Hawaiian War Chant," "The Tin Roof Blues," "Music, Maestro, Please," "Sweet Sue—Just You," "You Must Have Been a Beautiful Baby," and "Boogie Woogie," which became Tommy Dorsey's all-time best-selling record. Dorsey's band was among the most popular in the nation, which meant that it did not have to spend as much time on the road as other bands. The band could settle down in big city hotels or ballrooms for long stretches, rather than be constantly scuffling on one-nighters. Purtill was never keen on traveling.

Purtill admired Dorsey's superb trombone playing, his over-all, professionalism and high standards, but found him difficult personally. He comments: "Tommy and I—you had to love him and hate him at the same time. . . . No one was going to outshout him." Purtill recalls that he quit and returned to Dorsey more than once.

"I quit Tommy at the New Yorker Hotel. Then I got a call from Glenn Miller. He was stuck doing one-nighters outside of Philadelphia, playing a ballroom," Purtill remembers. Purtill thought he'd drum with Miller for a spell. Miller had not yet broken through nationally. In late '38, he had yet to have his first hit record, and his band was hardly as well known as the bands of front-runners such as Benny Goodman, Artie Shaw, and Tommy Dorsey.

Miller had first formed a big band in 1937, but it had soon failed. Miller had then returned for several months to studio work, even playing in the trombone section of Tommy Dorsey's Band on some radio broadcasts, before forming a second band of his own in March of 1938. Tommy Dorsey, in fact, had loaned Miller a nice chunk of money so that Miller could start this second, and ultimately successful, band. (After Miller clicked, Dorsey thought he had invested wisely and now owned a piece of one of the nation's top bands. Miller, however, considered the money to have been a straightforward loan, rather than an investment in the band, and simply paid Dorsey back.)

Maurice Purtill. (Frank Driggs collection)

"I was drumming with Glenn that first night," Purtill recalls. "And then halfway through the night, Glenn said to me: 'I think you have to go back to New York. Call Tommy.' Davey Tough had been working in and out of Tommy's band. Now he had gotten sick and Tommy wanted me back. And Tommy was backing Miller. So I returned to Tommy for a while. And then I left Tommy again. This time, I stayed in New York, doing studio work and teaching."

Purtill accepted a second call to help out Miller in early spring of 1939. He had no intention of joining the band permanently. He simply planned to work for Miller while Miller was in the area. Miller was now booked into Frank Dailey's Meadowbrook in Cedar Grove, New Jersey. Purtill wound up staying in the Miller Band until it broke up roughly three and a half years later. "I just said I'd help Glenn because he was going to stay around New York. He had gotten a booking to play for that summer at the Glen Island Casino," Purtill remembers. Little did Purtill imagine then what he was getting into.

The Miller band, by April of 1939, had gotten much stronger than when Purtill had first heard it. Miller had added some better musicians ("heavyweights," Purtill says). And Purtill himself proved a significant asset. In his book, *The Big Bands* (New York: Schirmer Books, 1981), George T. Simon recalls catching a broadcast of the band from the Meadowbrook and being amazed at how the band was jumping. Simon telephoned Miller the next day to ask how Miller's drummer had suddenly improved so greatly. Miller explained that his old drummer had not improved; he had just gotten a new one: Moe Purtill.

Miller was now getting heavy radio exposure: 10 broadcasts a week from the Meadowbrook. "The band was on the air every time you turned around," Purtill says. "Radio made Glenn Miller. Not records, not movies.

"When I was a kid, you know, at night I'd put the lights out and I'd listen in on a little radio to sustaining broadcasts from all over the country. I'd hear a band from, say, the Blackhawk. And when you'd hear these broadcasts, your imagination would go to work. Now Miller's theory was: we go on the air as much as we can. He was paying for the lines, sometimes, to be able to broadcast from all the different places where the band would be playing. We'd shove the music down their throats. Then when the band toured and came to your home town, you'd say: 'That's that band we've been listening to every night.' And you'd want to see what the hell you had been listening to.

"Well, people would stand up close to the band and they'd call out for tunes we'd never recorded. They had heard them on our broadcasts," Purtill recalls. Miller would keep track of which tunes were being requested the most, and would make records of the ones the public was responding to. Bill Finnegan's arrangement of "Little Brown Jug," recorded for RCA Bluebird on April 10, 1939, was about the first of the Miller recordings to score big with the public (despite the typical Hollywood malarkey of *The Glenn Miller Story* which had the band playing the tune for the first time only *after* Miller's death). "Moonlight Serenade" (Miller's theme) and "Sunrise Serenade" were also recorded that month.

"We just did about 20 tunes at first, played those same 20 tunes over and over. Pounded them into you on the broadcasts. Glenn would say: 'If they've heard us, Moe, we're in,'" Purtill recalls. If this band didn't make it, Purtill notes, it would mean real trouble for Miller. "He owed Tommy so much money, he was in over his head."

Getting the Glen Island Casino booking for the 1939 summer season was a real break, because that was a major showcase spot. The initial sparse audiences were discouraging to the musicians. "But the band suddenly caught on. One night I couldn't park my car outside the Casino, it was so crowded. I didn't know what was happening. It was all of the air-time that did it," Purtill comments. (George T. Simon's recollection is that the Miller Band caught on during its stay at the Meadowbrook in the Spring of 1939, just prior to its stay at the Glen Island Casino. Simon recalls Miller's Glen Island opening night as being packed.)

Glen Miller. (Chip Deffaa collection)

"Then we went down to Washington, DC, broke all the records. It's amazing how this thing hit.

"I never heard of a five-day week with Glenn Miller. We worked seven days a week. We got Sunday off in New York with Miller—and then the bum would book the band for a one-nighter!" Purtill says with a grin. "If we had 40 one-nighters and one free day in our schedule, he'd be killing himself on the phone filling it.

"He was *always* booked. He was a smart businessman. I don't think there was a booker that liked him; he had a guarantee and got 60/40.

"We got our own radio show, sponsored by Chesterfields. The Andrews Sisters sang on it at first, too," Purtill says. When the first 15-minute "Chesterfield Show" was aired on December 27, 1939, the sponsors were apparently unsure if Miller's band alone would be a big enough draw; the Andrews Sisters were brought in as insurance. But as Miller's band established itself as the number one national favorite, it became clear there was no need for the Andrews Sisters, and the show—broadcast Tuesdays, Wednesdays and Thursdays on CBS at 7:15 p.m.—became the Miller Band's alone. The broadcasts continued through September 24, 1942.

"I remember, we were playing at the Pennsylvania Hotel. And we were doing three 'Chesterfield Shows' a week, with repeats. You had to repeat each radio show three hours later for the West Coast, because of the time difference. Then on top of that, Glenn accepted a booking at the Paramount Theater," Purtill recalls. For two weeks, the band was rehearsing for and broadcasting three radio shows per week (six shows, counting the repeats), playing four or five hours nightly at the Pennsylvania, and four or five shows daily at the Paramount. "And on top of that, we had record dates at 2:00 in the morning!" Purtill remembers. It was a grueling schedule. Musicians wondered how they could be expected to maintain the pace.

"In the end, it was Glenn who wound up in the hospital. He was the only guy in the band didn't make the job. Gene Krupa, Tommy Dorsey, Dick Stabile, Jimmy Dorsey all led the band for Glenn, while he was in the hospital. That was a busy band," Purtill adds.

"You'd figure with all the time we spent together, there'd be confrontations among the members of the band. There was none of that.

"I had a very good set-up with Glenn. I never did go through the manager. But we didn't socialize that much. He'd have a few people up in his room, and rap. He liked to rap. I just didn't bother with him that much.

"Glenn's attitude was: 'Do your job and be a gentleman.' We were so busy, there wasn't much time to think of anything else."

Purtill says of playing with the Glenn Miller Orchestra: "It was a good deal. We were swinging, we were having a ball. . . . But if anyone had said then 'the Great Glenn Miller,' you'd have laughed at them." It was a job. An excellent job, Purtill says. The band got a hero's welcome wherever it went. But the musicians, according to Purtill, did not think they were creating music for the ages. And the players *they* admired were the best jazz artists, not necessarily the musicians the public liked most.

Still, Purtill notes, it was a heady experience knowing your band was the most popular in the nation. The band made two motion pictures for Twentieth Century Fox, *Sun Valley Serenade* and *Orchestra Wives*. You couldn't go anywhere without hearing Miller music on jukeboxes. Record sales earned Miller a fortune.

Glenn Miller and Maurice Purtill. (Frank Driggs collection)

"And Glenn would also record his radio shots—he paid to have every live radio broadcast saved, even if it was from some hole-in-the-wall with the worst acoustics. He was the smartest bandleader of all of them—a smart cookie," Purtill says. Those airchecks Miller had made have been released on albums, Purtill notes, and still continue to produce revenues for the Miller estate, roughly 40 years after Miller's passing.

In concert appearances, Miller liked to showcase Purtill on "Bugle Call Rag," taken at a mile-a-minute clip. But the drummer did not play as prominent a role in Glenn Miller's Band as in some of the other big bands. Much of the Miller library was the sort of sweet stuff in which the drummer was not supposed to be noticed by anyone. Purtill did not get the attention that flashier drummers in more swing-oriented bands got.

The Glenn Miller Orchestra played for its last time at the Central Theater in Passaic, New Jersey, on September 27, 1942. Miller volunteered for the service, and the members of his orchestra went their separate ways.

"Glenn wanted me to go in the service with him," Purtill notes. But Purtill had no desire to be a hero. He headed to California, played for a while on Kay Kyser's "College of Musical Knowledge" radio show. Then he went to New York with Tommy Dorsey and his Orchestra. "Then I got drafted. And man, that was the end of that," Purtill says. "I played in a Navy dance band. Ralph Marterie had the dance band. Al Jordan, Doris Day's husband, played trombone. There were guys from the Philharmonic in it, too. We did a lot of bond rallies with Nimitz and Halsey, and we did a radio program, 'Meet Your Navy,'" Purtill recalls. For professional musicians like Purtill, who had long grown used to salaries of more than $100 weekly for playing in bands, it seemed strange to be paid $2.56 per radio show in the Navy band.

In the spring of 1943, Glenn Miller organized his well-remembered Army Air Force Orchestra, using outstanding musicians who had formerly been members of the bands of Benny Goodman, Tommy Dorsey, Artie Shaw, Will Bradley, Harry James, Jan Savitt, and Vaughn Monroe—besides a few alumni of his civilian band, and a full string section. Ray McKinley (with Frank Ippolito as alternate) handled the band's drumming superbly.

For almost a year, that band was stationed in the U.S., broadcasting weekly on NBC. In the spring of 1944, the band left for England. On December 15th, 1944, Miller set off for France in a small plane, to make advance preparation for the band's arrival there. He never reached his destination. The plane vanished over the English channel. Miller's mysterious death helped make him something of a legendary figure, a genuine American hero.

After the war, tenor saxist/vocalist Tex Beneke fronted an official Glenn Miller Orchestra for several years. Purtill drummed briefly with that band. "I came out of the Navy and I opened with Tex and the Glenn Miller Orchestra in the Capitol Theater in New York. It was mostly the Air Force Band. I was one of a couple originals. Tex had the strings, too. I didn't stay long, though. They had nothing but road work lined up. I had just gotten out of the Navy, and I didn't want to take the bus. With Glenn, I had always been sure I'd spend my winter in New York. Not on buses doing one-nighters in a snowstorm someplace, not outside someplace where it's 28 degrees below in the winter."

Others led non-authorized bands that played in the Glenn Miller style, trying to cash in on the popularity of the Miller music. Purtill recalls: "For a while, it was like: 'Will the real Glenn Miller stand up?'

"I stayed in New York. I played with Richard Himber, Raymond Scott. I did everything from bar mitzvahs to wakes. I didn't want to leave New York; I loved New York. So I taught and I freelanced. I went out once with Tex for six weeks." The tour, Purtill says, proved to be "a real turkey." The big band era was fading into history.

There were disagreements between Beneke and the Miller estate over the direction the orchestra should take. Soon Beneke was fronting his own orchestra; though he was still playing the Miller tunes, there no longer was an official Glenn Miller Orchestra at all.

But interest in Miller's music revived after the release of *The Glenn Miller Story* in 1954. In 1956, an official Glenn Miller Orchestra was re-organized, this time led by Ray McKinley. The orchestra, with various leaders, has been an ongoing entity ever since.

In 1973, Purtill moved to Sarasota, Florida, which he made his home for five years before moving to New Jersey. "You know, I was never in Florida until '73," he comments. "Big bands never played Florida. They played in North Carolina, South Carolina, Georgia, in tobacco warehouses—but never seemed to play in Florida."

In Florida, Purtill played in a quartet with fellow Swing Era survivor Jerry Jerome, who in 1937 had played sax in Glenn Miller's Band. "It was a good quartet. We'd play 'In the Mood.' We'd just play the intro—and these people would be standing like they're at the Philharmonic. For a lousy tune like that! We'd play it two, three times a night. 'String of Pearls' and some of the others, too." Sometimes old friends would drop by. Lee Castle sat in one night, Purtill recalls, adding his warm, Armstrong-inspired horn to the quartet. "Lee's a good guy," Purtill says.

Purtill professes to hate nostalgia. But when he looks back, he can't help thinking the old days were better in a lot of ways.

"There's only one theater in New York [Radio City Music Hall] with an orchestra today. Back then, you'd see bands at the Paramount, the Roxy, the Capitol, the Strand, Loew's State, the Apollo, RKO Brooklyn, and so on. And hotels. Every hotel had a band—there'd be a 10-piece band even in a broken-down hotel.

"There are no shows in New York where musicians can work, except your Broadway musicals. There's no work in New York, no studio bands. The business in New York—it's a sad situation. It's all changed. There are no places to go. The bars, the restaurants where all the musicians went are gone," Purtill says.

A handful of his old buddies, such as Tex Beneke and Lee Castle, continue to make appearances fronting big bands. The bands satisfy most listeners as they go through the old hits. But Purtill says such ghost bands cannot be compared to the bands of the Swing Era. He wonders if there's even any point in trying to keep the old sounds alive, if the music can't be performed as well as it was back then.

"There's nothing like an organized band. It gets tight, so closely knitted from everybody playing together night after night. When we played with Glenn, we didn't even take music out of the bus with us; we didn't have to," Purtill says. "But it's almost impossible to have an organized band these days.

"Today, if Tex Beneke appears someplace with 'his' orchestra, they're getting him local guys. I'm firmly against that. They introduce it as his band. But it'll never sound like an organized band. Poor Tex. He's a nice man. But there just are not that many places to book anybody.

"In a way, I resent Lee Castle and Tex and these guys. They try to get guys that can cut the charts on the budget. And man, they crucify some of these charts! Sometimes people say, 'the big bands are coming back.' But it'll never come back the way it was. It really can't."

Purtill enjoyed all of the top bands in their day: "Benny, Tommy (he was an excellent player), Basie and Duke," he says.

Occasionally he sees old musician friends. "They drop by, guys playing in the area. Buddy Rich and I are very good friends. He's one of the most phenomenal drummers I've ever heard. Other drummers I like include Joe Morello, Sonny Payne, Max Roach. And Louis Bellson—there's a gentleman. I saw Red Norvo just recently over in Hackensack, and Tex last year." Purtill was invited onstage when Beneke's Band played in nearby Hackensack. Playing in the specially-assembled band that night were two former colleagues from the old Glenn Miller Band: trumpeter Johnny Best and clarinetist Wilber Schwartz.

Over the years, the Glenn Miller Orchestra has acquired an almost legendary status in the eyes of some fans. A mystique. The romantic, immediately recognizable sound of the Miller band evokes an era like the music of no other band.

Purtill notes: "I still get letters from musicians and fans. One fan, a head heart surgeon at Mt. Sinai says, 'in case anything's wrong with your heart, I'll come right over.' I'll get letters from people, talking about seeing me in South Dakota or someplace. It's like 'American Patrol' is D-Day for them. Their big thing.

"They have their clubs, questionnaires, they're nutty," he says lightly. Purtill adds he sometimes tunes in the "Make Believe Ballroom" on WNEW AM. "[Disc jockey] William B. Williams plays that stinking theme ['Make Believe Ballroom'] we made in 1891!

"My wife is from Czechoslovakia. They put a Glenn Miller album on sale at nine, and at noon the store is empty. In Europe and Japan now, they treat the Glenn Miller Orchestra like I treat Charlie Parker and Diz. Or Mulligan and Getz. The greats.

"Not a day goes by that I don't hear a Glenn Miller tune. How long can this go on, where they're still playing that music? It's amazing."

Purtill says he is thinking about playing again. "What I'd really like would be a small group: three rhythm, alto or tenor and trumpet. Play some swinging things softly." But he's not working at all, at present.

Purtill's youngest son, John, enters the room, intrigued by the fact that someone has come to interview his father. John says he's nine years old, attends the Forrest elementary school. "I can sing," he says.

"He's a good hoofer, too," adds the proud pop.

The boy says his father puts on the old Glenn Miller records sometimes. "He starts playing the drums along with them," the boy says, "and I start singing."

1982

LEE · CASTLE

(Part One) A Trumpeter for St. Anthony

Back in the Swing Era, Lee Castle's fine horn graced the big bands of the very best, including Tommy Dorsey, Artie Shaw, Benny Goodman, Red Norvo, Glenn Miller, Jack Teagarden, Will Bradley and Ray McKinley. At various times in the '40s and early '50s, Castle also led big bands of his own, although without much commercial success. When Tommy and Jimmy Dorsey reunited in 1953, Castle became a featured trumpeter in, and musical director of, their combined band. Following the deaths of Tommy in 1956 and Jimmy in 1957, Castle inherited the band. Since 1957, he's appeared all over the country as leader of the Jimmy Dorsey Orchestra.

Castle's musical favorites include Louis Armstrong (he's one of Armstrong's most ardent disciples), Frank Sinatra, Benny Goodman, Artie Shaw, and of course the Dorsey brothers. Although his band bears Jimmy Dorsey's name, he plays music associated with both Dorseys. He was personally much closer to Tommy. He can—and periodically does—walk from his Elmsford, New York, home to Tommy Dorsey's grave. He believes TD's spirit senses his presence there.

Castle was somewhat reluctant to go through the interview process, he told me. Some years earlier, he explained, he had managed to get 12 hours of his life story down on tape by himself, for a projected autobiography. He had found the process enormously difficult; it had taken him years to get those 12 hours on tape, in spare moments. But then one night, someone had burglarized the band's bus, and among the items stolen were the tapes Castle had made. All of that work for nothing! Afterwards, he could never find the energy to repeat taping his recollections. He bought another tape recorder, and attempted to

Lee Castle. (Courtesy Abby Hoffer)

talk into it. But he was unable to get past the first sentence, he told me.

But nevertheless, we started chatting, first on the dock of his private pond—taking time out occasionally to watch a muskrat chase the ducks on that warm summer afternoon—and then, later, inside his home. Castle has a strong streak of the sentimental in him. As he began to reminisce, one story led to another. I asked him how he got started as a trumpet player. "Well, I'll take you further back," he offered. And he did just that.

* * *

Born February 28, 1915, Castle's real name is Aniello Castaldo. By the time he began working in name bands in the late '30s, he was known as Lee Castaldo. A band booker changed his last name to Castle in the early '40s.

"I was born and raised in Little Italy, in the Bronx. And I was a sickly baby," he tells me, beginning a story that he was told many times by his mother. "I was sick and at that time, they didn't know what the hell to do with a baby. And it seemed like I wasn't going to make it. So, my mother made a novena to St. Anthony, who was the Italian patron saint. And that night, they had a specialist come in—a black man, a black doctor. And he said, 'At 12:00 midnight, give him a drop of this medicine. And if he doesn't come out of it'—like I was in a coma or something—'then I'm sorry, nothing to do.'

"Finally, my mother and my aunt and my grandmother, they said, 'We've tried everything, and nothing seemed to work. Let's try giving him a hot olive oil enema. And if that doesn't work, let's forget it.'

"So they give me a hot olive oil enema and that enema really, boy, let everything out. And my mother said from that second on, I started crying and reached my hands out and she breast-fed me. And when the doctor came over—figuring it was too late—he was shocked. So it shows you; that was St. Anthony, I imagine, who made them think of that.

"So when I got well, there was an Italian priest who says: 'You know, St. Anthony helped you. Now you have to help St. Anthony.'

"So when I was a kid, they used to dress me up every St. Anthony's Day with a little white handkerchief in my hand. And I'd go around collecting pennies from different houses, and bring it to the church. And I always had the little St. Anthony's habit, or whatever you call it. . . . Then, I thought I was getting a little too old to do this. But the priest said, 'You're not through working for St. Anthony. Now you've got to get in the Sons of Italy Band.' So I got in the Sons of Italy Band—a brass band, a feast band. I played drums in the band, played for the funerals and the festivals.

"And my older brother Charlie—who probably taught me more

than anybody—was already working in the Sons of Italy Band. At that time he played baritone. Later he became the trombone player with Benny Goodman, and other bands, plus Toscanini and those guys. And one day my brother brought a record home of Louis Armstrong. And that changed my whole life around. And I said: 'That's it! I got to play trumpet.' And Louis Armstrong and Bix and those guys just knocked me on my behind. And that's when I started to play trumpet; my brother got me a trumpet." He was happy to serve St. Anthony, he recalls, by blowing his horn in street parades and festivals.

Castle appreciates Bix Beiderbecke and other important stylists. But no musician had the towering impact upon him that Louis Armstrong had. As a teenager, he listened to Armstrong's latest recordings so many times that he still feels that, in a sense, Armstrong taught him how to play. He remembers practicing over and over until he could

Louis Armstrong: a major influence on Lee Castle (as on so many other Swing Era musicians). (Courtesy RCA Records)

copy Armstrong's version of "Blue Turning Grey Over You," which is the earliest Armstrong record he remembers hearing. (Armstrong recorded "Blue Turning Grey Over You" on February 1, 1930. Castle was probably 15 years old when he heard it.) Only a few years earlier, Armstrong had been known primarily to jazz musicians and to urban blacks. But by 1930, his fame was reaching general audiences, and he was being billed as "the world's greatest trumpeter."

A bit later on, Castle recalls, "I went to see a Louis Armstrong movie short. Oh, for a whole week. Man, I tell you—I thought I'd go blind. 'Shine' was the thing he was playing up there." Castle watched four shows daily, until he had learned every note in Armstrong's sensational, breakneck performance of "Shine." (Armstrong's short, *Rhapsody in Black and Blue*, including "Shine" and "You Rascal, You," was made in September of 1932.)

In the early 1930s, Castle was listening to Armstrong's current records. These were typically bravura performances—often of pop tunes—in front of a big band. Armstrong's superb "Hot Five" and "Hot Seven" small-group jazz recordings of 1925-28 (which Castle would eventually come to love) had been released a bit prior to Castle's discovery of Armstrong, he notes. And thus he was initially unaware of their existence. Those sides are today considered classics and are well-known to all serious jazz listeners, but they were originally released as "race records," marketed to black buyers. It is not surprising that as a boy, Castle was unaware of them.

Castle explains how he came to discover those earlier, hotter Armstrong performances: "Artie Shaw and Tony Pastor—they turned me on to the real Armstrong records to listen to. I came in on 'Blue Turning Grey Over You,' 'Shine' [recorded by Armstrong March 9, 1931], 'Chinatown' [November 3, 1931]—all of those things that Louis made, you know. And when I joined Artie Shaw's Band [in 1936], Tony Pastor, who was the saxophone player, took me under his wing (his real name was Tony Pestritto); they loved when I played like, tried to play like Louis. And Artie Shaw said, 'Wait a minute, now, you're—listen to the *real, authentic* records.' He turned me on to the 'Hot Fives,' like 'Cornet Chop Suey,' 'Gully Low Blues,' 'Potato Head Blues.' All of those things. And that's how I got listening to that stuff. That was my bag."

* * *

Castle got his first professional job as a trumpeter in the early '30s when a group of Jewish youths, who had formed a band and were looking for work, approached the Sons of Italy Club.

"We had the Sons of Italy Club up here in my neighborhood, big guys were running it—*the boys*, you know, probably top mafia guys today," Castle says. "And they hired this little group, which consisted of four or five Jewish kids. And then they called me up: 'Hey Lee, come over the club tonight at eight o'clock, and bring your cornet.' I went over, and they told me, 'We have a little group going to play here, and we want you to play with them.' I said, 'Gee I can't read music.' They said, 'It doesn't matter.' And when the group came up, he told them, 'Either this kid plays with you, or you don't play.' So the kids said to me, 'Well can you read?' I said, 'No. Not yet. A little bit, maybe.'

"And they wanted the job, naturally. So they sat down and the first thing they called up was 'Keeping Out of Mischief Now.' And Louis made that famous [Armstrong recorded it March 11, 1932]. And I played a chorus—half of Louis Armstrong's chorus, you know, note for note. But these kids flipped out. 'Oh man,' they said, 'this is it; you got to be with us.' So I stayed with them and we'd get a half a dollar, a dollar, two dollars a job."

Castle gigged with them, not just in the Bronx, but in the Catskills as well. (He learned to play Jewish numbers for Jewish audiences there, he notes.) "And they were hep kids. They were all Louis Armstrong fans, and so I became pretty important to them. And the next thing you know, I'm eating matzoh balls and all this other stuff. And these fellows, incidentally, are still my dearest friends—oh, I keep in touch with them."

Castle soon moved on to bigger jobs. Paul Tremaine—who in the early '30s was a well-known leader—listened to Castle play, and offered him a job. Castle is a little vague as to when this occurred, but it was apparently around 1933.

"Now there's a guy who's on the air with a great band. Twelve o'clock: 'Lonely Acres.' He had Sunny Dunham, a lot of those guys in that band. And they were leaving, I guess," Castle says. "I told him I couldn't read music too well. He said, 'I don't care, you come on in.' So I went down to where he was working. And I would sit there, and every time there was a jazz trumpet solo, he'd say, 'Go.' And I'd get up, and play, and then he'd stop me. Today you can't do that; today you ask questions, like 'Hey, what key am I in? What are the chords?' But then, you're a kid, you had to *feel* it.

"So, I stayed with Paul Tremaine. Then a guy named Buddy Herrod took over," Castle recalls. The band played in a Chinese restaurant on Fordham Road in the Bronx. "Back then, Chinese restaurants were the place for big bands. Nowhere else. How they could afford them, I don't know." The late jazz pianist Teddy Napoleon, best known for his long association with Gene Krupa, recalled for interviewers that he got his start playing in a band with Lee Castle at a Chinese restaurant in 1933. And pianist Marty Napoleon, Teddy's younger brother, who is perhaps best known for his work with Louis Armstrong, recalls that when *he* was 12—which would have been 1933—he was an aspiring trumpeter, memorizing the solos of Lee Castle. He later switched to piano.

By 1936, Castle was reading music pretty well and playing in Paul Martell's house band at the Arcadia Ballroom (53rd Street and Broadway). One night bandleader Joe Haymes, his manager, and tenor sax player Bud Freeman dropped in. "Joe Haymes! I'd already been listening to him from the Village Grove," Castle recalls.

Haymes offered Castle a job. "And once I got in Joe Haymes' band, the rest is history. Haymes was the main guy; this guy was a stepping stone for all musicians. He'd had Gene Krupa, Pee Wee Erwin, Johnny Mince, all big guys in his band."

Haymes might be better remembered as a bandleader today, except for the fact that other leaders kept hiring away his best players. For example, Tommy and Jimmy Dorsey had jointly led a big band in 1934-35. Then when Tommy walked out in mid-'35, Jimmy took over their band. And Tommy hired virtually the entire Joe Haymes Band, to start his band in September of '35. Haymes then had to build up a whole new band from scratch.

The Brian Rust discography suggests that Castle replaced Chris Griffin in Haymes' band in mid-'36. The other trumpeter in the band at the time, it is interesting to note, was Zeke Zarchy, who would later work with Castle in Artie Shaw's Band and Tommy Dorsey's Band, and who still periodically works with Castle today, a half-century later. Recordings Castle made with the Haymes Band leave little doubt that he was an ardent admirer of Louis Armstrong. Castle's solo in the band's spirited recording of "St. Louis Blues" (July 27, '36) borrows from Armstrong's "Savoy Blues."

It was during Castle's tenure with Haymes that Castle happened to meet Jimmy Dorsey for the first time. The recollection makes him smile.

"You know, I'll tell you a funny thing—when you first meet these guys, it's something. I admired Jimmy—*Jesus*. And the first time I met Jimmy, he wanted to beat me up!" Castle laughs. "I had taken the girl I was going with to a club Adrian Rollini had. Joe Marsala had a little group down there. We're sitting at the first table. And Jimmy walked in and he was drunk—and I said, 'Jesus, Dorothy, look at this—Jimmy Dorsey!' And finally he tried to play trumpet, which he was a good trumpet player, but he was drunk. And I'm smiling at him, you know, and I guess he mistook that for laughing. So he come up and he shoved the trumpet right up on my chest. Said, 'Here, you son of a bitch. You think you can do any better?'

"So I got up and said, 'Hey, I'll wrap it around your—'

"Just then Adrian Rollini got him, sat him down and said, 'You're out of line, Jimmy.' And Adrian said, 'Sit down here and it's on the house.' I was so disappointed, I said no, we got up and left.

"That was even before I got to know Tommy. When I was with Joe Haymes' Band, that's when that happened." In later years, of course, Castle became good friends with Jimmy, although he always was closer to Tommy.

* * *

"I left Joe Haymes and went with Artie Shaw. Artie had a string quartet band and we worked with that. He's a dear friend, a lovely guy. I talk to him often," Castle says.

Shaw—then being billed as "Art," rather than "Artie" Shaw—was at the very beginning of his career as a bandleader. And he was using a most unorthodox instrumentation. His 13-piece band included a standard four-man rhythm section, a trombone, two trumpets, a tenor sax (Tony Pastor), a clarinet (Shaw), a cello, a viola, and two violins. This

Jimmy Dorsey. (Chip Deffaa collection)

was the instrumentation Shaw used, for example, when he recorded "Sugar Foot Stomp," with Castle on trumpet (August 6, 1936). Castle was the band's featured trumpeter.

A review of the Shaw Band by George Simon in the October, 1936, *Metronome* noted that "hot brass man Lee Castaldo delivers via a clear crisp horn; he certainly is one of the city's most improved musicians." Simon gave the band a strong "A minus" rating and predicted that it would only continue to improve as time went on. But this first band of Shaw's was not a commercial success.

Castle was in the Shaw Band, according to the Shaw discography by Bill Korst and Charles Garrod published by Joyce Music Corporation, for its recording sessions on August 6, 1936; September 17, 1936; October 30, 1936; November 30, 1936; December 23, 1936; and February 19, 1937.

Castle worked briefly with Red Norvo in the summer of '37. Then when an opening developed in Tommy Dorsey's Band, he joined that band. He says that actually, Dorsey had offered him a job while he was still playing with Shaw.

One night, Castle recalls, Shaw's band had been working at Frank Dailey's Meadowbrook in Cedar Grove, New Jersey. "And it was customary when a bandleader came in, you'd acknowledge him, and sometimes he'd come up and sit in. Well, that night Tommy Dorsey was there. So they got him up to sit in and he's sitting right there right beside me. And I'm playing, and I was frightened, you know—TD, the greatest trombone player in the world. And much to my surprise, he—and he always talked from the corner of his mouth, he said—[and now Lee Castle mutters out of the corner of his mouth, imitating Dorsey's voice]—'Listen kid, if ever you're looking for a job, look me up, will you?' Just like that. Man, my heart was beating! I never said a word to Artie or anybody. Then Artie broke up that little band, and he didn't know what he was going to do. So, I called Tommy Dorsey and—boom, in no time, I had a job."

* * *

When Castle joined Tommy Dorsey's band late in the summer of 1937, he was beginning an association that would have an impact upon the rest of his life.

The Tommy Dorsey Band was riding high in '37. On January 31st of that year, they had recorded "Song of India" and "Marie," which were released back-to-back on Victor #25523. That hit record had catapulted the band into the bigtime. A 1937 *Down Beat* readers' poll—the first contemporary music readers' poll by a national publication—named Benny Goodman's band the overwhelming favorite, followed by Bob Crosby's Band, and then—only three votes behind—Tommy

Dorsey's.

It was a real step up for Castle to go with Dorsey. As far as the general public was concerned, Artie Shaw was an "unknown" in 1937. (He broke through big, with a reorganized band, in 1938.) Castle had been a featured soloist in Shaw's band. He was glad to be joining Dorsey's band now, even though he understood he would rarely be getting opportunities to solo there.

Pee Wee Erwin was Tommy Dorsey's star trumpeter in the summer of '37. Andy Ferretti was the superb leader of the three-man trumpet section.

Castle recalls: "Tommy was the toughest man; he would frighten anybody. His opening words to me were, 'Listen kid, I'm going to tell you something. You're not going to get anything to play in this band, I'll tell you now. You're going to be a third trumpet player. . . . I want those two guys to know that if they don't stop drinking, that I got a kid here that'll play. . . . You keep your nose clean, and you'll be in this band as long as I got an asshole.' Man, but the way he said it scared the hell out of you.

"He was rough; he frightened me. I blamed whatever hair loss I had on him; I blamed my nerves on him, and everything. But he made a better musician out of me, and a better player."

Castle's first recording session with Dorsey was on September 8, 1937. He was in and out of the band into early 1941. His initial, and longest, stint lasted nearly a year and a half. He played on almost all of the records Dorsey made between September 8, 1937 and February 16, 1939. Castle was in the band when it cut such popular sides as "Josephine" (September 11, 1937), "Who" (October 14, 1937), "Little White Lies" (December 6, 1937), "Yearning" (March 10, 1938), "Music, Maestro, Please" (May 12, 1938), and "Milenberg Joys" (January 19, 1939). He was not soloing; he was simply contributing to the excellent overall sound of the trumpet section. Castle's first—and somewhat tentative-sounding—recorded solo with Dorsey was on "I Never Knew," recorded March 10, 1938. The late Pee Wee Erwin told jazz writer Mort Goode: "Lee Castle, when he first joined the band, was kinda bashful about being featured on almost anything. Andy Ferretti and I used to fight with Lee to get him to play more. I had a lot of things in the book, and Lee is a marvelous trumpet player, but he was always trying to beg off a solo. But Andy and I kept after his tail to get him to play. . . . I actually tricked him one day—hooked him into one of the Clambake [Seven] things. I acted like I had a bellyache, and Andy told Lee to take over because I couldn't make it."

Castle recalls: "Sometimes we'd be playing in a big blues thing, and Pee Wee Erwin would throw me the part. He'd say, 'This is more

Lee Castle on trumpet, alongside of Tommy Dorsey on trombone, in Dorsey's Band, 1938. Trumpeter Pee Wee Erwin recalled that Castle's good looks drew him more female admirers—including some movie stars—than any other member of the band. (Frank Driggs collection)

up your alley, Lee, than mine.' You know, a real Louis Armstrong sort of thing. They knew what belonged to whom."

Erwin has recalled how, when they were in the Dorsey Band together, Castle "would always get Louis' [Armstrong] lip salve. As long as he'd get that from Louis he'd be all right."

By this time, Castle had become friends with Armstrong. "I became sort of like a protegé of Louis's, you know. Like an understudy. I used to go around with him sometimes. From the time I met him, he and I were the closest of friends," Castle says. "He was the most humble man I think I've ever met in my life. He was like an Albert Schweitzer. He was close to the Guy Upstairs. . . . But I wonder if Louis ever knew how great he was. I just don't know. But he was humble. He was just beautiful."

* * *

At some point (Castle's memory is a bit hazy as to specific dates), Tommy Dorsey sent Castle to study trumpet under his father, Thomas F. Dorsey Sr., who had taught both Tommy and Jimmy when they were young. Both had initially played trumpet, as well as the instruments for which they later became famous. "Tommy saw a lot of potential in me. He said, 'I'm going to send you to my father [in Lansford, Pennsylvania] and I'm going to send you $50 a week. I want you to stay on that farm and study.' I said, 'All right,' and I did. I went out there and lived with Mom and Pop Dorsey; I became like a third son. As a matter of fact, they had as much interest in me as they had in them. Wherever I was, it was: 'Where's Lee? We haven't heard from Lee. What's he doing?' You know. And Tommy would call me up—later, when I wasn't in the band—and say: 'Listen, for Chrissakes, will you call the folks? What are you doing? Call them on the phone, Goddammit, what are you doing?' Stuff like that. And Pop Dorsey taught me a lot. He changed my embouchure. He did everything. And of course I came back with Tommy. I was obligated."

It is uncertain now exactly when Castle went to the Dorsey farm, and exactly how much time he spent there. The discographies indicate that Castle was absent from Dorsey recording sessions for the last three and a half months of 1938, and he may well have been on the farm in that period. Castle's recollection is that he spent perhaps a year and a half on the farm, but it may be that he thought he spent more time there than he actually did. The discographies show no gap in his recording career during the late '30s longer than that three and a half month stretch in late '38. He recorded again with Dorsey in January and February of '39.

On February 24, 1939, Castle joined the band of Glenn Miller, who had not yet had much success. Castle stayed only until March fourth.

"I guess I didn't like Glenn too much . . . or I didn't like his ways, or whatever," he comments. "And besides, Glenn didn't pay me, Tommy Dorsey paid me. Tommy said, 'Go to work with Glenn and I'll pay you your salary.' Tommy financed Glenn, you see.

"And then Glenn sensed that I was going to leave the band. So he says, 'Look, I got a chance to get a guy named [Mickey] McMickle. I got a funny feeling you're going to leave this band.' 'Yeah,' I told him, 'I got to have teeth work.' I had to say something. He said, 'Well, I'll get McMickle and the minute your teeth work is over, you come back.' I said, 'OK.'

"So, one day I was up at Nola Studios in a [Jack] Teagarden rehearsal and he had Charlie Spivak in the band. And I sat there, and that Teagarden just threw me for a loop! The only time I had that feeling was with Louis Armstrong, you know. And oh, Benny Goodman, too, gave me that feeling, when he'd play some jazz. Yeah, Teagarden. He sounded so good. So finally, he came up. I said, 'Jack, you never sounded better . . .' He said: 'No kidding? Well, would you like to hear more of it?'

"And I said, 'Yeah, go ahead.' He said, 'No, we need you to join the band, we need a trumpet player.'

"So I never went back with Glenn. I went with Jack Teagarden, and I did all the jazz trumpeting in his band. Glenn wouldn't talk to me for three years after that. Because he became very famous afterwards."

A June, 1939 *Metronome* review of the Teagarden band by George T. Simon noted that one Karl Garvin got occasional opportunities to solo on trumpet, but that "hot trumpet emphasis is placed upon the lips of the more driving and experienced Castaldo [Castle]." "Beale Street Blues" and "Muddy River Blues" give excellent samplings of Castle's playing at the time. He'd grown in strength and confidence since his solos with Haymes three years before.

The Brian Rust discography places Castle in Teagarden's band during recording sessions from April 28, 1939 through November 1, 1939. John Chilton's *Who's Who of Jazz* says that Castle stayed with Teagarden until December of 1939.

Teagarden's band, although praised by critics, never became a big commercial success. By the summer of '39, Glenn Miller had burst through to great commercial success. But Castle was far happier with Teagarden, who was a pure jazzman, rather than a commercially-oriented taskmaster like Miller. With Teagarden, Castle got to solo, and he got to play just the sort of jazz he liked. And hearing Teagarden's playing, night after night, was a personal thrill for Castle. (Teagarden was one of the all-time greats, in many musicians' eyes. When Tommy Dorsey and Teagarden were brought together for a 1939 all-star recording session, TD refused to play any jazz with Teagarden on hand.)

On June 26, 1939, Castle made some sides which have become jazz collectors' items. Released under the billing of Glenn Hardman and his Hammond Five, the personnel consisted of Glenn Hardman, organ; Castle, trumpet; Lester Young, tenor sax and clarinet; Freddie Green, guitar, and Jo Jones, drums. The personnel was assembled by John Hammond.

"That was an all-star thing," Castle recalls. "I was with Teagarden at the time, at the Blackhawk Restaurant, I think. And John Hammond called me and I asked if I could get off for four days. And that was a good break. Lester Young and I got along beautifully on that session." Castle calls Young the greatest tenor player who ever lived.

They recorded "Upright Organ Blues," "Jazz Me Blues," "China Boy," "On the Sunny Side of the Street," "Who," and "Exactly Like You." "Upright Organ Blues" gave Castle a chance to lay down one of his best solos to date, a wonderful thing, somewhat reminiscent in feeling of Armstrong's work on "West End Blues" or "Savoy Blues." "Upright Organ Blues" has been reissued on the widely-available Columbia Records double-LP set, "Count Basie, Super Chief." The liner notes quote Jo Jones as saying that when the recording date arrived, Castle "had been out all night and turned up drunk and with a split lip. Some chick's husband had come in, hit him across the hand with a .45 and he jumped from a second floor window. So he was pretty mussed up. Played OK, though."

Castle comments that he was aghast when he read the story on the record album; it was totally untrue, he says, and he mulled suing for libel. "I showed that to Basie. He said, 'Ah, that's terrible.' I've never been caught in bed with a gal and I don't drink, you know. And I was afraid my wife would read about it. Terrible thing. So my lawyer asked the man who wrote the notes where he got the story from. He said, Jo Jones. Well, Jo Jones is a drunk; he's incoherent, and nobody in his right mind would take any notes from Jo Jones. I figured let it go."

* * *

By late December of 1939, Castle was back with Tommy Dorsey for a spell—now as a featured trumpeter, replacing Yank Lawson. On broadcasts, Dorsey occasionally advised listeners to note a trumpet solo by Lee Castaldo (as Castle was then still called).

Early in 1940, Dorsey told Castle that another Italian fellow was about to join the band, and asked him to help make the newcomer feel at home. That other Italian fellow was a skinny, not-yet-famous vocalist from Harry James' Band: Frank Sinatra. Castle and Sinatra were roommates initially, he recalls. "Yeah, once—when he first joined the band. It was like two rooms with a connecting bath and you had to keep the doors open. But we were always together. The man's a beautiful guy. Frank hasn't changed. And Frank and I are still very good friends.

"He's great, the greatest thing we've had, believe me. And he sings better than ever, as far as I'm concerned. To me, he's like Louis Armstrong; his presence is enough. Not like these guys who shout. . . . Frank has got it. Yeah. He said, 'This is the reeds' [Castle points to throat] and he's right. Called it the reeds. Nobody ever said it that way. No, Frank is—even Pavarotti would sit back and listen to him.

"I was impressed with Frank right from the beginning. Listen, let me tell you, I don't have to say a word about Frank Sinatra. Just listen to any one of his records."

One story Castle loves to tell concerns "This Love of Mine," which became a big hit for Tommy Dorsey, with Frank Sinatra on vocal, in mid 1941. Sinatra co-authored the song, but he initially was unable to get TD interested in it. He then took the song to Jimmy Dorsey (whose band had forged ahead of Tommy's in terms of popularity, in 1941). Jimmy declined to record it but instructed Sinatra to tell Tommy that he *was* going to record it; that was one sure way of getting Tommy to record it. "And the minute Tommy knew that Jimmy wanted it, he jumped on it," Castle recalls with a laugh. He adds: "Of course, I wonder if it would have become a hit without Frank singing it, though."

There were a couple of new numbers in the Dorsey book, in early 1940, which provided solo opportunities for Castle. Unfortunately for Castle, however, Dorsey did not get around to recording them—and they both proved to be popular—until after Castle had left the band again.

"Sy Oliver made an arrangement called 'Quiet Please.' He put down: 'Lee, give me a big Louis job here,'" Castle recalls of one uptempo number, which ended with a great Buddy Rich drum solo. Oliver's lightly swinging arrangement of the ballad, "East of Sun," provided a beautiful showcase for the talents of both Sinatra and Castle. An air-check from February 24, 1940 shows Castle sounding romantic and lyrical, stretching out for a longer solo than was heard on the hit record made two months later.

But by then, Bunny Berigan—one of the greatest trumpeters of all time—had returned to the band, and Castle was out. (Berigan was drinking so heavily, Castle notes, that Dorsey considered hiring Castle back just for the record date, to play "East of the Sun." But Berigan came through, recording a memorable solo.)

Castle now made his first attempt at leading his own big band, a perhaps logical "next step" for a trumpeter who'd been featured with Shaw, Teagarden, and Dorsey. However, Castle's 1940 band proved to be short-lived.

The discographies show Castle was present in Dorsey's band again (apparently subbing for Ziggy Elman) on a January 6, 1941 recording session, at which Sinatra, Connie Haines and the Pied Pipers vocalized on "Oh, Look at Me Now."

* * *

The spring of '41 found Castle as featured trumpeter in the Will Bradley/Ray McKinley Band. He was in the band when it made such sides as "In the Hall of the Mountain King" (April 13, 1941), "From the Land of the Sky-Blue Water" (June 23, 1941), and "Basin Street Boogie" (July 23, 1941). He got plenty of solo opportunities in this band. His trumpeting fit in well with Bradley and McKinley's music. (McKinley didn't forget Castle; when McKinley recorded a sextet album for Grand Award in 1955, Castle—then featured in the Dorsey Brothers' Orchestra—was the trumpeter he used.)

Then Castle went back to work for Artie Shaw. Castle was in the Shaw band when it recorded such famous sides as "Blues in the Night" (September 2, 1941) and "St. James Infirmary" (November 12, 1941), both of which were star turns for trumpeter/singer Oran "Hot Lips" Page. Castle recalls being featured in the band on trumpet, although he was not featured as prominently as Page was. "I was a featured trumpeter and musical director there. I led the band for him and did shows and everything. And when he went into the Navy, he handed me the baton. I took over the band, but we couldn't get to first base."

The Shaw discography by Bill Korst and Charles Garrod has this notation following Shaw's recording session of December 23, 1941: "Shaw disbands again. Makes some jobs with Lee Castle's band." The discography indicates that Shaw recorded again in January of 1942 (with Castle in his trumpet section), and then enlisted in the Navy in April of that year.

Chilton's *Who's Who of Jazz* states that Castle organized a big band in March, 1942. An item about "Lee Castle's band" playing at Roseland in the June, 1942 issue of *Metronome* is the earliest reference in print I've seen to "Castle," rather than Castaldo. Castle comments: "Billy Shaw, a band booker, decided it should be Lee 'Castle' and not Castaldo. He said, 'You can't get the big name on a marquee.' And maybe the war had something to do with it."

A review of the Lee Castle Orchestra by George T. Simon appeared in the October 1942 issue of *Metronome*. Simon noted:

> Lee plays good jazz and good sweet. His greatest attribute is his tone. It's sharp, brilliant, and yet fat. As a result, he's able to impress both on jazz and on ballads. His hot style is primarily Armstrong, though he tosses in a few James licks here and there. His sweet style is much more like Harry's, though the Spivak influence is obvious. Both his styles are mighty impressive, especially when he doesn't try too much. Like Bobby Byrne on trombone, and like the late Bunny Berigan on trumpet, Lee tries to do a lot, much more than most of his compatriots do. To the average jazz follower, the consequent fluffs are excusable. . . .

Simon noted the band as a whole seemed rather green, and not particularly impressive at this stage. But he closed by saying Castle "has lots of stuff to work with there (including his own, very impressive horn), so there's no obvious reason why he shouldn't be hitting the jackpot one of these days."

However, such was not to be the case. For one thing, the American Federation of Musicians, unable to get an acceptable contract with the recording industry, banned all recording by AFM members, effective August 1, 1942. The recording ban, which dragged on through 1943 (and then into late 1944, for most companies) meant Castle was unable to record his new band. And without records, there wasn't much chance of establishing a new band's reputation.

Castle gave up trying to make it as a bandleader for now. According to Chilton, he signed his band over to Richard Himber late in 1942. He joined Benny Goodman's band as the featured trumpeter, a spot he

Benny Goodman, clarinet; Charlie Castaldo, trombone; Hal Peppie, trumpet; Miff Mole, trombone; Irving Goodman, trumpet; and Lee Castle, trumpet, in a publicity shot for the 1943 film The Gang's All Here *with Carmen Miranda, Phil Baker, and the Goodman Band*. (Frank Driggs collection)

held down throughout 1943. He was now being prominently showcased in one of the nation's foremost bands, but the record strike prevented him from getting the kind of exposure that Goodman's previous featured trumpeters, such as Bunny Berigan, Harry James, and Ziggy Elman, had received.

"I went with Benny. We made a couple of movies. Did you ever see *Stage Door Canteen*—the movie? See Benny Goodman's Band? See the trumpet player who plays 'Bugle Call Rag'? Thin guy, a lot of hair—that was me. I played all the jazz trumpet in the band. I played almost all the first trumpet, too. Benny made you work. But we had a long recording strike. That hurt me. That's why you never see me on any of the [Benny Goodman Band] records," Castle comments.

Castle's driving horn may be heard on V-discs and airchecks of "live" radio broadcasts by the 1943 Goodman Band (some of which have been released on LPs), playing such numbers as "Sugarfoot Stomp," "Henderson Stomp," "Seven Come Eleven," and "King Porter Stomp." Had it not been for the strike, Castle notes, he probably would have been heard as featured trumpeter on a lot of Goodman records. And he no doubt would made more of a name for himself.

Still, Castle was voted the sixth best trumpeter in the nation, in the annual *Down Beat* poll (reported in the issue of January 1, 1944).

Castle left Goodman to try again to make it as a bandleader. "But the record strike was on when I had my own band, too. The only good things I did were popular V-Discs," Castle recalls.

In addition to the V-discs Castle made for members of the armed forces, Castle did make some records with his band after the strike was over, cutting such sides in 1945 (for the Musicraft label) as "Jump it, Mr. Trumpet" and "La Rosita." Castle notes with pride that his record of "La Rosita"—a moderate success—outsold Jimmy Dorsey's.

Castle's recollection is that when Artie Shaw came out of the Navy in 1944, Shaw "took over my band at the Roseland and we went on the road together." Shaw soon put together his own star-studded band, and by late 1945, he too was recording for Musicraft.

Castle's band never became a hit. Perhaps he was not a big enough "name" trumpeter to the general public. Perhaps managerial difficulties hurt his chances. In any case, big bands were already fading in popularity. Castle was one of a number of fine Swing Era musicians (including Buddy Rich, who first tried forming a band in 1946) who found it hard to make the jump from featured sideman to commercially-successful bandleader.

Castle did some studio work. He turned up at various jazz jam sessions-type gigs where he could blow freely in the Armstrong-inspired vein he favored. (One photo, taken at New York's Stuyvesant Casino, shows him playing in the company of Pee Wee Russell, clarinet; Ray McKinley, drums; and Lou McGarity, trombone.) He also wrote two books (published in 1947 by Leeds Music Corporation) of Louis Armstrong trumpet solos for aspiring trumpeters.

In the late '40s and early '50s, he continued to try to make it as a bandleader. He recalls Mom Dorsey showing up for many of his opening nights, proud of the fellow she called her Italian son. Pop Dorsey had died in 1942. Castle was nothing if not persistent. He got Deane Kincaide, who had been a key arranger for Tommy Dorsey, when Castle had first joined TD's band, to write charts for him.

I wondered if Dorsey had ever tried to help Castle get established as a band leader?

"Tommy Dorsey was the only man in this world that wouldn't help me, or who would put obstacles in my way," Castle answers, as if still smarting a bit over the way TD—who he had thought the world of—sometimes treated him.

"And when I rejoined the band in 1953, when he and Jimmy merged, I reminded him of that. He says, 'I was a pretty smart guy.' I says, 'What do you mean?' He says, 'You're here, aren't you?' He always wanted me to be with him. But Tommy didn't want to see me succeed in any way. He did a lot of things, but I guess he was determined to have me in his band. In a way I'm flattered. . . . Maybe I wasn't ready for it [leading my own band]. I don't know. I believe in the Guy Upstairs, because I know what to do with it, now that I've inherited this. Before, maybe I wouldn't have known how to handle it that way; I don't know."

The spring of 1950 found Castle working once again with Artie Shaw. He was with Shaw for such big band recordings as "The Continental" and "Foggy Foggy Dew" (both April 4, 1950) and "Just Say I Love Her" (May 31, 1950). He is heard soloing on Shaw's Gramercy Five recordings of "Crumbum" (April 7, 1950) and "The Shekomeko Shuffle" (April 8, 1950). Castle comments: "I love Artie Shaw, he's a great guy. He's been up—not here, at the other house. And Artie's been up to my sister's wedding in Little Italy when we were young men. Brilliant musician. Beautiful guy."

Castle recorded an album, "Dixieland Heaven," for a small label, Davis Records, in the early '50s, playing numbers such as "When the Saints Go Marching In," "On the Banks of the Wabash," and "My Wild Irish Rose." He led a sextet consisting of such top traditional jazz players as George Wettling, drums; Bob Haggart, bass; Dick Cary, piano; Lou McGarity, trombone; Peanuts Hucko, clarinet. (On four numbers, Bob Wilber replaced Hucko on clarinet.)

Castle tried still again to make it with his own big band. He played a long stretch at Roseland in 1952. In April of 1953, Castle (then working at the Meadowbrook), got a call from Tommy Dorsey to join his band.

The jazz musician as pop star: Jimmy and Tommy Dorsey signing autographs for the fans. (Institute of Jazz Studies)

LEE • CASTLE

(Part Two) "The Third Dorsey"

Tommy and Jimmy Dorsey were reuniting. Ever since Tommy had walked out of the Dorsey Brothers' Orchestra in 1935—18 years before—there had been two Dorsey orchestras. Both had been enormously popular. Generally, over the years, Tommy had had the stronger outfit, but there had been a period in the early '40s in which Jimmy had overtaken him in terms of popularity and record sales. The reunited Dorseys would prove a potent box-office draw.

They would be co-leaders. Their band would play material from Jimmy's book when Jimmy conducted, and from Tommy's when Tommy conducted. New material would be commissioned, and old charts would be revised, to feature both of them together. Often Tommy would solo on trombone, with Jimmy providing lacy obligatos on alto saxophone. For big band fans, hearing them together was a dream come true.

Tommy had always been the more aggressive brother, and he had the upper hand now. Basically, Jimmy was giving up his band. He and two members of his band (trombonist Jimmy Henderson and featured tenor saxist, Buzzy Brauner) were coming into Tommy's band. Although radio and TV announcers would introduce them simply as "the fabulous Dorseys" (borrowing the title from their 1947 film biography), their band was officially billed at first as "Tommy Dorsey and His Orchestra, Featuring Jimmy Dorsey." By 1955, trade publications noted they were using an alternate official billing, "The Dorsey Brothers' Orchestra." To the public, it was both brothers' band, but to the musicians in it, Tommy—who conducted most of the time—was the ultimate boss.

Tommy hired Lee Castle to be more than just a member of the trumpet section. Castle would get a good deal of solo opportunities, particularly in a Dixieland small-group within the band. Castle would also rehearse the band, serve as an alternate conductor, and be a general go-between for the brothers, who still had one of nation's best-known cases of sibling rivalry. In hiring Castle, Tommy had hired not just an extremely qualified musician, but also someone who Tommy felt was securely in his camp. After all, Castle had spent more time working for Tommy Dorsey than for any other bandleader, and Castle had never worked for Jimmy.

Castle was in Tommy's band for Tommy's final recording sessions without Jimmy under his Decca contract. He was in TD's band when it recorded such sides as "The Touch of Your Hand" (which features a fine muted solo by Castle) and "Wunderbar" in May, 1953, and "Blue Room," "Juba Dance," and "Cheek to Cheek" in August. The Dorsey brothers began recording together, on the Bell label, in January of 1954.

"I became featured trumpeter and musical director of that band," Castle recalls. "When they weren't on the bandstand, I would conduct. At the Statler [Hotel in New York, where the band was based much of the year], I conducted like from seven to eight, Jimmy conducted from eight to nine, and then Tommy conducted the night on. Then when they were off the bandstand, I would conduct the band until one of them came back on. I conducted the shows, I conducted [Elvis] Presley and all those people for them. Because they had enough to do."

Were the Dorseys fighting much in this period?

"Sure. Damn right. That was no joke," Castle recalls.

And was he ever in the middle of it?

"Yeah, a couple of times I was, sure."

Castle's wife, Jean, interjects: "But they really loved each other."

"Sure they did. They fought over music, that was all. Nothing else, over music. But there was always that little tension," Castle says.

"I'd always worked for Tommy and not Jimmy. And when they merged, you know, I served both of them. And like every time Jimmy wanted to say something to the boys, he'd say, 'Listen, Lee, tell those guys that I don't like it when they do this and that.' I'd say, 'Jimmy, I'm a trumpet player in the band and the minute I do that I become a leader'—and, you know, then the guys in the band wouldn't even talk to you. I said, 'Why don't you tell them? *Jesus*.' He always wanted me to bawl the band out. I said, 'That's not my job.'

"So one day he called a meeting. Down at the Statler. So Tommy said, 'Come on, I got to go somewhere.' I said, 'Tom, Jimmy called a meeting, you know I got to go.' He says, 'He can do without you. Let him have his meeting. You come with me.' You don't say no to TD! He'd fire you right then and there!

"So we came back. See, Tommy would tell you off and buy you a dinner 10 minutes later. But Jimmy would carry that little grudge, you know. And like I walked into the Statler, there was Jimmy. He says, 'Where were you at the meeting?' I said, 'I had to go somewhere with Tommy.'

"'And if Tommy was having a meeting, could I take you somewhere with me?'

"I said, 'Jim, what do you want? What do you mean? I don't understand.'

"'No! You mean with me it's all right if you don't show up! But with *the brother*, you better be there, is that it?'

"I said, 'No, it's not it. He insisted I go with him and I went with him. Take it up with him—*Jesus*.' But that's the way it was, you know.

"Or: 'What about this, can you do that?' he'd ask.

"'I think it's going to be kind of rough, Jim, to do that,' I'd say.

"'What do you mean rough? If *the brother* asked you, you wouldn't find it rough, would you?'

"And that's the way it went. Other than that, sure they loved each other. When Tommy died, Jimmy was broken-hearted right to the end. So, that's proof enough."

Castle became quite fond of Jimmy, whom he found big-hearted and sensitive. Because Castle was born on February 28th and Jimmy on February 29th, they celebrated their birthdays together. But he always felt closer to Tommy. "I was with Tommy all the time," he notes. Tommy may have been temperamental, truculent—he could shower a friend with generosity one moment, then turn ice-cold the next—but Castle had tremendous admiration for him.

Castle adds that nobody but Tommy Dorsey ever intimidated him. "Because Tommy was unpredictable. You never knew what he was going to say in front of people. Or do. Right up to the end. He and I were buddies. Closer than friends. And still, one time—like he'd bawled somebody out, then out of the corner of his eye he'd look at me and say: 'And remember, nobody's married to me in this band.' You know. And the thoughts would come through my mind, I can't repeat! I'd say, 'Who the hell cares? Who the hell asked you.' But that's the way he was."

Shortly before he died, Tommy urged Castle to move from the Bronx, to build a house on property next to his own in Greenwich, Connecticut. When Castle said he couldn't afford it, Tommy answered that he'd take care of the down payment.

"That was some band. That was probably one of the greatest bands ever assembled. I mean it. Oh, just a great band. They were terrific," Castle recalls of the Dorseys. "I'm a nostalgia guy, Chip. I sit here and I think, and boy—how I miss those guys! And when I get a little despondent, if I'm around the Bronx I'll go on my father's grave, my brother's, and my sister's. And if I'm not going down in town or in the Bronx, and I don't feel well, I just walk up here, a ten minute walk, and I'm right on Tommy's grave. Valhalla, right here in Kensico. And I stand on his grave. I've always said that if two guys could ever come back, it would be my father and Tommy Dorsey! But I haven't heard from anyone, so I guess it's hard to come back. But I sense that if I'm standing over their graves, they know I'm there. Some people will tell you this is all nonsense. But I stand as good a chance as they do of being right—you know, how do they know?"

* * *

This is the way the band used to be introduced on radio. Announcer: "Those fabulous Dorseys! [Theme: "I'm Getting Sentimental Over

Lee Castle and Chip Deffaa at the grave of Tommy Dorsey. Dorsey was "the Sentimental Gentleman" onstage, rough and domineering offstage. "But he made disciplined musicians out of all of us," says Castle. "I miss him." (Photo by Nancy Miller Elliott)

You. . ."] From the Cafe Rouge of the Hilton-owned Statler Hotel in New York City, we invite you to the Dorsey Brothers Show, starring Tommy, the sentimental gentleman, and Jimmy, the world's greatest saxophonist—with their Orchestra. *Those Fabulous Dorseys.*"

And it *was* a fabulous, 19-piece ensemble. They could afford to hire the very best musicians. Buddy Rich came in on drums, followed by Louis Bellson. Trumpet great Charlie Shavers was featured on most of the jazz. Castle was lead horn in a spirited Dixieland combination, which included the Dorseys, Brauner, and the rhythm section.

"You didn't have to pick [musicians]. When you needed a guy, you'd go for the best you could get. Professional men. Oh sure. It isn't like now, you try a guy out. They'd come right in and they'd play," Castle remembers, a little wistfully.

The band was clearly superior to the bands either of the Dorseys had led individually earlier in the 1950s, as their recordings (some of which continue to be reissued by Columbia) show. (Castle notes that on some of the recordings Toots Mondello subbed for Jimmy, who was ill; the albums still credited Jimmy.)

Jackie Gleason, a great fan of the Dorseys, presented them on his variety show. (He also bestowed upon Castle the title, "the Prince of the Trumpet.") And he helped the Dorseys get their own TV program, called "Stage Show." It began as a summer replacement for Gleason's show in July of '54. In the 1955-56 season, the Dorsey brothers' show moved into the regular schedule, as the lead-in for Gleason's "Honeymooners" program; there were 67 "Stage Show" broadcasts in total. (It is part of jazz history that Charlie Parker died while watching one of the Dorsey Brothers' TV shows; he had always admired Jimmy's technical facility on alto.) The Dorseys' guest stars included Count Basie, Duke Ellington, Louis Armstrong, Tony Bennett, Ella Fitzgerald, Sarah Vaughan, Lionel Hampton, Bob Eberly, and Helen O'Connell. And on four shows, the Dorseys presented a young singer who had never before appeared on national TV: Elvis Presley.

Castle recalls: "We gave Elvis Presley his first start with Tommy and Jimmy. I conducted him, for Tommy. And Tommy didn't even want him. Here's a guy who shakes his hips. . . and they're stealing his bones, you know. If they want to steal anybody's bones, it should be Sinatra's. He's the greatest thing that ever hit our business. Him and Crosby. But Frank is the guy."

Frank Sinatra had left Tommy Dorsey's Band, on far from the best of terms, in September of 1942. But TD maintained strong respect for Sinatra's talent. Castle notes: "You know, I traveled with Tommy Dorsey for years and Tommy didn't like anybody, but when he fooled around with that radio and he came to a Sinatra record, it stopped there. And one day he looked at me while I was driving and he said, 'I got to give this dago credit. He's got good taste. He won't let anybody push him around.' So I said, 'I wonder where he got that from, Tom?' And Tom started laughing. You know. Which is true. I think a lot of TD rubbed off on Frank and I think Frank would admit it."

And what, I wondered, did Castle think of Elvis Presley?

"What any musician thinks of Elvis," he answers curtly. "The only thing I could tell you that impressed me was that he was a nice, hum-

Lee Castle with Frank Sinatra. (Courtesy Lee Castle)

ble guy. He wasn't really a singer, and he shook his hips. It wasn't our bag, you know. To me, when you hear a guy like Sinatra sing, you can sit back and listen to music. I can sit here, over this lake of mine and just sit on this pier and listen to Frank—either Frank or Louis Armstrong. Some of the records maybe with Tommy, you know. I never listen to my own records anyway.

"I'd rather listen to people like Debussy, Delius, you know, that's what I listen to. I love them. And Wagner. I love Wagner. 'Tristan and Isolde.' I got my little thing. Ravel, you know. 'Rhapsody d'Espanol.' I got little things that they did. Debussy, 'Afternoon of a Faun.' And 'Claire de Lune' and all that. The guys that put me on Delius were Axel Stordahl and Paul Weston—they put me on to him back when we were in Tommy's Band, in the late '30s. And Deane Kincaide. They were always playing Delius. Because they wrote like that. Sure."

The Dorsey brothers' network television and radio broadcasts had exposed them to a whole new generation of fans. They were enjoying renewed appreciation.

Fraternity Records approached Jimmy with the idea of making some records featuring him on sax. He demurred a bit, saying nobody was interested in an old-timer like himself. But on November 11, 1956, he went into the studio and cut four sides, backed by the Dorsey Brothers' Orchestra, minus Tommy and the trumpet section. The Arthur Malvin Singers were used in place of the trumpet section. Castle conducted. The tunes, released under the billing of "Jimmy Dorsey and His Orchestra" (the first under Jimmy's own name since he and Tommy had reunited), were: "Sophisticated Swing," "Mambo En Sax," "It's the Dreamer in Me," and "So Rare." On the issued take of "So Rare," while the drummer laid down a heavy beat, Jimmy moved through a gutsy, rough-edged solo, quite unlike anything with which he had previously been associated. The influence of rhythm-and-blues was evident. Tommy wasn't too thrilled by the recording. But "So Rare" went on to become, in 1957, Jimmy's last and greatest hit.

On November 26th, Tommy died unexpectedly. He had taken sleeping pills before going to bed. During the night, he had thrown up without awakening, and had choked on the food particles.

Jimmy was shattered by his brother's death. Without Tommy, he seemed lost. He cried every night. Leading the orchestra was of little interest to him. Castle conducted the band the night after Tommy died.

Jimmy told Castle: "Lee, it's all yours from here on in. I'll be with my brother in six months." And that's just about what happened.

In January of 1957, surgeons operated on Jimmy for lung cancer. The band kept working, but most of the time Jimmy stayed in his room at the Statler, while Castle conducted. The Dorsey Brothers' Orchestra was now, by default, Jimmy Dorsey's Orchestra, although it continued to play music from the libraries of both Dorseys.

"So Rare" was getting constant radio play, and focusing attention on the band. It was the first smash hit record by a big band in a long time. Fraternity was eager to record more sides, so that an album could be released. Plans were made for another recording session.

In March, Jimmy went to Miami Beach to rest, while the band continued playing in New York. His condition worsened and he was soon transported to Doctor's Hospital in New York. He never left the hospital. He'd talk often with Castle. He was eager to be sure that the band was playing "So Rare" at just the right tempo, and so on. Towards the end, Jimmy realized that he was not going to be able to make the recording session set for June 17, 1957. He told Castle to get saxophonist Dick Stabile (in whose big band Castle had also played briefly, back in the '30s) to play his solos for him.

A few days before Jimmy's death on June 12th, Castle presented Jimmy with a gold record, marking the fact that "So Rare" had sold a million copies.

The Dorsey Band, conducted by Castle, and with Stabile on sax for four numbers, made the record date as scheduled on June 17th, just two days after Jimmy's funeral. Earl Wilson reported that the musicians played with the feeling that both Tommy and Jimmy were there. The band recorded "Amapola," "Maria Elena," "Boogie Woogie," and others. Those selections, plus one more recorded in early 1958, were released on an album that made a splendid final tribute to Jimmy Dorsey—and helped to ensure the continuation of the band.

Mom Dorsey told Castle: "I still have my Italian son."

* * *

The Dorsey Band, directed by Castle, continued working in New York and on the road, filling bookings which had been made many months in advance—prior to the death of Jimmy, and, in many cases, prior to the death of Tommy as well.

The heirs of Tommy and Jimmy, who jointly owned the band and were sharing in its profits, disagreed over its future. Jane Dorsey, Tommy's widow, decided to pull out.

The Tommy Dorsey estate authorized the formation of a new official "Tommy Dorsey Orchestra," which was *not* composed of musicians who had played in Tommy's band, but which would have the right to play Tommy's charts. In early 1958, trombonist Warren Covington, who had had virtually no connection with Tommy Dorsey, was hired to front the new band.

The Jimmy Dorsey estate authorized Castle to continue leading what had been the Dorsey Brothers' Orchestra, and was now billed as the Jimmy Dorsey Orchestra. The band would have the rights to all of Jimmy's old charts. Both the Castle-led "Jimmy Dorsey Band" and the Covington-led "Tommy Dorsey Band" would have the rights to charts that had been jointly owned by Tommy and Jimmy after they had reunited in 1953.

Castle comments: "People feel the fact that I've got the Jimmy Dorsey Band, I worked for Jimmy. I never worked for Jimmy until Tommy and Jimmy merged. When Tommy died, the band became the Jimmy Dorsey Band, and I took it over. Then Tommy's widow split the estates. She pulled out, so I had to call this the Jimmy Dorsey Band.

"There's only been one leader in the Jimmy Dorsey Band. I've had the band longer than both of the Dorseys. But Tommy Dorsey's band has had several leaders since Tommy died," including Covington, Sam Donahue, Urbie Green, Murray McEachern, and Buddy Morrow, who leads it today.

Castle recalls: "For a long while, we continued with the same guys in the band. Then one by one they started to leave. Me and a guy named Tino Barzie [who had formerly been Tommy Dorsey's manager] were running the band, and we couldn't afford those guys anymore, because we weren't getting Dorsey prices. So Tino said, 'We'll have to interview a new band.'

Warren Covington. (Courtesy Abby Hoffer)

"I said, 'No, we'll call each guy in the room, and say, "What are you getting, $200? Will you take a hundred and a half? A hundred and a quarter?" And we'll give them all a cut. Some will stay and some won't. And the ones that won't, we'll replace them, but the ones that stay, at least we got most of the guys.' So we did, and nobody quit. We went on with that band. But then, one at a time, they got off the road, and you couldn't blame them."

* * *

Epic Records, which had signed the band, seemed uncertain as how to best market it. The first album they released, "Jimmy Dorsey's Greatest Hits," consisted of fresh recordings of numbers that Jimmy had originally recorded between 1936 and 1942. Noted tenor saxist and arranger Al Cohn adapted the original arrangements. The album was a mixed success. The band had fun with swing instrumentals "John Silver" and "Parade of the Milk Bottle Caps," with Castle recording spirited, first-rate open trumpet solos on both. It's a shame he hasn't been captured on record more often in that vein. And some of the old Bob Eberly ballads, such as "Maria Elena," "I Understand," and "I Hear a Rhapsody," translated beautifully into instrumentals. The melodies were good. The band got a great ensemble sound, and it made the most of changing dynamics on "I Hear a Rhapsody." Castle used first-rate musicians on his Epic dates, including Doc Severinsen, lead trumpet; Toots Mondello, featured alto sax; Urbie Green, featured trombone; and Gus Johnson, drums. But some of the other numbers had originally become hits only because of the vocals by Bob Eberly and/or Helen O'Connell; the new instrumental versions weren't nearly as satisfying.

The next album was better: "Jimmy Dorsey on Tour." The numbers here—including "Moten Stomp," "Autumn in New York," "Sweetie Cake," and "The Bells of St. Mary's"—were instrumentals that the Dorsey brothers had been playing in their last years. Records and tapes of radio broadcasts exist of the Dorsey Brothers' Orchestra playing these same arrangements. "The Bells of St. Mary," in fact, had been arranged by Bill Finnegan for Tommy's band as far back as 1949. This album has more of the flavor of Tommy Dorsey's last bands than most records made in this period by the "official" Covington-led Tommy Dorsey Orchestra, which was busy recording for Decca tunes such as "Tea For Two Cha-Cha"—without much of a Dorsey sound at all. Castle's virtuosity as a trumpeter was displayed on "What's New," which became a perennial highlight of his concert appearances.

He notes, however: "When the album came out, I discovered my introduction to 'What's New' had been cut out—you know, anything to get everything in. I said, 'I demand to know why I wasn't informed of this! This isn't the way this arrangement is.' But at that time, I didn't own the band. And you're fighting a losing battle."

Castle also found time to play on a recording session led by veteran trombonist Miff Mole (with whom he had played in Benny Goodman's Orchestra back in 1943). For this November, 1958 record date, Mole was reunited with fellow stalwarts of the New York white jazz recording clique of the 1920s, including Jimmy Lytell, clarinet; Frank Signorelli, piano; and Chauncey Morehouse, drums. Castle's crisp, clear horn fit in well with the music made by these older players. The numbers recorded that day, "Dreaming by the River," "Exactly Like You," "Original Dixieland One-Step," "For Me and My Gal," are still available on a Miff Mole album on the Jazzology label. Castle was always at home with this kind of traditional jazz, and no doubt would have recorded more of it, if he had not taken over the Dorsey Band.

For its third album by Castle and the Jimmy Dorsey Band ("Goodies But Gassers"), Epic records wanted contemporary "Top 40" tunes. So Castle and the band went in and cut their instrumental interpretations of "Don't Be Cruel," "Uh! Oh!," "Venus," "Personality," and other best-sellers of the previous five years. Castle was hardly thrilled about recording such rock 'n' roll and pop tunes. But he notes: "It's hard for a big band to get a record date. So if somebody offers you an album, you grab it. I thought, 'Well, why not? I still don't own the band; if I refuse, they'll do it anyway.' And I thought, 'Maybe I ought to come out of this thing and get in with these new songs.'"

One of the new songs actually proved to be a terrific vehicle for Castle. "Kansas City," written by Jerry Lieber and Mike Stoller, swung. With the band chugging beneath him and building tension, Castle rode upwards in a memorable arc-like open trumpet statement. The number—which was over all too quickly—closed with Castle growling down on muted trumpet.

He remembers with enthusiasm: "Now 'Kansas City' was good!" You know, I make a thing—go way up to a high D in 'Kansas City.' Whoeee—I can't do it now!" Though he wasn't big on playing most of the other new tunes, he kept that chart in his books for a long time.

"Then they made me record a thing called 'Big Bad Train.' The A and R man at Epic said, "This'll be a hit!" We did a single on that. It died," he recalls.

Castle acquired all rights to the band in the early 1960s. He notes: "Jimmy's daughter Julie is still alive. But she has nothing to do with the band anymore. She's in Europe most of the time. I own the band lock, stock, and barrel.

"I took care of Mom Dorsey till she died. I buried Mom Dorsey. I paid for everything. No relatives, nobody showed up.

"I'm in touch with Julie and whenever I can see Julie get a few dollars, I see to it that she does, you know. And I'm always here in case they need me, they know that."

In 1969, Castle was glad to be offered a record contract, even though—once again—he was being told what to record. Pickwick Records released two albums by the band: one of music by Burt Bacharach and Hal David, the other of music by the Beatles. Arranger Bugs Bower, who wrote the charts for the albums, conducted. For these sessions, Castle used top pros including trumpeters Johnny Amoroso, Dick Perry, and John Frosk—all of whom had worked in the Dorsey Brothers' Orchestra in the '50s. On one selection, "Yellow Submarine," Castle got to blow a bit of Dixieland trumpet. But on other sides, he generally played straight melody, following arrangements that might have been played by any band; there was nothing particularly Dorsey-ish about the music.

Those albums of contemporary pop tunes hardly represented the actual "sound" of Castle's Jimmy Dorsey Band as it worked, night after night, playing dances and concerts.[1] Castle didn't really try to keep the band sounding contemporary. He mostly enjoyed playing material from the Dorseys' libraries. The actual sound of the band has been better captured in its occasional TV appearances than in many of its recordings.

Today, Castle maintains he's interested in staying up with current pop tunes, but his heart clearly lies with the older numbers. He's happy playing the music from his era (and especially happy when he has a chance to play it in the company of some fellow musicians from his era). Of course the Dorseys played far more tunes throughout their long careers than can be maintained in a band's working library. The "newest" addition to Castle's working library at any given time is more likely to be an old arrangement that he's taken out of storage and reintroduced, than a brand new tune.

"I know I need pops," Castle professes. "I want to get some of the current things. But what are the current things? . . . I've got 'Night Fever' in the book, but we never use it.

"I've got two great books here—Tommy's and Jimmy's. The ones that they had when they were together, you know. And I just put 'Street of Dreams' [originally a hit for Tommy in 1942] in there—I didn't get a chance to go over it yet—and a few others. Those arrangements were made by Howard Gibeling. And that's hard to beat him, you know." Gibeling did a number of the rich instrumental charts for

[1] Nor does the band's most recent album, "Dorsey Then and Now" (Atlantic, 1987), which even has Castle doing a rap number.

the Dorseys when they merged in the '50s—both brand new tunes and revisions of earlier hits. The Dorseys hired the best arrangers available. Castle may not be breaking much new ground, musically, but he is preserving a body of arrangements well worth preserving. (He has to shy away from overly-difficult charts, however, because he has got to have music that any third trumpeter he might pick up for some out-of-town date could sight-read satisfactorily.)

Castle is a pragmatic dance band leader, eager to give his audience what he believes it wants. "I play a lot of sweet solos because the people have to have the melody. Tommy Dorsey did, very successful. I remember Glenn Miller once saying to me, 'The easiest business to make a million dollars in is the music business.' And I said, 'How do you figure that?' He said, 'Well, never distort a good melody and you've got it made.' And he was right," Castle declares.

"We've got about 200 some odd arrangements we travel with. And we only play 30 or 40 a night maybe. I carry a lot of that because I like to be able to play requests. If I've got it, I'll play it. If I don't, if it's that important to you, I'll have the piano player play the first chorus of your song, then we'll go into something else. Anything to make the people happy. After all, you know, all they want to hear is the melody."

Castle runs the band in a business-like fashion. "In the school I came from, Tommy, Benny and these guys—at a dance, you always played the first hour and a half without getting off. They give you a lot of music for those four hours." Tommy, he notes, didn't even allow the sidemen to wear watches; their job was over when the leader called it a night, not when the clock struck any particular hour. And Castle is strict about the appearance his musicians make. "There are a lot of things I won't tolerate. I don't go for this crossed-legging on the bandstand or keeping your jackets open or smoking on the bandstand or drinking a little vodka on the bandstand."

Castle's band helps keep alive many of the Dorsey brothers' hits, as well as quite a few numbers from their libraries that never became hits but are certainly worth hearing again. What it does *not* do anymore, however, is play new jazz originals. The Dorseys always played a wide variety of music, including current pop tunes and evergreens. But right up until they died, they also kept on introducing new jazz instrumentals, which showcased soloists within the band. In the mid-'50s, Tommy acquired a number of new charts from Ernie Wilkins, who had helped create much of Basie's new sound. (Castle still plays some of them today.) TD also took at least one chart from a promising young trumpeter/arranger in Basie's Band named Thad Jones. And when Louis Bellson (then drumming for the Dorseys) or Charlie Shavers (then trumpeting for them) came up with a new number, the band would dig into it eagerly. There was always room for jazz originals.

That tradition of adding new jazz originals has fallen by the wayside. (Nor does Castle have the soloists to equal a Charlie Shavers or Louis Bellson.) Castle is happy to front a fine dance band—he strives for a good ensemble sound—featuring Dorsey music. Castle certainly knows how the charts should sound, and his trumpet, at its poetic best, remains a joy to hear. The band is far less jazz-oriented, however, than the bands the Dorseys led.

* * *

In 1981, suffering from angina, Castle underwent heart bypass surgery. He had to abstain from trumpeting while recuperating. The band continued playing dates in his absence. Castle worried that the layoff might affect his playing; some older musicians have found themselves unable to play again, after having been forced to lay off for a while. But he made a full recovery.

"You come back. You have to practice," Castle comments. Nights when he is not working, he says, he tries to get in an hour or an hour and a half of practice. He plays solos, scales, whatever he feels he needs. "I sit home. My wife goes to bed maybe ten, 11 o'clock. I wait a little bit. Then I close the doors, I put the TV on a little louder, I may have a ballgame or good movie, and I'll sit there and I'll practice while watching the movie. That's the only way I could do it."

Lee Castle and the Jimmy Dorsey Band. (Chip Deffaa collection)

Trumpeting night after night with a 14-piece big band, "is hard work. And after the bypass it comes harder," Castle says.

He comments, too: "It's tougher for a leader [than for a sideman], because when you're in the band, you're constantly playing; you're always warmed up. And if you got six, seven brass and somebody makes a mistake, you hardly notice it. That gives you confidence. It's like 500,000 guys in an invasion on the beach. You figure: '500,000 guys; I stand a chance of not getting hit.' But when you're alone up there and the horn's been laying on the stand, then you come across a tune and you've got to play a solo right away. You've got to pick it up. That horn's cold. Your lip is cold. And you know this. And you know your lip is cold and you know how your lip feels. And you see 5000 people. Now you're starting to get nervous. Once you get through the first two bars, OK—but to start getting into it, that's hard."

Castle has always had a reputation among his musical colleagues for being something of a worrier. Drummer Moe Purtill recalls him from the old days, affectionately enough, as a hypochondriac.

The late guitarist Carmen Mastren told jazz writer Mort Goode: "I won't say he had a lot of imaginary ills, but he had a pill for almost every hour of the day or night. Nothing any stronger than aspirin, but he could feel good and bad all at the same time, it seemed."

And Pee Wee Erwin, who considered Castle a marvelous trumpeter, said that Castle "always griped" about his lip.

Castle still is quite the worrier today, still seemingly capable of feeling good and bad at the same time, as Mastren put it. He gets a brilliant, pure sound from his horn that would be the envy of almost any brass player. But he declares: "You're never satisfied. You're always striving. You're always trying to find a better way. And then you have teeth problems, you got to worry about that. Right now, I've got teeth problems; I don't know whether to have them filed shorter. I don't know whether they're too short or wide or too thick, and it's bothering my playing. And you have to feel your way around to see. I've never bitten my tongue so much in my life as I'm doing now. So apparently these teeth are too long. The caps. But then if you file them too short, then you can't play again. So you don't know.

"Pee Wee Erwin was a *fantastic* trumpet player. Oh, my God! I wish Pee Wee were around now, I'd ask him what the hell is happening to my lip. Heh-heh! I think he would know, more than anybody."

Advancing years generally affect the technical prowess of a trumpet player. Young Louis Armstrong, for example, could hit a hundred high C's in a row, a feat he could hardly duplicate as he got older. But technical prowess is only a small part of a jazz player's artistry. With the passing of time, Armstrong found different ways of doing certain numbers. He didn't need the pyrotechnics to reach his audience.

Castle likewise has found it harder to hit certain high notes, or to hold them as long as he once did. He is bothered, at times, by that notion that he cannot always perform certain numbers the same way that he once did; he's lost some flexibility. He tries to analyze the problem. Is it his caps? The mouthpiece of the trumpet? Or something else?

Several nights prior to this conversation, for example, he and the band had played in a major outdoor concert in Brooklyn. There were probably 5000 people there. He comments: "One number that I should have played the other night—which I don't dare—is 'What's New.' I don't do it on account of these damned caps. I don't know. I've tried doing it in here. I've tried practicing. I used to hit a high B flat and hold onto it for almost a minute—and then continue the phrase. Last night I tried hitting that thing and I keep falling off of it. And I say, 'What the hell is wrong?' So I don't dare do it. I thought of doing it, then I thought, 'Aw, I'll get nervous and dry'—I'm getting dry now thinking about it.

"'What's New' is something that I would do if I had a couple of drinks and was doing a dance job. Because people are dancing, not paying attention to you. But you get out there and try to play 'What's New'—with people looking at you, you know, and you know that you have problems, you can't tell them that. So I stayed away from that tune. I was thinking of playing it but then I thought, 'Jesus, I'm afraid that I'll louse it up.'[2]

Castle admits he feels "bugged" at times by the notion that he may not be able to play everything the same way he once could. He's unsure how much of the problem may be just a matter of confidence. But then, his voice filled with determination, he vows: "I'll tell you—35 years old, 65, 70 or 80, 85 years old—I'm still going to beat it, because I want to play! And which I intend to do."

Castle is probably his own harshest critic. It is doubtful that people listening to his current work—unless they've been following his career with an exceptional degree of attentiveness—would have any way of knowing that he might not be able to hit notes quite as high, or hold them for quite as long, as in his earlier years. For sustained high notes are not central to his art. What Castle chooses to play, he plays well. Given a melody he likes, he can do much with a brief, descending

[2] Since this conversation, Castle has returned to playing "What's New" regularly at his concerts. A September, 1987, concert in New Jersey found him playing it brilliantly, with more feeling than on his Epic recording. He finished the tour-de-force, thanked the audience for their applause, and said: "I don't know how many more years I can play that."

phrase in the middle register. He can solo succinctly on "This Love of Mine," for example, creating a moving, vulnerable-sounding passage that captures both the beauty and the sadness in the tune. A passage that echoes in the listener's mind after the concert is over. He can take those short solo spots in the middle of the arrangements of "Green Eyes" and "Tangerine"—spots originally filled by Jimmy Dorsey's alto sax—and enliven them with zesty, crackling trumpet work.

There are countless young schooled musicians who can play higher notes or hold them longer. Technical skills can be learned and honed by practice. But the ability to create something interesting, something memorable in a brief solo spot—that can't be taught in school.

* * *

Overall, Castle has not been much impressed by the direction jazz trumpeting has taken since the advent of bebop. He longs to hear more of the lyrical playing that predominated in his youth. Castle watches the younger jazz stars of today with mixed feelings. He comments: "You got this new trumpet player, what's his name, Marsalis? Last night I sat down and listened to him for a while on TV. And boy, he's a hell of a trumpet player. I watched his mouth and everything—and he's just perfect. He plays some classical things that scare you! But when it came to the jazz, it didn't mean anything to me. Because, I get the impression either they're trying to create a new style—which you can't do—or he's listening to the boppers, you know, that play a million notes in one bar. Where Louis would play four quarter notes and swing like—

"But it didn't impress me. Jeez, my hat's off to him, he's one of the greatest soloists I've heard in the technical field." But to Castle's ears, Wynton Marsalis—as well as many other younger players—is missing the beauty that can be found in jazz. Castle recalls hearing Marsalis' recording of "Stardust" on the radio. "I'm listening for the melody and I couldn't—it seemed to me like he was playing the harmony notes to the melody. I sit back and say to myself: 'Well, maybe that's the way music's going to be. Remember now, take your age into consideration.' But to me, it's still like throwing salt in your coffee.

"This guy's a hell of a trumpet player. But I wonder if this guy's ever heard of Louis Armstrong? And why wouldn't he want to play something like Louis Armstrong? Nobody plays like Louis.

"Yet if you think of a trumpet, you got to think of Louis Armstrong and not Harry James. Harry James and I used to hide behind poles to hear Louis. . . . A guy like Louis Armstrong, I always felt that when he died. . . one nickel a musician would have built a hell of a monument. But he went down by the wayside. A talented genius."

Castle also recalls listening to his car radio one night, "and I heard a guy that played pretty good. I said, 'This guy plays like a black man and he's got a lot of little Louis things in there.' Which is good. And it surprised me." It turned out to be Ruby Braff. "I was elated to hear that. I said, 'Jesus, I'm glad to see Ruby keeping this thing a little alive, because nobody dares play a Louis Armstrong lick'—why, I don't know. Charlie Parker said: 'The better you play, the easier it is for me to chase you back to Louis Armstrong.' Anything that you play real good, Louis's played it. So I can't understand why you don't hear much of that. All you hear is [Castle scats a million-notes-a-minute modern jazz lick]. . . . What about a little something tasty?

"But maybe that's the way things have to be. I'm not putting it down. Certainly I don't have the facilities to play that way. Because those kids that play that way are pretty good trumpet players; otherwise they couldn't play that way. A lot of technique. But it's a sin, a pitiful thing, that they wouldn't go back home and play a Louis Armstrong record for a change. I think they might change their mind a little bit. . . .

"It's all right if you want to improve on the old, but how can you improve on the old if you never knew it? And that's what I feel some of these kids are doing today.

"And yet I meet some kids that shock me the other way around—they sound like Bix Beiderbecke. And that's very gratifying; that's really lovely to listen to, you know."

Castle enjoys listening to records by Armstrong and by Sinatra. "And to *good* Dixieland players. Like Teagarden. Of course, Benny Goodman, Artie Shaw. Whatever bands I'm listening to will always bring back a pleasant memory. Because nine chances out of ten, I've been with those bands, and I have a beautiful memory for all of them. Tommy, of course, I've been with him for many, many years. Benny Goodman used to thrill the hell out of me when he played. Artie Shaw would thrill the hell out of me, and I used to hang around with Artie. And you learned a lot from him, intellectually. He's an intellectual guy."

Castle enjoys speaking with Shaw periodically today. "And Cab Calloway lives right up the street. He comes down here a lot," he notes. He stays in touch with Sammy Kaye and Buddy Morrow, and others from his day. He wears an old hat that he got from Jimmy Durante. Castle has a strong sentimental streak.

"I can never understand one thing," he adds. "Jimmy's a hell of a jazz player. Yet you don't see—like the night guy on WNEW, he plays all these jazz records. . . but never once does he play a Jimmy Dorsey record or even a Tommy."

* * *

If Castle gets nostalgic at times for the old days, you can hardly blame him. In the late '30s and early '40s, big bands were America's favorite form of musical entertainment. And Tommy and Jimmy Dorsey led two of the most popular bands. They could afford to hire the very best available instrumentalists, vocalists, and arrangers. Until they died, the Dorseys maintained impeccable musical standards.

But times have changed. And Castle has had to deal with a different set of economic realities. He found not long after Tommy and Jimmy had died that the band could no longer command the same fees; thus he could no longer afford to pay sidemen the same wages. Ultimately, he knew, he would have to settle for lower musical standards.

In the three decades since the Dorseys died, Castle has fronted some excellent bands (as well as some rather disappointing ones). He has kept going, often against the odds, on a demanding schedule of one-nighters. The Dorseys got extended location dates—months on end at the Statler in New York and prolonged gigs in other major cities. Bands rarely get such chances to settle down anywhere anymore. The Dorseys had network radio, and eventually, television, contracts. When the brothers died, the band lost its broadcasting outlets.

But Castle has hung in there. He's dedicated to the big band sound.

Is he generally satisfied with the quality of musicians he gets these days? "Some, yeah. Most of them, yeah. But some, a little green yet, you know," he answers. "But as long as you got your strong key men, you're all right." It must be frustrating for him at times—although he doesn't say it—to work with musicians who aren't always up to his level.

Castle likes to call a couple of Dixieland tunes a night. He features a seven-piece band-within-the-big band, the "Dorseyland Dixieland Jazz Band," on numbers such as "Indiana" and "Sweet Georgia Brown." When he played those same numbers 30-odd years ago, Tommy Dorsey stood beside him on trombone, Jimmy Dorsey was on clarinet, Buzzy Brauner was on tenor sax, and Buddy Rich was on drums. The players he's usually working with these days are *not* the equivalents of Tommy and Jimmy Dorsey and company. In some cases, they don't even seem comfortable with Dixieland.

"Dixieland's an art. And if you don't really have the right guys for it, it's rough," Castle comments. He's happy when he gets an occasional chance to play Dixieland with first-rate older players who know and love the music. "The Lotus Club on Fifth Avenue hires a Dixieland band once a year. I did it for about four years. I would always bring in Cliff Leeman with me, and my dear, dear friend and roommate Carmen Mastren, who died. He did a couple with me there. George Masso, the trombone player. Bobby Pratt I'd bring in on piano. All of these guys who know what Dixieland's all about. And when you start playing Dixieland with them, a guy like Cliff Leeman starts playing the drums, notes bounce out of your horn. But when you've got a group of guys that don't know what Dixieland's all about, notes don't bounce out, and you can't get them out of your horn. You're struggling.

"A long time ago, when I was with Tommy Dorsey, Lou McGarity and my brother [Charlie Castaldo] came to my room. They were Miff Mole fans. I told them, 'You guys would do yourself a good favor if you bought some Jack Teagarden records and listen to them, because Jack plays certain phrases that fit into any tune.' And they did. You know, Lou McGarity sounded like Teagarden himself. So I try to tell these kids today. But when they're not working with me, they're out listening to all these beboppers."

He adds: "Sometimes I've thought, I'd just as soon leave the big band home and somebody just give me the right good Dixieland players, and I'll just go on tour with them, because—no headaches, you just play what you want to play."

* * *

In the Swing Era, countless big bands criss-crossed the country in buses. All of the well-known leaders maintained organized road bands,

Lee Castle and the Jimmy Dorsey Band, Rockefeller Center concert, 1979. (Chip Deffaa collection)

with musicians on a regular payroll.

Today, economic considerations have forced most of the leaders to switch to a different system. Only a handful of bands (Woody Herman's, Lionel Hampton's, Buddy Rich's, the Tommy Dorsey Band, the Count Basie Band, and the Glenn Miller Band) are actually road bands that feature the same personnel on all dates, from coast to coast. And even most of those bands lay off periodically.

I've enjoyed catching Castle's Jimmy Dorsey Band many times in concert in New York and New Jersey. But what I've enjoyed might more accurately be referred to as his eastern band. For he uses one crew, consisting of musicians who live in New York, New Jersey, and Delaware, for his eastern U.S. gigs, whether they're in Florida, Virginia, New York, Rhode Island, or wherever. The key members make nearly all of the bookings. But all members take other gigs besides their work with Castle, since playing in the band is not a full-time job for them. Then he's got a Chicago-based crew that works with him in Chicago and on other midwestern bookings. He's got a West Coast crew that he uses for West Coast dates. And in various big cities, he can pick up local musicians as needed, who are often alumni of the big bands of Tommy and Jimmy Dorsey, Benny Goodman, and so on. Castle likes hiring such alumni when possible; he favors more experienced players generally.

"They'll come in and play better than the guys that you want to drag on the road with you everyday, and have to break in and teach them how to play," Castle declares.

There are advantages and disadvantages to Castle's system. He saves on transportation costs, which are so expensive that a full-time road band has to be working practically every night of the week, to be profitable. And he can accept short-term bookings in out-of-the-way locations, which he would otherwise have to turn down unless he had enough gigs along the way to justify the traveling.

In addition, Castle can get older players to work for him, who would not want to go on the road full-time. The players in the Woody Herman Band and the Glenn Miller Band today, for example, are virtually all in their early 20s. They're just out of school. They don't mind living on buses and planes for a stretch. They'll eventually settle down someplace, to be replaced on the road by new youths.

You'll see more gray heads, white heads, and bald heads in Castle's bands. He'll get older players who are glad to do a certain number of dates with him a year, without having to spend too much time away from home. And they're generally better at playing his type of music than even more technically proficient younger musicians would be.

Castle is delighted when he can get some fellows from his era on a gig. "I use Zeke Zarchy [trumpet] in California, Babe Russin [tenor sax] who died, I used Don Lodice [tenor sax], Jack Sperling [drummer]. I use all the guys," he says. Zarchy, Russin, and Lodice all played with Castle in Tommy Dorsey's Band circa 1940. Sperling drummed for Bunny Berigan, Tex Beneke, Bob Crosby, and others.

"And Chris Griffin—who was in Joe Haymes' Band just a little before me—I took Chris to Australia with me recently. Chris is a beautiful guy. You know, me, him, and Zeke Zarchy—all these guys, we played in the same band, the same era. We like the same players, the same taste in music. And I took Jack Leonard with me, I took Johnny Mince." Leonard was Tommy Dorsey's vocalist and Mince was TD's featured clarinetist, when Castle first joined TD's band. For Castle, reuniting with such old friends is great. The vibes onstage are good. "And you don't tell these guys how to play!" he exclaims. "They were there when I was there."

For the music Castle likes to play, that's important. Every time I've heard Castle's band in recent years, for example, I've been impressed by the well-rounded sound of the sax section. It gets a *pretty* sound—of the sort that you hear all too rarely these days. Young saxists generally get a harsher tone today; they don't *try* to get the tones that were sought in the Swing Era. The young saxists in Woody Herman's Band, the Glenn Miller Band, Artie Shaw's Band, and Buddy Rich's Band produce the metallic sound you commonly hear in college jazz ensembles today. Castle's saxists produce more of the sound of a good 1940s dance band. Having some older players in the section makes a difference.

Herman takes talented young musicians and lets them play the type of contemporary jazz that they want to play. That works out fine for him. (Occasionally *he* seems the odd man out, soloing in an older style than the others in the band.)

The Glenn Miller Band takes talented young musicians and makes them play 1939-42 charts which many of them aren't really interested in. They don't sound as good as the original Miller Band, whose members *wanted* to play that music, nor do they sound as good as the current Woody Herman Band, whose members are playing the music that *they* want to play. They're professional, but their lack of enthusiasm shows.

Castle gets a core of musicians who enjoy playing the music he likes to play, and who play it well. They get a warm, well-rounded ensemble sound.

Castle's eastern crew gets a lot of work. Which means that the band sounds *together*. Not as together, naturally, as a band that's on the road full-time, but far more so than a pick-up band that's just been assembled for an individual booking. These players know Castle's book forwards and backwards. And some of them have worked with him, off-and-on, for years. "That's a fantastic band you heard the other night!" Castle says. "I use these fellows all the time."

If Castle wanted to save more money, he could use strictly pick-up bands, and eliminate almost all transportation expenses. There'd be players in any union local capable of sight-reading the charts efficiently enough to satisfy many listeners.

"I'd rather make much less money than to want to crawl in some hole and get sick over it," Castle declares. "It's a pleasure to go up there

Lee Castle, 1988. (Photo by Nancy Miller Elliott)

and give a downbeat and know everything is coming out. But to go up there and say, 'Who is this guy? I wonder how he plays?' Or, 'I don't like the way he holds that horn; I know he can't play.' (I can tell by the way the guy holds the horn whether he can play or not.) That's sickening. I'll wind up back in the hospital. I don't do it. Pay the extra money for the transportation. Got to have great guys or I don't work. The office knows I don't work."

No doubt Castle would prefer it if he could take an ideal band on the road on a full-time basis, the way Tommy and Jimmy did years ago. But since that option is not economically feasible (and since he's not sure his health could stand full-time life on the road anymore), Castle is happy to work with contractors who maintain bands for him in various parts of the country. And if he can occasionally get some of his Swing Era cohorts gigging with him, he's really at home.

Castle is not a perfectionist like Shaw or Herman. He is not trying to reach new heights artistically with his band. Nor is he pouring all of his profits back into the band. He has made a good living by playing the music he likes. He's comfortable with his repertoire, and so is his audience. And, despite his occasional protests to the contrary, it's obvious when he's onstage that he loves to play, especially when he gives the audience a longer show than the contract requires him to. And he's the last of the Armstrong-inspired trumpeters still out there, regularly fronting a big band.

A typical concert by Castle's band today will open with a drum roll and cymbal splash, and Castle's brilliant trumpet cascading down Jimmy Dorsey's theme, "Contrasts." His tone is penetrating. After introducing the melody, Castle turns it over to the alto saxophonist, to more specifically recall Jimmy Dorsey.

On ballads such as "This Love of Mine" and "Deep Purple," the saxes strain heavenward. Castle solos sweetly. He may stray from the Dorsey repertoire, briefly, to offer a lyrical Italian number (a reminder of his own heritage), or to play a hit associated with Goodman, Shaw, Miller, Herman, or Ellington. He sings occasionally, too, in an amiable way: perhaps "It Happened in Monterey" or "All of Me." (He subbed once or twice with the Pied Pipers in Tommy's band years ago.)

And always, he parades out the Dorsey favorites: "So Rare," "Maria Elena," and "Boogie Woogie" (with calls of "One more time" and repeat endings in the Basie manner). How many times has he played such numbers!

"My Prayer," "I Hear a Rhapsody," and "Serenade in Blue," are joined in a medley featuring the reeds, to create a beautiful sustained mood.

A 10-minute medley linking hits of both Dorseys proves a surefire close to a set: excerpts from Jimmy's "Amapola," "John Silver" (the whole band shouting out Ray McKinley's original break: "15 men on a dead man's chest"), "Green Eyes," and "Tangerine," plus Tommy's "Marie," "Song of India," "On the Sunny Side of the Street" and finally—with the entire band rising to its feet—the driving Sy Oliver arrangement of "Opus One." If the trombonist on "Song of India" is not the equal of Tommy Dorsey, the audience doesn't seem to mind. Their applause is as much for the memory as for what they are hearing at this moment. You watch Castle conducting the sax section on "Song of India," getting the phrasing just right; you think of him conducting the number some 30 years ago (when the Dorseys were alive), first playing it (as a sideman in Tommy's band) nearly 50 years ago.

The band puts on a great show. The musicians have worked together enough to become a strong ensemble. They get a smooth, full, polished sound. Drummer Tim Laushey kicks along the charts in classic style, and may occasionally interject a comment during Castle's between-the-numbers bantering with the audience; he's been with Castle enough years to do that. On some of the bigger dates, Helen O'Connell is paired with the band.

Is it hard getting work for a big band these days?

"I don't know. I've found I'm turning things down, now," Castle answers. "I don't want to work, really. I'm tired. I really am. I'm tired of putting that horn to my mouth every five seconds. . . . I'm working, I don't know, maybe, maybe 35 weeks, 40 weeks a year.

The whole band rises to kick out "Opus One." Castle is from the old school; he knows that showmanship helps put across the music. (Chip Deffaa collection)

"I'm a little on the despondent side because I took on too much. I'd like to cut down a little bit. Because I'm all over the country, traveling. Still yet to go to, let's see—Flint, Michigan, Detroit, Chicago. We were just in Milwaukee for five days with Sergio Franchi, playing a big Festival Italiano. I've still got Buffalo to go to, Cambridge, Mass., to go to, Waterbury, Denver, California. Good God! You know—too much. I want to sit here for awhile and do nothing."

Castle's home, in an expensive section of Elmsford, New York, is not far from Little Italy in the Bronx, where Castle was born and raised. Where his mother, 70 years ago, beseeched St. Anthony to let her son live. Castle has never strayed too far from his roots, geographically or musically.

"There's a big fiesta going on there [in Little Italy] now, a big feast," Castle says. "I was there last night and that's why I'm tired." This trumpeter for St. Anthony still feels very much at home in the old neighborhood.

And that, finally, is what brings this day's visit to a close. He notes as we say goodbye: "I want to go down by the Italian feast."

1985-1986

PANAMA · FRANCIS

From Swing to Rock 'n' Roll and Back

"This should be the busiest band in this country, because wherever we play, man, we upset 'em," declares Panama Francis, swing drummer *par excellence* and leader of the Savoy Sultans. "Wherever we play, people are sitting on the edge of their seats, whether it's concerts or whether it's for dancing. But we can't get arrested. If it wasn't for the Rainbow Room, there wouldn't *be* any Savoy Sultans. The Rainbow Room is responsible for the group staying together."

About half of the year, Francis' Savoy Sultans (nine musicians plus a vocalist) may be found playing at New York's posh Rainbow Room. When not at the Rainbow Room, they'll get occasional quality bookings: perhaps a few weeks in Europe, or a night in Atlantic City, or an appearance at the Kool Jazz Festival. But the key word is *occasional*. Francis has been unable to get even a fraction of the out-of-town dates so many "ghost" big bands get, although there's no denying his nine men can outswing most of them. It's frustrating to him that despite the acclaim his band has received in Europe and in the New York area, he has been virtually unable to get any national exposure in the U.S. If the band is good enough for the Kool Jazz Festival, why aren't offers pouring in from lesser festivals, or from colleges?

"I had the number one record in France; it was number three in England.[1] I was nominated twice for a Grammy," declares Francis with more than a hint of frustration. Every night that he's at the Rainbow Room he can see how dancers appreciate his music. Why aren't booking agencies pushing his band?

Francis' Savoy Sultans carry on, in a sense, the tradition of the great black swing bands of the '30s and '40s: bands such as Chick Webb's (Francis' original idol on the drums), and Teddy Hill's, and Lucky Millinder's, and Willie Bryant's, and of course Al Cooper's original Savoy Sultans, from which the band takes its name. The senior members of Francis' band, alto saxist Howard Johnson and guitarist John Smith, were both members of Teddy Hill's band fully 50 years ago, and were active throughout the big band era. Johnson ultimately wound up in Dizzy Gillespie's big band, Smith in Cab Calloway's. Pianist Sammy Benskin played with the original Savoy Sultans. Francis himself played briefly in the big bands of Roy Eldridge and Willie Bryant, and for much longer periods in the big bands of Lucky Millinder and Cab Calloway.

"You look. There are no black bands around anymore," Francis says with regret. "The only one that's in existence now is Count Basie's Band, and that's not going to last but so long. And there's Mercer Ellington, but he doesn't play his father's music the way his father did," Francis says.

In the '30s and '40s, it was big band swing drumming all the way for Francis. In '40s jam sessions he witnessed the development of bebop. But the new approach to jazz was not for him. He didn't change his style of drumming; he didn't move with the current towards what became known as modern jazz.

When the big band era faded, Francis moved into rhythm-and-blues, rock 'n' roll, and pop music recording sessions. He became known, to his surprise, as *the* rock 'n' roll drummer. He was a rock 'n' roll pioneer, copied by other drummers. The music didn't always thrill him, but it certainly paid the bills. Between 1953 and 1963, he is certain he was on more hit records than any other drummer.

Eventually, however, he came full circle, back to the music of his youth, to the big band swing that he liked best.

The band Francis leads today came into existence almost as a fluke. In 1975, he put together a New York jazz repertory concert re-creating the swing-era music of both Lucky Millinder and of Al Cooper's Savoy Sultans. He used 14 musicians—as Millinder had—for the Millinder

[1] "Gettin' in the Groove" won the Grand Prix du Disque from the Hot Club of France for 1979 and placed third in England's *Jazz Journal's* critics' poll—behind "two dead guys," as Francis puts it: Louis Armstrong and Sidney Bechet.

charts, nine musicians—as Cooper had—for the Savoy Sultan charts. Francis was certainly familiar with the music of both bands. He had powered Millinder's big band from 1940-46, and during those years the band had often played opposite the Savoy Sultans at the Savoy Ballroom. The Sultans were the house band at Harlem's famed ballroom; they successfully challenged many bigger, better-known bands that played opposite them over the years. The concert was originally sup-

Panama Francis. (Photo by Nancy Miller Elliott)

posed to be a one-time-only event, but a couple of French impresarios proposed that Francis bring his new "Savoy Sultans" to Europe. In 1979, Francis' group played in Europe for three weeks, and recorded its first album for the French record label, "Black and Blue." The musicians played eight original Savoy Sultan arrangements; the rest of the time they played head arrangements of Swing Era numbers. Francis returned to the U.S. and found sufficient demand for him to keep the band going.

At the Rainbow Room, particularly earlier in the evening, when most people in the room are dining, the band must exercise a certain restraint. It offers superior dance music. But if you want to really see what the band can do, you'd best try to catch it in a concert or dance away from its base.

You'll hear occasional new jazz originals, such as "Funky Willie" (co-authored by Panama Francis and Fred Norman, who has arranged most of the current material in the band's book) and "Stolen Sweets" by Wild Bill Davis. You'll hear plenty of big band-era favorites; the nine musicians play like a big band, not like an informal jazz combo, in which one soloist is heard after another. The three saxes and two trumpets can create call-and-response patterns like the reed and brass sections of a larger band, or create surprisingly full ensemble backgrounds for soloists. Occasionally, Francis will play an original arrangement of Al Cooper's Savoy Sultans, or of Chick Webb's big band (adapted to Francis' smaller instrumentation). He likes honoring Webb's memory in this way—no one else plays those Webb arrangements today. But such charts are used sparingly. The emphasis is *not* on recreating anyone else's music. The band plays mostly its own charts. It has its own identity, one that is firmly grounded in swing era tradition. Francis' resonant, steady drumming gives the swing era numbers an authenticity that is lacking when most bands today try to play them.

At a Jersey Jazz Society concert, Francis sets the tempo with a call: "One, two—one, two, three, four." And the band is off. The saxes are making circular figures, punctuated by brief trumpet statements. The foundation is Francis' solid four-beats-to-the-bar on the bass drum. Vocalist Julia Steele, a full-bodied and full-voiced woman, swings into "I Cried for You," her voice rising above the saxes, pulling back and forth on phrases the way a jazz instrumentalist would. "I cried, I cried I damn near died for you," she calls out, while the band riffs in the background. Trumpeter Spanky Davis, the baby of the band and, incidentally, its only white member, stands for a crackling solo, and Francis provides great, strong drum accents under Davis' statement. The whole band is rocking now, sending out pulses of energy, and the audience is caught up in the rhythm. It's so rare that you hear this kind of simple, strong swing anymore. Big band jazz became more complex in the mid-'40s. The changes were generally seen as advancements. Maybe so; but this earlier, simpler approach to the music packs an emotional punch contemporary orchestrated jazz often lacks.

Francis quiets things down with an instrumental version of "I'll Get By," the saxes hovering in close harmony. He offers "Let's Get Together" from the old Chick Webb book (which prompts an older man sitting near me to recall nights spent dancing to Webb at the Savoy). And then a seven minute stretching-out on "Sentimental Journey," the band propelled along by an irresistible, march-type of rhythm Francis sets down.

Francis appears tremendously happy sparking his band along. It's a good band. He knows it. The audience knows it. He only wishes that the band could be working steadily, year-round. He tells you later, quietly, "There's no band business anymore." And laying off between bookings doesn't sit well with him. Panama Francis is not the type who's happy just "relaxing." He was practically born to be a big band drummer.

Panama Francis and the Savoy Sultans. Spanky Davis solos on trumpet. (Chip Deffaa collection)

"I've been into music all my life," Francis tells you. "I never wanted to be no ball-player or lawyer or nothing, I wanted to play music. And that's what I did; I lived and breathed music. It's my life. When I was growing up, I never played ball because I was afraid of hurting my hands." Francis has been a professional musician for some 55 years, since shortly before his 13th birthday.

David "Panama" Francis was born in Miami, Florida, on December 21, 1918. He cannot remember a time when he was not interested in music. All kinds of music.

As a boy, he spent countless hours listening to his parents' Victrola. "I can remember listening to my first recording, I guess I was about four years old. My father was a record collector. He was a plain laborer, but he just loved music. Daddy used to go out and buy records; he didn't buy nothing else. And the first record I heard was a one-sided Victor record by Ferde Grofe. And the woman's name was Miss Virginia, that's all that was on the record, Miss Virginia. This record was 'Running Wild'—[he sings softly:] 'I'm running wild. . .' I was crazy about that record.

"Oh, I used to listen to Eddie Cantor and Gene Austin. And Jolson. And all of the blues records. Bessie Smith, Mamie Smith, Ethel Waters. Ethel Waters made a recording of 'Make Me a Pallet on the Floor.' And I used to love that record, because it opens up with a monologue, and she's talking to this man who is her pimp, her old man. And she's doing real bad, and she knocks on the door. She says, 'It's me, Daddy.' And he says, 'Get away from that door.' And she says, 'Daddy, I been out in the front yard eatin' that short grass.' And he says, 'Well go to the back yard, where it's longer.' And she says, 'I knew you when you was sick and you couldn't eat. Will you listen to what I have to say?' And then she sings the patter of the song, 'Make me a Pallet on the Floor.' I used to *love* that record. Play it all the time. I also liked, 'You Been a Good Old Wagon Daddy, But You Done Broke Down,' by Bessie Smith. I used to play *that* all the time.

"I had records of Sousa, Sousa marches, and used to listen to them—'Stars and Stripes Forever.' The only music that I didn't pay any attention to was classical music. I never was into that bag until I got old. But as far as the marching bands, and the popular music of the day and everything, I was into that.

"And I've been hooked on Louis Armstrong since I heard his record of 'Memories of You.' I know all the Louis Armstrong records. . . . But I had a fire in my apartment, where I lost over 2500 78s. I had every—you name it. I had my father's records, plus the ones that I bought after I became grown.

"I always loved to listen to music. That's why I can play all the different styles. I can play Dixieland, I can press-roll and everything. Because I came up listening to these things. I've never limited myself to just one bag.

"My mother told me that when I was a little boy, like two, three years old, she said, after I finished eating, I used to start to beating a rhythm of some kind on the table with my spoon. And whenever they asked me what I wanted Santy Claus to bring me, after I learned to talk, why I always told them I wanted a 'dum.' Instead of saying 'drum,' I used to say 'dum.'" Francis got his first drum when he was perhaps four years old.

"By the time I was eight years old — although I couldn't read music, I had a good ear — I was the number one drummer in the drum and bugle corps that I belonged to. All the other kids were like 11 and 12.

"Then at the age of 10, I started playing with the marching bands around Miami. I used to play for all of the lodges. When the Masons and the Oddfellows would have their parade, I was in the marching band. And all of the churches in Miami had bands. Miami was a very, very musical city. A lot of action in Miami. Miami was the playground of the United States. That was before Las Vegas and all this got on the map. Everybody came to Miami during the winter season; *everybody* was there. There wasn't a show or band that never played Miami.

"So I was in the St. Agnes Church Marching Band band from the age of 10. I was the only youngster in the band. All the rest of the men in there were like old enough to be my father and grandfather.

"Then I played my first gig, my first dance gig, July 4th, 1931. This was a combo consisting of banjo, tuba, piano, and a trumpet, and I was on the drums. I was going on 13. The others were adults." Francis' parents were followers of the black leader Marcus Garvey, so Francis' first job was at a dance for members of Garvey's organization.

"I played in combos from when I was 13 until I was 14, and then a fellow by the name of George McCaskell had a big band. I think George was like 21. But the rest of the guys was like 17, 18 years of age. And I was 14, the baby of the band, when I joined them. We played around Miami. And then we started traveling, too. When school closed for the summer, we went on the road. We played all over Florida, Georgia, Alabama, Mississippi. We went as far north as North Carolina, and as far west as Mississippi. We were saving money for a band bus. But we caught George McCaskell with his finger in the pile, and we kicked him out of the band and we made George Kelly (the tenor sax player) the bandleader. George Kelly was my roommate on the road when I was 14." (Kelly eventually went on to play with Al Cooper's Savoy Sultans in the '40s, and with Panama Francis' Savoy Sultans from 1979-83.) Francis drummed in that big band, led by McCaskell and then Kelly, for six years.

Francis also made money gigging, from time to time, with a saxophone player, Lee Guster Allen, known as "Sonny Boy." "During those days there were a lot of farms, and they had a lot of migrant workers, and on Saturday night, we used to play for them. The places we played, they called 'em juke joints; they were the kind of places where the very low class of blacks (as we considered them) went to. Low class, 'cause they were the whiskey drinkers, fighting. They were shooting and cutting, and all that; I saw all that kind of stuff when I was like 14 years old. They'd call 'em a juke joint. The guys'd get out on the floor and grind.

"I didn't have a teenage childhood. That was one section of my life that I missed, and I used to envy my kids when they became teenagers because of the things that they were enjoying and doing—I never got a chance to do that; I was always 'grown.'"

Black bands, such as those led by Don Redman, Fletcher Henderson, Claude Hopkins, and Chick Webb, were swinging strongly in the early '30s. The white bands lagged behind. As far as Francis was concerned, the only white band that could rival the black bands on hot numbers in the early '30s was the Casa Loma Band. He also felt George Olsen had a fine early band. But the black bands pretty much had the lock on swing. They were anticipating by several years the style of playing that Benny Goodman and other white bandleaders would popularize later in the decade.

"My influence on the drum was Chick Webb," Francis says. "His band used to come on the radio, every afternoon around three o'clock, from the Savoy Ballroom. And when I heard him, I went, 'wow!'

"And I liked Sid Catlett. Sid Catlett was very nice man. I remember he came to Miami with Don Redman's Band around 1935. And he spent his whole intermission with me. I'll never forget that. I was so honored, man. I just went up to him and told him that I was playing the drums, and I liked the way he played, and I asked him questions."

In 1938, Francis briefly joined Charlie Brantley and his Florida Collegians in Tampa. He played with them from May through July. But work had slowed up in Florida. Francis had to find a way out.

"My mother and father had separated when I was 12, and my father had gone to New York. I got the bright idea to write him, about him sending for me to come to New York. And I *lied* to him, and told him that the people around here were saying how great I was, that I should be in New York, which was the Mecca of show business. The next week, my father sent me a bus ticket. I rode in the back of the bus from Florida to New York. It took two days and two nights," he recalls.

Francis went out jamming every night at the uptown clubs where so many musicians congregated. "About the fifth night, I was jammin' at a place called Massapequa, and Tab Smith heard me. He said, 'Well I got a job over in Brooklyn, at the Rosebud. Would you like to join me?' 'Yeah.' Five days after I was in New York, I was working with Tab Smith!

"This was at a nightclub. And they had a couple of singers that used to go around to the tables and sing to the tables. That was the first time I saw this act of a female picking up a dollar with her vagina. Which is a trick thing. They don't really pick it up with—they pick it up with their thighs, you know, the thighs, but it's so close, it looks like that. And they used to go to tables and be singing, and the gangsters and all them type of people used to put the money on the edge of the table and like that, and watch them pick it up with their vagina. Almost fell off the drums there when I saw that!" He laughs at the recollection.

* * *

"One night, the next year [1939], I was out jamming. A man came into the jam session where I was playing, and he heard me, and he said, 'Would you like to play with my band?' I said, 'What's the name of your band?' And he says, 'I'm Roy Eldridge.' I almost dropped on the floor! I didn't realize who I was talking to. Roy was at his zenith then. I told him, 'Yeah.' He says, 'We're playing at the Arcadia Ballroom and rehearsal's Tuesday at one o'clock.' So I was there, sitting on the bandstand. I had on a panama hat. Well, unbeknownst to me, Joe Glaser, who was Roy's manager, had hired Big Sid Catlett to join the band. I don't know what happened between Roy and Sid Catlett. When Joe Glaser walked in to the rehearsal, he looked up, he asked Roy, 'Where's Big Sid?' And Roy says, 'I don't know.' And Joe Glaser said, 'Who's the drummer up there?' And I guess Roy didn't remember my name, but I still had on my panama hat. He says, 'Oh, that's Panama.' And I was too scared to tell the fellows in the band that that wasn't my name. And they started calling me Panama. That's how I got named 'Panama.' My real name is David.

"Roy had 10 pieces. The Arcadia Ballroom, at 54th and Broadway, was almost like a dancing school. We used to have to play 15 minutes of Viennese waltzes, 15 minutes tango, 15 minutes of fox trots, and that's how I learned to play the different rhythms for dancing. Roseland Ballroom was much more popular but the Arcadia was much more sophisticated."

Francis made his first recordings with Eldridge's band. At his very first recording session, in 1939, Francis says, they cut sides of "High Society" and "Muskrat Ramble."

In January of 1940, Francis moved on to Lucky Millinder and his Orchestra, opening with the band at the Savoy, the huge ballroom which stood on Lenox Avenue between 140th and 141st Streets. The band played frequently at the Savoy in the six years Francis stayed with it.

"You see, how I know about the Savoy Sultans is because we were both working at the Savoy at the same time. They were on a different bandstand. The Savoy always had two bands. The Savoy Sultans were organized by a fellow from my home town, Miami: Al Cooper. His younger brother, Grachan Moncur, the Savoy Sultans' bass player, and I had played in the same band back in Florida that George Kelly was the leader of."

Francis always enjoyed watching the dancers at the Savoy. Some of the Lindy Hoppers were fantastic. Even to this day, Francis says, he prefers playing for dancers to playing for seated concert-watchers—

Lucky Millinder and his Orchestra, Savoy Ballroom, New York, 1941. Left to right: Ernest Purce, baritone sax; George Duvivier, bass; Ted Barnett, alto sax; George James, alto sax; Panama Francis, drums; Stafford Simon, tenor sax; Freddy Webster, trumpet; Nelson Bryant, trumpet; Trevor Bacon, guitar, vocals; Archie Johnson, trumpet; George Stevenson, trombone; Joe Britton, trombone; Don Coles, trombone; Lucky Millinder, leader, vocals. Not visible in picture: Bill Doggett, piano. (Frank Driggs collection)

although he adds he rarely sees especially good dancers anymore.

Often the band played in theaters. "When they used to have the big black shows all over, I used to love to play for tap dancers like Bunny Briggs and Bill Bailey (Pearl Bailey's brother) and Red and Curly, Walter Green and all these guys, Buck and Bubbles, the tap dancers," he recalls.

"I spent six years with Lucky. I made all of his recordings from 1940 to 1946. He had many a hit record. They were mostly vocals. 'Sweet Slumber,' 'When the Lights Go On Again (All Over the World),' 'Big Fat Mama,' 'Shout, Sister, Shout,' with Sister Tharpe, 'Rock Daniel' with Sister Tharpe. Those were some of the hits that I was on."

Francis made some film shorts with Millinder's band, too. And, he recalls, he was also filmed to provide the opening image—"just like the lion is with MGM, that's the way I was"—for a series of band shorts made to be used in a kind of jukebox with film, which never really caught on. "They called it the Panorama machine. You used to put a dime in it, and first you'd see this guy beating on the drum—that was me—and then it was a fade-out. And then the feature attraction came on. They made things with Fats Waller and Duke Ellington, Don Redman, and all of the performers, black and white. They'd have these machines in the bars. It was backed by President Roosevelt's oldest son, James Roosevelt; he had a share. But I guess people wasn't ready for it."

* * *

There were plenty of places to jam in those days. "The union stopped jamming, although I think it's the worst thing they could have done, for they should have had a place or a hall of some kind, where the younger musicians could go and jam, and older guys probably would be there and help them. They don't have that anymore, which is a shame, because they've taken the jazz and put it in the schools, and nine out of ten people that are teaching the jazz are classical musicians," Francis says.

At uptown clubs such as the Massapequa, Jock's, and the Rhythm Club, musicians could gather to jam. If they were between jobs, they could show up early. Others would arrive after they finished their paying jobs for the night. Francis jammed with many of the best who were working out new ideas in music, from guitarist Charlie Christian to bass player Jimmy Blanton.

The club that became known as *the* top place for jamming in the early '40s was Minton's Playhouse. "See, Minton's was run by an ex-bandleader, Teddy Hill. And Teddy Hill was the kind of bandleader that all the fellows liked. He was like one of the boys. He never let you know that he was the bandleader.

"Minton's was not the only place that we used to jam. But Minton's was where all of the, like, the top-notch guys used to go to jam. That's why it got such a reputation. Because Charlie Christian used to go in to jam, Roy Eldridge. Carmen McRae was the intermission piano player at Minton's at one time. And Billie Holiday used to come there. And Ella. Everybody who was anybody. And it was because of Teddy Hill for one reason. And then Dizzy [Gillespie] and them came there. Dizzy had played in Teddy's band."

Francis witnessed the evolution of a new form of jazz, which would become known as bebop. At jam sessions at Minton's, a crew of younger musicians were creating the new sound. Dizzy Gillespie (a former member of Teddy Hill's band), Charlie Parker, Kenny Clarke and others were at the center of the activity. Francis was not impressed. He still believes bebop gained its vogue due largely to the promotion of it by certain influential, intellectual jazz critics.

"I mean, a lot of the new styles and the new names and things really were cop-outs," Francis declares. "See, like the whole bebop era. The whole bebop crew were rejects. Big bands were very popular then. These guys were rejects from the big bands. Well, you could listen at the music, you could tell just what kind of mentality went on with these guys. And they were all guys that bandleaders wouldn't have in their bands, because they were bad actors. Personally. And they had strange ideas, too, about music. People don't know this.

"The bebop era was really born from the intellectuals. When the bebop era came along, it was something that they could analyze. Something that they could feel that they were part of. And they pushed it. They were in a position. They could write the books, they knew how to use words, and that's how they got it off the ground. 'Cause bebop is—oh, jeez, listen to the music—it'll tell you, something strange about it.

"They made [Thelonious] Monk a—like he was a genius or something like that. I was shocked when I heard people talking about Monk—Monk was the world's worst piano player! He couldn't even sit in a jam session. He did everything wrong. You know, and he couldn't read. He came in a band that I was in, with Lucky Millinder's Band, and he lasted *one set*. Now if you're talking about Bud Powell, now Bud Powell was a musician. But Monk wasn't. But the intellectuals made him a genius.

"Musician's styles are developed from shortcomings. Take Charlie Parker for instance. The reason why he played like he did is because he really didn't have a good sound on the horn. His sound wasn't considered a good sound. He didn't have that big sound like a Benny Carter or a Johnny Hodges or those type of people. So he had to cover up by playing fast. You've never heard him hold a note out. He was always moving.

"And that was to cover up for that sound that he had. *He* even talked about it himself. One time, he and I were at the bar across the street from the Metropole. He says, 'I don't mind them copying my style, but I sure wish they could find another sound on their horns, instead of copying my sound.' Because he wasn't too happy with it.

"But that's how styles are born. Like another guy can just take a few notes and make it sound like something. Another fellow has to move, has to have a lot of technique. So when Charlie Parker and Dizzy Gillespie came on the scene—both of those guys had almost the same problem. The trumpet players that Dizzy had to work with used to give him hell because he couldn't play with a vibrato. He played with a straight tone. He got the technique that would cover up for him not being able to have a pretty vibrato on the horn. One of the things that made Charlie Parker so outstanding, was that the white musicians had been struggling for years to try to find a style that they could emulate. They had had problems. So few of them were able to emulate the black musicians, because the black musicians were playing more from feeling, instead of technique." Parker's manner of playing, Francis believes, was easier for white musicians to copy.

"Dizzy and I played in Lucky Millinder's Band together. That was when Dizzy was finally finding himself. He used to play just like Roy Eldridge. He used to sound just like Roy, note-for-note. Because Roy was fast. And then he finally found his style that he developed," Francis recalls. "That riff of his, 'Salt Peanuts'—da-dada-dada-duh—that was a riff that he made up on the blues. In fact, we got a record, a Lucky Millinder record called 'Little John Special,' and that's the riff behind the saxophone players.

"Dizzy is one of the luckiest men in the world. Every trumpet player that would have been competition for Dizzy, something happened to him. Joe Guy died from drugs. Fats Navarro died from drugs. Clifford Brown got killed in an accident. You go down the list. Dizzy's the luckiest man in the world.

"But all of those [bebop] guys were really rejects that big band leaders didn't even want to see them in their bands. Because Dizzy was a character. Kenny Clarke was a character. He felt that the drum was not supposed to just sit and play a supporting role. He felt that the drums should be out front, just like everybody else. That's when he started dropping bombs. They called it dropping bombs. And he'd play 'Ka-CHUNG-a—BOOM!' The bandleaders didn't want him in their bands, because of the style of drumming that he played."

As bebop caught on, almost all drummers shifted to the style developed by Kenny Clarke, Max Roach and others, in which time is kept on the ride cymbal rather than on the bass drum, and the bass drum is used only for occasional heavy accents—Clarke's so-called bombs. Today, it has become the norm, both in small-group and big band jazz. Clarke said that the style originated this way: In 1937, he was playing in Teddy Hill's Band at the Savoy. Hitting four-beats-to-every-bar on the bass drum proved too much for him, especially on the mile-a-minute flagwavers. His right foot, which worked the bass drum, gave out. So he shifted to only occasionally hitting the drum for accents. In the next few years, he honed and developed what became known as bebop drumming.

Francis' band today rides on the sort of solid foundation you rarely hear anymore. Francis formed his style well before the advent of bebop and modern jazz. His model was Chick Webb, and—his numerous rock 'n' roll records of the '50s and early '60s not withstanding—he remains one of the great exponents of classic swing drumming.

"These bands, you hear 'em today, and it's all top and no bottom," Francis complains. "That's because there's no bass drum. Just a bass fiddle. And no bass fiddle has been able to give a jazz band bottom, like a bass drum can do.

"See, 'cause I'm one of the few drummers that's left—me and Freddie Moore, I guess—one of the few drummers that's left, that still plays time with our bass drum. I never changed. It's not easy to play a bass drum. That's one of the reasons why, when Max Roach and Kenny Clarke and those came along, dropping bombs and things, that was an escape. Because they couldn't play time on the bass drum," Francis says.

"It's *hard* to play time on the bass drum, because you have to have control and you have to have that stamina. Playing time is an art within itself. That takes years and years of learning how to control that bass drum—you should be able to *feel* it more than you hear it—to play four beats to a bar, or two beats to a bar, on a bass drum. And that's the reason why so many drummers will sit up and say, 'Well, you don't have to play time on the bass drum; you use the bass drum to accent.' That's a cop-out. Because he *can't* play time.

"Max Roach couldn't play a bass drum. That's why, as far as I know, I think Max Roach has only played in one big band, Benny Carter's. He never played in no big bands. He had great hands, because he was one of the young black drummers that was schooled. (When I was coming up, most drummers weren't schooled.) He knew rudiments, and so, what he couldn't do with his foot, he did with his hands—cymbals and things. He found a way out. You know, styles are developed from shortcomings."

* * *

In 1946, Francis joined Willie Bryant's band. Francis stayed six months, until he got an invitation from Cab Calloway to join his band. Calloway was making a motion picture, *The Hi De Ho Man*. Francis's very first day with the band was spent before the cameras. As soon as they finished making the movie, the band went into the recording studios to record "The Hi De Ho Man (That's Me)," which became one of Calloway's signature numbers. Other recordings he made with the band that year included "The Calloway Boogie," "Two Blocks Down, Turn to the Left," and "Everybody Eats When They Come to My House."

By now, bebop had reached full flower, but Calloway would have none of it. His band played the same straightforward swing it always had, which suited Francis just fine. In the early '40s, Calloway had reportedly chastised Dizzy Gillespie for trying to introduce bebop ideas into his band, with the line: "I don't want you playing that Chinese music in my band."

The emphasis, of course, was always on Calloway's singing. Calloway himself was so dynamic a personality that it is sometimes forgotten

Cab Calloway. (Chip Deffaa collection)

what a great band he had. Among the 17 musicians in his band in 1947, for example, were such top players as Jonah Jones, trumpet; Keg Johnson and Quentin "Butter" Jackson, trombones; Hilton Jefferson and Sam "the Man" Taylor, saxes; and Milt Hinton, bass.

But on any given night, Francis says, the band would play only a couple of the instrumentals in their book. "I don't know how he did it, but that man [Calloway] could sing for three and a half hours. Mostly we were backing his vocals. We had a takeoff on Lionel Hampton's 'Flying Home,' and we had all the things Chu Berry used to do when he was in the band. But we'd only do two instrumentals a night.

"I was featured, too—but Cab never featured me in New York; he always featured me in the boondocks. We'd play the Strand Theater and he would feature Jonah Jones. But then when we got outside of

The Cab Calloway Band on tour in Panama, circa 1949. Jonah Jones, trumpet, is fourth from left; Milt Hinton, bass, is fifth from left; Calloway is fifth from right; and Panama Francis is second from right. (Frank Driggs collection)

New York, I was featured with the band, doing a drum solo with a tune called, 'Coasting with Panama.' It was originally made for Cozy Cole—'Coasting with Cozy'—they just changed the title.

"Cab was the greatest bandleader I ever worked for. I must say that I never lived liked that. I always said that if I ever had a band, I hoped I'd get in a position to run it like he ran it.

"We had our own pullman and baggage car. First time I ever rode a pullman in my life was with Cab Calloway's Band—1947. And they arranged to travel right into the town, and they pulled us along the side and we'd go play the dance or play the theater. We'd get back on our pullman. We had seven changes of uniforms, which we never bought or even had them cleaned. He paid for *all* of that. Every show we had on a different uniform. And in Cab's band, if you didn't have your shoes shined, it cost you $25. That's the only things he didn't furnish. He furnished our socks, our shirts, ties, and suits that we wore. Two sets of drums for me.

"We always knew where we would be playing on New Year's Eve with Cab. On New Year's Eve, we always opened the Sherman Hotel in Chicago. And I may be wrong, but I *think* that Cab Calloway was about the only bandleader that gave his men a paid vacation. We got the month of August off with pay. And we got the last two weeks in December off with pay, and our Christmas presents. His birthday was on Christmas Day.

"We never played for many blacks. Most of our work was for whites, in the theaters. Mostly theaters. I think out of the whole six years I was with the band, I think we played two black jobs. All the rest of the times was for whites, and in the theaters. I think he appealed more to the white audience than he did to the blacks. He was like, accepted, because of 'Minnie the Moocher,' and he used to sound like a Jewish cantor, singing the hi-de-hos, and on the end of the thing, he'd sound like a Jewish cantor. He was very well liked by the Jewish people. They still do, they're still crazy about him. But the hi-de-ho thing was mostly. . . white audiences. They liked him."

In 1948, the big band business collapsed. A recording strike that year contributed to the demise. Many bands simply folded. In the spring of '48, Calloway announced he was cutting down to seven men. He hated giving up the full-sized band. But when the seven included such players as Jonah Jones, Sam "the Man" Taylor, Milt Hinton, and Panama Francis, the music was still bound to be first-rate. Francis recalls touring the Caribbean Islands with Calloway's septet around 1951. And they made several film shorts, with Calloway singing "St. James Infirmary," "Minnie the Moocher," and "I Can't Give You Anything But Love."

Cab Calloway's Cab Jivers, Strand Theatre, New York, circa 1948. Left to right: Dave Rivera, piano; Milt Hinton, bass; Jonah Jones, trumpet; Panama Francis, drums; unidentified musician; Lucky Thompson, tenor sax. (Frank Driggs collection)

Ultimately however, Calloway realized the marketplace would no longer support his touring, even with a seven-piece band. He took bookings with a trio. He finally concluded that his future would be as a "single." When an offer came in mid-1952 for him to go into a Broadway revival of *Porgy and Bess*, he took it. Francis remembers one final big band date with Calloway in '52, with a full band re-assembled for the occasion. Then the Calloway band was no more.[2]

It was hard on many musicians when the big band era ended. Some had nowhere to go. Many had assumed there'd always be big bands. But big band jobs were few and far between.

Some former Calloway sidemen, such as Jonah Jones and bass player Milt Hinton, moved easily into small-group jazz work.

When Calloway went into *Porgy and Bess*, record producer Teddy Reig got Francis into Birdland, where he worked for a stretch with Slim Gaillard, and also did some gigs with Charlie Parker. And then, more importantly, Reig got Francis into some rhythm-and-blues recording sessions. Former Calloway Band sideman Sam "the Man" Taylor joined him on many of the dates.

Francis didn't realize it, but he was embarking upon a whole new career. He was getting into rock 'n' roll on the ground floor.

* * *

"There was a little guy, Leroy Kirkland, who was writing all of the rock 'n roll things, and he was doing some things with Teddy Reig," Francis recalls. "I knew how to play gospel, gospel rhythm. And the average drummer was not involved in anything like that. I knew the church rhythm. And I knew how to play the triplets, with the backbeat.

"Leroy Kirkland and Jesse Stone are really the fathers of the rock and roll scene. They were the ones that started writing out the triplets and bass. Jesse Stone was a songwriter and an arranger, and so was Leroy Kirkland. They were both black; all of the musicians, at the start of it, were black."

Who would Francis credit as being some of the important people in the beginning of rock 'n roll? "Well, like Ruth Brown, La Vern Baker, the Platters, Clyde McPhatter, Chuck Willis. These are all the beginning. But they were actually rhythm-and-blues singers, gospel singers, that's what they were. Jesse Stone and Leroy Kirkland were writing the music in the background, and the musicians were like Mickey Baker (guitar), and Al Williams at first and then Ernie Hayes (piano), Lloyd

[2] On a couple of occasions in the 1980s, Francis reunited with his former boss as the Savoy Sultans backed Calloway in concert. And in 1988, Francis was one of a half dozen former sidemen who returned to pay tribute to Calloway at his 80th birthday celebrations in Carnegie Hall.

Trotman (bass), Sam 'the Man' Taylor (tenor sax), and I was the drummer. And that was it. Sometimes we used Dave McRae on baritone sax. We backed up lots of different singers. We were the ones that were doing all of the dates. We were the originals. We were the backbone of all of those records made at the time.

"Rock 'n' roll was nothing but rhythm-and-blues. There were no white artists at first; they were all black. It was not until the white kids started listening to it, and it started getting popular, that the Frankie Avalons and the Connie Francises and the Fabians appeared. And when they brought Elvis Presley, that was *it*. And Elvis Presley . . . Elvis Presley was nothing but a carbon copy of Otis Blackwell.

"But like they do in America, especially in the arts, as soon as a white learns what the black is doing that is popular, they shove the black aside. And they bring the white out front and give him all the publicity."

Francis recalls, for example, how in the early days La Vern Baker, who was black, would make a recording and Georgia Gibbs, who was white, would immediately make the copy—and walk away with the big bucks. Major record companies often used white artists to "cover" records first released by black artists on smaller labels when those records began enjoying any degree of popularity.

"The guy that wrote all of Elvis' first big hits, was a black guy, Otis Blackwell," Francis says. Francis played on demos of songs Blackwell wrote. The demo recordings were made in New York, then shipped to Presley in Tennessee.

Francis places on the turntable the original 78 r.p.m. demo recording of "Don't be Cruel," one of Presley's biggest early hits. Blackwell is singing the song he wrote.

"Well, now you listen to this, and see if there's any difference in the two voices. See how close they are." He plays the Blackwell demo, then Presley's RCA Victor recording of the number, then the demo again. Presley appears to have copied just the way Blackwell sang it on the demo: the emphasis, the phrasing, the feeling. Moreover, Blackwell's voice is in the same range. Their timbres are similar.

"It's amazing, isn't it. I just want you to hear. It's the demo that we made. . . . Elvis sang it in the same style, same exactly like Otis. That's why Otis Blackwell is suing the estate now."

* * *

Francis found himself, to his surprise, becoming *the* drummer in the early years of rock 'n' roll. Between 1953 and 1963, he recorded with an astonishing array of artists. He figures he was easily on more hit recordings in those years than any other drummer. But the countless rock 'n' roll and pop sides he recorded didn't always thrill him. He would have rather been playing big band swing.

"I used to come home and my wife would ask, 'Well, what did you record today?' And I'd say, 'I don't know.' And I didn't—because it was just a job. But I recorded with La Vern Baker, the Coasters, Eddie Cooley. I recorded with the Four Seasons. 'Big Girls Don't Cry' and all those things—that's me. I recorded with Wayne Newton, James Brown, the Kirby Stone Four, Mitch Miller, Bobby Darin—I did his big record, 'Splish Splash'—Neil Sedaka, Connie Francis, Frankie Avalon, Fabian, Della Reese, Paul Anka, Perez Prado, Roy Hamilton, Ray Charles, Mickey and Sylvia, the Platters, Jackie Wilson, Tony Bennett, Brook Benton, Dinah Washington, Buddy Holly, Sarah Vaughan, the Tokens, Johnny Mathis, Bobby Freeman, Joe Turner, Bobby Lewis, Little Willie Jones, Sam 'the Man' Taylor, the Flamingoes. That's just some of them.

"From 1953 to 1963, I was like the number one drummer. If a date was on a Tuesday and I couldn't make it, if I could make it Thursday, that's when they set the date up, for Thursday. I was doing like three and four record dates, sometimes five record dates a day."

The earliest rock 'n' roll had a certain musical integrity which much of the commercially successful stuff produced later in the '50s lacked. Francis was particular about getting the time right, about playing with feeling. And he had a great deal of respect for his friend Sam "the Man" Taylor, whose saxophone was an important voice in early rock 'n' roll. Taylor, and fellow saxophonist King Curtis, could create solos worth listening to. It was hard for other musicians to imitate their work.

"So then that's when the saxophone players started honking," Francis says. "They didn't play like Sam 'the Man' Taylor or King Curtis; they started honking and playing all of the funny notes that didn't even belong in the song. Because the white saxophone players couldn't play the blues. And that's when they started telling 'em about honking on the horn. Like Lubinsky, from Savoy Records, used to tell the saxophone player, 'Play crazy.' He'd be sitting up there, and he would tell 'em to play crazy, and make all kinds of funny sounds and things on the saxophone. Because the white saxophone players could not play the blues. I mean with the *feeling*. Because to play the blues, you have to feel it."

The saxophone pretty much vanished from rock 'n' roll, as electric guitars took over. Francis believes the saxes vanished because of the inability of most white sax players to play blues well. It was easier to play the electric guitar.

"Musicians found out that they could escape with the guitar—take the guitar in and hold one note—pling, pling, pling, pling, pling—and you didn't have to really swing with the guitar, like Mickey Baker used to do. So that's how the solo guitar came into its own."

Even the phrase "rock 'n' roll," popularized by Alan Freed, was taken from a black disc jockey, Al Benson, according to Francis.

"Al Benson had a radio show in Chicago, and he was very popular; he played rhythm-and-blues. But when he opened the show, he used to say [now Francis intones deeply, in the cadence of a black preacher]: 'And now, ladies and gentlemen, we gonna rock and we gonna roll this afternoon. . . so-and-so-and-so-and-so.' And so Alan Freed picked it up in Cleveland, and beating on the telephone book, along with the record that was playing, and he says [Francis intones the phrase in a faster, lighter, voice]: 'Yeah, we gonna rock and we gonna roll—' and *that's* how the label came about. That's how the records got labeled rock 'n' roll'—but it was rhythm-and-blues records that were being played, by black artists.

"They crucified Alan Freed when the payola investigation came about. *Everybody* was getting payola. I overheard producers and record owners saying, 'Well we have to give so-and-so a piece of this tune, so he'll play it on his radio show. Or, we'll put it in his publishing firm.' Alan Freed *was* taking payola—but these other people was taking payola too. But they crucified him, because he had a TV show, and a radio show.

"You know, the sponsors of his TV show wanted him to make the show with three white artists and two black artists. And Alan Freed just told them, 'No, I mean this is these people's music. If it's going to be anything, it'll be three blacks and two whites.'"

Francis, who played drums on that short-lived pioneering rock 'n' roll show, recalls well why the show came to an abrupt end. "On one of the shows, Frankie Lymon [a black singer] danced with Connie Francis [who is white] on the finale, and they took the show off the air right after that. Although we got paid for the 13 weeks, the show I think lasted something like two or three weeks. Because of the interracial dancing, they scuttled the show."

* * *

Francis was in demand for rock 'n' roll studio work. But there was a downside to that success. "I got labeled 'the rock 'n' roll drummer.' So I never got a chance to play any big band jazz like I'm doing now. Ever since I was in my teens, I had played in big bands. All of a sudden I woke up, and I was a 'rock 'n' roll drummer.' I was hurt and I was frustrated. It was an injustice to me because I could also play the big band drumming—because what was I doing in Lucky Millinder's Band? What was I doing in Cab Calloway's Band, that all of a sudden I couldn't play big band jazz anymore? That all I was called for was rock 'n' roll?

"On the weekends, I was at the Central Plaza with Conrad Janis, playing Dixieland. At least I was close to playing like a big band. You know, I was able to swing, instead of playing just triplets and backbeat," Francis says.

He recalls other musicians often introducing him as "Panama Francis, the rock 'n' roll drummer." The phrase seemed demeaning to him. He was an all-around drummer. And so many jazz musicians held rock 'n' roll in contempt. Francis adds that plenty of drummers who initially looked down on rock 'n' roll moved in as soon as they realized there was good money to be made in rock recording sessions.

Francis found some white record producers and contractors who seemed to prefer throwing work to white musicians. They hired him initially because he seemed to be about the only one that could get the rhythms they wanted, but when they found white drummers who could play the parts, they hired the white drummers.

"Sometimes they brought drummers in as percussionists on record sessions I was doing, so that they could watch me. And they were able to write down what I was doing," he recalls. They started writing out rock drumming parts, which any technically proficient drummer could then play. "They had written it out so the white drummers could play

Panama Francis, 1960s. (Courtesy Panama Francis)

it. Although they still couldn't play it with the *feeling* that I had. They were playing it technical. I woke up one morning and I wasn't being called by certain producers and record companies anymore."

Francis is well aware of how important rhythm is to the success or failure of a number. He is certain that some numbers he drummed on would not have been hits without his contributions. He believes, for example, that Perez Prado's record of "Patricia" clicked only because of the rhythm he came up with, and added in an overdubbing. "And when Ray Conniff, for whom I have great love and respect, got ready to do his first album, if I had played the drum part like it was written, the record would never have gotten off the ground. I was the one that established that rhythm. And Conniff tells people that. Out of all of the people that I came up with and helped, he's the only one that still remembers me. Whenever he gets a job to go anyplace in the world, he calls me first. Because he knows that I am partly responsible for the rhythm that was used on his records."

In 1963, Francis drummed for Dinah Shore when she played at New York's Plaza Hotel. She invited him to travel with her as her personal drummer. He accepted, and stayed with her for five years. "She was one of the greatest persons I ever worked for, and that was one of the greatest jobs I ever had. She is just a beautiful human being," Francis says.

Bernard Purdy and Gary Chester had by then succeeded him as New York's favored studio drummers. And the young rock groups pretty much all had their own drummers. Rock 'n' roll had evolved, growing farther and farther away from its rhythm-and-blues roots. From Francis' viewpoint, "Rock 'n'roll just didn't swing any more. It became like a technical thing."

He quit drumming for Dinah Shore in 1968. Shortly afterwards, she got her TV show, he adds, and he regretted having left her. He had decided to settle in California.

For the next five years, he worked only sporadically. He was in his 50s now—an old man in the eyes of the people making most of the popular music. His past accomplishments meant little to the Los Angeles contractors. Studio dates were going to a new crop of drummers.

"I was like hitting and missing, and drawing on unemployment insurance. The only person out there that remembered me was Ray Conniff," Francis says. He got so discouraged that for the first time in his life, he considered taking a day job. By 1973, Francis' contributions to early rock 'n' roll seemed like ancient history. And there was little point in trying to tell a young contractor about Lucky Millinder and the long-gone Savoy Ballroom.

"Then I said, I'll take a chance and come back to New York. And when I came back to New York, I joined Sy Oliver, and I stayed with him from '73 until '75," Francis says. With Oliver, he was back playing the music he grew up with.

In New York in the mid '70s, there was a flurry of interest in jazz re-creations. Francis was glad to get the chance to do a concert re-creating the music of Lucky Millinder and of Al Cooper's Savoy Sultans. The concert turned out to be everything he could have hoped for, and more. There were slides of Lindy Hoppers at the Savoy. Francis recalled, too, how blacks in Harlem held formal dances at the Savoy. And the music that night was right on the money.

Francis never dreamed there'd be anything beyond that one concert. But two French impresarios arranged for Francis to bring his Savoy Sultans to Europe for a three-week tour in 1979. And the band has been rolling along since.

Periodically, the band has worked with older singers, such as Jimmy Witherspoon (with whom it recorded an album, available on the Muse label), Herb Jeffries, and Maxine Sullivan. Most often, it has worked alone. Its last two albums, for Stash records, have been instrumentals.

The Rainbow Room has been Francis' main employer of late. He notes: "I don't play the original Savoy Sultans' music up there at the Rainbow Room, because the people up there don't know nothing about the Savoy Sultans. I have to play standard songs up there. But they're good arrangements, and people dance to it.

"The Rainbow Room gave me a chance, and that's why I'll always feel obligated, as far as the Rainbow Room is concerned. Because they're responsible for this band being in existence.[3]

"The people that's running the business now do not want any more black bands. I don't have an agent, I don't have a manager. It's really a conspiracy out there. There'll be no more black bands. I can see the handwriting on the wall."

In his youth, Francis saw black bands pioneer in the swing idiom, and then white bands make far greater money playing the same music. In the '50s, he saw the process repeat itself, as blacks pioneered rhythm-and-blues and rock 'n' roll, and white imitators so often went on to greater fame and fortune.

"That's about what has happened through the years, with this music. It's all been a case of race. Race. One of the illnesses of this country," Francis declares.

[3] In 1987, the Rainbow Room closed for extensive renovations. After the room reopened, a new house band was hired. Since then, Francis' band has freelanced, and he has also worked on his own in jazz concerts.

"I'm very sensitive about things like this. And it's a bad scene," he says, emotion filling his voice. "It shouldn't be that way. It should be that a person is accepted for their ability, and not because of what color they are."

Francis wonders about the future of the type of music he likes best. His sidemen, for the most part, are hardly youngsters. His guitarist, he notes, played alongside him in Cab Calloway's band, 40 years ago. They're playing the same sort of music they've played since they were young. They don't go for the frantic flagwavers, of course, that once were part of the swing repertoire. But aside from that, they're carrying on the spirit of the Savoy.

What happens when these older musicians are gone? It worries Francis that he isn't meeting young black musicians who can play this type of music the way it should be played. A heritage is being lost. "Believe me! I can't find a young black musician that knows any tunes outside of the bebop tunes. They don't know the standards," he says.

Francis is skeptical, too, about how much jazz musicians can learn in school. The greats from his generation and before, he says, did not learn jazz in school.

"Trying to teach somebody how to play jazz," he declares, "is like trying to teach somebody how to perform sex. You cannot teach nobody. You can give 'em an *idea*, but you can't teach no jazz. Just like you can't teach nobody sex. You can give 'em an *idea*. You have to have the potentials and learn by experience, because after you get the fundamentals, you still have to have the experience of knowing what to do with what you got. That's why we've got so many mediocre musicians today in jazz. Because nine out of ten of 'em has never had any experience. They think they *know*, because they went to school, and got a degree in music. . . . There's more to it."

1985

STEPHANE • GRAPPELLI

Parisian Swing

It doesn't take Stephane Grappelli long to answer the question: Who are your all-time favorite jazz violinists?

"Me!" he responds simply, with a laugh. He then adds that he is just kidding—but he offers no other names. And perhaps that is as it should be.

Today, at age 80, Grappelli continues to dominate jazz polls on violin. He maintains an arduous touring schedule, playing for listeners who, for the most part, were not even born when he first broke through to international fame with the "Quintette of the Hot Club of France" recordings which he made with Django Reinhardt in the 1930s.

Grappelli has been a jazz violinist for nearly as long as the concept has existed.

"Because with Joe Venuti, we arrived before everybody," he declares in his charmingly French-accented speech. "He was in America, I was in France. Mind you, I was told there was some violinists there, but they played more grass music than jazz."

A number of critics have inferred, from listening to Grappelli's earliest recordings, that Venuti must have been a major influence upon him. But Grappelli maintains that Venuti was not. He wants to be recognized as an original.

When he started out as a musician, as a youth in Paris in the early 1920s, he says, "it was quite difficult to get some records from America. The first time I heard Joe Venuti, I was 23 years old [which would have been in 1931]. See, that's late. So nobody can say I copy him, you know.

"The first time I heard Venuti on a record, he was playing a beautiful violin. Actually, very beautiful—a lovely sound.

"But me—I have not the training he had, because I never studied (I played by ear, you know)—and I couldn't see the music like that. Me, I was interested in black musicians. That's why the first record I heard that was black musicians, that I said, '*That's* the way I want to play.'"

"And I transposed what I hear on the saxophone, trumpet, anything—I transposed that on the violin. I transposed what I hear from . . . black artists."

* * *

We've met in the office of jazz booking agent Abby Hoffer in New York. Grappelli makes himself comfortable, stretching out on a couch. He says he is not feeling well, but his eyes are bright and lively. He kibbitzes a good bit, before getting down to the interview proper. When I mention I have some French ancestry, from the region of Lorraine, he banters about the beauty of that area. He speaks in an easy, relaxed way, often provoking laughter in the room. Eventually, finally, we get to his own career.

Grappelli's childhood was apparently rather bleak. He was born in Paris on January 6, 1908. His last name was then spelled "Grappelly." He changed the final "y" to an "i" in the 1960s. His mother died when he was three, and his father, who couldn't handle raising him alone, placed him in an orphanage.

When he was six, his father enrolled him into Isadora Duncan's dancing school, the first place where he ever heard live music. But then World War One started. The school was closed, his father went off to war, and he went into a different orphanage. There, he had to sleep on the floor, and never had enough food to eat. He fled, and lived on the streets.

After the war, his father took him in, and bought him a violin: three-quarters standard size, appropriate for a boy of 12. He still has that treasured first violin today. Father and son studied solfeggio together, using a music book borrowed from the library because they couldn't afford proper lessons. He learned piano, too.

Although the violin is by far Grappelli's preferred instrument today, he will often include a piano interlude when he appears in concert: "I do five minutes to amuse the tourists."

He got a job at age 14, playing piano in the pit band of a movie house. That was to remain his main source of income until Al Jolson made *The Jazz Singer* in 1927, and by ushering in "talkies," ended the use of live musicians at movie houses.

In the meantime, American jazz was invading France. Mitchell's Jazz Kings, a septet led by expatriate drummer Louis Mitchell, was a sensation in Paris. In 1922-23, they recorded more than 50 sides for Pathe. Grappelli was particularly enthralled by their recording of "Stumbling" (1922). At the movie house, he would play that tune when Charlie Chaplin would come onscreen.

Grappelli was too young to get into night clubs then, but just to stand outside the door of a club and hear a pianist, drummer, and

Stephane Grappelli. (Courtesy Abby Hoffer)

saxophonist play a number like "Hot Lips" excited him. This brash new music from America moved him in a way that European music did not.

He recalls his first opportunity to sit in with musicians from America.

"When I was 19, I was engaged to play in a band at the casino in Deauville, the north of France. And in Deauville, there was an orchestra from a university from America. I don't know which university it was. There were about 20 young guys. And I was amazed at the quality of the music they were playing. It was all those beautiful tunes that they were playing at the time. 'Thou Swell' and all those. I was always asking to play 'Thou Swell.' I couldn't pronounce—but they understood.

"And I began playing with them. I was playing the piano at the orchestra where I was working. And sometimes the pianist from the American band was so drunk that I used to deputize for him. They called me. 'Steven'—they called me Steven—'Please come in,' and I'd play. He was so drunk, he was sleeping under the piano. He was young, too: 19 or 20. Because this was during prohibition in America, and now in France, they can drink what they want to drink. All those boys there—drunk like hell! They don't speak French, I don't speak English. But you see, that's proof that with jazz music, you don't need to speak."

And then when Paul Whiteman's Orchestra hit France, he got to meet the Dorsey brothers, Bing Crosby, and others in that aggregation. He remembers shaking hands with George Gershwin, too.

By now, the violin was becoming more important to Grappelli than the piano. He was studying classical violin and considering a career in that field. "I was wondering, if I study a bit, then I can go to the opera one of these days, like a second violin or something like that, to make a bit of money."

But the lure of American jazz proved irresistable. He heard a jazz record by Bix Beiderbecke, Frankie Trumbauer, and Eddie Lang. "That was the beginning of my decision to play jazz forever, when I heard those three artists. So I give it up, the studying."

Bix influenced his piano playing. Art Tatum, a few years later, was another influence. Louis Armstrong influenced his overall sense of swing. "I got a knock in my face, when Louis Armstrong came to Paris [1934]. And it was not his trumpet . . . it was the way he was singing. In spite I didn't understand a word what he was singing, I was in another world when I hear him!"

Joe Venuti, judging from Grappelli's early records, appears to have been more of an influence upon Grappelli's violin style than he acknowledges. Jazz authority Dan Morgenstern notes that Venuti heard a good bit of his own style in Grappelli's, too.

Joe Venuti and Eddie Lang had made their first records together in 1926. In the next few years, they established that a violin and guitar could make a most effective jazz combination.

* * *

Grappelli first met Django Reinhardt, the Belgian gypsy jazz guitarist, around 1929. They crossed paths a few times in the next few years. In 1934, they both wound up, by chance, in an orchestra in the Hotel Claridge in Paris. They started fooling around backstage together one time, and found that they clicked as team.

The quintet which they soon formed had a unique instrumentation: three guitars, a bass, and a violin. French jazz critics Hugues Panassie and Charles Delaunay were so impressed when they heard it, they decided to make it the official band of their hot jazz club: hence the title, "the Quintette of the Hot Club of France." Their elegant, small-group swing caught on quickly. Record contracts, radio broadcasts, and a steady job at Bricktop's popular nightclub quickly followed.

Grappelli and Reinhardt may have been ideal partners musically, but on a personal level, they frequently clashed. Grappelli was businesslike, methodical. He was personally fastidious, invariably punctual for appointments, and prudent with money. Reinhardt was rather sloppy, impulsive, and careless with money. He was apt to show up late—or not at all—at the club or recording studio if a game of billiards, a bit of drinking, or a nap appealed to him at the moment. Grappelli often found Reinhardt to be exasperating. And yet there *was* a bond between them. Though Grappelli was just two years older than Reinhardt, Reinhardt gave him the respect due an elder in gypsy society, Grappelli recalls.

When they met, Reinhardt was illiterate, though eventually he learned to read. Grappelli handled the business for both of them; Reinhardt trusted him implicitly. Grappelli recalls that Reinhardt didn't want anyone to know he couldn't read—he was self-conscious about the fact—so he would pretend to read contracts after Grappelli had read and approved them. One time, however, when Reinhardt pretended to read a contract a producer was offering for London booking, he tried to make his simulation more convincing by pointing to one line and declaring *it* was unacceptable. Grappelli glanced at the contract, saw that line guaranteed that they would be given first-class airfare to and from England—and told Reinhardt to shut up!

The personal disagreements never mattered once they were onstage. For Grappelli and Reinhardt always swung—in an era when very few European musicians did. They were the first European jazzmen to match, and even influence, pre-eminent American jazzmen.

Their 1934-39 recordings remain classics. They co-composed such numbers as "Are You in the Mood," "Djangology," "Tears," "Minor Swing," and "Oriental Shuffle." And they recorded their versions of American standards such as "Dinah," "Japanese Sandman," and "Sweet Georgia Brown." Each made records released under his own name, in addition to those released under the Quintette's name. Sides they made with Coleman Hawkins' All-Star Jam Band, featuring Benny Carter, helped win them greater international renown.

Reinhardt, being the more colorful of the two, drew more attention than Grappelli. The fact that he was a gypsy, living in a gypsy caravan, rather than an apartment or hotel room like other musicians, made him seem exotic to some fans. Many were awed by the fact that he got such an unusually sure and precise attack even though he had a partially paralyzed hand—it had been damaged in a fire. Reinhardt and Grappelli were co-leaders of the Quintette, but Reinhardt's name was billed first, and to some extent he overshadowed Grappelli. Many fans no doubt presumed, back then, that Reinhardt was the more important musician. But history has judged Reinhardt and Grappelli to have been equally important to the Quintette's brilliance. Significantly, the records that they both made on their own during the Second World War were not nearly as successful as those they had made together.

Even though these were Depression times, Reinhardt and Grappelli earned a fortune in the late '30s. Tips at Bricktop's club were large. Grappelli, who had known what it was like to be hungry as a child, had no qualms about being wealthy now. He ate well, drank well, and began collecting antiques.

Grappelli recalls, too: "We played in evening dress. Always. And I remember, it was awful to play the violin in the summer, with the starched shirt—like an armor. And with that collar—that was the worst part, the collar. With the button there. And the more you pushed the violin, the button goes to your throat. It was an agony!" Grappelli is glad that today he can perform in the same casual, colorful open-collar shirts that he favors offstage.

The onset of the Second World War ended their partnership. Grappelli was in England, and naturally decided to remain there, when the Germans invaded France. Reinhardt had no choice but to stay in France. He hired a clarinetist to take Grappelli's place in the Quintette. Grappelli formed an English band which included young George Shearing on piano. He learned English now, so that he could communicate with his musicians, and his audiences.

After the war, Reinhardt and Grappelli tried to reunite, but it proved impossible to recapture the past. There were sporadic reunions, and in 1949, they made some first-rate recordings together. But the great partnership belonged to history. "At the end of his life, Django used to disappear," Grappelli recalls. "You know, he liked to go to the country. He don't like to work too much, you see. And he was getting old soon. He died only at 43 years old [in 1953]. But he was looking much more than that, unfortunately, because he was not careful with his health. He died with a brain hemorrhage."

* * *

In the 1950s and '60s, Grappelli's career fell into something of an eclipse. He was playing as brilliantly as ever, but the attention of many critics and fans was fixed elsewhere. Like so many other players who had been stars of the Swing Era, Grappelli was now being treated as something of a holdover from the past.

After bebop came into vogue, many critics and fans concentrated so wholeheartedly on the new style, that the masters of the older style were neglected. Grappelli, Joe Venuti, Benny Carter—such past masters all suffered some neglect in these years.

Grappelli continued doing what he did best. Bebop was never his thing. And eventually, for Grappelli—as for Venuti and Carter and others—the critics and fans came around again. He was re-discovered and lionized anew.

In the past two decades, Grappelli has re-emerged as a giant on the international jazz scene, universally lauded. He made his first,

Stephane Grappelli. (Courtesy GRP Records)

long-overdue visit to the United States in 1969. He had put off making the trip, he says, because he did not like flying.

His nimbly swinging, beautifully poised manner of playing, which some bebop fanatics might have judged "dated" in 1948, seems instead to be timeless, classic, in 1988. And his pure tone remains unsurpassed among jazz violinists.

Grappelli's approach is flexible enough to work with seemingly any collaborator. He has jammed and/or recorded with a wide range of stylists (Duke Ellington, Miles Davis, Jean Luc Ponty, Joe Venuti, Bucky Pizzarelli, Stuff Smith, Oscar Peterson, Yehudi Menuhin, Phil Woods). But he most often works just with his own trio, leaping through many of the same numbers—"Them There Eyes," "I Got Rhythm," "Honeysuckle Rose"—which he first recorded 50 or more years ago. He had made occasional explorations into contemporary music, trying his hand on, say, a Stevie Wonder tune. But his preferences clearly lie more with the melodies of the '20s, '30s, and '40s. His most recent album, "Stephane Grappelli Plays Jerome Kern" (GRP) is an honest reflection of his interests.

Grappelli remarks, almost as if he's surprised by the idea, that he's heard that the Quintette's original recordings are still in print. Indeed they are, I note. They continue to touch new listeners. I add that a quintet has just been formed (with guitarist Frank Vignola and violinist Bob Mastro taking the roles of Reinhardt and Grappelli) to re-create "the Quintette of the Hot Club of France" at Michael's Pub in New York.

Grappelli is unmoved by news of this salute. "Well, I'm not very interested in that because I get no money out of that."

Grappelli is looking forward to a celebration of his 80th birthday at Carnegie Hall. The concert, sponsored by the Grand Marnier Foundation, in association with Pat Philips and Ettore Stratta, will feature an eclectic gathering of notables, including classical cellist Yo Yo Ma, pop singer Maureen McGovern, the Juilliard String Quartet, composer Michel LeGrand, and such jazz artists as Roger Kellaway and Toots Thielemans.

The plan is to have the various artists perform numbers in homage to Grappelli in the first half, with Grappelli and his trio finally coming out to play in the second half.

Grappelli seems interested in stepping off of the pedestal his producers have planned to put him on.

"We must have a kind of jam session," he declares.

"No, no," says Stratta. Most of the other musicians will be there just to *honor* Grappelli, not to play with him. "You'll do something with Yo Yo. A little piece. Something written for cello and violin. And that's it. And you'll play your own things."

Grappelli, undeterred, insists he wants to do more than that.[1]

Finally, the conversation must come to an end. Grappelli's getting a bit thirsty, he says. And he explains he has caught a cold flying in from France. "I take that damned plane, and now I'm going to get dressed like a trapper in Canada."

He adds, though, that—cold or no cold—he is happy to be back in America. "What is the best public in the world? Well, I must say the American, because they understand what they are listening to. They've got that in their blood. But in other places, sometimes one in 20 understand what is going on. You see them scream 'bravo' in the wrong place." And as I bid him goodbye, he nods, picks up his violin, and begins gently plucking out the notes to "Sweet Lorraine."

1988

[1] At the concert, Grappelli *did* get everyone—including the Juilliard String Quartet—to jam on a couple of numbers with him.

MEL · TORME

"I Wanted to be a Big Band Leader. . ."

Mel Torme is one of the master singers of our time. But his original goal, he surprised me by mentioning one day, was *not* to make it as a singer, but rather as a big band leader. He expected to do some singing with his band—although he didn't think he had that great a voice—but also to play the drums, and write all of the arrangements. That was his fantasy in the late '30s and early early '40s. He never quite realized that dream, although for a brief spell—when he was the drummer, vocal-group arranger, and third vocalist in Chico Marx's big band—it looked like he was well on his way.

What altered his goal? "Frank Sinatra broke loose and changed the world. He placed bands in the low visibility position. Before him, big bands were the number one element in all of music." In late 1946, as big bands were fading, a manager urged Torme to try and make it as a single. His records clicked. "People began to think that I sang OK. I didn't think so—honest to God, I hated my singing. I was blessed with some great arrangements. It breaks my heart that the singing wasn't as good as the arrangements. I had kind of a callow sound. And my voice hadn't deepened yet."

Mel Torme. (Courtesy Henry Luhrman)

Torme feels so strongly about that, that when one record company executive told him a few years ago that they were planning to reissue some of his old recordings, he made an extraordinary offer: "'I've still got all of the arrangements. Let me come in for free. Let's do them again.' But I couldn't get the guy to budge."

Torme acknowledges, too, that he can sing a song such as "Stardust" with more feeling today than in his youth. "Well, that's called three divorces and a lot of scars, a lot of heartaches. . . . I sang 'Stardust' when I was 19 years old and it was a joke. What the hell business did I have singing 'Stardust' then?" In the past five or so years, he reflects, he's found himself able to get much more out of that song.

It's within the past decade that Torme seems to have fully realized his potential as a singer; *these* are his peak years, even if his records do not enjoy the mass sales that they did in his youth when, promoted as "the Velvet Fog," he became a pop star. He sings more tastefully now. And with his perfect pitch, flawless rhythmic sense, and an unusual, immediately-recognizable timbre that has only gotten more attractive with age, Torme has garnered, in recent years, as much critical acclaim as any singer could ask for.

And yet he hasn't entirely forgotten his original goal. When I first telephoned him for this piece at his California home at nine a.m. his time, he had already been up for several hours—typically for him—writing music. Few realize it, but Torme, unique among singers, writes all of his arrangements. He's also been known to occasionally conduct bands he's worked with, even for other singers working with him. And he'll sneak in a number at the drums if given a chance, as well. (He owns the drums Gene Krupa used at the famous 1938 Benny Goodman Carnegie Hall concert.) When opportunities arise, he enjoys working with the best of the big bands. He's particularly proud that after a recent date with the Count Basie Band, some of the musicians in it asked him if he'd write an arrangement for the band: "That's like a Congressional Medal of Honor for me."

When I told Torme I was working on a book on Swing Era survivors, he asked to be included, even before I got a chance to ask him if he'd *like* to be included. In his usual animated style, he was soon telling me of the multitude of old 78s he still had and citing obscure ones by Charlie Barnet and Jimmie Lunceford that he particularly liked. He named for me, from memory, every single member of Artie Shaw's great 1939 Band—right down to the third trumpeter and third trombonist, names that even a jazz historian would be hard-pressed to recall. He spoke of bandleaders such as Shaw and Tommy Dorsey, Glenn Miller and Duke Ellington with the near-reverence of one who was, after all, a mere youth when they were the reigning heads of the music world. Did he warm to the subject of the big band years? You bet!

A few days after our telephone talk, Torme arrived in New York, to open a highly-successful four-week engagement at Michael's Pub on the East Side. The recollections that follow have been distilled from a couple of lunches we had together during that engagement, as well as a bit of between-sets kibbitzing in his dressing room.

* * *

"The heyday of the big bands," Torme recalls wistfully, "—that era lasted from 1935, when Benny broke loose, until 1945, the end of the war. By that time, Frank's roots were deep, and Dick Haymes had broken loose, and then Bob Eberly was going on his own—and now the day of the singer had arrived. And during that 10-year period, that was the most extraordinary development of music in our country, from the standpoint of a high-quality kind of musical scene.

"And the real sadness—and I know this sounds like sedition, this could be seditious of me as a singer to say—but I just feel that the era of the singers ushered in the beginning of the end, as far as great quality music is concerned.

"Because music wasn't being dominated by arrangers and musician/bandleaders, like Artie Shaw and Tommy Dorsey and Benny Goodman. And when they were relegated to second position, so to speak, lower visibility, second billing, you know—I just feel that it started to go to hell in a handbasket. It broke my heart to see it happen."

In Torme's judgment—and he knows he'll get a lot of flack on this from aficionados of today's rock and pop—the big band era represented the golden age in American music.

* * *

When did Torme's own love affair with big bands begin?

Well, he notes he sang with his first big "name" band as far back as 1929, when he was just four years old (he was born September 13, 1925). And he's been at it, more or less, ever since.

Four years old? That calls for some explaining. And Torme is happy to oblige.

"My favorite toy was the radio. I had my trains, and my tinker toys and all that. But at an incredibly tender age, I fell in love with the radio, and with music.

"And the Coon-Sanders Orchestra was an orchestra that I listened to all the time on the radio. Because they had an early broadcast. Sometimes these remote broadcasts would be 11:30 at night. And I used to sing all their arrangements around the house." Carleton Coon and Joe Sanders co-led one of the peppiest and most popular dance bands of the late '20s. Torme still has some of their records today.

"One night my Mother and Dad took me for a treat to the Blackhawk, where they were playing. And I'm sitting there in the front row, a droll little boy in a sailor suit, and they're playing. And they see me singing along with the band, 'Oh, you're driving me crazy. . .' [and Torme sings the words now, with an irresistible verve, in a little boy's voice]—and I'm all over the table. And finally Joe Sanders or Carleton Coon walked over and said, 'This little boy seems to know everything we do.' My mother says, 'Oh yes, he listens to the radio.' On a whim, they got me up. I sang 'You're Driving Me Crazy.' And it went over very, very well. Carleton Coon, who was the drummer, came over later and picked me up and brought me back to the drums and sat me on his bass-drum knee while he played. That may have been the first time I ever fell in love with drums, I don't know.

"And they said, 'What about bringing little Melvin in here on Monday nights, and we'll make him a Monday night feature? We'll give you $15 on Monday night, and dinner for the family'—which was really important, because the Blackhawk had great food.

"I did that for just under six months. I'd always sit at the ringside. Carleton Coon or Joe Sanders would say, 'And now, little Melvin Torme is going to come up here and sing for us. Come on, Melvin. You finished with your dinner?' And I would come up and sing usually 'You're Driving Me Crazy,' or a song called 'Pretty Little Baby.'"

His name, he adds, was then pronounced TOR-mee; it was not until he was in high school that his parents added the accent mark to the second syllable, changing the pronunciation to Tor-MAY.

Word got around town that little Melvin was a good novelty act. Over the next couple of years, he sang on occasion with trumpeter Louis Panico's Band, Frankie Masters' Orchestra, and finally with Buddy Rogers' Orchestra. Torme notes: "A couple of years ago, I ran into Buddy Rogers at a party in California. I sang and he said, 'Aw gee, Mel, that was—' And I said, 'You used to call me Melvin.' He said, 'What?' And I said, 'You don't remember me, do you?' And when I told him, he said: '*You* were that same little kid?' That was fun."

Torme then sang in child vaudeville units for a couple of years. He was still doing "You're Driving Me Crazy"; that had become "sort of a standard with me. I also did a song called, 'Whose Sweet Patootie Are You?'"

After winning a singing contest at age eight doing Al Jolson's "Going to Heaven on a Mule," complete with Jolson-like recitative between choruses—he had just seen Jolson's film, "Wonder Bar"—Torme landed work in radio. A great deal of live radio then originated from Chicago.

He played innumerable parts in soap operas, dramas, and action serials of the day. For a brief stretch, he entertained fantasies about making it as an actor and getting into pictures. When he actually made his first motion picture, in 1943, he adds, that killed whatever interest he might have had left in acting: "I was bored stiff. I'm just not geared to waiting, waiting, waiting, waiting, waiting around, to get up and do 30 seconds worth of film, and then wait some more. It drove me crazy. I used to pace the sound stages."

Torme began drumming, initially in a grade school drum-and-bugle corps when he was about eight. "I just thought the drums were a real macho instrument. I was slight, and I felt it would help my image around school with the guys. I was doing radio, and they resented it; I was getting out of school early a lot. The drums were a way of trying to be one of the gang, and be a little bit athletic. But in those days, drums were really just on the side. I didn't really get into drums until I was about 12 or 13."

When did he first think of becoming a singing-drumming-arranging big band leader?

"I'll tell you *exactly* when it was. My Uncle Art, God bless him, was a very very well-known lawyer in Chicago. He handled the famous and a few of the infamous. . . . And one of the guys in Chicago was a sweet man—probably mob connected—who had one of the biggest juke box operations in Chicago. You'd go to his jukebox warehouse: *tons* of records, I mean *tons* of them. I was about 12 or 13, I can't remember. And he said, 'Do you like music, kid? Go, look, and take. See what you want.'" He let Torme loose in his jukebox warehouse, and Torme—who had always been immersed in music—felt like he was in heaven. He took free records of Charlie Barnet, Cab Calloway, Duke Ellington, Count Basie, Artie Shaw — the beginnings of the sizable collection of Swing Era 78s he still has today.

"Then my education began in earnest. This was like 1937-38. And of course, at the same time I was immersed in the Benny Goodman-Gene Krupa mystique. Gene Krupa lived literally four blocks away. I lived at 7827 Essex Avenue, right off of 79th. On the corner of 74th and Kingston was a grocery store, with a green awning and thick white letters on it. I used to stand in front of that grocery store, just to look at the name: 'Lykke and Krupa.' Gene Krupa's dad owned that store. That's where Gene lived. I got to meet him at a very early age, and I fell in love with the guy. He's one of the nicest human beings God ever put on earth. Really a neat guy.

"And that began it all. And then because I'd been playing in the drum and bugle corps, my Grandpa bought me a set of drums . . . the Ray Bauduc combo, with the picture of the bobcat on the front of the bass drum. And every day after school — I couldn't wait to get home. I got it about '38, I was about 13 years old. And the Bob Crosby Band — with Ray on drums — was now playing the tea dances at the self-same Blackhawk restaurant where I used to work. And I went to see them.

"I just got utterly immersed. I would sit in school, with my notebook, and I would draw bass drum heads, and try to reproduce the crests of Jo Jones with Basie, and the 'GK' crest of Gene, and Buddy Rich, and the Bobcats . . . . I've still got that stuff at home.

"That is truly where the big band education really began. It just became a way of life. I really, desperately, wanted to just be a big band leader. Because for obvious reasons, the big bands were . . . they had the prime visibility in those days. Singers were band singers; they *worked* for the big bands, you know. And every once in a while, they'd get up out of their chair and come and sing. But until Sinatra broke loose — other than Bing and a couple of people like that — the big bands were it in music. They were *it*.

"The big band era, that was the best musical era this country ever knew. It was the highest level of sophistication music had reached. Not only the big bands, but the songwriters who were extant at the time." Torme himself began writing songs, on the side, when he was about 14.

Torme's father happened to be friends with bandleader Ben Pollack — "one of the protean drummers of all time," Torme says — which helped open a few doors in the music world. Word was beginning to get around that young Torme was becoming a pretty fair drummer and singer.

By now Harry James, who had gotten his start in Pollack's Band, before becoming a star in Benny Goodman's Band, was leading his own band. It wasn't too successful in its first two years (1939-1940) when it stressed hot jazz; James' Band only really found its mass audience in mid '41 when James began stressing romantic ballads.

Torme was just 15 when, in 1940, Harry James said he was interested in adding Torme to his band; the youth could sing and play drums. Torme told a friend of James' interest; the high school newspaper ran a big story about how he was going to go off with James. Then, as time passed, and nothing happened, Torme's classmates accused him of having made up the story that Harry James was interested in him.

In the meantime, Torme had been getting letters from Harry James: the band didn't have the money at present to take on an extra player; there were difficulties involved in carrying someone so young on the road. The offer was put off, and finally cancelled.

By now, most of Torme's classmates had turned on him. They'd taunt him, he recalls: "'Here comes the liar,' 'Here comes Harry James' ex-drummer—everybody rise!' That was something that a girl said on a trolley car going home. And there must have been 10 or 11 of my schoolmates on that car, and they all rose and gave me the mock bows. And it hurt a lot."

And then, just as nearly everyone was convinced he had invented ever having had anything to do with Harry James, James decided to record a song Torme had written, "Lament to Love."

James cut the record, with Dick Haymes on vocal, on June 10, 1941. Torme was then 15; his recollection is that the record was released, with his name, naturally, on it as composer, just after he turned 16 in the fall. "A lot of the kids had not believed me—until this song became a hit; it made number seven on the hit parade and stayed there for about three weeks. That was enough to finally convince them that I hadn't been lying. But by then, it was too late. I had gone through enough. They really put me through hell. You know, when your school and your friends are your whole life, it's pretty big stuff." Torme still can feel the pain of being rejected by his high school crowd.

In the meantime, Torme was furthering his musical education by going to a club on the South side to catch a drummer he admired, Red Saunders. "Or going to the State and Lake or the Chicago or the Oriental [theaters], every single weekend. My best friend and I would go downtown with our girls. If there was a great band playing, we might go to the early show and stay for two shows; sit through the movie and everything. Be done at about 6:00, and then go to the Panther Room, and have dinner; it was not very expensive in those days. And watch the Gene Krupa Band, or Jimmie Lunceford, or Duke Ellington, or Charlie Barnet, or Artie Shaw, and stay the whole night. Wouldn't get home until 1:00. Be downtown all day—Saturday was music day."

One afternoon, Ben Pollack took Torme downtown to the Panther Room to meet Glenn Miller, who had played in Pollack's band back in the '20s. "I brought some of my tunes. Because already 'Lament to Love' had been on the air, now. They were all lousy. But he couldn't have been nicer to me. Instead of putting me down, he said, 'I want you to see something, Mel. I'll give you a copy of this and I want you to study it, because if you're going to write lyrics, you really have to write. You can't just write Moon, June, Tune, Spoon. This is a brand new song.' And he walked up to the piano and brought back 'That Old Black Magic.' And there wasn't even a lead sheet on it yet. This was February or March of 1942. He said 'We just got it. Ray Eberle's just learning it. But I want you to look at the lyric.'

"In August of '42, I went off to join the Chico Marx band. And Skip Nelson—he always used to go call me 'Junior'—was the romantic singer with the band. He was damned good." Then Glenn Miller and Ray Eberle had a falling out; Miller fired Eberle, and hired Skip Nelson as his replacement. Torme watched with some amazement as Nelson

Mel Torme, singing with the Chico Marx or Ben Pollack Band, Lakeside Park, Denver, 1942. (© 1988 Frank Driggs collection)

got to do the vocal on the Glenn Miller Band's recording of "That Old Black Magic." It was a hit.

Torme was originally hired as a third singer (after Skip Nelson and Elise Cooper) and vocal-group arranger in Chico Marx's Band. "It was Ben Pollack's band, really; Ben had put it together. Chico just fronted it. And then when George Wettling (the drummer) left, Ben knew I played drums, and he thought they could save a lot of money by putting me in. They promised me $50 a week more. I was making $75 a week; they promised me $125. Then I started playing drums with the band—but the extra money wasn't forthcoming. And I felt it was unfair. I said, 'Get another drummer. I'll just keep singing.'

"I was with the band a year; I joined them in August of '42, and the band broke up the end of July of '43. I played drums with the band for about a month, toward the end." Because Torme's tenure with the Chico Marx Band fell within the 1942-44 recording ban, he did not get to make any records with them. Doing vocal-group arrangements for the band was good practice for his later orchestral arranging; writing

Mel Torme drummed in Chico Marx's Band, which was actually organized and run by Ben Pollack. In this photo, taken at Lakeside Park, Denver, in 1942, Pollack is on drums in the front row, Torme is on drums in back row, and Barney Kessel is on guitar. (© 1988 Frank Driggs collection)

for a vocal group, Torme says, is like writing for a sax section.

Torme and his parents emigrated to Hollywood. He appeared in the entertaining film musical, *Higher and Higher* (1943), starring Michelle Morgan, Jack Haley, Frank Sinatra, and Victor Borge. And around the same time, "Ben located an organized vocal group of four kids, then going to City College, who didn't have an arranger. I was an arranger without a vocal group. We just fit each other's needs." The group, with Torme added as lead singer and arranger, became known as the Mel-Tones in September of '43.

They were so naturally talented, Torme says, that sometimes he didn't have to do any arranging at all. They could begin singing a song, perhaps while riding in a car, in perfect five-part harmony. "The Mel-Tones were very special."

The Mel-Tones appeared in two teenage movie musicals: *Pardon My Rhythm* (1944), with Gloria Jean and Bob Crosby and his Orchestra, and *Let's Go Steady* (1945), with Skinnay Ennis and his Orchestra. But making movies bored Torme.

He could be found almost nightly, when his schedule permitted, checking out the big bands at the Palladium. He was also drumming when he could, at various clubs around town.

Three major "name" bandleaders sought to hire him as their drummer, Torme says. "Tommy Dorsey was the most relentless. But the other two offers were: number one, from Gene Krupa, who said: 'Mel, look, I play two numbers a set. I come out and play the opener. Then I'm in front. You'd get a chance to play, and you could sing with the band. But mainly I want you for your drumming.'

"And the other one was Stan Kenton. Aw, he drove me batty. That's how I got to know my future manager, Carlos Gastell, who managed Stan at the time. I used to go and sit in with Kenton, who was having terrible drummer problems—because he was not a strong rhythm pianist. So all you had was the bass, Eddie Safranski, who was really more interested in doing solos than in walking the band. I would get up there and sit in for a whole set and play 'Intermission Riff' and 'St. James Infirmary,' and hold the band together. This was 1944 and '45. Kenton called me up one night and said, 'Look, I know you can't leave the Mel-Tones, but we're doing two weeks at Frank Dailey's Meadowbrook, and it's the most airtime we've ever had. It's really important to me that the band shine. Would you just come and play drums for two weeks? I'll give you $300 a week,' and in those days, that was pretty good money." But the Mel-Tones were committed to Armed Forces radio broadcasts, plus camp shows, and Torme couldn't accept Kenton's offer. "Believe me when I tell you, I was really torn. Because I loved playing drums.

"The Tommy Dorsey thing, of course, was the real challenge, but I knew in my heart that even if I didn't have the Mel-Tones, there was no way to fill Buddy Rich's shoes." By then Torme and Rich, who had also gotten started in show business in childhood, were friends. Torme admired Rich's drumming so much, he says he became a kind of Rich clone, modeling his playing style on Rich's.

"By that time, Buddy and Tommy had become very disaffected with each other. Buddy was always being very naughty with Tommy. And Tommy said, 'I won't replace you, I won't let you go, I won't free you from your contractual obligation, unless I can find somebody that'll please me.' Well, who the hell can please anybody after Buddy Rich gets done playing drums for him?"

Rich engineered it so that Dorsey would have a chance to hear Torme play drums. The Dorsey Band was just about to go on for a radio broadcast, but Rich—to Dorsey's irritation—was not there. One of the

Left to right: Marcy McGuire, Mel Torme, Dooley Wilson (piano) in the 1943 motion picture, Higher and Higher. (Frank Driggs collection)

other sidemen suggested to Dorsey, as Rich had instructed him to, that Mel Torme, who was in the studio to sing with the Mel-Tones, could fill in for Rich on drums.

"I played that day and Tommy liked it," Torme recalls. "And then he began the campaign." Dorsey, who was drinking heavily in that period, called him at all hours.

Dorsey invited Torme over to his house to discuss the drumming proposition. There Dorsey introduced Torme to his then-wife, starlet Pat Dane. He startled Torme by remarking that she had the best pair of tits in Hollywood—and by then directing her to show them to Torme! With no enthusiasm, she complied with her husband's request. A naive and uncomfortable Torme took in the view.

"After the Pat Dane thing, Tommy called I think once more. And I said to my mother—I mean I never thought I'd ever say this about *Tommy Dorsey* [and now Torme whispers]: 'Tell him I'm not home.'" Needless to say, this was one recollection of the Sentimental Gentleman of Swing which Torme did not share on the 1987 PBS TV tribute to Dorsey, which Torme co-hosted and wrote.

"You know, Tommy and I became great friends after that. He stopped drinking. He was really a lovely guy." In fact, Torme eventually wound up marrying an aspiring actress named Candy Toxton, whom he first met at one of Dorsey's parties; she was actually Dorsey's girlfriend at the time.

Does Torme ever regret that he didn't take up Tommy Dorsey's offer and play the drums with that great band?

"You bet I do," he says. "You bet I do."

When Torme sang at a concert with the Tommy Dorsey Band, conducted by Buddy Morrow, a year and a half ago, he surprised a lot of the musicians in it by opting to play drums for the finale. He also got to drum for one number, while Buddy Rich sang, on the 1987 PBS tribute to Dorsey.

In choosing to concentrate on singing, Torme has necessarily had to put aside his interest in drumming. But his background in drumming has helped his singing. Note the way he'll lag behind the time—and then suddenly catch up, producing a slight sense of elation in the listener—when he performs "Just One of Those Things" in concert. He will sing, "If we'd thought a [pause] bit. . ."—and now he's fallen behind the beat. He catches up, later, compressing the words: "we'd have been aware. . ." He can utter words in a seemingly random way, and know he'll still come out right on the beat at the end of a phrase, because he's maintaining such a strong sense of time internally. His drumming background helps here, as well as in his arranging.

* * *

Torme's big break as a singer came when he recorded with Artie Shaw in 1946. He had never before recorded as a solo vocalist, without the Mel-Tones.

"Albert Marx, a very wealthy guy who loved music, started a new company called Musicraft Records. And Ben Pollack—I still had the Mel-Tones, then, and Ben was our manager—told Albert: 'Look, you haven't got a vocal group on the thing and the kids have been doing this and that. . .' P.S.—He signed us.

"Now he wanted to kick the label off with something spectacular. He'd signed Artie Shaw, and it was Artie's idea to do Cole Porter. Artie Shaw said, 'Let's really do this well. Let's get a concert orchestra together.'

"The first time I met Artie Shaw ever was at his house to rehearse. Of course I was an idolator from the year one about Artie Shaw. I always thought that he had the best taste in music of any bandleader I had ever run into. All those great show tunes that he did with the '39 band. God, I loved them. So I was in heaven.

"And he said, 'I like the way you sing. I like the way you sing solo. Why don't you do "Get Out of Town" on this album?'

"I said, 'Are you kidding!?' He said, 'No.'

Buddy Rich. (Chip Deffaa collection)

"Originally, it was just going to be the Mel-Tones recording with him. I was under contract as a vocal group arranger and leader. Artie Shaw gave me my first chance, when he let me sing 'Get Out of Town,' solo on the record. And he went around at that time—and he says he still does it—saying, 'This kid's my favorite singer. I like the way this kid sings.' And that's why I made all those records with Artie. And that really began my solo vocal career in earnest."

On ten recording sessions between April 29, 1946 and November 8, 1946, Torme sang by himself on nine records with Shaw's Orchestra (including "They Can't Convince Me," "Get Out of Town," "For You, For Me, For Evermore," and "I Believe"), and with the Mel-Tones on an additional six records with Shaw's Orchestra (including "What is this Thing Called Love?," "And So to Bed," and "Guilty"). On the first session, Shaw's Orchestra included 15 strings; but soon Shaw had upped that to two dozen strings, plus two bassoons, an oboe, a flute, and four French horns. Torme couldn't have asked for a finer showcase.

Torme notes: "That band was a studio band. My relationship with Artie Shaw was purely a recording relationship then. The first time I ever appeared 'live' with Artie Shaw was in 1985 at the Hollywood Bowl."

By 1985, Torme was the bigger name, as far as the general public was concerned. He received top billing at the Hollywood Bowl. Just how that may have set with Shaw, who, after all, had helped launch Torme's solo career, is open to conjecture.

Torme recalls: "I get to the Bowl for afternoon rehearsal. And a producer runs up to me, frantic: 'Oh Mel, I don't know how to tell you this. Oh God! Artie Shaw took your name off the main dressing room, and put your nameplate on the back dressing room, and he took your dressing room! I don't know what to do.'

"I said: 'Don't do anything. He's Artie Shaw. He's my hero. And he was my mentor. And if he wants that dressing room, of course.' I never said a word about it to him. And he never said, you know, like, 'Gee, I didn't think you'd mind.' He just automatically—*I'm Artie Shaw*. I happen to love the man. I adore him.

"And then we got on the stage. And I'm waiting to rehearse my numbers with the band, and he says, 'Mel, you don't mind, I've got a couple of things I want to do.' And he rehearsed the band—with things that they weren't even going to do at the Bowl. He said, 'Why don't we try this. . .?' And I'm waiting. . . .

"So my band rehearsal was cut down to—but I don't care, it was a great concert, we got wonderful reviews. Artie is a very special human being. And he's my mentor. We still talk all the time."

If Torme has his way, he says, his next PBS TV special will also star Artie Shaw and his Orchestra. "Yeah, absolutely, that's what I'd like to do. And it's a *wonderful* band. But Artie doesn't like to wallow in the past. He's very, very strong about that. 'I don't want to sit around and wallow in nostalgia.'

"I said, 'But Artie, you're an icon. You really are. You're a religious icon, man. You know, you can't escape it. You created something that...' We talk long, hour-long talks on the phone. But he's very adamant about it. He says, 'Mel, I didn't like it even then. I had the hot band in '39; we were the swing band of the year, with Buddy and Georgie Auld and all those guys—I didn't like it. I don't like being a performer. I'm not a public personality. I never liked being in front of the camera.'

"I say, 'God, that's amazing because you were so terrific.... Well look, co-host it with me, for Christ's sake.'

"He says: 'All right. But I want to be apart from the band. I don't want any attachment to the Artie Shaw—You can have the Artie Shaw Band on.' I say, 'Artie, how the hell do we do that? Are you going to do a dissertation on the Satyricon?...' So it's a slight impasse. But I'm hoping that I can bust him down. Because I think, gee, that would be a great show. I've idolized him. I knew Tommy, I liked him a lot. But I idolized Artie Shaw. He and Duke Ellington were my two major musical big band leader idols."

* * *

By 1946, Torme saw the way things were going. Big bands were on the wane. Singers were on the upswing. Sinatra, it seemed to him, had turned the music world upside down. Torme, however, still had not tried making it on his own as a singer. He didn't have a big name then, like Dick Haymes or Bob Eberly.

"But then one night, around Thanksgiving of 1946, Woody Herman and Les Brown got into kind of a long session with a manager named Carlos Gastell, who at that time managed Nat Cole, Peggy Lee, and Stan Kenton. They said, 'You know this squirt that has this vocal group, the Mel-Tones?' He says, 'Oh yeah, Mel, I know him very well.' 'Well, Jesus, maybe he could make it on his own. What do you think, Carlos? You're always looking for new things.'

"The three of them were sitting in his office playing those records that I'd made with Artie Shaw. And Carlos was known to take a drink or twelve. So he called me at 2:00 in the morning, and he said, 'Get down here!' I said, 'Carlos, it's 2:00 in the morning, my Mom and Dad are asleep!'

"But I met with him the next day and he convinced me that there might be a career for me as a solo singer. We went to New York, to set a deal at the Copacabana, in December of '46." The timing was right.

The "young squirt" vocalists were replacing the bandleaders in the public's eyes. And Torme's velvet tones caught on.

The bebop and "cool jazz" musicians of the late '40s and early '50s left an influence on Torme's vocal style, particularly in his scat improvisations. He won the respect of jazz critics. But never got so far out as to lose the general listener.

* * *

As the Swing Era was receding into history, Torme's own career as a single was really just beginning.[1] But in Torme's judgment, the passing of the big bands marked the beginning of the decline in American music. Singers became the prime focus of attention, and then rock 'n' roll groups. And the consummate professional musicians he had idolized—the distinguished bandleaders who had once set the standards in music—fell by the wayside.

"But during that golden period of time—and the big band era really was, no kidding—there was generated a kind of silver thread of excitement every day." A boyish enthusiasm rises within him. "I mean, think about this. All of the girls I went to school with—all those great-looking chicks in Angora sweaters and saddle shoes—couldn't wait to read *Down Beat* every week. Those girls knew the names of all the trombone players in the Glenn Miller Band. Those guys all had fan clubs. And it was a sweet thing to see.

"I listen to the music—the Glenn Miller arrangements by Jerry Gray and by Bill Finnegan, and the things that Billy Moore Jr., who was my favorite, did with the Lunceford Band, and of course Sy's arranging for Lunceford and for Tommy Dorsey. Glenn Miller himself was a master arranger. The harmonies, the sounds were so beautiful. I mean, absolutely lovely stuff.

"And it simply broke my heart that we got to a position in life where the electronic field took over. And with the electronics came a new perception of what it meant to be important. And what it meant to be important was to make a physical statement—whether it was the clothes you wore, or the way you didn't cut your hair, or the earings that dangled from your ear, you know. But that has very little, if anything, to do with music.

"And it hurt me deeply to see people like, for instance, Johnny Mercer, wonder whether he'd ever have a hit again because the age of the rock singer/song writer had come along. And the songs are so puerile, so uninventive, so unartistic. The lyrics don't rhyme. There's no craftsmanship to those songs. Because the market they're going for is a

[1] For further details of Torme's career, read his autobiography, *It Wasn't All Velvet*, published in 1988 by Viking/Penguin.

very, very young market. They don't really discriminate, from the standpoint of whether a song is workmanlike or not. Johnny Mercer got discouraged because he loved great lyrics; he loved writing them, and he loved hearing them. And now he suddenly hears all of these kids come along with these—not just that they're suggestive lyrics, sometimes downright descriptive lyrics, but also bad lyrics, *bad* writing. Childish.

"When Elvis Presley first started, I was so incensed at rock 'n' roll in general, and what I felt was a total amateur kind of approach to music. Some interviewer said to me, 'What do you think of this new kid, Presley?' I said, 'I think he's terrible. The guy's got a totally uncontrolled vibrato. He sings out of tune. I don't think he contributes a damned thing, except I guess the little girls like him. I've been through that period, where the little girls liked me. And then they didn't like me any more, they liked Vic Damone. Then they didn't like Vic Damone anymore, they liked, you know—we all go through that. It serves a purpose and I understand it, but don't ask me to comment on what a good singer he is, because he's not.'"

But if Torme thought things had gotten bad when Presley rose to fame, things seem much worse to him today. He says that when he heard one singer come out with a song called "'Do it to Me One More Time,' I began to think: 'This is the end. This is the decline and fall of the Roman Empire.'

"I'm glad I'm the age I am. I'm glad I was born when I was. I'm glad I grew up under the influence of the big bands. And under the kind of behavior that was exemplified by the likes of a Harry James and an Artie Shaw and a Gene Krupa, who was a perfect gentleman—and even Tommy (in his drinking days, he was kind of a two-fisted guy). For there was a set of rules that you lived by. And that was one of the great things about the big band era, as far as I'm concerned."

The young now seem, to Torme, to have too much control in our culture. "Young kids are given money—far too much—to indulge their fancies, and they all of a sudden began to control the cosmetics industry and the clothing industry, fashions and music, and of course, TV. Where I am, at the Kimberly Hotel, we've got 36 channels on the TV. But every other channel is a music TV channel, with all nothing but rock 'n' roll stuff. It's maddening. You just can't find anything decent to watch."

He worries about the sociological changes that he's witnessed in his lifetime.

"When I was going to high school, if Miss Baumgarten said, 'Melvin Torme, you get up, you go to the principal's office, and you wait there!'—I got up and I was terrified. Now the kids run the schools, the teachers are terrified. It really is like some macabre nightmare, what's happened to our country."

The uneasiness, the unhappiness that Torme is voicing now, comes as something of a surprise, if only because Torme's onstage persona is so blithe, insouciant, unflappable. Offstage, too, he is a model of congenial graciousness to strangers who recognize him. He believes that, as a public figure, he bears a certain responsibility to behave well. To maintain standards.

* * *

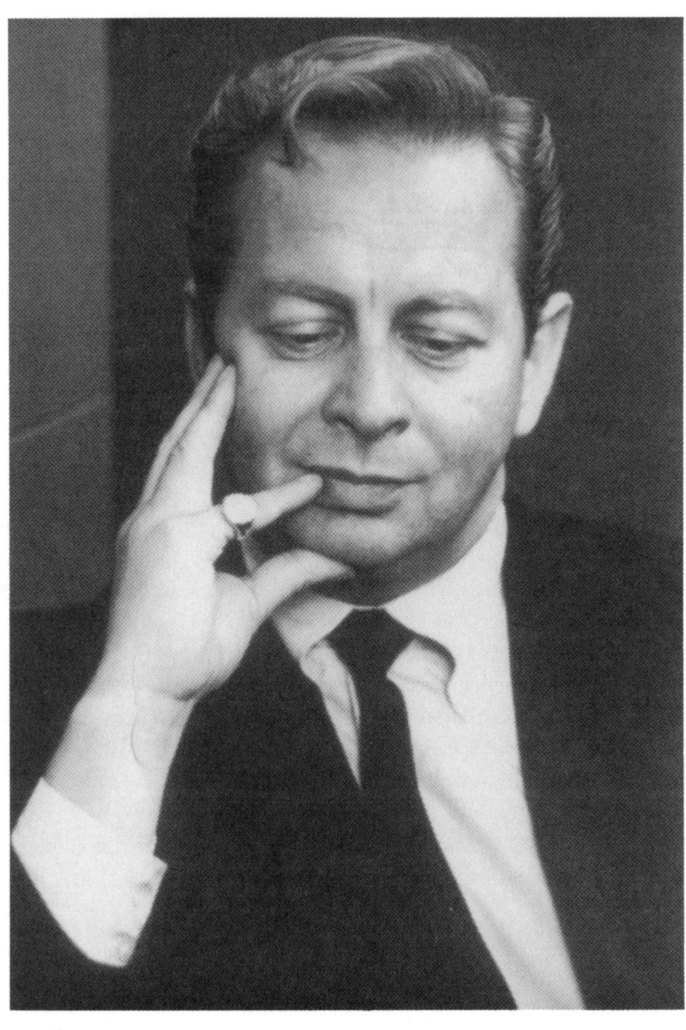

Mel Torme, 1960s. (Frank Driggs collection)

Torme works steadily these days: tony supper clubs, major concert halls. He gives freely—almost too freely—of himself to his audiences. He'll finish "Stardust"—ending in head tones of such awe-inspiring silvery purity that this listener would welcome five minutes of silence to simply savor them. Then he'll proceed almost at once, as if unaware he's offered us anything special, into an uptempo rouser. He kids with us, scat-sings to music of J. S. Bach, takes care to acknowledge Ella Fitzgerald, Bing Crosby, and the all-but-forgotten Leo Watson as among his scat-singing influences. He offers a tribute to Fred Astaire, whose savoir-faire he so greatly admired, and then sings a song which he recalls Buddy Rich asked him to sing the day before Rich died: "Here's that Rainy Day."

And after the "final" number of the set, Torme comes back perhaps a tad quicker than he should, to offer his pre-planned encores, including a bit of "Autumn Leaves" *in French.* He doesn't tend to make the audience beg him, coax him with applause the way a diffident Frank Sinatra might. Sinatra, in a sense, leans away from his followers. Torme leans towards them; he seems more eager to please, and to be liked.

Torme is at the top of his craft now. He has earned 13 Grammy nominations and two Grammies. He is widely admired, almost universally praised by critics. But there has been a rock revolution since he started out. And now, in his maturity, he cannot expect to sell the quantities of records that he sold in his youth. He is a superb singer of classic American songs. But today's teeny-boppers, he knows, probably would not recognize his name.

Torme maintains a frenetic pace of productivity. He is now working on his fourth book, a biography of Buddy Rich. He has written more than 300 songs, the best-known of which, "The Christmas Song," has been recorded 500 times.

Torme writes entire shows for himself. If you see a concert at which Torme is the host or chief participant—whether it's saluting Gershwin, big bands, or 60 years of singing in America—chances are he's put the whole thing together. He'll write the lines he utters on TV specials, too, but won't take a writing credit.

He arranges the music for his concerts and record dates. He is adept at coming up with imaginative medleys and special material for himself.[2] An embodiment of the old-style work ethic, Torme says he

[2] However, this critic feels Torme would be better showcased if he generally hired the best available arrangers, instead of trying to try to write so many arrangements himself. Torme is one of the greatest of all living singers; he has not achieved the same level of distinction as an arranger. Nelson Riddle and other master arrangers have writttten more memorable charts for Sinatra than Torme has written for himself, and have thus helped create more fully-realized albums. To my ears, the arrangements Marty Paich wrote for Torme in the 1950s set him off better than his own arrangements today typically do.

feels guilty if he so much as takes a Sunday afternoon off to see a movie: he isn't *accomplishing* anything in that time.

Torme, with great gusto, is forever revising his act. By the time many performers reach their 50s or 60s, their acts are *set*, typically focused on past hits. But if Torme ever found himself resting on his laurels, he says, he'd quit. He wants his audiences to keep coming back to see him, knowing that they'll see a substantially new show each year. And there are simply too many new songs to discover, too many old songs to rediscover, for him to stand still.

Mel Torme. (Chip Deffaa collection)

He says he doesn't like wallowing in nostalgia, any more than Artie Shaw does. He doesn't want to be seen as some kind of a relic from the past. He remains a vital contributor to the music world today.

But he can't help feeling some nostalgia for the so-called good old days. For deep down, in many ways, he really does believe they were better.

In Torme's dressing room tonight, in his break between sets at Michael's Pub, George T. Simon is telling him the lyrics that Edward Heyman *originally* wrote (not the lyrics by Mitchell Parrish that were published) for "Moonlight Serenade"—or "Now I Lay Me Down to Weep," as Heyman would have titled it. And as Simon speaks each long-forgotten line, Torme sings it back to him, in that flawless, clear, cool voice, to the familiar sentiment-laden melody.

"They're good lyrics," Torme says simply, after they've gone through the entire song, line by line. The words are bittersweet. The Glenn Miller melody, of course, is nostalgic as hell. You know Torme could do a superb job with it in his ever-changing act. He asks how he could get a copy of those lyrics.

1987

HAROLD • ASHBY

Remembering Duke and Ben

n his spartan Manhattan Plaza apartment, Harold Ashby picks out the notes on his Casiotone 501 portable electronic organ with care. Strains of "Mood Indigo"—rich, dirgelike—fill the room.

It has been 10 years since Ashby, a gifted jazz/blues tenor saxophonist from Kansas City, last played with the Duke Ellington Orchestra. In the past decade, he has played with some great musicians, most notably Benny Goodman. He's been periodically reunited for brief gigs with other former members of the Ellington band, such as Cat Anderson, Booty Wood, Norris Turney, and Wild Bill Davis. He's cut a few albums. He's led quartets in the U.S. and Europe. And last fall he presented his own special concert, with a grant from the National Endowment for the Arts, at St. Peter's Church in New York. But in talking with him, you have the feeling that he'd chuck it all in a minute if he could somehow play one concert again with the extraordinary orchestra that the late Duke Ellington led.

You catch Ashby leading a quartet at the Cornerstone Restaurant, a base for traditional jazz in New Jersey. He swings into "Take the A Train." He makes the most of the tune, and the audience interrupts his playing with applause. But you can't help remembering how it once sounded, when Ashby blew in a sax section along with Johnny Hodges, Russell Procope, Paul Gonsalves, and Harry Carney.

In a break, Ashby flicks open his saxophone case to show you something. Pinned to the inside of the case are two red-white-and-blue buttons that read, "Duke Ellington, USA," buttons which he recalls giving out by the handful when the band toured the Soviet Union. He mentions that someday he'd like to record an Ellington album of his own. And that he's written several never-recorded numbers as tributes to Duke.

"Duke died May 24th, 1974. I stayed with the band till February eighth or the ninth of 1975. Then I left. It couldn't be the same," he declares firmly. "You know, Duke Ellington had died; that's it—it can't possibly be the same thing. Duke Ellington's band—and *that's it.*"

Ashby loved to solo with that band, he tells you, on the numbers that Duke Ellington had determined were *his*, such as "Chinoiserie," "Just Squeeze Me," "Acht O'Clock Rock," and "I Can't Get Started." For Ellington knew each of his players' special talents, Ashby says; he knew just how to set each player off to greatest advantage.

Sure Ashby misses being a part of that band at times. "Hey man, it was beautiful playing this music," he says simply. "It was beautiful."

* * *

Ashby is a distinguished-looking fellow. His hair has turned white; it becomes him. He speaks slowly, sparingly. His apartment has a rather ascetic feel. In his refrigerator right now, there is fruit juice, but not a good deal else. He believes in the positive value of periodically fasting, and he has been fasting lately. Except for the newly-acquired electronic organ, a TV, a record player and a surprisingly small number of albums—some Charlie Parker, some Ben Webster, some Ellington—the apartment seems rather empty. He has a single shoebox in which he keeps miscellaneous personal possessions and mementoes. And, oh yes, there is the case containing his saxophone. Ashby has never been one for acquiring things. Music quite literally has been his life.

Ashby was about 15, he recalls, when he first saw the Duke Ellington Band in Kansas City in 1940. Sitting in the sax section were such legendary players as Harry Carney (who had first joined the band back in 1926) and Johnny Hodges (who had joined in '28). Little did Ashby dream that more than a quarter of a century later he would be playing alongside both of of them. The soloist who most impressed Ashby that night, though, was tenorman Ben Webster. Webster was universally admired for his big, warm tone, as well as for his unusual sensitivity on ballads. He may be best known to general listeners for his work on such famous Ellington recordings of the early 1940s as "All Too Soon," "Cottontail," and "C Jam Blues." Little did Ashby dream that Ben Webster would someday take him under his wing, record with him, and bring him to the attention of Duke Ellington, in whose band Ashby would

Harold Ashby. (Frank Driggs collection)

inherit some of the solo spaces that had once been Webster's.

Ashby was born in Kansas City, Missouri, on March 27, 1925. The city was a hotbed of jazz and blues in the late '20s and the '30s. Ashby was too young to appreciate the emergence of the Count Basie Band in Kansas City in '36, but he was not too young to witness that band's return, on tour, to the city as a national favorite, just a few years later.

There were clubs everywhere in the city. And swarms of musicians, both amateur and professional. By the time Ashby was 13, he notes, his best friend was into the clarinet in a big way, learning to play "Sing Sing Sing" like Benny Goodman. One of Ashby's brothers was an alto player; the other was a trumpet player. "Now the trumpet player also had a clarinet. So I got his clarinet and went into the orchestra program at Lincoln High School, an hour a day," Ashby recalls.

"And then I'd baby-sit for my brother. And he had all the records. Like Coleman Hawkins' 'Body and Soul,' and Lester Young's thing; I put them on and listened to them. In 1940 I went on to Lincoln Junior College. Then when I was 17, I went to R. T. Coles Vocational School, where I really learned how to play tenor. And that's when I went for music three hours a day, and all the fellows used to be, you know, *playing* in the music class. They knew all the solos. That's when I got into the music, really. That's when I started going to the dances, listening to bands that would come there, like, every Sunday. I saw Count Basie when Lester and them were playing, I saw Erskine Hawkins when Paul Bascomb played the tenor. Saw Louis Jordan, when Louis Jordan was really into it. And I saw Duke—I saw Ben [Webster] come out there and play 'Body and Soul.'

"I bought a saxophone. It cost about a hundred dollars, and I was paying for it. It was a Conn. I used to work after school. My uncle was a real estate man, so when they'd have apartments, I'd clean them up. Before that, I was a grocery delivery boy, because my mother died when I was eight, and my father was like a janitor, so I was doing a little bit of everything."

Ashby's home was close to clubs, he notes. "I lived on 13th and Euclid. I'd walk across to 18th and Vine, and 19th. I saw Don Byas jamming in there at the Kentucky Tavern. I saw Charlie Parker. I'd see the Spook Breakfasts on Monday morning." On Monday mornings, when clubs and taverns could legally re-open, after shutting down at 1:30 in the morning, they would offer "Spook Breakfasts," with plenty of music. Ashby says that the years of the most intense musical activity in Kansas City were a little before his time. But there was still a good deal of action for him to catch in Kansas City before he went into the Navy in July 1943, and just after he came out in December 1945.

"When I was in the Navy, though, I pawned my horn, 'cause I was gambling," he recalls. "And then I sold it after I was shipped to Chicago."

By now, Ben Webster had quit Ellington's band, and was working instead with small groups. "In Chicago, they had a place called the Downbeat Room—that's where Ben was playing around '44-'45. Ben and Don Stovall and J.C. Higginbotham and Red Allen. I was on the ship. When I went in town, I'd listen to Ben and them play.

"When I got out of the service, I went back to Kansas City, and I was gambling. I was going to the pool hall and to the dice games and all that, and I was losing. So I went and bought a horn. Fellow told me, 'Man you better buy a horn.' I wasn't going to make it gambling. And I started playing with Tommy Douglas' territorial band.

"Then I started playing with Walter Brown, a blues singer—sung 'Confessin' the Blues,' the one with Jay McShann, with Charlie Parker on the first record. And then with John Jackson, who was a hell of an alto player, and his band. And at that time, John Jackson had played with Billy Eckstine, so I was picking it up from there."

And he was getting to know Ben Webster. About 1949, he recalls making a recording date with Walter Brown. And the next day, Webster was at the same studio, recording with a quartet. "Around there in '49, I was playing with a little group, and Ben used to come around and sit in with us. We was young kids then, we was like 24. And Ben wanted to be around the young cats then, so he'd come around and sit in with us. That's the way we began to know each other. So when I went to Chicago after that, he knew me," he recalls.

Ashby became something of a musical disciple of Webster, and a lasting friendship developed. "Ben drove me up to like Elkhart, Indiana, one time, to take my horn up there. And the man fixed my horn and gave me a *cut rate*. You know, because I was with *Ben Webster*. The man overhauled the horn. Then Ben drove me back up there to get it. Yeah, Ben was a good friend, man.

"At first I was trying to play like Ben. You know, I liked the way Ben played. Ben had a beautiful sound. Ben had a pretty sound. Anybody can tell you, you listen to him and hear Ben play, and that's *it*. You know, I got all these records of Ben. He got that *pretty* sound. And I was trying to play like Ben. You have to be inspired by someone. I heard all of them play, and I liked Ben. When I heard him—that was it.

"In Chicago, in the early '50s, I started playing with Willie Dixon and Memphis Slim; I used to make records for Chess: Willie Mabon, and Otis Rush, the blues thing in Chicago. I was involved in the blues, the blues records. [Jimmy] Witherspoon. Lowell Fulson. Chess Records made all them. I played with Sonny Boy Williamson, the harp [harmonica] player. Then I left Chicago and came on here to New York."

The blues, and rhythm-and-blues Chess records that Ashby played on may not have been big commercial sellers. But a lot of rock 'n' rollers *did* listen to those records, and then offered their audiences diluted, more commercialized versions of that music. Listen to the album, "Willie's Blues," Prestige/Bluesville 1003, recently reissued by Fantasy. Willie Dixon plays bass and sings in an appealing, if crude, style; Memphis Slim is on piano; Wally Richardson is on guitar; Gus Johnson Jr. is on drums. Ashby's buoyant, vital sax work contributes a great deal. The links between this type of music and rock 'n' roll are apparent. But the album has an honesty about it that you don't sense on the popular rock 'n' roll records.

"When I first met Ben Webster, you know, I was like 15 years old; I saw him playing in a dance with Duke Ellington. And I met him again in Chicago. And then when I came to New York in December of '57, I met Ben again.

"And he used to call me up and ask me, did I need any money and all that kind of carrying on, you know. In New York City, when I first came here, I remember one time when I had no money. Yeah, a couple times, I didn't have no money. I've found out now that I can go a long time fasting, just drinking water. But when you don't have any money, then you worry about eating. The thought in your mind is, 'What am I going to do?' I got broke a couple times, man." Webster invited Ashby to move out where he lived.

"I moved out on the Island with Ben and Big Miller, the blues singer. The lady had a house, and her basement was divided like in three bedrooms: Ben, Big Miller, and me," he recalls. Ashby was proud when Webster invited him to record with him. They made an album in 1959. "This is Ben's date, Ben used me on it. Ben wrote the tune called 'Ash' on this date. Ben wrote about three tunes for me over the years." Ashby flips through his stack of albums, until he finds another of Webster's. This one has a tune Webster wrote, entitled, "Ash's Cap." The liner notes state that it was "dedicated to a close friend and disciple who once recorded with him." Ashby later returned the compliment, recording an original number entitled, "Lullaby for Ben." Ashby finds an old photo of Webster, and points out the distinctive, large rounded ring Webster wore. He owns that ring now; it is in his shoebox of mementoes. It was given to him after Webster died in Amsterdam. He says softly: "Ben was something else." And it was Webster, he tells you, who introduced him to Ellington in the late '50s.

"One time Duke was playing at the Apollo Theater, and Ben went up there to see all the fellows. He took me up there and introduced me to Johnny Hodges and Duke Ellington," Ashby notes. Ashby wound up getting a job substituting in the house band at the Apollo Theater.

And he was also getting to know musicians in the Ellington circle. Sometimes Ellington sidemen would record small-band jazz sessions on their own. Ashby recorded first with Lawrence Brown's All-Stars; in the next few years, he would record with Johnny Hodges, Russell Procope, and others.

But openings occurred far more infrequently in the Ellington Band than in other bands. The personnel, particularly in the sax section, remained remarkably the same from one year to the next. Ellington first invited Ashby to play with the band, substituting for Paul Gonsalves, for two nights in 1960. Over the next eight years, Ashby filled in from time to time, on a temporary basis. He became a permanent, full-time member of the band in 1968.

Ashby notes that the first time he played with the band, in 1960, "was *very* special. I remember the first time when Duke called me on the phone. Duke called me early one morning, man. I used to work on 125th Street, at the Celebrity Club with Milton Larkin. I used to play weddings, and then, on a Sunday night, you'd play from seven to 11. And then I'd go around to clubs. So I got home that morning around five o'clock, and I went to sleep. And about eight o'clock, the phone rang. It was Duke Ellington, saying, 'Harold Ashby? I want you to work with me tonight and tomorrow night.' I was kind of groggy, and I figured this was somebody playing a joke. I said, 'Well look man, I'm tired right now. I ain't woke up yet. I'll see you.' And hung the phone up, you dig? So Duke called back, and said, 'Look, this is *Duke*. I want you to work tonight and tomorrow night.' So I said, 'Yeah, OK, I'm scared.' I used to live at 925 St. Nicholas Avenue. That's 156th and St. Nicholas. And Duke used to live at 935, right next door, and I never knew it. So Duke said, 'The bus is down there at 155th street. Go down there and catch the bus. Right away.' So, I went to take a bath. He called you like this, and you get nervous and scared, you know. Because I had never been in a context like that before.

"And then Duke called again, said: 'You haven't left yet? Go catch the bus!' So I got my clothes on and went on down and caught the bus. And everybody's on the bus, going to make this trip, *everybody*—Johnny Hodges, all up and down, they're all there. Jimmy Hamilton and I think Sam [Woodyard], Procope and all those people are on the bus. Ain't nobody says nothing. I just walk on back there and get on the bus. I'm scared to death.

"And that particular night, when it come time to play, I walked up on the stand. Procope was sitting on the stand. I was looking through the music, I don't even know nothing about playing in a . . . you know, I'm looking through the music. I've never had no . . . I played *the blues*.

Duke Ellington and Harold Ashby in Moscow, 1971. (Courtesy Harold Ashby)

I could play the blues, you know, in a blues band.

"So Procope says, 'You know, this band isn't like any other band. Just blow.' And that's it. And so Duke came out there and starts playing. The fellow sang some blues. And Duke told me to play. And that was it. I got across because of *my sound*, you know what I mean? My sound. The sound that I had was, you know, compatible with their type of thing. So that's what that was all about. So I just made it," Ashby recalls.

By then, Ashby had developed his own, immediately recognizable sound. It was a full sound, silvery, but sometimes soft and misty around the edges. A sound that was sometimes colored by pathos. Ellington, who picked his reedmen for their sounds, not just their technical facility or ideas in phrasing, knew Ashby could fit into his band. There was no opening in the reed section at the time, and wouldn't be for eight years, when Jimmy Hamilton left; sax men, in particular, seemed to stay with Ellington forever. But Ashby did get to play on some small-group recording dates led by members of the Ellington band. He was now part of the extended family of Ellingtonians.

In January of '61, Ashby cut an album with Paul Gonsalves, "Tenor Stuff." He notes: "It's like a two tenor thing: Paul, Harold Ashby, Sir Charles Thompson played piano, Aaron Bell, Jo Jones on drums. During that period, I made all these kind of records. Johnny Hodges used me on a lot of his dates. I did one with Johnny called 'The Smooth One.'

"And then in 1963, I played with Duke's second band, which he had in Chicago, for the *My People* show. Duke wrote all the music. Alvin Ailey choreographed it. Duke was right there, but Jimmy Jones conducted the band. And Billy Strayhorn. It was like a Billy Strayhorn band, and he was in charge of it. But you know, this was Duke's thing; he was commissioned to do the show." In 1966, Ashby played on an Earl Hines big band album ("Once Upon A Time," still available on MCA), which included a number of Ellingtonians. "Then I started playing with Duke Ellington regularly July fifth, 1968."

Ashby says that when he watches the news on TV, and they show trouble in Poland or Nicaragua or Ethiopia, he remembers playing in all of those countries with the band. He picks up a Polish Duke Ellington album. He finds photos taken in Ethiopia. One shows Emperor Haile Selassie giving Ashby a present. Ashby doesn't remember what it was; he sent it to his sister. But he remembers the huge crowd in Addis Ababa, and knowing that somewhere, far back in the darkness, was Selassie. And the time he and some friends from the band sat in with some African musicians. And giving out the Ellington souvenir buttons in the U.S.S.R. He remembers, too, trying unsuccessfully to mail albums to someone he met while in the U.S.S.R.; the albums were returned to

Harold Ashby accepting a present from Emperor Haile Selassie of Ethiopia. (Courtesy Harold Ashby)

him. And so many jazz fans in Europe tape-recording their concerts. And playing Thailand, and Australia, and throughout South America. And Westminster Abbey, for a sacred concert. And Japan, where he was given a saxophone, in exchange for his endorsement of that brand.

And mostly he recalls the music. "The 'Chinoiserie' was one of the big things that I played. It's on the album, 'The Afro-Eurasian Eclipse.' Or, if you listen to the record of Duke's 'New Orleans Suite,' I play 'Thanks for the Beautiful Land on the Delta.' Duke wrote music for each individual. When he wrote something, to have you play it, I mean it was for *you*. Yeah, it wasn't for anybody else. He wrote it for your capabilities, what you could do. 'Cause some people are liable to have more technique, one may have more feeling. He would write for your thing. So it was something else.

"Duke was like one of the fellows, that's the way he was. He was a regular person. You could talk to Duke Ellington. Yeah, he was a nice person," Ashby says.

"I don't think Duke Ellington played jazz. He played *music*. You can't categorize that. Like Duke Ellington said—'*Beyond Category.*'

They put labels on it. Well, I'm not a jazz musician. I'm a *musician*."

Ashby started working on his own in the New York area, after leaving the Ellington Band in 1975. His quartet played periodically at the West End Cafe. He cut an album (with a not very distinguished rhythm section) called, "Presenting Harold Ashby," for Progressive Records. It has some nice moments, "Over the Rainbow" in particular, but overall it is not nearly as satisfying as a much harder-to-find album called "Scufflin'," which Ashby recorded in France for the Black and Blue label, during a 1978 tour with fellow Ellington alumni including Booty Wood (trombone), Aaron Bell (bass), and Sam Woodyard (drums). Having the right sidemen can make quite a difference. And Ashby and Wood sound great together. Ashby's exceptional sensitivity with a ballad is demonstrated on Antonio Carlos Jobim's "Quiet Nights." He moves on "Get Down," one of his originals.[1]

Ashby likes playing in Europe. "Last March, I went over there on a tour with [blues-based jazz pianist] Junior Mance's group; we went through France and Spain, Belgium. And I went to Barcelona from October 20th to November 8th. I played Waterloo the year before last. Last year I played up there at Carnegie Hall with a Duke Ellington alumni band." He's worked sporadically.

"But I don't go out and try to get no jobs today. I did that a long time ago, and I'm tired now. I can't be running around out there now," Ashby says. With a smile, he suggests: "It's like, a prostitute sits by her phone, and when it rings she goes out. Same thing with a musician."

He's enjoyed playing occasional dates with Benny Goodman. He comments: "Benny Goodman, you know—he can play. He's something else. He won't be jivin.' He'd be playing the clarinet—that's for sure." A photo shows Ashby with Goodman, Warren Vache Jr., John Bunch, Chris Flory, Phil Flanigan and Urbie Green at the Kennedy Center in 1982. A clipping on the concert reports: "Ashby's 'Body and Soul,' breathily erotic and with emotional abandon, brought applause second only to that awarded the headliner."

Ashby enjoys long-favored records. "I listen to *Ben*, Johnny Hodges, Charlie Parker, Lester Young—the masters." Other than that, he says, "I'll go down and take a swim, sit in the sauna, something like that. That's about the only thing I do. And I watch my diet. You know, I haven't eaten any meat in a long time. I got a whole bunch of apple juice over there. And I fast. I got every book on fasting. You feel better." And sometimes he plays his sax, or picks out themes on his organ.

[1] At the 1985 Nice Jazz Festival, Ashby reportedly went over best on the uptempo things. A December, 1985, cover story on Ashby in England's *Jazz Journal International* called him the "revelation" of the Nice festival.

He is due—overdue, really—for a rediscovery. He notes: "I got a whole bunch of tunes, man. I wrote a whole bunch. I would like to get a record date so I can record some of them. But the only way I'll ever record, I guess, is if I go overseas or something. 'Cause I don't think they're going to record 'em over here. The way I play horn, you know, I go to Europe."

1985

Remembering Count Basie

don't dig that two-beat jive the New Orleans cats play. Because my boys and I got to have four heavy beats to a bar and no cheating."

—William "Count" Basie

The Kid from Red Bank, as Basie liked to call himself, never cheated the cash customers in his life. He offered honest, hard-hitting, four-beats-to-the-bar, big band jazz. Duke Ellington may have created works of greater profundity and mystery. The Dorseys may have treated ballads more romantically. But when it came to simply making a band swing, getting the band to really move in a way that satisfied both musicians and the public, nobody—but nobody—surpassed Basie.

From 1937 until his death on April 26, 1984, at age 79, Basie spent virtually all of his life on the road, traveling from gig to gig with his band on a bus and, later, a plane. Basie was hailed as the man who brought Kansas City style jazz to the rest of the country. And there was truth in that, although Basie never let anyone forget he was born in Red Bank, New Jersey.

* * *

Basie might have become a professional drummer, he often said, except for the fact that he realized while in his early teens that he was the second-best boy drummer in Red Bank. And if he couldn't even be the best young drummer in a small town like Red Bank, he didn't see much future for himself on that instrument. So he switched to piano, and left the drumming to his Red Bank rival—Sonny Greer. Greer went on to become one of the most renowned big band drummers, working with Duke Ellington for three decades.

After Basie became famous, newspapers often printed that he had played in boys' bands in his youth, before going on to playing in vaudeville. But in a tape-recorded interview in the oral history collection at the Rutgers Institute of Jazz Studies, Basie said he never played in any boys' bands. Kids in Red Bank simply did not have bands when he was growing up, he said. He started work as a professional musician, with adults, while in his mid-teens, first in Red Bank, then in Asbury Park, then in New York, and on tour. And he did not play piano in vaudeville, he added. Although he *did* play for burlesque shows.

Count Basie. (Courtesy Willard Alexander, Inc.)

In Harlem, Basie heard the newest developments in stride piano and Fats Waller gave him instruction on the organ. He got a steady gig as a pianist in a six-piece band at Leroy's, a popular club for blacks owned by Leroy Wilkins.

Basie headed west with a touring show and got stranded in Kansas City, Missouri, which in the 1920s was one of the four great cities for jazz, along with New York, Chicago, and New Orleans. One wonders how jazz history might have turned out differently, had Basie been stranded in another part of the country.

Thanks to the collaboration of political boss Tom Pendergast and Johnny Lazia (Kansas City's version of Al Capone), Kansas City was wide-open. It touted itself as America's best good-time city. Clubs which paid off never worried about being raided by the police for illegal drinking or gambling. All applicants to the police force were referred for approval to Lazia.

And jazz flourished. By the late 1920s, it has been estimated there were from 200-500 nightclubs of various kinds operating in Kansas City.

Basie played clubs with great swing bands: first with Walter Page's Blue Devils, then with Bennie Moten's Band. By 1936, after Moten's death, Basie was leading his own nine-piece band, which included the best of Moten's players, in Kansas City's Reno Club. Here, Basie and his men developed on the bandstand numbers which would eventually become jazz classics. Customers who could not afford marijuana (three sticks for a quarter) could sit in the balcony and get high from the fumes of other customers—and musicians—smoking below.

When jazz enthusiast John Hammond chanced upon a broadcast from the Reno Club over an experimental short wave station, he persuaded agent Willard Alexander to book the Basie Band on a national tour. The band's rhythmic pulse, Hammond felt, was irresistible. Basie, with his band expanded to 13 men, arrived in New York in 1937. Within two years, his band was a national institution.

It was gutsy, earthy music in the early days: the blues that were popular in the southwest, with plenty of riffs by the brass, and battles by Basie's star tenors, Lester Young and Herschel Evans. Over the course of five decades, the band grew more polished and sophisticated, and in later years, arrangers became increasingly important. But the blues always remained an important part of the band's legacy.

* * *

Over the years, Basie periodically went home to Red Bank to visit his parents at 229 Mechanic Street and childhood friends. Sometimes he brought his band for benefit concerts.

The last time was just a year before his death. "You don't know what a pleasure it is to be back home again," he told the crowd, at the start of a concert to benefit the A.M.E. Zion Church, which has served Red Bank's black community since 1833.

Basie is remembered now with a Count Basie Park in Red Bank. And the nearby Monmouth Arts Center has honored Basie by renaming its theater the Count Basie Theatre—the same facility Basie played to a sold-out audience only a year before his death.

But Basie's best memorial is his music. And as long as public interest remains, Basie's adopted son, Aaron Woodward, intends to see that there's a Count Basie Orchestra, playing the Basie favorites like "Jumpin' at the Woodside," "One O'Clock Jump," and "Shiny Stockings." And, of course, two Basie classics that beautifully showcased his inimitable "Kansas City style" at the keyboard: "The Red Bank Boogie" and "The Kid from Red Bank."

1984

Nat Pierce and Woody Herman at the funeral of Count Basie, 1984. (Photo by Nancy Miller Elliott)

THAD·JONES

Straight-Ahead with the Count Basie Orchestra

"We intend to move ahead, carrying on a tradition that Basie lived his life in and gave his life for. I don't think that Basie would want us to be preoccupied with the past—you know, he was not like that. He would want the band to move forward," declares Thad Jones. He is a vital, energetic man. He has slept but three and a half hours in the past two days. He is just coming off the road for a breather after his first two-and-a-half-month cross-country tour as leader of the Count Basie Orchestra. He has four hours between planes and seems eager to use them to talk about the band, and his life.

"It's been beautiful, beautiful, traveling with the band. Difficult—because primarily it's been a trip of one-nighters—but the results are very encouraging and inspiring," he says. "Everybody actually feels refreshed, and ready to go on. Ready to get into it, in a much deeper sense."

This is a critical period for the Basie Band. The band is generally acknowledged to be the finest large touring jazz band in the world. Will it be able to maintain that position?

Thad Jones. (Institute of Jazz Studies)

There seems to be no more difficult a challenge in music than sustaining the quality and spirit of a big band after its leader has died. If a new leader changes things too radically, he risks losing the public, who'll say it no longer sounds like the same band. And yet if the new leader strives primarily to keep the band *from* changing—forever preserving the sound exactly the way it was when the old leader died—he risks losing the band's most creative members, and turning the band into a ghost of its former self, dealing in nostalgia. We've all seen name bands that can execute beautifully their 40-year-old charts, but can no longer offer much that is new.

If there is anyone who can find the proper balance between holding onto the past and reaching out for the future needed to truly maintain the proud tradition of the Basie Band, chances are it is Thad Jones, who took over as leader of the band in February, 1985. No other Basie alumnus could have brought to the band his combined strengths as a musician, successful bandleader, and arranger.

In the early '50s, Charles Mingus was raving that Jones was the greatest trumpet player he had heard in his life. Basie hired Jones in '54 and for the next nine years—an outstanding time in the history of the

Basie Band—Jones was a key member of the organization.

From 1965 to '78, Jones fronted the Thad Jones-Mel Lewis Orchestra, which in that period came to surpass Basie's Band in terms of musical adventurousness, repeatedly reaching the number-one position in polls. Since 1978, Jones has made Denmark his home, leading the Danish Radio Orchestra and teaching at the Royal Conservatory in Copenhagen.

And then there is Jones the arranger. There are those, such as Marty Kriven, Coordinator of Jazz Studies at William Paterson College in New Jersey, who will tell you: "Jones is *the* most important living arranger, the continuation of Duke Ellington. He's an original." His music can be complex, moody, in the Ellington tradition. And he now enjoys the privilege Ellington once enjoyed, of being able to write for—and hear his creations immediately brought to life by—as fine a large jazz ensemble as may be found.

Jones has no intention of having the Basie Band play old arrangements he wrote for the Thad Jones-Mel Lewis Band. But he has already begun writing new music for the Basie Band. A new chapter in the band's nearly 50-year history is beginning.

* * *

At first, after Basie's death in April of '84, the band operated without any publicly designated leader. Eric Dixon served as the unbilled musical director, quietly giving the downbeats from the saxophone section where he had sat for so long.

Aaron Woodward, Basie's adopted son, recalls that for months he resisted the idea that the band needed anyone out in front. "But the late Willard Alexander, who had booked dad for years, told me we would have a great deal of difficulty continuing without a leader," Woodward says. The Basie Band is an institution—but it is an expensive institution to keep in operation. And the band, Woodward says, simply was not getting the bookings it needed to ensure that it would survive.

Alexander prepared a list of possible leaders. Woodward discussed the alternatives with "the senior council" of the Basie Band—guitarist Freddie Green, trumpeter Sonny Cohn, trombonist Bill Hughes, and reedman Eric Dixon. "They've all been in the band 25 years—Freddie's been in it nearly 50 years. They are the bearers of the flame," Woodward says. "And Thad Jones was the only person that all of them individually and unanimously recommended as leader."

Jones had commitments to conclude in Denmark. He would be permanently leaving the country that he, his young Danish wife, Lis, and their five year old son, Thad Jr., considered home. But he was eager to take on the challenge.

On February 10th, 1985, Jones started—rather gingerly at first—

as leader. Almost all of the musicians had stayed on with the band following Basie's death. "It's more than a band, it's a family," says Woodward. To some members of the band, Jones might initially seem like an outsider. He did not want to ruffle any feathers.

In his first weeks with the band, Jones took only one token solo per night, on "Shiny Stockings." After two and a half months as leader, he had upped his quota to three numbers per night.

He comments: "The solos have been distributed throughout the band before I got here. I'm just going to have to be patient and find certain things that a person of my 'inexperience,' you might say, would be able to kind of fumble through. You know, with all of those fantastic players up there, I'm a little intimidated in the beginning. So I'm just going to have to take it easy, and if I see a little opening, I'll cautiously move in. But I won't jump in!

"The music that the band is playing is a music that's been accepted

Thad Jones and the Basie Band's "Keeper of the Flame," Freddie Green, 1985. (Chip Deffaa collection)

totally by the public for years. They're considered sort of standard compositions in the jazz repertory. So you *must* play these numbers. You know, we never take anything away from this band's book—we just add to the book.

"I've asked for contributions from Frank Foster and Ernie Wilkins, and I've received some very positive 'yeses.' For most of the years when I was with the band, with the possible exception of a period when Neal Hefti was the focal point of interest, Frank Foster and Ernie Wilkins created about 75% of the band book. And Frank Wess is another one who I'd like to get some music from; he is another one of the great—and unheralded—arrangers. These men have sort of a spiritual tie to the band, no matter where they are or how long they've been away from it. Whatever music they contribute will be with this mental picture of Basie in mind.

"In recent years, Sammy Nestico, another very fine arranger, has contributed a tremendous amount of music. Eric Dixon, a fantastically gifted writer, has been doing a great amount of writing. And Dennis Wilson has made some very strong and important contributions to the band book," Jones notes. "What will happen musically will only be a forward movement and an expansion of something that's already there."

* * *

Thaddeus Joseph Jones, 62, is the middle brother of what may well be America's first family of jazz. His older brother, Hank, is a distinguished jazz pianist; his younger brother, Elvin, makes everyone's list of top drummers.

"Originally, I played trumpet—my Uncle William gave me my first one—but trumpets were not allowed in the Pontiac High School Concert Band—you had to have a cornet. And after I tried the cornet, I liked it so much that I never got away from it. For me, the cornet is more natural than the trumpet; it feels better," Jones says.

Jones' first professional dates were in his native Pontiac, Michigan, at age 16 in 1939 with the grandly-titled "Arcadia Club Band." The 10-piece unit was organized by his Uncle William; his brother Hank played piano. "Our uniforms consisted of some white Eton jackets that we ordered through Spiegel's catalog. I don't know where we came up with the name 'Arcadia Club Band.' We probably got it out of one of those catalogs, too. Everybody in the band, with the exception of the drummer, was related to somebody else in the band.

"We were going to high school and we'd take the jobs whenever they came up—sometimes we played consecutive weekends. For a night's work, we would sometimes get a dollar and a half or two dollars per person. Two dollars and fifty cents, three-fifty was a big night," Jones says. "But that's when money went as far as it was supposed to.

You could pay eleven cents to get a bottle of milk. Bread cost you eight cents a loaf.

"I wrote my first arrangement for that band, on 'Little Coquette.' I presented it at a rehearsal, and after the first two or three bars, the band just broke up and started laughing. Because what I had done—I had written all of the instruments in a different key.

"Louis Armstrong was my hero then, as far as the trumpet was concerned," Jones notes. (Among other trumpeters whose artistry he's admired over the years since, he says, are Dizzy Gillespie, Miles Davis, Freddie Hubbard, Wynton Marsalis, Snooky Young, Joe Newman, Bobby Hackett, Wendell Culley, Harry "Sweets" Edison, and Clark Terry—a list notable for its stylistic diversity.)

"And I listened to *all* of the bands then. There must have been 50-60 different successful bands that you could consistently hear on the radio in that period. And they were all top-flight.

"Well, naturally I enjoyed Ellington and Basie, Lunceford, and Woody Herman. There was a band that used to play at the amusement park not too far from where we lived, Sonny Burke. And there was Red Nichols—a hell of a cornet player; his band also played at that park. I heard Sam Donahue's Band. I listened to Guy Lombardo and the others, Sammy Kaye, Kay Kyser, Spike Jones." Jones enjoyed those commercial "sweet" dance bands, he makes clear, "just as much as I enjoyed listening to anything else! The music was challenging, and the bands were stocked with very, very, very good musicians. Every one of them. You know, a lot of times they played the type of music that they played for commercial reasons, but every now and then they could break down and play just about as good a jazz as any old band you'd want to listen to. There was Horace Heidt and his Musical Knights—used to feature a lot of triple-tonguing and double-tonguing in his trumpet section. There were so many bands. There was Dick Stabile, who was the first saxophone player that I heard that used to play in the high register consistently. There was Noble Sissle, Andy Kirk, Erskine Hawkins. The country was really rich in music then. And all of this was transmitted to us via the radio.

"Our family was poor. We couldn't afford to get around to all these places to see the bands in person. I went to see Duke Ellington once. And I saw Nat Cole with a band; he came through my home town—he was playing with a big band, with a show called *Shuffle Along* which was quite good, and at a very acceptable price, and I went to see him. It was the first time I'd ever seen a man wear draped pants. They're just the opposite of bell-bottoms—the large part is in the knee and the small part is in the cuff. I was fascinated.

"I went out on the road in '41, and started traveling with Connie

Connell's Band through the south. We found out that the road wasn't all it was made out to be. The jobs weren't plentiful. And we were having pistols stuck in our faces by cops. We lived under the threat of the gun the whole time we were in the south. Because you never knew when one of these irrational people would just go off and decide to use that weapon that they always carried. The society was very permissive in that area—against blacks, that is. There was a lot of killing going on. We sort of traveled in fear for a large portion of the trip. It was very seldom that that thought ever left us.

"I was inducted in the army in 1943. I didn't play with any organized army bands—by the time I got in, the band cadres were rather complete," Jones notes. But he played frequently on an unofficial basis.

After his discharge in 1946, Jones went barnstorming, "playing wherever the jobs came. I played carnivals, burlesque shows—I did the whole thing. We used to go around town on these open flat-bed trucks, performing what they called a 'bally'—short for ballyhoo—just to let people know that the carnival was in town. Most of the playing was done in the open air, which did a lot to develop power. At one time, I had a reputation for being quite a loud cornet player."

Jones wound up in Oklahoma City where he joined—and soon took over the leadership of—a 10-piece territory band. That was his first taste of leading a big band (late 1947 or early '48, he says). But the heyday of the big bands was coming to a close. And soon he was forced to give up the band, and gig instead with small groups. Just how bleak things were in the big band business is indicated by the fact that in 1950, even Count Basie was forced to give up his big band and tour with an octet instead. He re-formed his big band in '52.

Jones was working at the Bluebird Club in Detroit in a quintet with his brother Elvin and pianist Tommy Flanagan ("We were beboppers all the way then") when Basie hired him in '54.

"I took Joe Wilder's place in that band—well, I didn't take his place, nobody can take *his* place, Joe Wilder being as great as he is. But he was leaving the band, and they needed somebody to kind of fill up the space," Jones says with a rich laugh, "—and so they asked me to join. After about two seconds' hesitation, I said yes.

"I was there at the birth of that phenomenal Basie Band in the '50s. When I joined the band, Ernie Wilkins was still playing alto saxophone in the band and writing an enormous amount of music. Every one of his contributions was par excellence. If you weren't careful, you'd think it was Ernie's band because just about all of the music that I played was arranged by Ernie Wilkins. Johnny Mandel spent some time in the band and contributed some music to the Basie book. There was a guy named A. K. Salim who wrote the "Blee Blop Blues," which was one of the mainstays of the Basie repertory. Frank Foster was contributing another tremendous portion of music to the repertory. And I think Frank Wess was beginning to get interested at that time in doing a lot of writing. We eventually wound up with Sonny Payne as a drummer and Snooky Young as a lead trumpet player. The band had really gotten together, had gotten very tight. And when Joe Williams got there, it was just like the finishing touch."

The band enjoyed a period of great commercial as well as critical success. For a time, it was even getting bookings on the rock 'n' roll circuit. It was turning out hit records at a time when everyone said big bands were dead. At least one new Basie Band album was released during each of the nine years Jones was with the band; one year saw the production of four albums. Many of the titles remain familiar to jazz buffs nearly 30 years later: "The Atomic Mr. Basie," "Chairman of the Board," "Basie at Birdland." It seemed as if Basie could do no wrong.

One of the band's biggest hits was "April in Paris" (1955, arranged by Wild Bill Davis), with its oft-copied "one more time" repeat-ending. Jones created a brief but catchy "Pop Goes the Weasel" solo on the

The Count Basie Band at Paramount Theatre, New York, 1957. Left to right: Joe Newman, trumpet; Benny Powell, trombone; Wendell Culley, first trumpet; Thad Jones, trumpet; Reunald Jones, trumpet; Henry Coker, trombone; Bill Hughes, trombone; Eddie Jones, bass; Freddie Green, guitar; Sonny Payne, drums; Basie, piano; Marshall Royal, lead alto sax; Bill Hughes, alto sax; Frank Wess, tenor sax; Frank Foster, tenor sax; Charlie Fowlkes, baritone sax. (Frank Driggs collection)

number. He had to re-create that solo in live performances so many times after the record became a hit that he finally asked another trumpeter in the band to take over the spot for him. He adds he has no desire to ever play that solo again.

Rarely did Basie take protracted solos, although Jones adds that when conditions were right, Basie could play so much piano it was astonishing. The band in these years included such fine soloists as Joe Newman, Al Grey, Eddie (Lockjaw) Davis, Billy Mitchell, Sonny Cohn, Frank Wess, Frank Foster, as well as, of course, Jones. But it was really the overall sound of the band, more than the work of any particular stars, that people seemed to be responding to. (Jones got additional opportunities to show his own soloist abilities on small-group modern jazz albums that he recorded apart from the band, with the likes of Thelonious Monk and Pepper Adams.)

Basie liked music to be comparatively simple; he felt that simple charts swung best. If his musicians found an arrangement difficult to play on its first run-through, he assumed the material was not for the Basie Band. He *didn't* want charts his players would have to struggle to execute. Jones' writing tended to be more advanced, more complex than that of the other writers for the Basie Band, and as a result, Basie did not use Jones' arrangements as much as those of the others. As time went on, Basie became somewhat more receptive to Jones' offerings, although his own preferences were still for simpler music.

By the time Jones left the Basie Band in 1963, he says, he had developed strong and lasting emotional ties to it. But he felt he owed it to his family to give up life on the road. And perhaps at some level he realized that if he wanted to express himself completely, he could not stay on indefinitely as a Basie sideman.

Jones took a staff job at CBS in New York and also played with George Russell and Gerry Mulligan, mostly in the city. An invitation to join Duke Ellington's band was too tempting for Jones to turn down cold. Jones has always had unbounded admiration for Ellington. But Jones concluded almost immediately after he said "yes" that he could not in good conscience really take the job. "I had just left Basie's band because I had two young children that needed both parents there," he explains. "And although the offer from Ellington was attractive, I couldn't take it because it would just mean going back out on the road and denying the young ones.

"I stayed with Ellington about 10 days. I was there for the premiere of Ellington's *Night Creature* in Detroit, Michigan, and that was one of the most moving experiences of my whole life," Jones says. "The premiere was performed with the Ellington Orchestra and the Detroit Symphony Orchestra. It's incredible what developed between Ellington and the conductor of the Detroit Symphony, Walter Poole. Poole and Ellington were like two mystics who just communicated with each other without saying a word. They just looked at each other and every now and then, like they would nod their heads as though they were really talking together—and I'm sure they were, in some way and on some level that the rest of us really didn't understand. And at the end of the performance, the band got a standing ovation, not only from the audience but from the symphony as well."

Jones notes that Ellington has always been the biggest influence on him as an arranger. "I don't know whether I write like him or not, but believe me, it's not because I haven't tried," he says. "I can't think of anybody who was able to use the material available and to mold it and create such fantastic musical tapestries. It's almost like watching a moving mural, to listen to one of his arrangements. All of the different colors. All of the different intangibles that you feel, emotionally. And all of it, say, reflecting on this mural that just moves continually. Constantly changing, but always reflecting the deep sense of commitment and personality that Ellington had, insofar as the music is concerned. There's no other arranger or creator or composer that has approached this. None," Jones says. "But at the same time," he adds, "I also know that was Ellington's way. And each person has his or her own voice that they have to speak with, if they want to speak the truth. Although I was inspired and influenced to a great extent by Ellington, I felt that my voice had to be spoken, in order to make the music meaningful."

In 1965, Jones and drummer Mel Lewis, who had been with him in Gerry Mulligan's group, formed their own modern, star-studded, New York-based big band. Jones recalls that when they decided to form a band, "we started calling musicians, and nobody turned us down. We didn't have a prospect of a job in sight. The only place we could get to rehearse was A and R Studios, which Phil Ramone operated, because he said he'd let us have it free, after midnight. That was convenient for the players because a lot of them were doing studio work in the daytime. We had about six rehearsals, and the word got around, and all of a sudden there was a lot of interest being shown in the band. Monday in New York at that time was a day when none of the club musicians worked. We always used to call it 'Blue Monday.' All of the clubs were usually dark on Monday night. So I said, 'Why don't we do it on a Monday night?' Just because nothing was happening didn't necessarily mean that people didn't want something to happen. And when we finally opened on our first Monday at the Village Vanguard, you couldn't buy your way in there, with any amount of money. Every nook and cranny was filled. They were lined up on the stairs, four and five across. You couldn't go down the stairway, there was no way you could get by all those people. They were lined up around the corner, for about almost a block and a half, the same way, of people waiting to get into the club." The band included players of the caliber of Snooky Young, with whom Jones had worked in Basie's Band ("Snooky, to me, is the greatest lead trumpet player in the world, bar none," Jones says), Jimmy Maxwell, Bill Berry, Bobby Brookmeyer, Jack Rains, and Pepper Adams. "And that was our introduction to Monday nights. And we established a tradition on Mondays that exists today, not only in America but all over the world. You know, a lot of people in Europe, for instance, have established Monday nights as performance night." The orchestra, which since 1978 has been led by Mel Lewis alone, continues to hold down the Monday night gig at the Village Vanguard 20 years later.

The band, playing mostly Jones' own music, was a great critical success from its very first album. It elicited more praise from critics than even the Basie Band, which by then seemed to be getting into somewhat of a rut.[1]

Jones notes: "We were voted the number one band in the country—about five or six years in a row, wasn't it?[2] But economically, we never saw it in our pockets. Success to us meant the respect we got from our peers. We didn't make any money from the band." Jones also taught jazz in the '70s at William Paterson College.

Then in 1978, while touring with the band in Yugoslavia, Jones was the victim of a freak incident. He was seated in a taxi cab, he recalls, when "a drunk, a crazy, who knew karate," wildly slammed a fist through the side window. Jones did not realize at first how significantly he had been injured by the flying glass.

There is no greater fear for a musician than permanent damage to the chops. As time passed and Jones' lip did not heal satisfactorily, he grew deeply depressed. He wondered if he would ever be able to play at all well again.

"Glass got embedded in my lip and cut the major muscle on the top of the lip that controls the movement as you play," Jones says. "Before I found out that the muscle was cut, I tried to play, but I knew something was wrong—because I couldn't get any stability in the top

[1] Basie's reluctance to play Thad Jones' music may have given Jones an incentive to form his own band. Longtime Basie trombonist Grover Mitchell recalled in 1987 that Jones had written the arrangements for an entire Basie Band album, but at the last minute, record producer Teddy Reig convinced Basie to record Chico O'Farrill's arrangements instead. The charts which Jones had prepared for the Basie Band wound up being the first ones recorded by the Thad Jones-Mel Lewis Orchestra.

[2] Actually, the Thad Jones-Mel Lewis Orchestra won the *Down Beat* Readers' Poll from 1972-1977, and the *Down Beat* Critics' Poll from 1974-78.

lip. I had it examined by this guy, and he just felt in there, and said, 'The reason you don't have any stability is the muscle was cut. One end's over here and one end's over here.' And after three operations—the last one was about three, three and a half years ago—everything seems to be pretty much back to normal. Fortunately, I had a good plastic surgeon in Denmark, who did all of this. I've been assured full mobility and returning strength, and his prediction seems to be right on the money. And it'll get better. I went to Carmine Caruso in New York, the renowned trumpet doctor, and he has given me some fantastic help. In effect, you know, I had to learn how to play all over again. Which *ain't easy*. After you're inactive for that long, things go out of balance. So I had to sort of put things back in balance again. Now it seems to be working pretty good."

Mel Lewis, who today heads the Jazz Orchestra co-founded by Jones and himself in 1965. (Courtesy Abby Hoffer)

Jones had long been considering moving abroad, he says, when the severed lip muscle seemed to trigger the final decision. Like so many other notable black jazz musicians before him (Ben Webster, Oscar Pettiford, Ernie Wilkins, etc.), Jones felt greater personal and professional acceptance in Scandinavia than he had felt in the U.S. "A lot of musicians—just from the lack of respect that they get for their art in this country—have migrated to other parts of the world. And our culture has suffered as a result. In Denmark, I was recognized as a jazz musician; they understood my contribution to music," Jones says. He directed the Danish Radio Orchestra and taught jazz. He had time to listen to music he enjoys (including operas, symphonies and jazz piano—he rarely listens to other trumpeters for pleasure). Meeting Lis, who is now his wife, did much to restore his spirits. After his chops healed, he gigged and also recorded a couple of albums in Europe.

Jones says that since returning to the U.S. this year, he has been struck by signs of an increase in the respect being shown jazz in this country. He has noted such things as Jazz Halls of Fame, which did not exist when he left the U.S. eight years ago, and the Hollywood-style stars now in the sidewalk in Kansas City, Missouri, honoring jazz greats. He has been impressed, too, by finding that Basie has been honored with such things as a Count Basie Ballroom in Kansas City and a Count Basie Theatre in New Jersey. Signs that jazz is appreciated here, he says, might help persuade some jazzmen to stay in the U.S., rather than move to Europe.

Jones adds: "Jazz, to me, has been the most vital and progressive music of the last 200 years. In the short time it's been in existence, it's created more diverse forms, from just this one, simple musical structure, of any music in existence today. A jazz musician of the caliber of a Freddie Hubbard or a Miles Davis can create more in two minutes, spontaneously, than some orchestras can in 25 minutes. That's a marvelous gift that shouldn't be allowed to die and to wither. It should be nourished—especially in America, where jazz really was born."

And as for the Basie Band, Thad Jones expects it to continue to be a vital and ever-evolving contributor in the world of jazz. "If you don't progress," he says, "then you may as well give it up; what you're there for is not being accomplished at all. . . . This is *not* a 'ghost band,'" he emphasizes. "This band intends to move forward."

1985

The Basie Band After Basie

Does it still *sound* like Count Basie's Band?" That's the first question most jazz buffs would probably want answered.

Having heard the Count Basie Band in three separate 1985 New York-area engagements (at the Blue Note, at the Glen Island Casino, and at a Mercy College "Battle of the Bands" with Woody Herman's Herd), I can assure you the answer is an unqualified yes. Whether they're playing a laid-back blues or an uptempo rouser, an old standby or a new tune whose title you'd have no way of knowing, there's just no way you'd mistake the band for any other. The broad, confident ensemble sound, the distinctive attack of the brass, the way they'll bend notes, the frequent changes in dynamics, the recurring flashes of wit—all of these things combine to tell you that you're listening to the one and only Basie Band. Would that there were more bands with so strong a sense of identity. Even Woody Herman—great as he is—will sometimes take out bands filled with kids, fresh out of Eastman and North Texas State, whose playing is clean, accurate, and well-rehearsed, but frankly non-distinctive. They'll get a sound not all that different from any number of first-rate college jazz ensembles. But the Basie Band plays with real authority and an unmistakable sense of identity. In conversations with members of the Basie Band, one thing that comes through loud and clear—whether you're talking to veterans in the organization or to the very youngest members of the band—is a real commitment to the music.

Having a rather stable personnel no doubt contributes highly to the band's strong sense of identity. When Thad Jones took over as leader in February, one might note, he found in each section of the band a musician who had been in the band when he had been in it—even though he had left fully 22 years before!

When Basie died in April of 1984, there were those who believed that the band would soon die with him. Why continue without Basie, some argued, for Basie's inspired playing and guidance had made the band. But the band continued filling its engagements as usual, with pianist Tee Carson occupying Basie's chair as he often had done during Basie's illnesses in the preceding four or five years. Replacements well-versed in the Basie idiom were found for the few musicians who left. And when the band played New York's Blue Note for a week in January of '85, music critic John S. Wilson noted with some surprise in the *New York Times*: "The band is playing with more spirit and fire and fun than it has shown in years."

Eric Dixon comments: "I remember Basie saying long before he died: 'Whenever I go, keep it going as long as people want to come and

Battling tenors have long been a Basie Band tradition. Kenny Hing and Eric Dixon are the tenors, Thad Jones the conductor in this 1985 concert. (Chip Deffaa collection)

listen to it; you all keep it going.' And that's what we did. From the time he died, it's been going, and we've tried very hard to keep it in that Count Basie vein. So far it's been working."

* * *

Fifty-four-year-old Dixon (who had played with Cootie Williams, Quincy Jones and Johnny Hodges before joining Basie in 1961), served quietly as musical director of the Basie Band for nine and a half months after Basie's death before Thad Jones was brought on board. He states: "I was a temporary leader. It was never my desire to really be a leader, but in order to help the organization, somebody had to do it, and somebody that was down front. Anybody in back of the first row would have had to come down front, to be seen. But it's like—you don't really need nobody to *lead* this band. All you need is a downbeat and a cutoff. The band has played itself ever since I was a little boy. I think the band's in excellent shape right now. I'm not being braggadocious. It's a band that always fired itself up. Even before I was in it, it used to amaze me to watch it, how the fellows would just want to play."

The two youngest members of the band (who might be said to symbolize the band's future), lead trumpeter Byron Stripling and alto sax player Danny House, both of whom are 23, make it clear that they "want to play" no less fervently than any of their predecessors in the Basie Band.

Stripling joined the organization about three months after Basie's death, having previously played in the big bands of Lionel Hampton, Woody Herman, and Clark Terry. How did he get picked for the Basie Band? Stripling explains: "I had been following the band so much—I was writing different guys in the band letters. They'd known me since I was in junior high school because I'd follow 'em around and I'd say, 'Hey, I'm Byron,' and they got to know me. And I got their addresses, a couple cats, and I would write them letters. Kind of a little kid, just bugging them. That was in Minneapolis, when I was in junior high and high school. Whenever they would come around, I'd always be there. They'd be waiting for me. I've just been following them around. So when I came into the band, it was like joining some people that I had really known for 10 years. Bill Hughes and Sonny Cohn, basically those two people were the ones I got to know. Some of the other ones I got to know, too, have left. And those were two important people in the band.

"They gave me tips on playing with this band. For instance, Sonny Cohn has gone through for me—You see, with the Basie Band there's a foundation, a trumpet legacy that's been established, a tradition that's been laid down, starting with Buck Clayton, and then you go to Joe Newman, and then you have Snooky Young. In fact, the section that played the 'Basie at Birdland' record: Snooky Young, Sonny Cohn, I think William Johnson, and Thad Jones, that was a very important section in jazz big band playing. Because that section, on the Roulette records that they made, was very important for style concepts of all bands. People would say, 'Play like the Basie trumpet section.' Because of the way that they played. And it would be like the same with the sax section. Marshall Royal became important not only to this band, but to music in general, so the influence went beyond just this band.

"Well, I had studied the band's music and I must have seen the band 10-15 times before I joined. Obviously, I was familiar with the records. Because you can't come into the organization without having a strong familiarity with the style concept with which the band plays. So if I were to walk in here cold—I mean, it's possible on other bands, and I did it on other bands, where I wasn't familiar with the music—but here the stylistic concept has been established throughout the years. For instance, with the trumpet there'd be like Snooky Young in the chair I play. He laid down how that was supposed to happen, how you're supposed to play lead trumpet with this band. So I had to study his style in order to perform this music."

Danny House, who joined the band a month after Basie's death, notes: "I had seen the band many times before Basie died. I was recommended by Chris Woods, who was the alto player before me. I knew Chris, and knew a couple other people in the band. I grew up in Santa Barbara, California, and went to school in Los Angeles, and worked around Los Angeles a lot. In '81, I had played in Clark Terry's Band."

Being in the Basie band is "great, couldn't be better," House affirms. He adds that before joining the band, he *thought* he was familiar with a lot of the band's music and arrangements. "But when I got in the band, it became obvious the music's always sort of evolving," he says. "And a lot of it isn't, can't be written down, like where the end of a note should be, how late, how early, how long of a drop, and stuff you can't really write down. You play charts with other bands and you think, 'Oh yeah, I'll be able to handle Basie'—but this is a whole different ballgame. You get here, I mean you got to listen a lot. You really have to listen."

Stripling declares: "The band's whole concept of phrasing—really, a lot of it came from Lester Young. The way he would—[Stripling scats a Lester Young type of phrase]—*'buh-bah, buh, bubba-bubba-dudit—uhhh-uh.'* And the way he would lay back on a phrase set the style of phrasing when the band got music. Because this band originally played without written music. And you have like 16 cats sitting up there, everybody killing with no music. That's because the Afro-American tradition is based on the oral tradition. Okay, then things got a little bit more complex. The band progressed with jazz, and it also helped jazz progress." It is often said that superior arrangements have been the key to the success of the modern Basie Band. But new members of the band, Stripling emphasizes, truly learn the Basie tradition from the rest of the band, not simply from reading what's on paper. For the often-played stuff, he notes, no one is referring much to the paper anyway.

"Now for me, playing lead trumpet, there was no reason to really look at 'One O'Clock Jump,' for example, because I had heard it so much," Stripling says. "And also, because the way that we play it cannot be notated. Because notation is really inadequate for what this music tries to express. You can't notate—[and Stripling scats a typical Basie trumpet section lick]—*'split 'n doodle dooh-ah—dow, bip boodle a dee—ow.'* How do you notate that? You can't put it on paper, and a composer will tell you that. That's why people have to sing what they want me to play."

Dixon says that new members are typically brought into the band on the recommendation of present and/or past members of the band. "They pick somebody that they know could play to suit the Basie Band. Somebody could be a heck of a player, but maybe his playing doesn't fit with Count Basie's style. And that does make a difference. Clark Terry and Chris Woods recommended Danny House, for instance, which I consider to be a very good recommendation. He's young, but he's thinking in the vein that we're playing. Young people are needed. People like Freddie Green, Bill Hughes, Sonny Cohn and myself—we can't do it forever. Let's hope we can get a group of young ones to think in the same vein. Maybe when we're finished, there'll be a group of them under us that can set up the next bunch of youngsters. And maybe this thing can really go on forever, as far as this sound."

Has the band changed since Basie's passing? Trombonist Dennis Wilson, who has been with the band eight years, answers without hesitation: "It's still a cookin' band. The only change is that we're missing one person, that's all. It's the same band, the same band."

Duffy Jackson, who had drummed in Basie's Band in 1979 and '80 and then returned earlier this year to fill in as drummer for several months (the present drummer is Dennis Mackrel, who had also drummed with the band before Basie's death), says he believes that the '85 Basie Band plays with more excitement than the band had shown in the final years of Basie's life. Jackson's belief is that the spirit of the band had simply reflected the spirit of its leader. And, he says, when Basie started going into his physical decline around 1980, the band started to sound tired at times, too. Jackson adds that he had found himself restraining his drumming back then, out of concern for Basie's poor health. "You had to be aware of things when you played, you know. He was uncomfortable. Rim shots were actually painful for him then. The last eight weeks I was in the band in '80, I think he played only two gigs with us. He was getting very sick."

Dennis Wilson says that the band's schedule has gotten tougher since Basie's passing. Previously, the Willard Alexander booking agency had worked periodic breaks into the schedule to allow Basie chances to rest and regain strength. "It was *easy* before. Now it's getting hard. We're doing a lot more. I don't know if I can take this," Wilson adds with a laugh. "But then, there are those who think maybe the band's not working, so it's almost a necessity to work more, so people find out you *are* working."

* * *

At the Glen Island Casino, a dance instructor from the local Arthur Murray School is imploring Thad Jones to have the band play a waltz. Jones, who has only recently taken over as leader, asks Dixon: "What waltzes do we have in the book?" Dixon answers that they don't have any. Jones decides that they'll fake the old Wayne King favorite, "The Waltz You Saved for Me." The older musicians in the band will all remember it, anyway. No one in the audience seems the wiser as Jones and Sonny Cohn begin playing the melody straight, and most of the other musicians in the band pick it up. At a table near the bandstand, Jones' Danish wife, Lis, sits with friends. Their five-year-old son, Thad

Thad Jones conducts at the Glen Island Casino, 1985. (Chip Deffaa collection)

Jr., is obviously enjoying his father's music. He's out on the dance floor now, dancing to the sweet melody with one of his parents' woman friends.

"Dad thought highly of Thad. Dad had a great deal of respect for him," Basie's adopted son, Aaron Woodward, comments. And the feeling was certainly mutual. Jones named his youngest son Thaddeus Joseph *William* Jones, Jr., he notes; the "William" was put there in honor of William "Count" Basie. "My son loves Basie! He recognizes Basie's picture everywhere he sees it," Thad Jones tells you. "You know, when I took him to see Miles Davis in concert recently, I asked him how he was enjoying the music. He answered, loud enough for everyone to hear him, 'I like Count Basie!'"

Maintaining the Count Basie Band—19 topflight musicians—requires a steady flow of quality bookings. Is the band's future now secure?

Woodward states frankly that it is not. And then he brings up a curious reality. The Basie Band is, he says, the finest institution of its kind in existence in the world today. You find Basie charts played by stage bands and jazz ensembles in high schools and colleges from coast to coast. "So many colleges play our charts. And yet the band, right now, can't crack the college/university touring circuit," Woodward notes with concern. "If we could just do that—just get a good flow of college bookings—*that* would secure the band."

1985

FRANK • FOSTER

Back Home with The Basie Band

"It's a pleasure being here, back home again after 22 years. Now I'm the old man. I'm so overcome with happiness at this occasion and what this means to me and my family—so I'm going to announce the first number and get out of the way." With those brief remarks, on the night of May 31, 1986, Frank Foster made his first appearance as leader of the Count Basie Band. The fans who had turned out for the concert in the stadium at New York's Hofstra University had had no idea that they would be witnessing a moment of musical history. No word had yet appeared in the press that Foster was replacing Thad Jones as leader. The Basie organization explained after the concert that Foster was officially taking over as leader, on a full-time basis, effective as of June 17th, but his schedule had permitted him to appear with the band on May 31st, so he had chosen to do so.

Foster had been a vital element in the great Basie Band of the '50s and early '60s, both as a tenor sax soloist and as a composer/arranger of such numbers as "Shiny Stockings" and "Didn't You." In recent years he had worked as a single, or in tandem with fellow former Basie-ite Frank Wess, billed as "the two Franks" (their album, "Two For the Blues" received a Grammy nomination in 1984), or as leader of his own New York-based big bands. He had also continued to write arrangements for the Basie Band as time permitted, as well as for artists ranging from Frank Sinatra to George Benson, earning himself another Grammy nomination in the process.

Foster made it clear early on in the concert that he had no intention of serving merely as a conductor. "I ain't here just to wave my arms, y'all. This is *all right*—but I have to do something else, too," he said after simply leading a couple of numbers. He picked up his sax and surged into Thad Jones' "One to Another." A bit later on, when tenormen Kenny Hing and Eric Dixon went into their familiar battle on "Jumpin' at the Woodside," Foster jumped in unexpectedly with them, making it a three-way—and raising the exciting promise that the Basie tradition of battling tenors was about to be re-invigorated.

* * *

No explanation had been given to the public as to why Thad Jones was stepping down as leader of the band, other than that he had decided to return home to Denmark to pursue other plans. But members of the Basie Band knew his health had deteriorated. He had lost an alarming amount of weight while touring with the band in early '86. An announcement was made that he was going to record a Thad Jones-Mel Lewis Jazz Orchestra reunion album, but his health prevented him from going through with the project. On August 20, 1986, he died of cancer in Copenhagen.

* * *

When Foster officially took over the reins on June 17th, he knew there would be a busy schedule ahead. But he didn't realize just how much would be happening so soon. Within his first few months as leader, the band played all through the U.S. (including concert dates with Sinatra), toured Europe from England to Poland, cut a radio jingle, and appeared on the Bill Cosby TV show. And just one week after Foster officially took over as leader, the band went into the recording studios to cut a compact disc.

The session, which had been planned while Thad Jones was still leading the band, was important because the band would be making its first American recording since the Count's death in 1984. (The band, led by Jones, had recorded one album in Europe backing singer Caterina Valente, but that album had been released only in Europe.) A strong new album was essential to remind jazz buffs worldwide that the Basie Band was still here, still contributing to the jazz scene.

The atmosphere was relaxed as musicians began gathering at the Power Station studio on 53rd Street in New York around one o'clock, on June 24th. Plenty of rock groups had been recorded here, but not big bands. It soon became apparent that the young studio personnel were not familiar with the Basie Band.

From the recording booth, an engineer asked: "Does the conductor want click?" Meaning: Did Foster want to hear a click-track—the equivalent of a metronome—in his headphones, as an aid in keeping

Frank Foster. (Courtesy Willard Alexander, Inc.)

time? No one bothered answering. The idea of the Basie Band needing electronic gimmickry to keep time was ludicrous.

A bit later, the engineer told Foster confidently that he'd see to it that the band got "the Power Station sound." Foster replied cordially, but seriously, that he just wanted a *Basie Band* sound.

The musicians took their seats, and the engineers asked each to play something, so they could make sound checks. After 75-year-old Freddie Green strummed a typically brief bit, an engineer asked if "the guitar player" could give him some more.

The guitar player relied curtly: "Ain't got no more."

With the exception of a few months in 1950, Green has been in the Basie Band continuously since 1937. He remains the heart of the rhythm section—some would say the heart of the band. Deftly, evenly playing his unamplified instrument (he virtually never takes a solo), his contributions are intended to be felt rather than really heard by listeners. He also serves as a kind of "spiritual director," as a keeper of the flame, who knows what the Basie Band is all about.

Green has uncompromising standards. Foster may have been the actual leader, but if Green thought anything was going down less than perfectly during the session, he never hesitated to speak out.

The band began recording "Good Time Blues." Green stopped the take almost immediately. "Hold it! Hold it a minute!" he broke in over his mike. He told bassist Lynn Seaton: "Don't come in so quick. Give him [pianist Tee Carson] a little chance. Then you come in." They started again, with Seaton letting Carson play a bit longer piano intro.

A little later on, everyone seemed satisfied, listening to the playback of the first take of "Corner Pocket." But Green felt that drummer Dennis Mackrel needed to fill up one spot more. "You're capable of doing it," he prodded. "This sounds like a cop out." The second take met with Green's nod of approval.

As the band ran down "You Got It," an old Frank Foster number being revived for the session, Green interjected: "Why are we running away with the tempos? Why don't we *groove* some of these things?" He was right: The band *was* pushing the number; it sounded forced, rather than confidently swingin' in traditional Basie manner. In most bands, the idea of a guitarist interrupting a number because he was unhappy with the tempo would be unheard of. But after nearly 50 years in the band, Green feels he's earned his say about how things are played.[1] And as the session continued, it became apparent that members of the Basie Band generally seem to feel more of an investment in the band than musicians in most bands. They all care about the end results.

Dennis Mackrel rehearsed the band on a new number he had written for the session. When one musician questioned if that was the tempo

[1] Green died March 1, 1987.

at which they'd be recording the number, Mackrel said it was the tempo *he* preferred, but that the decision "is up to us."

At one point in the two-day-long recording session, Eric Dixon briefly took over as conductor, and Foster took Dixon's place among the reeds. They were running down "April in Paris." Foster had played the number countless times during his original tenure in the band, but in the years since, the ending had evolved slightly differently, finishing with chords that musicians noted were reminiscent of "Jingle Bells." So Dixon led the band as they recorded the ending, conducting by motioning with his saxophone, while Foster simply blew in the sax section.

Most numbers were done in just two takes; a couple in single takes. The players went in and did a job, like they do somewhere almost every night. "We're together, onstage and off," Sonny Cohn commented during a break. This *isn't* a band with one or two superstars, he explained. All of the players are stars, in a sense. "But they're all thinking as one; they all want the same sound."

A Basie Band recording session is an event. Among onlookers who turned out to catch portions of it were Albert Murray, who had collaborated on Basie's autobiography; Yasuki Nakayama, editor of Japan's *Swing Journal*; Nancy Miller Elliott, who had collaborated on Buck Clayton's autobiography; and David Hartman, host of ABC TV's "Good Morning America." "I used to trail Basie around," Hartman said. "I keep the band's schedule—they send me their itinerary—and I try to zip in when I can."

The musicians were justifiably confident about how the band would sound. Their only concern was how well it was being recorded. Some of the older members recalled albums that had been ruined, in their estimation, by recording engineers or sound-mixers. As baritone saxist John Williams noted when telling the recording engineer that he was anxious the sound be captured just right: "People will be listening to this 30 years from now."

Spirits were high as they listened to the playbacks. "Frank's burnin' on that one," said Dennis Wilson as he savored an extended Foster solo. "That makes *me* want to dance—and I've got five left feet," said Foster as he dug one of the new tunes the band had just tried. The session brought back memories for Foster's wife, Cecilia; the last time she had been to a Basie Band recording session, she recalled, had been in the early '60s, when Frank had been a sideman.

* * *

Frank Foster remembers well when he was originally asked to join the Basie Band. The invitation came like a bolt out of the blue. He was just 24 years old, in the spring of 1953, and had just returned to the U.S. after serving with the army in the Korean War.

"I was not even out of the army yet. I was just on a weekend pass, in Detroit, and I ran into an old hometown buddy of mine who said, 'Count Basie's looking for you,'" Foster tells me, marveling a little about how the chain of events began, which ultimately aled to his leading the Basie Band. "I said, 'How does Count Basie know I'm out here? Because I'm not even out of the army yet.'

"I found out that Ernie Wilkins and Billy Eckstine had recommended me for the band. They didn't know where I was, but they had recommended me to take Eddie 'Lockjaw' Davis' place. And luckily, the very day I got to Detroit was a day that the Basie Band was playing there. All this seemed to happen quite by chance—but I like to think it was divine providence."

Foster had done a gig with Billy Eckstine prior to his being drafted in the spring of '51. And Jimmy Wilkins (brother of Ernie Wilkins, who was now playing sax in, and arranging for, the Basie Band) had been the leader of the Wilberforce Collegians big band when Foster had been a student at Wilberforce about five years earlier.

"Basie was looking for another tenor player, so they had recommended me. I went down to the place where Basie was working, and they let me play a couple tunes. And then he said he'd get in touch with me, which he did a few months later. This must have been May of '53, and in July of that year he sent for me. Lockjaw hadn't really terminated yet when I saw the band there in Detroit. I guess he terminated around the end of July.

"I started with Basie in New York on July 27th, 1953, which was a Monday night. Well, actually, that was my first night in town and the Basie Band left town the next day, the 28th. So that was like a night off. A friend of mine took me to Birdland that night to see Charlie Parker and I sat in with Charlie Parker that night."

Foster laughs as he recalls Parker having him sit in. "He put me to an extreme test, like masters will do young upstarts. By playing a commonly-played jazz tune at that time, playing it like almost two and three times as fast as it's normally played, just to see if I would keep up. And the tune was hard enough for a mediocre musician in the normal tempo. But in the tempo that he played it, which was at least twice as fast, that would make it doubly hard. Well, I kept up with him, and I gained his respect. That was 'Dance of the Infidels.' That wasn't the only tune we played, but that's the only one whose name I remember—because of that test he put me through."

I wondered if Foster had tested younger players in a similar fashion, in the years since? "Yes, yes. With pleasure!" he interjects, smiling broadly. "Some of them haven't fared so well, either."

Fresh out of the army, with few important credits to his name before his army stint, Foster really felt as though he were starting at the top. And Basie made things pleasant for musicians in his band. "It was the best life I'd ever led."

Foster notes, however: "The band wasn't doing exceptionally well at the time, because this was prior to Joe Williams and prior to the 'April in Paris' hit and the 'Everyday' hit, and the band was really struggling. Basie had just reorganized the band, I think a year before. Because he broke up the big band for a couple of years (1950 and '51) and then he started the band again in 1952. That was the band that I joined. But the band wasn't really a hot item at that time. They were just gaining momentum, but still struggling. But for me, getting $150 every week, which was something I had never done before—you know, I was on top of the world. I mean, I'd gotten a regular pay as a private first class in the army, but—forget that!"

And there was also some extra money for each chart Foster wrote for the band. He made important contributions right away.

"I started arranging as soon as I joined the band. In fact I brought one arrangement to the band that I had done while I was in the army, and they used it. It was like a simple mambo chart, for dancing.

"Two of my first arrangements for the band were 'Down for the Count' and 'Blues Backstage.' They were actually written in 1953, although they were recorded a year or two later. I wrote 'Shiny Stockings' in 1955."

Foster notes, though, that he has always been a rather painstaking writer of arrangements. He works slowly. He is known for the quality of his writing, not for the quantity. Basie never told Foster he wanted any particular number of arrangements, never pushed him.

"No, he just left it to me. He would advise me on what he wanted. Most of the advice was: 'Keep it simple and make it swing.' Well, the band made anything swing. Mostly it was 'Keep it simple.' Not write too many 'pregnant nineteenths,' as he called them. But he didn't give me a quota or a number or anything that had to be written by a certain time.

"And there wasn't that much excess money floating around, even to pay for arrangements at the time. When recording companies would later hire Billy May or Quincy Jones or anybody else to write arrangements for the band, they would pay the arrangers off. But the band, in the early '50s, didn't have much of a slush fund for paying arrangers.

"I got paid extra for writing arrangements, but not much. It really wasn't important, the amount I got for an arrangement. What was important was actually hearing the arrangement.

"And Count Basie got along marvelously with musicians. He didn't demand much. All he asked was that everybody pull their weight. Play your part. Look decent. And be in shape.

"He was a wonderful leader to work for. But he would take advantage of a situation in which a person had had a little too much to drink. I remember there was this one trombone player who might have had too much to drink. And Count Basie would call one of his feature numbers. Well, during my first couple of years there, I developed a bad habit of being late from time to time. And lots of times I would miss bus leavings, or come in late for engagements. . . . He would have the habit of calling my feature number as soon as I walked in. And if you walk in cold, then you have to play without the benefit of warming up. And he used to like to do that. He stopped doing it when I rose to the occasion, though."

The Basie Band shot up in popularity in the mid-1950s, winning its first *Down Beat* critics' poll as the year's number one big band in 1955. What does Foster think caused the band's dramatic rise in the '50s, long after big bands were supposed to have fallen from general favor with the public?

"Well, I definitely would say that the recording of 'April in Paris' and the recording of the Neal Hefti things, especially 'Li'l Darlin',' 'Whirly Bird' and things like that, as well as some of those Thad Jones arrangements, and some of my own. I like to think that 'Shiny Stockings' helped heighten the popularity of the band. But definitely the recording of 'April in Paris,' which happened to just catch on. And the added push given by Sonny Payne. He was very flashy and very visual, and a *strong* drummer. And of course Joe Williams and his hit 'Everyday' and 'All Right, OK, You Win.' Those things accounted for the band's rise in popularity during the '50s.

"The personnel at that time was just—it was a boss lineup. They had Joe Newman, Thad Jones, Snooky Young on trumpet; Henry Coker, Benny Powell, Bill Hughes on trombone; Marshall Royall playing lead alto, Frank Wess, myself, and at one time or another, Billy Mitchell or Budd Johnson or 'Lockjaw' Davis playing tenor. And finally, Eric Dixon came in the early '60s.

"With that personnel, the band should have done it whether there was a big hit or not. And it did do it, as far as our staunch fans are concerned; the fans that don't care about the hits, that just love the music, period, and the Basie Band personnel. But we got many more fans as a result of the exposure through that hit on 'April in Paris' and Joe Williams' hits on 'Every Day' and 'All Right, OK, You Win.'

"And also," Foster recalls, "a command performance for the king and queen of England in 1957 didn't hurt. And being selected to do TV shows like the 'Jackie Gleason Show,' the 'Perry Como Show,' Hoagy Carmichael's show, the 'Dinah Shore Show,' the 'Garry Moore Show,' the 'Steve Allen Show.' The whole band would be on these shows. And then one time, Basie himself was on the 'Tonight Show' and he just took a few key men with him, and I was one of those. Those things did a lot to heighten our visibility in mid and late '50s.

"Plus the engagement at Birdland got to be very strong. In that time, we would play like three or four times a year at Birdland, most notably during the Christmas holiday season; we were always there. And Basie was one of the big drawing cards in Birdland at that time. Of all the artists that came there, the Basie Band drew more. . . .

"We'd be booked for two to four weeks. Most of the time, they would be two weeks, but sometimes three and four weeks. And clubs like Birdland in other cities, like Storyville in Boston, the Blue Note in Chicago, the Crescendo in Hollywood, those were the places we really loved to play. And those places flourished during the late '50s. And we enhanced our reputation through performances at those places. Because the band was always fired up when we played those places. We liked playing those places more than being on the road just playing one-

Members of the Basie Band relaxing during a late 1950s European trip. Among the members are two future leaders of the band: Thad Jones (fifth from left in back row) and Frank Foster (eighth from left in back row). (Institute of Jazz Studies)

nighters and dances."

What was the difference?

"The audience, mostly. The audience and the chance of sitting down in a major city for more than a few days at a time. Because you had a chance to get into the cities. We got to know Boston by being there at Storyville for two weeks. We got to know Chicago, by being there at the Blue Note for two weeks. We got to know Los Angeles by being at the Crescendo in Hollywood for two weeks. Also we got to know other artists. Appearing on the bill with us there was Lenny Bruce, for instance, in Los Angeles. And we got to know Professor Irwin Corey. People like that, from time to time, would appear on the same bill with us. People like George Kirby and Dick Gregory, when he first came out as a comedian, we got to know him. One of his earlier performances as a comedian was on the same show with the Count Basie Band. That was in Robert's Show Lounge in Chicago.

"The club scene is a lot different now. There are far fewer clubs. There aren't as many clubs that can support big bands. Some of them don't have space. And the budgets are so astronomical now. I imagine a club like Birdland could afford the Basie Band back from '54-'60. But here it is, like over 20 years later, and you know the economic scene, how everything has gotten so high-priced. The price of big bands has kept up with the inflationary trends. Clubs, most of which are just made for small groups, can't afford to have big bands.

"The '50s was a good era for big bands playing in clubs like Birdland. There were a handful of clubs across the country. In every major city, there was one club. In Philadelphia, there was a club called Pep's, where we played. Chicago had—on the south side, it had Robert's Show Lounge for a while. On the north side, it had the Blue Note. In the '50s, in the major cities all over the country there were these clubs that could hire big bands *and* pay them. It's a situation that I'm sorry had to come to an end. At least I got to experience it."

* * *

Benjamin Frank Foster was born September 23, 1928 and grew up in Cincinnati, Ohio.

In looking back, he can barely remember a time when music wasn't extremely important to him. "I really started loving the sound of music when I was like four to five years of age," he says. His brother Charles, who was six years older than him, got him interested in big bands, such as those of Basie, Lunceford, and Ellington. His mother got him interested in "serious" music.

"When I was four and five—I started listening to music and appreciating classical music at that age. My mom started taking me to operas, I would say, by the time I was about seven or eight. Until I was about 13 or 14."

Initially, Foster maintained a lively interest in both classical music and jazz.

"I chose to go the jazz route. And there was one unfortunate thing that probably propelled me into the road which was left open. Blacks couldn't go to the Cincinnati Conservatory of Music when I graduated from high school in 1946. And that was sort of a deterrent to getting into classical music. Although there was a very fine conservatory up at Oberlin, where I could have gone, and probably to Juilliard, but family finances didn't really permit. We were what might have been called middle-class colored folks. It was a family where the father and mother had to work. And the cup didn't runneth over at that time. My father was a postal worker."

He made the switch from being just a listener to being a player of music around 1939-40.

"At age 11, in answer to a newspaper ad by Wurlitzer, I took up the clarinet. At that time they were charging $3 a week: a dollar and a half for lessons, and a dollar and a half toward paying for the instrument. And the reason I took up clarinet is very simple: there was a picture of a clarinet on the ad. If there had been a picture of a trumpet, I may have taken up trumpet, I don't know. At age 12, I knew I wanted to be a professional musician.

"And at age 13, I took up alto saxophone. I played with local dance bands until my last year in high school. Then I organized my own big band and wrote all the charts. We played gigs for money. Like we made about $3 apiece. Or $5 was big money in those days, for high school kids."

His main influences on alto sax were initially Johnny Hodges, Willie Smith, and Benny Carter. He first heard Charlie Parker in 1945, and was knocked out by what Parker was doing. When he switched to tenor sax in 1948, Dexter Gordon and Sonny Stitt were his main influences among tenormen, until he became interested in John Coltrane in the late '50s. But Foster's basic style was formed long before he began appreciating Coltrane; he sounds nothing like the commonly-encountered Coltrane-influenced player today.

The band Foster led as a high school senior was not intended to sound like any name band. "I wanted to write all the music, and all original music, so I guess we didn't sound like anybody. I didn't have any big influences, arranging-wise at that time. Later on, Tadd Dameron and Jimmy Mundy and Gil Evans and Sy Oliver were influences. I guess maybe Sy Oliver might be a first influence. From his work for Lunceford and Tommy Dorsey."

After graduating from high school in Cincinnati, "I went to Wilberforce, which later became Central State, in Wilberforce, Ohio, for three years, before going to Detroit.

"For three years, I was one of the main people in the Wilberforce Collegians jazz band. I wrote most of their arrangements. I played lead alto first year and then switched to tenor for the remaining years because they had enough alto players but not enough tenor saxophones to fill the section.

"It was like a college jazz band. And we were on a partial scholarship. Most of what we made was to pay for our scholarships. Which was a nice arrangement.

"A gig came up with Snooky Young in Detroit that summer, at the end of the third year. Young had about 10 pieces, a very good band. And I took the gig, with the idea of coming back before school started in September and going for my fourth year. But I already knew that I was doing so poorly in my non-musical studies that I wasn't going to graduate in four years. And then something happened. I had three instruments stolen! And I used that as an excuse to remain in Detroit, to try to track those instruments down. That's how I got out of going back to Central State my fourth year."

Now Foster became a full-time professional musician.

"I had no instruments at all. And my mother and father had invested in those that were stolen. They weren't too happy. So I stayed in Detroit—this was '49—living with an aunt at first, and I used borrowed instruments for maybe a year."

He also got to meet rising young musicians on the scene, such as Barry Harris, Kenny Burrell, Tommy Flanagan, Doug Watkins, Paul Chambers, Donald Byrd, and Thad and Elvin Jones.

"Then one guy named Little John Wilson, who had a band called 'Little John and his Merry Men,' he got a job in Ohio, and he paid for an instrument out of a pawnshop for me to use, which I used until I went to the army in 1951.

"During the time I was in Detroit, I met a very great number of good musicians. I didn't meet Charlie Parker, but I heard him live, and I met Sonny Stitt. I met and played with Wardell Gray and Milt Jackson. I had this job in a club called the Bluebird Inn, and whenever Milt Jackson came to town, he automatically had a gig, the same with Wardell Gray. That's how I got to play with them. This continued until I was drafted into the army in March or April of 1951.

"I eventually got to play music in the army, but not until I got all the way to Japan. I took basic training in the United States and then I went AWOL [absent without leave] for about a month or so.

"I just wanted to hang around San Francisco. I was trying to put off being sent overseas because I knew that I had a military status as an infantry rifleman, which was nowhere resembling a musician. If I'd gone over there, I would certainly have been done in, in that war. So I was just trying to hold off being sent overseas.

"And I hung out for a little over a month in San Francisco, during which time I met Dexter Gordon and Phineas Newborn, and Lester Young. And ran into a very great number of musicians hanging out in San Francisco during that time. I was *playing*."

He kept a pretty high profile for somebody who was AWOL, he acknowledges with a laugh.

"Somehow the military boys didn't check this place I was hanging out in too much. A place called Jimbo's Bop City. All the musicians would go there and jam after hours. Didn't too many servicemen come around there. The servicemen mostly were looking for girls, so they went other places. This was strictly a jazz joint. There *was* an officer who was hanging out there, but he didn't know I was AWOL.

"Sometimes the owner of the club put me up in the hotel he owned, across the street from the club. Other times, I stayed with one of the other couple of ladies I knew.

"The main lady that I was going with persuaded me to turn myself

Frank Foster. (Courtesy of Cecilia Foster)

in so that I wouldn't have to spend too much time in the stockade. As it was, I spent five days in the stockade before going overseas.

"Everybody who suggested to turn yourself in after going AWOL would say, 'Well go see the chaplain, maybe he can help you.' So, for some reason or other, just following their advice, I went to see a local chaplain at the base where I was stationed.

"I remember telling the chaplain that I was a jazz musician. And I remember the chaplain telling me, 'That's not good, son. You're going to have to give up that jazz. If you're going to stay in music, you should play church music and religious songs. But you're going to have to give up that jazz.'

"So much for the chaplain. Needless to say, I didn't take his advice."

Overseas, he managed to get himself into an army band that played dance music, as well as military music. "And then they had several combos that would go out to entertain officers and enlisted men. So I played with a jazz combo and a dance band."

After the Army, the invitation came to join the Basie Band. Traveling with the band was his life from 1953-64. He added excitement with his solos on uptempo numbers. And he wrote such frequently-played arrangements as "Easin' It," "Discommotion," "In a Mellotone," and "Who Me?"

He also found time for occasional outside record dates, with the likes of Milt Jackson, Donald Byrd, Tony Scott, Thad Jones, and Thelonious Monk. As his outside record dates suggest, Foster's own interest in the early '50s leaned towards more of a modern hard-bop style than towards the traditional Basie style. Older players in the Basie Band initially blocked Foster from soloing on ballads, saying he hadn't yet developed the proper tone for ballads.

Basie helped shape Foster's direction, signaling his approval whenever Foster's playing sounded closer to an older great like Ben Webster than to Sonny Stitt. Foster gradually came to fit in better with the band—Basie and the rest of the ensemble really helped mold him—with a style that he viewed as a cross between Webster's, Stitt's, and Wardell Gray's.

"I was very happy with the Basie Band. The only thing that made it less than happy was the fact that I started a family—well, I got married a year after joining the band, but I started a family around '57. And in the early '60s, my kids from this first marriage were early school age, and being on the road, away from them, constituted a slight hassle. They were back in the New York area. I was having a family grow up without having much to do with raising the children. So, that was one of the reasons I finally left the band in 1964.

"Another reason was, I began to feel like I wasn't going anywhere musically. And I wanted to keep up with the music scene that was going on outside the band. And I wasn't getting fulfilled. I wasn't getting enough playing. I was still young then and I wanted to play a lot.

"There's just too many people in a big band to feature everybody on every song. So I wanted to play more and I wanted to be close to my family. So for those two basic reasons, I left in 1964."

Foster also had some arranging ideas of his own that might not have fit in with the Basie Band of 1964. He acknowledges: "I guess I wanted to branch out into my own sort of big band concept. Apart from the Basie idiom, so to speak."

Foster formed his own 18-piece band, which made its debut at Birdland in 1965, and shortly afterwards appeared in concert at Town Hall, with vocalist Ernestine Anderson. Foster also arranged and conducted a Sarah Vaughan LP in '65. But his hope of establishing himself as a big-name bandleader, comparable to Basie, wasn't in the cards.

"I formed my own big band, but it didn't work that much. And that was sort of a letdown. So for 22 years, I had career highs and career lows, but no steady things that went along on an even keel. It was always up-down, up-down. One gig or two gigs for the big band, then a couple months of drought. And then another gig, and then a couple more months of drought. And then another gig. And then maybe three or four months of no activity with the big band."

He tried alternatives to the 18-piece ensemble, hoping that a less-costly unit would be more readily booked.

"In the late '60s, I started 'Living Color' with the idea that maybe a smaller group would still have the sound of a big band but get more bookings. And it did a few things but not that much more than a big band. Then I started the 'Non-Electric Company Quintet,' which worked on-and-off and recorded some. But I still wasn't happy because what I wanted was a career as a big band leader, working regularly with a big band. And that was the thing I was missing, for 22 years after leaving the Basie band.

"I had Monday nights at this place called Ali's Alley, in New York, and that lasted for 13 months in 1977-78. That was the longest series of engagements with one group that I had ever done. But that was like working off the door, so the musicians weren't really getting a salary. We worked once a week, every Monday night—the same, concurrently, with Thad and Mel at the Vanguard.

"And when that stopped happening, then I went through another period of not much happening at all with big bands, until I finally took 'Living Color' to Europe in 1978. And that was a pretty good trip. But then after that, not much activity back here, either. And my musical activity was really dealt a kind of a crippling blow when I took a position as an assistant professor of music up at the State University of New York at Buffalo, in 1972, for four years. So, between 1972 and 1976, my activity on the New York scene was limited by the fact that I was commuting once a week to Buffalo to teach. And not too much fun in that. I met a lot of great people, but it was not so rewarding. Because it was a lot of hassles. Especially getting to and from Buffalo when the weather was bad."

In 1970, he composed a number called "The Loud Minority," which he eventually adopted as the name for his big band.

"That title rose out of the militant '60s. It was a reaction to 'the Silent Majority.' It was used as the title for an album, and later on, in the mid '70s, I decided to just name the band 'the Loud Minority.' We didn't get too many jobs, and I often wonder if it was because of that name or just the fact that it's just going to take a lot of juice to get a big band started with a relatively small name.

"You take the name Count Basie. That's a *big name*, as far as big bands are concerned. You take the name Frank Foster, that's not a big name as far as a veteran bandleader, a successful bandleader. When I started my band, big bands were on a nose-dive."

Foster would have liked to have had the degree of success that Thad Jones and Mel Lewis had enjoyed with their band. But even that band, he notes, was far less successful financially than the average onlooker might have surmised.

"Thad and Mel started their band at the Village Vanguard, and the band has played there for over 20 years. That has all the markings of success. But they paid a lot of dues with that band. Not being able to work but so many gigs. Not really being able to pay musicians top salary, working there. But they were working regularly. I never got a chance to work regularly with my own big band, except that one time for that 13-month period at Ali's Alley.

"Also, I never went to a booking agency. I always thought maybe I could book the band myself. But I found out very differently," Foster notes. The Basie Band, like most of the big name bands, has long been handled by the Willard Alexander Agency.

Currently, there's more big band activity in New York than there has been in years. "Yeah, there's been a resurgence in big band activity and I'm glad to see that," Foster reflects. As we talk, the band is about to go into an eight-day run at the Blue Note, as part of a 1986 Blue Note big band festival. But still, he cautions against interpreting the overall scene too optimistically. "It's not really as healthy as it may appear to be on the surface. Because a lot of these big bands are working off the door, playing for a percentage of the gate or whatever, and not paying the sidemen very well.

"The sidemen are working for the love of the music and the love of the sound of the big band. And the love of participating in the big band experience, which every jazz musician should aspire to. Because it's a different thing from a small combo. The big band has infinitely more possibilities, orchestrationally. Not necessarily more fulfillment for the individual player. Because small groups afford each player a lot of solo space. Big bands don't afford each player a lot of solo space, but most big bands have principal soloists who get featured a lot. And just the thrill of playing big band charts—some of it's just, you know, a great feeling.

"Composing and arranging a big band is just a composer and arranger's dream. To—with the ideas in your own mind—shape the direction of this musical vehicle, and try to make it sound different from the next big band—it's quite a challenge."

Foster has been particularly adept at writing and arranging blues numbers ("Blues Backstage," "Blues in Hoss' Flat," "Misunderstood Blues," etc.). There are plenty of successful big band arrangers who cannot create a memorable, authentic-sounding blues.

"Being inspired by a particular positive or negative situation, the artist comes up with something that relates to that. Whether it would be understood as such or not," Foster observes. "I might write a real

Members of the Basie Band listen to playbacks during a June 1986 recording session in New York. Back row, left to right: Frank Foster, leader; Freddie Green, guitar; Dennis Wilson, trombone; Lynn Seaton, bass; John Williams, baritone sax. Front row: Ralph Peterson Jr., and Malcom Pollack, engineer. (Photo by Nancy Miller Elliott)

funky blues to depict how things look up in the South Bronx or up in Harlem. Not every listener may make that association, but it's there to be made anyway. Same with the South African thing, which has been of deep concern to me for a long time.

"It just seems like there's an effort to destroy the black community. And this crack epidemic is the latest curse upon the community that I see as family-destroying and community-destroying. It's things like these that are of concern to me, that may perhaps come out in some of my music.

"And I've been following the South African thing ever since 1949. I'm not a Johnny-Come-Lately. My indignation at that is not something that's come out of the last five to ten years of publicity on that. Mine goes back a long time.

"But as I'm concerned about South Africa, I'm also concerned about Northern Ireland. So I'm not exclusively concerned about the rights or the welfare or the condition of blacks alone, throughout the world. I'm concerned about the condition of everybody, especially everybody that's poor, homeless. This homeless situation disturbs me a lot." Foster lets his feelings emerge in his music.

* * *

Over the years, Foster has taken a wide variety of freelance composing and arranging assignments. After leaving the Basie Band in 1964, he continued periodically supplying arrangements for the band. He is proud, too, to have been commissioned to compose a suite dedicated to the 1980 Winter Olympics. He conducted a 20-piece orchestra in the debut of his "Lake Placid Suite" at the Olympics. He is currently reworking portions of that suite into numbers for the Basie Band to play.

He was glad, also, to write some charts for Frank Sinatra's "L.A. is My Lady" album and video. "We can credit Quincy Jones for that. Every now and then, Quincy calls me with a nice, juicy one, and this is one of the juiciest. He called me and said they wanted to do this album, and wanted me to do a couple charts. And wisely, he asked me to do just a couple, rather than doing the whole album, or six or seven, because I'm a slow, deliberate worker, and I just can't turn out charts like a mass production line—six or seven charts in a day's time, or a couple of days. I need two weeks to get one good chart out. So Quincy asked me to do two: 'Mack the Knife' and 'After You've Gone.'"

As for his work with George Benson, Foster notes: "George wanted to do an entire album with himself and a big band, patterned after the Basie idea. Actually, we wanted to hook up a George Benson-Count Basie affiliation. But Basie's health was rapidly declining. We wanted to hurry up and try to hook it up before Basie passed, but tragically enough, Basie passed before we could hook it up. But in the meantime,

I did get a couple of charts written for George Benson, one of which he included on his album, '20/20.' The arrangement got nominated for a Grammy, best original arrangement behind a vocal. We lost out to Nelson Riddle and the Linda Ronstadt thing. That was this year's nomination, '86. In '85, the 'Two Franks' album, 'Two for the Blues,' got nominated in the best performance by a small combo category."

Foster enjoyed periodic club appearances with his former Basie band-mate, Frank Wess. They were billed as the "Two Franks," which was also the title of a number they used to play with Basie.

As a freelance composer/arranger/soloist/leader in his years after Basie, Foster was always busy. But he did not feel he received the general recognition he should have. From 1964-86, his life had plenty of ups and downs. In that period, he never found a career opportunity he felt fully utilized his abilities.

"For 22 years after I left the Basie Band, I marked time, waiting for that right thing to come along. And when it came along, it wasn't what I expected. I didn't expect it to be the leadership of the Basie Band. But since that's what it is, I love it. . . . Oh yeah! I love it. I'm having big fun.

"I'm glad to be back now. And I realize that I wouldn't make but so heavy an impact on the music field playing with a combo, because there's so many great combos around. Like from the Marsalises to the

Diane Schuur sang with the Basie Band in concerts and on a 1987 GRP album which topped Billboard's *jazz charts for an unprecedented 33 weeks.* (Courtesy GRP Records)

Art Blakeys to the Terrence Blanchards and Donald Harrisons, there's just a number of great combos around. I never had much of a statement to make with a combo.

"My statement has got to be made with a big band. That's what I grew up with, when I was a teenager developing musically. The big bands were the thing. Combos weren't happening. Combos didn't come along until after Uncle Sam broke up all the big bands. By the mid '40s, when combos really started emerging, especially with Charlie Parker, Miles Davis, Dizzy, etc., etc., I had already been big band oriented. And though I enjoyed playing with combos, and played *a lot* with combos throughout the rest of my career—except for the years when I was with the Basie Band—the big band sound never left me. Nor the desire to really fulfill myself within a big band."

Foster had made both small-group and big band records under his own name, before returning to the Basie Band. But he has no plans for such outside recording activities now.

"I'm exclusively devoted to this orchestra. I'll be busy enough with the band and I would just be extending myself a little too much if I allowed too many outside interests to come in at this time."

And what does the future hold in store for the band? Foster comments simply: "I'd like to see the band, in addition to upholding the Basie tradition, sort of expand on the Basie style—but not get too far away for too long."

Foster is justifiably proud of the band, which was voted the number one jazz orchestra in the world in both the 1986 *Down Beat* International Critics' Poll and *Down Beat* Readers' Poll. He is concerned with maintaining the band's artistic standards; he lets the band's manager and bookers concern themselves with the business end of running the band.[2]

Foster notes: "These men who've been out here for decades—at least four members of this band have been there for 25 years—you can't compare this band to no studio band. This band has a *sound*. If we played some of the same music that some of these studio bands played, you'd hear the difference in the distinctive sound. The distinctive sound of our lead players comes out in this band's presentation, and the way we blend vibratos and things. A good studio band's going to play clean, crisp; it might even be more precise with some of the notations. But the *sound*. . . ."

[2] The band's precarious financial position became evident in 1987 when Count Basie Enterprises, Inc. filed for protection from creditors under Chapter 11 of the bankruptcy law. The band continues to work a heavy schedule, with bookings running nearly a year in an advance, hoping to get out from under debts. Whether it will be able to do so remains an open question.

I wondered, though, if it is ever difficult for Foster to be leading a band that's still somebody else's band?

"There's a challenge—but it's not difficult. I mean, what I'm doing is quite easy—standing in front of the band, directing. Most of the direction is not needed, it's just for show. It's fun. And it's exercise. The fact that it's the Count Basie Orchestra—I'm actually thrilled by that fact. And I like to think that I'm doing a job on his behalf.

"I also like to think that I'm doing a job that he'd be happy with. I have no problems with the fact that it's the Count Basie Band, rather than the Frank Foster Band. I don't want it to be the Frank Foster Band; I *want* it to be the Count Basie Band. I want it to remain the Count Basie Orchestra and go into perpetuity as the Count Basie Orchestra, under the direction of Frank Foster—that makes me very happy. It's like a marriage, you see, and I'm born under the sign of marriage, Libra."

1986

Frank Foster. (Courtesy of Cecilia Foster)

MERCER • ELLINGTON

Pop Left Him Harry, Cootie, and a Few Scraps of Paper

When Duke Ellington died on May 24th, 1974, his son, Mercer, inherited his band. Jazz writer Leonard Feather had an opportunity to interview Mercer, just five days after his father's passing. They were in Bermuda. Mercer had brought the band down the night before, in the best "show-must-go-on" tradition, to honor a commitment his father had made to have the band play at an IBM convention. Mercer was forthright in declaring his goals as the new leader of the Duke Ellington Orchestra: "Several things are certain. We are going to stay together; we're going to beef up the personnel; and the music of Ellington will live on like any of the classics, like the works of Debussy or Schoenberg. What's most important for us now is that his contributions be authentically represented."

His intentions were good, but he was over-reaching a bit with that declaration: "We're going to beef up the personnel." Five days after his father's death, Mercer was asserting that now that *he* was in charge, it was going to be a better band. Some band members must have wondered which of them were considered not up to snuff.

In reality, it proved impossible for Mercer to *maintain* the quality of the band he had taken over, let alone to improve upon it.

Mercer inherited a band that had been working constantly, day-in and day-out, year after year. In May of 1987, he acknowledged frankly to me: "We're working comparatively less than we've ever worked. We work an average of five to eight dates a month."

The Duke Ellington Orchestra no longer exists as a permanent, ongoing road band. And for anyone with an understanding of the importance of Duke Ellington in jazz history, that is unfortunate. One can't help wondering if things might have turned out any differently if leadership of the orchestra—which had long been considered the world's foremost jazz orchestra—had passed to a musician other than Mercer Ellington. The Glenn Miller Orchestra works 50 weeks a year today. Granted, in his heyday, Miller enjoyed greater popularity than Ellington. But still—given the richness of the Ellington repertoire, the Ellington Orchestra *should* be working more than five to eight dates per month.

In fairness to Mercer, it must be noted that his father, whom Mercer usually refers to simply as "Ellington," did not leave him in an easy position. Duke Ellington left no will. Family members had to work out for themselves how to divide the estate. Sister Ruth got Ellington's music publishing company. (Ellington had used royalties from his many compositions, which were often recorded by others, to help subsidize his band.) Mercer took over a band with some aged stars who were in poor health themselves, and with surprisingly-incomplete written documentation of the wealth of music the band had played over the years. Exaggerating only slightly, Mercer has said his father left him Harry Carney, Cootie Williams, and a few scraps of paper.

As musicians took ill, quit, or died, Mercer struggled to hire acceptable substitutes. The band continued filling bookings that had been made before Duke's death. But word of mouth spread quickly: the band no longer sounded like the Duke Ellington Orchestra. Some blamed Mercer; some felt it was simply fate.

The band had gotten its sound from the highly distinctive voices of specific players, so that when those players were no longer there, and without Duke Ellington himself in control, there was almost no way the Ellington sound could be perpetuated. Even Cootie Williams, who continued in the band for a bit after the Duke's passing, remarked one day that the band now sounded to him like a bunch of guys *trying* to sound like the Duke Ellington Band.

Within a few years after the Duke's passing, the band had lost much of the respect it had once enjoyed from critics. One critic, who saw the band not long after Ellington died, told me in horror that the band had played *rock* tunes; he couldn't understand why the band wasn't playing more early Ellington specialties. He didn't realize that—although many of Ellington's later compositions and orchestrations had been preserved, in at least partial form—most of the band's early arrangements no longer existed. Ellington, particularly in his earlier years, had often been too busy getting on with the next thing, to worry about saving arrangements for posterity. Posterity could take care of itself.

Mercer has tried to regain past respect in the years since, gradually rebuilding the band's library and personnel, but it has not been an easy task.

* * *

We sit in Mercer's Manhattan apartment—the living room dominated by three larger-than-life-size portraits of his father—on May 24, 1987, 13 years to the day after his father's passing. He is cautiously optimistic that a new recording being released this week, "Digital Duke," will help revive the band's flagging reputation. He recalls clearly the many hardships he faced in trying to maintain the orchestra immediately following his father's death.

"That gruesome date, when we played our first date [after Ellington's death] for the IBM convention, I barely had enough music to represent the old man. Because we had also lost so many people in the band themselves.

"Paul Gonsalves died the week before Ellington did. And some of the guys were sick and whatever. And all of this was carried in their heads, and the thing that held them together was Ellington himself. Now with him gone, there was no piano book. There was no drum book, because he didn't like drummers who read. And there was no bass book, because he always had a bass player with him he felt was adequate, and who knew the book well-enough."

The reed section, which had always been crucial to the Ellington ensemble sound, was soon totally decimated. Tenor saxist Gonsalves, who had been a key member of the band since 1950, died on May 14th, 1974. Alto saxist Russell Procope, who had first joined the band back in 1945, decided to quit when Ellington died. Baritone saxist Harry Carney, who had anchored the reed section since 1927, died on October 8th, 1974. Tenor saxist Harold Ashby, who had joined in 1968, quit in February of 1975. And alto Norris Turney, who had taken Johnny Hodges' place, upon Hodges' death in 1970, likewise decided he'd rather strike off on his own.

The inimitable trumpet soloist Cootie Williams, whose association with Ellington dated back to 1929, quit the band in the fall of '75. And various other, less-important members of the band decided to pack it in, as well. Without the reed players, without Cootie Williams, without the piano contributions of Duke Ellington himself, how could Mercer convey to listeners the magic that had once been the Duke Ellington Orchestra? With the personnel he had had, Duke Ellington could offer listeners anything—from an extended jam on a basic blues to a new Broadway show tune—and it would automatically sound Ellington-ish. With a band filled with substitutes, Mercer had a hard time making the band sound at all distinctive, much less like his father's band.

Some fine, younger pianists took their turns with the band, and Mercer gave them freedom to improvise as they chose. He had little choice in the matter; there were no written piano parts. What they played did not necessarily sound like Ellington's style. Years passed before Mercer managed to identify a fundamental problem.

Mercer Ellington. (Courtesy Willard Alexander, Inc.)

"Sometimes, you know, you can be so close to everything and be so dedicated but. . . one thing gets away from you. And it suddenly dawned on me that what was missing from the band was Ellington himself. I mean, we knew that physically. But we needed him *verbatim*. And so, what we've done, the piano parts you'll find now, if you go through the book, you'll find his music is transcribed on the piano parts."

So now pianists in the Duke Ellington Band will—at least some of the time—re-create Duke Ellington's own piano playing, as it has been transcribed from recordings. Which is essential if the band is to approach getting the sound of the band Duke himself led.

"I don't insist on it sometimes," Mercer acknowledges, "because we'll have a piano player and he's only going to be there for a day or two. I have to wait and watch him. And if he does have the tendency to relate to Ellington, and work, and begin to sound like him, then I start demanding that he gets into the book and plays things, the way he has them."

Ellington's piano style was rooted in an era long before today's younger pianists were born. Many of today's pianists—who would be far more likely to name McCoy Tyner as a major influence than Ellington—would have difficulty really suggesting the feel of Ellington's playing. A pianist could be an excellent sight-reader, but unless he's got a fundamental sympathy towards Ellington's style to begin with, he's probably not going to be able to play a transcribed Ellington solo with the same conviction and ease Ellington himself would originally have had. And, of course, no pianist—if left to his own devices—is going to improvise in the same way Ellington would have.

Ellington, naturally, continued improvising throughout his life. He was not about to sit down and play exactly the same thing on the piano every time his band went into a frequently-played number. He had no interest in re-creating, note-for-note, what he might have played on the studio recording of a particular number. Live recordings of the band preserve variant piano solos on many numbers. Certain representative Ellington phrases will recur, of course, in different solos, or in different tunes. A skillful pianist can *suggest* Ellington, without copying his recorded work note-for-note throughout, by incorporating such Ellington licks into his own playing.

"All through the book, now, you'll find Ellington transcribed. That was one of the things that made working with Roland Hanna [on the "Digital Duke" album] so enjoyable. Roland can see around the corner, and he plays what you put in front of him, if you tell him that's what you want. And you say: 'OK, Roland; this is when I want to hear Roland, and this is when I want to hear Duke Ellington.' And whichever way you want to go, he does it.

"On this album, for instance, on 'Do Nothing Till You Hear From Me'—that's definitely transcribed. And also with 'In a Mellotone.' Those things are done, and they're taken from Ellington, plus the licks. Plus licks, you know, little things that he inserts. . . a small part of a melody or something that Ellington put in. We'll put 'em there. And then, if he picks up on it, great. If not, then we just move on. But Roland, whenever there was something to pick up on, he was there—that was one of the great things about him—and he makes it sound very natural. That makes a big difference."

Sometimes, for a particular date, Mercer will have to make do with a pianist who does not have any special feel for Duke Ellington's music. The band as a whole will sound noticeably less Ellington-ish on such occasions.

Mercer has also had arrangers reconstruct arrangements that had been lost over the years, transcribing note-for-note what had been played on original 78s.

"For these 13 years, we've been expanding as best we could. When I say expanding, I mean *authenticating* what we wanted to represent with Ellington. It's not up to us to innovate, in order to represent him; it's up to us to keep these gems restored, as best we can. And therefore we take tunes like 'Hot and Bothered' and 'The Mooche,' 'Birmingham Breakdown,' etc. and put 'em down note-for-note, including the solos. So that, *if* there was somebody who had been around at that time—and they're getting to be very few—but even so, those who listen to the record will realize that we're not out there to misrepresent what we've come to play that was Ellington's."

The emphasis is on re-creation, not jazz improvisation, when the band plays such numbers as "Hot and Bothered" and "The Mooche." Mercer found that if he hired players who could simulate the distinctive *sounds* of famous predecessors in the band, they typically could not also improvise along the same lines. So Mercer decided he would seek players with the right *sounds*, and give them note-for-note transcribed solos to play. The function of the band has thus changed since the days when his father led it.

Mercer has also stressed the playing and replaying of his father's hits, more than his father did.

"In our appearances, particularly the dances. . . we start off with 'The A Train' every time. We're going to do 'Satin Doll' two times, at least a couple times that night; we're going to play 'Sophisticated Lady.'

"I used to worry about: how could I get through the night and represent Ellington properly when there was only so many numbers we had? Well, the answer's come in the repetition of that number. For instance, one time we'll play 'Solitude' in its original form. The next time we play it, the girl sings it. And it's another arrangement. So that a person who came into the dance at 9:30 will come up and say, 'I want to hear "Solitude,"' and we've played it already. We don't have to sort of make it monotonous to the person who's heard it already, so we come up with another arrangement of 'In My Solitude.' And we have that. We have a samba arrangement of 'Sophisticated Lady.' So we can make a variance in that."

Mercer's practice of offering alternate versions of famed numbers is questionable. Is the samba version of "Sophisticated Lady" as authentic a representation of Ellington as the original arrangement would be? Hardly. But let's set aside the issue of authenticity for a moment (because Mercer *is* also continuing to play the original arrangement). The question remains: Is this new arrangement of the same quality as the original? To my ears, the answer is clearly no. Mercer does not seem to have the same sense of taste that his father had.

"We have a reggae version of 'Queenie Pie.' 'Queenie Pie' was written by Ellington, but never performed by him. So the result is, we can do it any kind of way we want to, and not be open for criticism.

Mercer Ellington rehearses the band, along with vocalists Anita Moore and Jimmy McPhail. (Chip Deffaa collection)

But if we were to take something and, say, try to make a rock version of 'Mood Indigo,' I mean, you know—we're in for it! Hah! Hah! And I'm not about to."

Of course, some Ellington purists would still question whether his reggae treatment of "Queenie Pie" is the best, most authentic way that number could be offered.

What does Mercer Ellington feel is the biggest challenge he faces in running the orchestra?

"Well, the hardest part is getting recognition from the existing generation, without crossing over. We do things that, in a sense, are oriented a little to rock, or whatever you want to call it—but I can't get too far out there. We go to dances, and then they say, 'Well, when are you going to play some funk?' Or, 'We want to hear such-and-such a tune' or whatever. . . . We have a few things that we can get onto, that Ellington actually wrote, which are rock 'n' roll tunes. I can play, say, one of the tunes from 'Change of Mind,' which was a background he wrote, in rock, to a motion picture. And as long as it *is* Ellington, I can get away with it. But if I try to develop new things, and say, try to get to the place where I'm going to get a hit in rock, then that's it.

"If we do just anything, then we're just another orchestra. If we play rock, if we do just all original jazz concert things—I've got a million things over there I've been writing; I keep writing—but, as far as the public is concerned, this is entertainment. We're there to entertain, not to educate. If I have an opportunity now to get on a record date, then I'll introduce something." But he doesn't see introducing new music as a primary responsibility for him.

And so Mercer forges ahead, trying to play his father's music as best he can. He has redefined the purpose of the Duke Ellington Orchestra. The Duke was always interested in offering new material, so much so that he'd sometimes use medleys to get through, as quickly as possible, the old hits that the public demanded. He always said that a key reason he maintained the orchestra was so that he would be able to hear his new compositions played as soon as he wrote them. Mercer feels the orchestra has enough to do in preserving his father's music, without worrying too much about offering *new* compositions. And so long as the band plays famed Ellington numbers—even if they're played in versions far different from those his father favored (as in the case of the "Sophisticated Lady" samba)—Mercer believes he's continuing the Ellington tradition.

Mercer has received friendly criticism from jazz writers who love Duke Ellington's music, and in some cases may actually be more familiar with the Duke's early work than Mercer himself is. They are saddened when the band doesn't sound as Ellington-ish as they'd like. Mercer continues to have old recordings of his father's band transcribed, increasing the number of authentic Duke Ellington Orchestra arrangements the band can now play. "Every time I have an occasion," Mercer says, "—I try to become more Ellington than we are."

Mercer inevitably gets compared with his father. Which is to say that—and perhaps it's unfair to him—he is judged by a higher standard than the average bandleader is. In 1987, there are plenty of ghost bands bearing the names of deceased or retired leaders—not just the Dorseys and Miller, but Guy Lombardo, Russ Morgan, Sammy Kaye, Xavier Cugat, Jan Garber, Dick Jurgens, and even Henry Busse. It does not matter if Mercer leads a band better than most of those (and he does). No one ever considered the commercial dance music of a Jan Garber or a Dick Jurgens or a Henry Busse to be "art." Mercer is not competing with other bands so much as he is competing with memories of his father's band—and, for that matter, his father's band *when it was at its very best*. Duke Ellington's Band of the early '70s was not the equal of his band of the early '40s. But most jazz fans are familiar with the superb recordings made by the Ellington Band of the '40s, which have been steadily reissued.

And many fans feel Ellington's finer compositions are something like sacred texts—to be altered only at great risk. If the Jimmy Dorsey Band plays pop tunes such as "Maria Elena" and "June Night," listeners are satisfied so long as the band evokes the general feel of the past recordings. Ellington's numbers, however, tend to be subtler, more complex; nuances are more essential. If Mercer's band doesn't get just the right tonal blend and feeling on "Mood Indigo," the effect of the original recording is lost. And he *will* hear: "It doesn't sound like Duke's band." He is in a difficult position.

* * *

Born March 11, 1919, Mercer Ellington was just eight years old when his father broke through to the big time, opening at the Cotton Club on December 4, 1927. He was just 11 when his father first recorded "Mood Indigo," only 14 when his father enjoyed his first European tour.

Mercer was too young to fully appreciate those early triumphs of his father. What he could appreciate, though, from his earliest years, was his father's intense commitment to his work.

Some men are said to live for their families; Duke Ellington was not one of them. Whenever his muse beckoned, he listened. Maintaining an unsurpassed jazz orchestra, composing brief and extended musical compositions, recording them—such activities all seemed to take precedence for him over family life.

He saw to it, of course, that his son had the best of everything. But if his son was clamoring for his attention, so too were any number of composers and musicians. And he often seemed to attend to their needs first. There were a lot of egos to deal with in that band. Getting the best out of that disparate group of players, and keeping them together the way he did, year after year—that took energy.

Sometimes the son of a famous man who doesn't give the son as much attention as the son might wish, will react by rebelling—by trying to become everything the father was not. Mercer, however, went the other route. He tried to align himself with his father, to be as much like his father as possible. Perhaps he imagined his effort would bring him closer to his father, would make his father more interested in him.

For Mercer, his father was not just the ultimate authority on music, he was the ultimate authority on life. As the son put it, he couldn't think of another way of *dressing*, other than the way his father dressed; as far as he was concerned, his father set the standards. His father was

Duke Ellington: For Mercer, he set the standards in dress, in music, in everything. (Chip Deffaa collection)

a dominant, imperious presence.

Mercer attended Columbia University for a while, and also the Juilliard School of Music. But he was most eager to prove himself on his father's own turf: as a band leader.

In 1939, when he was just 20, he formed his first big band, which included such rising talents as Dizzy Gillespie and Clark Terry. Writing arrangements for the band was a 23-year-old named Billy Strayhorn. Later that same year, Strayhorn began his long tenure as arranger *par excellence* for Duke Ellington's Orchestra. Duke Ellington and Strayhorn enjoyed a close relationship. Strayhorn took up residence in Ellington's home. He became a kind of musical alter-ego for the Duke; they worked so closely together on compositions that often, neither one could recollect for sure who had contributed what. Mercer must have envied—at least a bit—this contemporary of his who seemed to become so much closer to his father than he was.

Mercer never enjoyed much commercial success as a bandleader. The Ellington name both helped and hurt. It helped in that it no doubt got him some bookings which would not have gone to an unknown 20-year-old trumpeter/composer named Smith or Jones. But it hurt in that Mercer would be compared to, and found inferior to, his famous father. And in the early 1940s, Duke Ellington and his Orchestra were at a zenith of creativity.

Mercer *was* a talented composer/arranger. He enriched his father's library with a variety of memorable charts in the early 1940s. But he had trouble establishing an identity of his own. If he wrote a successful number for his father's band, or for a small group led by one of his father's sidemen, it became known as his father's number. His father cast a long shadow.

It was Mercer—not Duke—who wrote one of the best-known tunes in the Duke Ellington Orchestra's repertoire: "Things Ain't What They Used to Be." First recorded on July 3, 1941 by a small group under the nominal leadership of Johnny Hodges (the septet, including Duke Ellington on piano, was drawn entirely from the Duke Ellington Orchestra), it became a tremendous success. The average swing fan today would probably identify Duke Ellington as its author—just as the Duke is often mistakenly given credit for writing "Take the A Train," which Strayhorn actually wrote, and "Perdido," which Juan Tizol actually wrote.

Among Mercer's other compositions for his father's band in this period were: "The Girl in My Dreams Tries to Look Like You," a minor and rather difficult-to-sing number (recorded by Duke on October 17, 1940); the better-known "Jumpin' Punkins," featuring some dissonant chords with a blues/gospel tinged setting (recorded by Duke on February 15, 1941); "Blue Serge," perhaps the moodiest, most somber of all Ellington recordings (recorded by Duke on February 15, 1941); and "Moon Mist," a lovely piece, created when Duke gave Mercer a series of harmonies and told him to compose a melody to them (recorded by Duke on January 21, 1942).

The years 1940-42 were extraordinarily productive for Duke Ellington and his Orchestra. Among the unforgettable numbers introduced and recorded by the band in this period were: "Concerto for Cootie" (later known as "Do Nothin' Till You Hear From Me"), "Never No Lament" ("Don't Get Around Much Anymore"), "All Too Soon," "In a Mellotone," "Warm Valley," "Flamingo," "Take the A Train," "I Got it Bad And That Ain't Good," "Rocks in My Bed," "Chelsea Bridge," "The C Jam Blues," and "Perdido"—an unprecedented outpouring of critical and commercial successes. Mercer wished more of his compositions could have become hits, but so many strong numbers were coming out from the Duke Ellington Band almost simultaneously, that the market reached a saturation point.

Mercer was in the Army in 1943-45, spending some of that time in Sy Oliver's Band. After his discharge, he led his own big band again until 1949. This one included two more musicians his father would later use, Butch Ballard and Wendell Marshall, plus a not-yet-famous Carmen McRae on vocals. She made her recording debut with Mercer's band, attracting no attention at the time. He also found time to study the Schillinger method of arranging at New York University.

Leading his own big band, of course, also gave Mercer a regular outlet for his compositions and arrangements. Throughout his career, he also did freelance composing and arranging for others, from musicians to singers to nightclub shows to dance companies.

But by 1949, the bottom had dropped out of the big band business. If times were hard for the biggest names in the business, like the Dorseys, Woody Herman, Count Basie, and Duke Ellington, they were impossible for Mercer Ellington. He gave up his big band.

For a few months in 1950, Mercer played E flat horn in his father's band. But after having led his own bands, it must have been frustrating to have to work as a sideman for his father once again, the professional equivalent of moving back in to live with your parents, after having had your own apartment, because you're unable to make it financially on your own.

From 1950-52, Mercer tried running a record label ("Mercer"). In 1953, he was outside of music, working as a salesman. In 1954, he toured as road manager and trumpeter in Cootie Williams' Band. From 1955-59, he worked as a general assistant for his father. In October of 1959, he gave big band leading another shot, leading an ensemble at the top-rated New York club, Birdland. Two albums by Mercer Ellington and his Orchestra, released on the Coral label in 1958-59, featured personnel drawn mostly from his father's band.

In the early '60s, Mercer worked for three years as a disc jockey on a minor New York radio station, WLIB. In 1965, he rejoined his father's band, as a trumpeter (not a soloist, just a section man) and band manager. Duke Ellington was getting older—he turned 67 in 1965 (Mercer turned 46)—and he could use his son's assistance in handling the orchestra.

* * *

I ask Mercer if it had been intimidating, growing up the son of someone who everyone said was a genius? Had it been a burden?

"Not really," he answers. "I mean, how can it be a burden, when you never had to worry about eating? And when, in the process of going through show business, and peoples' homes, like I came up through the Depression period, and I found out how bad off some people could be—I mean, from that point on, you could never feel that you had any kind of a thing that you were suffering. I didn't feel bad, and feel that my father was doing things to destroy my existence when he gave me a Ford automobile at my graduation; he wasn't doing anything to turn me against society. . . . I felt that was great, and it was. I had the best of clothes. I went to the best teachers and best schools.

"So the only handicap I had was within myself or within our little realm, because in a sense I had to vie for a position along with Billy Strayhorn. I had to compete with Duke Ellington himself, in order to get a number played by the orchestra that was going to be sustained or whatever. And the only thing I felt was a difficulty, was doing something that was worthy of gaining Duke Ellington's attention. And I think we all go through that, growing up. You want your parents to be proud of you, and to look at what you want to do."

Mercer composed just one instrumental which became a smash hit: "Things Ain't What They Used to Be." He reflects: "I look at 'Things Ain't' like a freak. That's just like winning a lottery or something. But the things that I was very pleased with and would have liked to have had more success with, were things like 'Moon Mist' and 'Blue Serge.' And probably 'Jumpin' Punkins' and things of that sort. But they always just happened to happen at the wrong time. There was something else that might have been going on. 'Things Ain't' broke through at the same time as 'Take the A Train' did, but he had other things that were making it, too, and as a result there was only so much Ellington that the industry was going to accept, and that's the way it went."

And some numbers, I suggest to him, become musicians' favorites rather than commercial hits. "Jumpin' Punkins" and "Blue Serge" might have fit into that category.

"Yeah, that's it! Well, of course that's the great thing about Billy Strayhorn's work. As time has progressed, his works have become more and more standard, you know, and more accepted. I mean, in those days everybody was scared as hell to do something like 'Lush Life.' But now all the singers want it to be part of their repertoire."

He hasn't gotten the recognition as a composer he has deserved. Does it bother him that sometimes people think songs *he* wrote were written by his father?

"I take that as a compliment. I used to play things around him, and he used to steal 'em. And I used to be very happy that I had done something that was good enough for him to want to claim, or to write.

Three Generations of Ellington: Duke Ellington (far right); his son, Mercer (far left); and his grandson, Edward. (Institute of Jazz Studies)

And so, as a result, little by little as the years go on, I felt confident that I was capable of doing something.

"And I think—there's always an event that sets you over the hill. The doubt as to whether I could put myself in the midst of musicians and be successful without having people know that I was Duke Ellington's son, came as a result of an arrangement that I made for Della Reese. She called up one night—I had known her for years—and she said, 'I want you to make an arrangement for me, and this is the way I want it. I want the rhythm on the first chorus, I want it to build, I want you to bring in something that makes it a little bit more exciting, but save the last chorus so that it's exciting.' Anyhow, by the time she got here, I went over to the Copacabana and rehearsed it with her. The song was 'Bill Bailey, Won't You Please Come Home,' and it sold a million records. So, by the time we got through I knew: Here's something no one associated, and it didn't make it because it was Duke Ellington's son that wrote it, it made it because it was a damn good number and somebody who was damn good sang it. And they must have thought something of me, to have me do it for them.

"So with that, I just felt from that time on that I was capable of doing things, and didn't have the feeling that I was in a position because my father had put me there. And in fact. . . I felt that many times I might have gotten further ahead, if I hadn't had him to fight. Heh-heh-heh. But that was it."

* * *

From 1965 to 1974, Duke Ellington and Mercer Ellington were together, traveling all around the world with the Ellington Orchestra. In these final nine years of Duke's life, they spent more time together than they had in Mercer's youth.

Duke was increasingly interested in creating longer musical works, such as his sacred concerts and a proposed opera for public television, entitled *Queenie Pie*. Sometimes he'd ask his son's advice on what to write next in a piece of music. Mercer would suggest something. And Duke would jest that he now knew what *not* to write. But occasionally he *would* incorporate suggestions his son made, which pleased Mercer.

Mercer was 55 when his father died in 1974. He inherited the responsibility of maintaining his father's overall reputation, not just the Duke Ellington Orchestra. He announced he would be resurrecting some of his father's early gems, which the orchestra hadn't played in many years. He said he also felt a responsibility to bring to fruition some of the unfinished projects that his father had been working on in his last years, such as *Three Black Kings* and *Queenie Pie*. And he wanted to see that his father's longer works became part of the repertoire of symphony orchestras, respected as notable pieces of serious music.

He told interviewers that he envisioned the orchestra going on in perpetuity. He brought his son into the orchestra as a guitarist; maybe his son could someday take it over after him, just as he had from his father.

He had ambitious plans. But he was juggling more balls in the air than he could comfortably handle. Duke Ellington had been able to lead a full-time road band, compose long and short pieces of music, and work on recording, theater, film, and television projects simultaneously. He was, of course, a genius. Mercer was hard-pressed to continue moving simultaneously in all of these directions.

Initially, it looked as though Mercer was going to make leading the band his top priority. In the fall of 1974, the band fulfilled a European tour commitment, and also played during the Superbowl, which gave them national TV exposure. There were quality bookings, such as Ravinia with Sarah Vaughan. The band was working all the time.

In 1974, the band recorded an album entitled "Continuum." Cootie Williams and Harry Carney were still in the band at that point, giving it a real connection to the old band. But soon they were gone, along with so many others. Mercer was struggling to make do with substitutes. Without Duke Ellington and the famous sidemen, the band could no longer command the fees it once had. Record companies lost interest in the band. And as Mercer devoted some of his energies to other projects, maintaining the band seemed to become a lower priority.

It was important to him to complete *Three Black Kings* (a 17-minute piece in three movements, designed to be played by the Ellington Orchestra in conjunction with a symphony orchestra), which received its premiere in 1977. The conclusion to the piece, which Mercer wrote, seemed to some a let-down after the drama of his father's writing. Mercer tried hard to figure out how his father might have intended to end it, but he felt he had been left in the dark. His father had long been superstitious about not writing down the ending of a piece of music until the day of its first performance.

Mercer also found time to co-author, with jazz authority and longtime Ellington-devotee Stanley Dance, *Duke Ellington in Person*, which Houghton Mifflin published in 1978.

Mercer then got sidetracked by the idea of doing a Broadway show using Duke Ellington's music. He no doubt envisioned the show refocusing public attention on the Ellington legacy. But as Mercer got more involved in *Sophisticated Ladies*—which wound up emphasizing Duke Ellington the songwriter rather than the all-around giant of jazz—the band suffered.

In the early 1980s, Mercer conducted an augmented version of the orchestra for *Sophisticated Ladies*. It had a slick, glossy Broadway—rather than specifically Ellington-ish—type of sound. The one-of-a-kind Ellington Orchestra had been reduced to Broadway pit band status, being used now primarily to accompany featured singers and dancers. The orchestra, which had long routinely topped the *Down Beat* International Critics' Polls, wound up no longer even showing up in the listings.

From a jazz aficionado's point of view, it's a shame that someone else—a top jazz musician with a real feel for the sound of the Ellington Band—could not have been given leadership of the Ellington Band, allowing it to continue touring worldwide, while Mercer conducted the Broadway orchestra for *Sophisticated Ladies* and worked on his other Ellington-related projects. During the two years that *Sophisticated Ladies* ran, there was no "Duke Ellington Orchestra" on the road, playing concerts and clinics and dances. Had there been an Ellington Orchestra on the road, it certainly could have picked up bookings, which went to Basie's Band, Buddy Rich's, Woody Herman's, and the Tommy Dorsey Band, etc. in its absence.

Mercer found his involvement with *Sophisticated Ladies* to be frustrating. He had hoped the show would perpetuate his father's music to a greater extent than it did. He had also expected that—after having spent a lifetime in the music business—he'd be respected more as a consultant to the show rather than being treated simply as Duke Ellington's son.

"I wasn't happy with the way *Sophisticated Ladies* turned out because we had a show which should have gone on for years. And it only lasted, successfully, two years, between New York and Hollywood," Mercer notes. "And the reason for that is, the producers did not listen to my concept of what the show should have been like. And that was, number one, that we should have screened talent and found great talent, but not *bought* great talent. But what they did, they went shopping in William Morris' office, so that by the time they got through paying salaries, the show was top-heavy. And unless it played to absolutely full crowds, it couldn't make a nickel. Consequently, when we wanted to turn it over to somebody like the Nederlanders, or the Shuberts, or whoever, they were too road-wise to buy something that was top-heavy. And therefore the show couldn't exist.

"So they stopped the show with the intention of re-creating it a year later when the contracts were void and so forth, but then by that time, all the people who had helped produce it had gone in their varied directions. And interest lagged. And so that was it. So what was a very good show, I thought, had been allowed to bite the dust.

"In addition to which, I wanted it to be a book show and not a review, which would have given it possibilities of being used in Hollywood or whatever. And that was ignored. We had a book, and it was scrapped. All of sudden, panic of trying to get a show put together, and then everything with pace was kept in, and everything that was slow was kicked out.

"We had a very fast-moving, exciting show, except for one thing—you only heard the title tune once, in 32 bars. I raised hell about it, and they finally made a production number of it.

"But—what the hell do you spend some 50 years in the business doing, that that cannot be accepted as enough time and experience to know what to do, and how a show should be run? Which is the length of time I've been here—from the early days of the Cotton Club shows, straight through to working with La Moulin Rouge, which I wrote two shows for. Also working with Alvin Ailey, and before that having written some music for Katherine Dunham. You know, I've been laying—like they say—in the cut, watching show business and being a part of it. And someone comes along and says, 'Well, you don't know the field.' How the hell can you not know the field if you come up through all of that. . . and you're still facing audiences. And with that, the next time, we don't have a show unless we do it *my* way."

Mercer's experience with *Sophisticated Ladies* left him a little gun-shy about the world of the theater. But still, he wanted to see *Queenie Pie* produced. The project had intrigued him for years.

"I've been kind of curious about *Queenie Pie* from the time that Pop was working on it with Maurice Peress in the Rainbow Grill at nights, in between sets.

"Here was a project which was supposed to have been aired by WNET [public television]. But after it was finished and everything was readied, it was determined that the budget for it would be $400,000. And in those days, that became a bit much for WNET to handle, and so it became unfinanced, and the project was dropped. But from that time on, I always felt that it was one of the things, and one of the directions Ellington went into, that should be pursued. And I kept talking *Queenie Pie*.

"Of course the other thing that was a great help, was WNET itself. Because they gave us a special on Ellington, with three excerpts from *Queenie Pie*. And with it, we had Patti LaBelle to demonstrate one of the songs. Now, during the time he was still alive, Pop had demos made by Robert Guillaume. So, when we wanted to exhibit the tunes, we had these two great people—at least they had become great, you know—but the prestige of these people, pushing a tune by Ellington; I mean, it wasn't like you had to go out there and had a hard sell. It was a matter of mentioning it,. and immediately you got interest.

"And as a result, we got our two performances, in Philadelphia and Washington. But then, I began to lose control of the concept, and many things happened which I felt were derogatory. We had a native scene. And I wanted this whole thing to be—I mean, you can be humorous, but you can still be prestigious as far as culture is concerned. So, I don't plan to have natives coming out there with bones, and spats on their feet and all that kind of crap, which is what happened. Also, the dialogue was bad, and the presentation of it was bad. The costumes were bad. I wanted to see costumes that were real. Either something that the Watusi wore, or the Masai, or whatever. And then you could still put humor on top of this. But at least it's something believable, and it's not being derogatory, as far as the culture is concerned.

"I wanted it to not just be another flash in the pan like *Sophisticated Ladies*—that if and when it was launched, whether it was successful or not, it would be a work that was a proud thing, and could be reproduced or re-done, and it would be artistically successful. It was the one time I wished for an artistic success, even though the financial part had to be sacrificed. And so, I would just as soon have it done properly and be an off-off-Broadway product, than to have it regaled and shown all over the place, and come in like a Grade B Tarzan movie.

"They also took three songs out of the show that were written by Ellington. And they put in one that was written by Maurice [Peress]—or he claims he wrote it. . . ." Mercer smarts at thought of an Ellington work being presented with songs credited to someone not named Ellington.

Will *Queenie Pie* ever be produced in New York?

"Oh yeah, I think we'll get here. But I just think it's one of those things where if you don't stick to your guns, you're going to get trampled. And by now, I think that they are very aware of the fact that I'm serious about it.

"But with absolute interest and ability to have it produced as a show in New York, I turned down every offer. Because, it wasn't the money alone that I was after. And it was very successful, and we had great reviews [out of town].

"We had a proposal from two producers already who were willing to come in. And everything about the show was right, from the standpoint of backing, money. But when it came to agreeing as to how it was going to be done—first off, the orchestra was not going to have an opportunity to be a part of the show. Which I thought was ridiculous, because that's one of the things that makes Ellington's music Ellington. I don't trust anybody else to play it. Especially headed by Maurice Peress.

"And then the other thing is, I felt that we should mold it to what is available. For instance, when Pop wrote it, his thoughts were Lena Horne in the lead—which would have been a great idea. But I felt that if I could interpret what he was saying, and also knew that this show was written around Madame Walker, who was a beauty products queen—not a beauty queen, a beauty *products* queen—then you don't need Lena Horne.

"You need a woman, who. . . attributed her success to God. And this is an excellent opportunity to display Ellington in what he did, Gospel-wise. So, I felt that we needed a type like Patti LaBelle, who represents this strong woman, who was very much like Madame Walker. She becomes a millionairess. And as a process. And we need to start up with that vein of Ellington's which he became so interested in—the church. And there's nothing un-commercial, or against starting off with God.

"They felt that this was not commercial. And so I said, 'Well, to hell with it.' And they made changes, which I did not agree to, and as a result just ran rough-shod and felt that the money was going to be enough alone to make everything OK. They found out differently. But you will see *Queenie Pie*. Believe me."

Mercer sees himself as carrying out his father's wishes, completing his father's unfinished business. But then, he's often offering *his* interpretation of what the music should be, and it's not necessarily the same as his father's would have been.

* * *

Mercer has plans now to augment the Duke Ellington Orchestra so that it can sound more symphonic for certain concerts.

"What I'm planning on doing at some given occasion in the concert field, is to go after playing versions of Ellington in the full spectrum of the way they were created, by adding certain things to our orchestra as it exists, with the help of the machines and the other things.

"For instance, I plan to put in a string quartet, to also have a French Horn player and an oboe player or someone with double reed ability, in addition to what we have. And as result, I feel that we can then play everything that's expected, and give you some sort of a perspective of what, say, *Night Creature* is like, when played by a full [symphony] orchestra. And we don't have to play a watered-down version of it, or we don't have to play the original version of it until they had made the concerto grosso arrangement. So this time, we can go in and we can play our things like *Three Black Kings*, or *Harlem*, or whatever, as if it were a symphony.

"[We'll use amplification]. . . so that if I have four violins sitting up there, I can give them the ability to compete with the brass or the trombones or the full orchestra itself, and still have—in other words, to create studio conditions onstage. This is what my definition is of the old days in music, and the new days in music. In the old days, when you went into the recording studio, you went there to duplicate the sound heard in the dance hall. Now, when you go into the dance hall, you go there to re-create the sound that's heard from the recording studio.

"You have all the reverberation, or what they call echo. Or you can spread them, you can accentuate the highs, you know, the tonal quality. And this can change and be necessary, depending on the acoustics of the hall you're in. Some halls will give you a nice faithful reproduction, but because of the way some other halls are built, they may dampen all the high sounds, and make the orchestra sound like it was sitting in a second room or next door or something like that. We'd add the strings for selected dates. Mostly concerts." (He makes it clear that he has no plans to use synthesized or pre-recorded strings: "I still believe in the live musician.")

He adds: "And the other thing we're doing, we're also developing the music for the church, which was done just for the orchestra. So that it will now be enhanced by the classical instruments—strings, oboe, French horns and so forth."

There seems something a bit presumptuous about his planning to add strings to music that his father had written for the church *without strings*. And perhaps something a bit bourgeois in his belief that "classical instruments" would necessarily enhance music that had been written for a jazz orchestra.

Does Mercer feel good about the future of the band?

"I feel like the baseball players feel: You're as good as yesterday's ballgame. Today is another one. You've got to keep at it, you've got to keep the clientele and the personnel satisfied. And keep the guys interested. Interest in the band is also relative to the people you have playing the music. And when they look and see people around who are very *capable* of playing this music, then they play it, and they play at their best. So, we don't take any chances. We start at the top—and then if that man can't make it, then we'll take the next best person we can think of. And as the days go on, our personnel has gotten—I'd say, very good, very capable."

But not exceptional, as typically might have been said of Duke's bands. When I attended a rehearsal of the band, Mercer mentioned to me with pride that his band included musicians who played lead in Broadway pit orchestras. Duke Ellington would have felt that their playing in *his* orchestra was a higher distinction than playing in a Broadway pit orchestra.

"The band plays mostly one-nighters. We're working comparatively less than we've ever worked. We work an average of five to eight dates a month. But the dates are all very heavy, very important. For instance, we will be going to Texas on the third, and we will be working for ex-President Carter and the President of France, with an organization down there. We just played in California at the Queen Mary, for that festival they had out there. And as it goes on in the summer, it generally picks up more, because of the festivals. We'll be in Yugoslavia for three days. . . . We're also going to France for 10 days in July. And these dates are inter-woven with other single dates, and so forth."

It's curious hearing him remark about the importance of the people the band has played for, as if *that* illustrated the worth of the band. Duke Ellington judged it by whether it met his own musical standards, not by external standards such as whether it played for "important" people.

Would Mercer like to be working more steadily?

"I would like to be working more steadily, but not too much more. Because when you're working consistently, like we used to do with Pop—he had to be a fanatic in order to keep creating, and he was able to, because of the genius that he was—but when we worked 30 days a month, it was quite demanding, and it doesn't give you time to really slow down in order to move on and do new things. Doesn't give you a chance to rehearse the band, doesn't give you a chance to write properly.

"And as a result, this way I can get into things that are more important. For instance, what could be more important than documenting Duke Ellington? So that in the future, you know, he's been a composer—but we want him recognized as a classicist, as well as a jazz writer. Many of his works approach symphony. Especially his creations for the church. I want these things documented, so that anyone can take them, or send for them. It doesn't require the [Duke Ellington] Band, they can just do them with their own facilities. And for that reason, we've started, with the Schirmer Music Company, publishing his extended things like *Harlem*. They will have *Black, Brown and Beige*. And they have the *Three Black Kings*—things of that sort, which for years, the conductors are saying, 'When can we get our hands on this music?' Well, now they can. *Night Creature* and so forth."

Each year from 1943-50, Duke Ellington presented new extended works at Carnegie Hall, such as *Black, Brown and Beige*, *Deep South Suite*, *Blutopia*, *Blue Belles of Harlem*, *Liberian Suite*, and *The Tatooed Bride*. *Harlem* had its premiere performance at the Metropolitan Opera House in 1951. *Night Creature* was first performed with the Symphony of the Air in 1955. *Such Sweet Thunder* debuted at Town Hall in 1957. *Suite Thursday* received its premiere in 1960 at the Monterey Jazz Festival. Ellington debuted *The Golden Broom and the Green Apple* in 1965 with the New York Philharmonic. His *First Sacred Concert* was in 1965, the *Second Sacred Concert* was in 1968, the *Third Sacred Concert* was in 1973. His *Togo Brava* suite was introduced at Newport in 1971.

My own feeling is that Duke Ellington was often much more successful in creating short jazz pieces ("Rockin' in Rhythm" is perfectly constructed) than in creating extended ones (*Black, Brown, and Beige* strikes me as episodic and rambling). Creating a perfect jazz miniature is a more important accomplishment than creating a flawed suite. Ellington's position in jazz history would have been secure even if he hadn't written any of his suites and sacred concerts. But Mercer feels strongly about the importance of highlighting his father's extended works. They are closer to the world of symphonic music. And he has been successful in casting continued attention upon his father's most ambitious undertakings.

Mercer Ellington. (Courtesy of Willard Alexander, Inc.)

Making his father's extended works available to the public has become a high priority for Mercer. Transcriptions have been made from recordings of the numbers by Duke Ellington and his Orchestra. And if variant performances exist, a decision has to be made as to which is the best representation of Ellington. The earliest recording of *Black, Brown, and Beige*, for example, is incomplete. Mercer had to compare later recordings, and the score that existed, to determine how the definitive text should go.

Published scores enable orchestras to perform the Ellington numbers by themselves (or, in some cases, if they wish, in conjunction with today's Ellington Orchestra). Mercer hopes to make as much of his father's output available as possible.[1]

Some, but not all, of the transcriptions have been done by Maurice Peress. Eric Kunzel, for instance, re-created *New World A-Comin,'* going back to the earliest recorded performance of it, rather than a later revision. "We have Kunzel's version in Schirmer. We worked that with the New Mexico Symphony. They had the material first, and then they sent for us to come down and be a guest on certain of the tunes, with the orchestra," Mercer notes.

"That's the type of thing that we do, now. The occasions are much more specialized. And we are being booked ahead of time, so we can be programmed. Such as the various heavy organizations require. Wolf Trap, and so forth. If they're going to have someone, they have to be able to say a year and a half before that they're going to be there. And that, I think, is sort of a tribute to our having become standardized. They now figure we're going to be around."

It's important to Mercer to maintain an Ellington Orchestra which is comfortable playing as much of the Ellington repertoire as possible. He pays his musicians well. He wants the best he can get.

Mercer has had to learn to conduct his father's music, particularly the extended works, since he never conducted the band while his father was alive. (Peress, who had had considerable experience conducting, as well as writing for larger orchestras, has helped rehearse the band on some of the extended works.) And rehearsals are a must. For the nuances in the music are not all down on paper. Mercer must coach the musicians to be more explosive at times, or to bite off the notes more sharply elsewhere, or to play more lazily in certain passages.

Mercer recalls that his father told him he wanted him to keep on playing his music. "I think the greatest school I went to was Duke

[1] In 1988, Duke Ellington's archives —including several thousand original and orchestrated pieces of music—were acquired from his estate by the Smithsonian's National Museum of American History. The collection is expected to be made available to researchers in 1989.

Ellington," he reflects. "I went to Juilliard at one point. And then after the war, I studied composition at NYU. But my greatest lessons, like I said, came from the old man." Sometimes, he notes, he feels as if he's been absorbed by his father. As if his father's ego has become his own. Continuing his father's work has become *his* work.

He wants all of his father's creations to be documented and brought to light—even the very last pieces of music his father was working on at the end, in his hospital bed.

Mercer has accepted the responsibility of perpetuating his father's music—although there still seems to be a small part of him that insists on periodically making alterations, if only to protest a bit that he *is* an individual with his own life, not just an extension of his father.

He is now in his upper 60s. Has he ever mulled the idea of retiring?

"Well, I get to the place where my father's answer to that question becomes more and more logical. Retire to what? What am I going to do if I stop playing music, or stop going on the one-nighters?"

* * *

Mercer has hopes that the Duke Ellington Orchestra's new album, "Digital Duke," on the GRP label, will give the band a boost in prestige.

GRP had opted to do the album as a follow-up to their best-selling "In the Digital Mood" recording, which they claimed had sold 150,000 units by July of 1987.

Mercer comments: "We hope very much to have the success that the Glenn Miller album had. But, you know, you just put that word Glenn Miller up there, and the people just flock. If you had to name any one person who had the greatest appeal around the world, it had to be Glenn Miller. The most unfortunate thing is that he didn't live to become even greater. A wonderful man. There was something about his music which was—not *too* intelligent. This is not a derogatory remark, but it was built for the layman. You hear a Glenn Miller tune and you could hum it and you could sing it." By contrast, Mercer notes, most of Ellington's music is more complex and subtle—and thus may not appeal to as large a number of people. For this album, then, a decision was made to stress Ellington's most familiar works, in the hopes of reaching as wide an audience as possible.

The idea for the album, Mercer acknowledges, did not originate with him. When GRP did the Glenn Miller Band album, they did not use the musicians who then comprised the authorized Glenn Miller Band. They assembled a crew of the best studio musicians they could find, put them under the direction of trombonist Larry O'Brien, who was then the leader of the Miller Band, and had them play the classic Miller charts.

The original idea behind "Digital Duke" was to play classic Duke

Ellington numbers, using an all-star studio crew including surviving former members of the Duke Ellington Orchestra. When Mercer got involved, an agreement was reached to use members of his current Ellington Band, past Ellington stars, and a couple of today's younger jazz stars (Branford Marsalis and Eddie Daniels) as sweeteners.

"Basically the idea for the album was [music publisher] Lou Levy's, who's been a friend of mine. When Dave Grusin [of GRP Records] got onto the idea, he started thinking in terms of Ellingtonia and people who were related to it. And said, 'Let's see if we can gather a few of those people around. And if not, people who are interested in the school.' There was a combination of who thought up the names.

"We didn't call anybody unless they had some kind of a feeling for Ellington himself. Result: We got Clark Terry, Roland Hanna. Britt Woodman, as well as Norris Turney, who I consider made a great contribution. And, to our great surprise, Louis Bellson said he would love to be on the date. We wound up with some of the greatest names housed

"Digital Duke" won a 1988 Grammy Award, spurring renewed interest in the Ellington Orchestra. (Courtesy GRP Records)

in one studio. Lew Soloff, J.J. Wiggins (who's been with us on bass for years), and his father, who had been playing piano for years with Helen Humes. We had people who really belonged to the school of Ellington.

"These people finally were in one room together—who knew so much about Ellington, loved him, and enjoyed playing. And I think that that's sort of evidenced in the tunes that we played. 'Cause there's just a feeling of happiness in it."

How did Branford Marsalis come to be involved?

"That was through Dave's influence. You got a man who knew the school of Ellington. And so he was invited. We started at the top, and the worst that could happen was they could say no. Branford said yes. You can tell, by the sound of him playing 'Cottontail,' that he had to have had knowledge of Ben Webster, which meant having knowledge of what Ellington represented. And it wasn't by accident because his father is a very highly capable musician. We worked with him, he knew Ellington, he loved Ellington. And that made it logical for us."

Mercer had known Ellis Marsalis, the father of Wynton and Branford, before the sons were even born. "We played Al Hirt's. And Ellis Marsalis was Al Hirt's piano player, in the club down there. We played together with him, in the old days. I met every one of those kids when they were tots!"

Eddie Daniels, perhaps today's hottest clarinet star, is on the album because Mercer asked for him. "If you look up on an album which I did with Teresa Brewer [in January of 1985], you'll find out that Eddie Daniels was the clarinet player on it. And I never forgot it.

"But when we started off, it really basically was not my date. It was a date that was proposed by Lou Levy, an all-star date. And since I was of the house of Ellington, I was invited. So I just brought the rest of my gang, that wasn't fulfilled by the all-stars, and suddenly it became an orchestral date; it became the Duke Ellington Orchestra, for the most part. Because of our arrangements. And the depth of transcribing that was attended to, by mainly Barry Lee Hall [who joined the orchestra's trumpet section shortly before the Duke died, and has been a key element, both as a transcriber of old arrangements and as a soloist in the Cootie Williams tradition, ever since].

"My favorite of all the numbers on the session, of course, is really like 'Do Nothing Till You Hear From Me,' because it's so reminiscent of the first days when I heard the band, and Cootie was there, at his greatest. Then, in addition to it, there's a nuance, because Barry Lee plays Cootie's part. But in addition, you have the flavor enhanced with Clark Terry as well, doing his contribution on plunger solo. And it's really Ellington."

Indeed it is. Even the reeds sound more authentic on this number than on most of the others. The number really has an Ellington-ish flavor. The presence of Norris Turney in the reeds is a major asset; it's a pity they could not have included Harold Ashby as well. Too often, in both live and recorded performances, Mercer's bands have had a Las Vegas or Broadway kind of slickness, rather than the honest *feeling* that his father's band had at its best.

"'Prelude to a Kiss' is another one that I enjoyed very much, and I think will have a great success, because of Norris and his ability to remind you so much of Johnny Hodges. And also, the concept that J. J. Wiggins—old man Wiggins, the father—has of Ellington."

The album also includes an obscure bit of Ellingtonia, which has been retitled for this album, "Twenty Two Cent Stomp."

"Actually, it's an old number of his, one of those blues things that, you know, Ellington used to toss off his shoulders about every other month. And I particularly liked this one. And we wanted to sort of acknowledge the graciousness of the United States when they put the stamp out, in the name of Ellington. So we re-titled one of the old tunes, so we could have it dedicated to the stamp. And a long time ago, the old man had another number, he used to call the 'Three Cent Stomp.'"

What was the number originally called?

"'Slammer On D Flat,' I think; I'm not sure. But he's so cryptic. I have to get some of the chroniclers to explain Ellington to me, more than I know him. Because they know every little nuance, every change of a title. For instance, 'Do Nothing Till You Hear From Me,' as most people know, originally was 'Concerto for Cootie.' But he's gotten much deeper than that. And a lot of things. If you look at the music and you hear the tune, you'd have no idea that these two would be connected. He's got some strange hieroglyphics there, to designate it."

Ellington purists may be surprised at liberties taken with a few of the numbers. "Take the A Train" now moves at a slower clip than on the original recorded performance, a bit too slow for my tastes. And making it a display piece for Branford Marsalis' tenor sax changes the overall feel of it considerably. Gone is the memorable, climactic Ray Nance trumpet solo. On "Cottontail," a sax section interlude from the original recording has been relocated to the beginning of the number for the 1987 recording. "Perdido" is taken at a tempo faster than on Ellington's first recording—but much slower than the way he generally played it in later years. (Ellington often changed the tempos of numbers.) The goal was not strict note-for-note re-creations of the best past performances, but the creation of valid new performances of these classic numbers. And on those terms, the recording works. The players sound like they care about the music, much more so than those on the

Glenn Miller Band recording.

Some of the charts were readied specifically for this record date; the band had not been carrying them in their library, although they certainly will be carrying them now.

Mercer saw to it that the guest stars were only used on selected numbers. He wanted the musicians who regularly work with him—such as trumpeter Barry Lee Hall, tenor saxist Herman Riley, and drummer Rocky White (who joined the band shortly before Duke died and has been with it much of the time since)—to have their chances to be heard, as well as the guest stars.

"I didn't want the session to get so far afield that it would be completely unrelated to the orchestra that I'm going to have when we do our one-nighters.

"Our band is truly an international band. One of the things that can really infuriate me is to have someone come up and say, 'Where did you pick this band up?' We don't pick the band up. And one of the reasons for our price is the fact that I have to get them from so many distant places. I have two people in Texas: our singer, Anita Moore, and Barry Lee Hall. In California, we have Buddy Collete, Charlie Owens, and Herman Riley. In Ohio we have Booty Wood and Chuck Connors. And I get Britt from out of New York, and so forth." It is to Mercer's credit that he has not tried to cut costs by simply picking up local musicians.

He adds: "Thank goodness for the airplane wars. I've been able to do this now, and juggle it around, for I'd say easily two to three years. It's my band. We have our own identification, especially guys who have solo responsibilities.

"The day after we recorded, people in California were calling me up and saying, 'I hear you had a great session yesterday.' This is like the second day; it took three days to record it. By the time we had finished up on the third day, I got a call from my friend Billy Moore [the arranger] in Copenhagen, Denmark. He says, 'We've heard about that record date you had, and the Danish Orchestra challenges you to a battle of music.' So I called everybody who was on the record date and asked them, would they go with me over to Copenhagen, and we got quite a few. So, we went over there, and we played back and forth to each other. And they played very emphatically, the Danish Radio Band, which is among the best of the European bands. Their music is impeccable and well-disciplined. And we went over there our rowdy selves, and played, I guess, as funky as you could imagine it. And as much as we could involve soul. It was a great contrast, and the crowd enjoyed it very much."

Mercer feels things look better now than they have in years. The band's library is certainly much stronger now than it was when Mercer first took over. If the orchestra is not the equal of his father's orchestra, it is a solidly professional orchestra with some seasoned and dedicated players, nonetheless. And the new recording is creating revived interest. He notes that the band was recently booked to play 28 days in Japan in the fall of 1988. And the first-ever Ellington video (made to the band's recording of "Perdido") was released shortly after the album. And there seems also to be a growing interest in Ellington's music, generally. In New York these days, it is not unusual to see tributes to Ellington (by orchestras other than the Duke Ellington Orchestra), whether at Cooper Union, the Cat Club, or Lincoln Center.

Mercer Ellington believes the "Digital Duke" album could be the thing to put the Ellington Band over the top again. He adds a note of uncertainty, though. "It's like going to Vegas. You know, you gamble, and just when—if you can win one more bet, you'll have it made. Well, I've been there, and many a time during these 13 years I've thought we're just about to make that big step and get into stardom. And here is another situation.

Mercer Ellington rehearses the Duke Ellington Orchestra and singer Jimmy McPhail on a number from Queenie Pie, *New York, 1985.* (Chip Deffaa collection)

"But if ever there was a time when the future looks very bright, it's because of GRP, and the record date they've given us. And also the promotion which is behind it. So this gives people a chance to know that we are still here. And then, it's even more important that they know that the band that is playing Ellington, is playing Ellington as they've heard him, and expect to hear him."

1987

In 1989, the Ellington Orchestra released an ambitious—and at times, superb—album entitled "Music is My Mistress" (Musicmasters). It featured the most authentic-sounding sax section work in years, and—marking a new departure for the band—showcased the composing and arranging skills of Mercer Ellington no less than those of his father.

WARREN • VACHE • JR.

A Hot Cornet for Today

Going strictly by the photos on the wall, you might think you're in the study of one of the old-timers of jazz. You notice first a 1930s-vintage shot of Louis Armstrong and his Orchestra. Armstrong is also represented by a statue. Then shots of greats such as Muggsy Spanier, Vic Dickenson, Bobby Hackett, Sweets Edison, Buddy Tate, Doc Cheatham, Buck Clayton, Benny Goodman, Jack Teagarden. These players—half of whom are now dead—first made their marks in the 1920s or '30s. Warren Vache Jr., whose study this is, was not born until 1951. The photos, Vache explains, are a mix of musicians he's known and played with, along with others that he has never met but has admired and has been inspired by.

Vache may well be the finest cornetist of his generation. Just a few years back, he recalls, he was voted number one in a readers' survey conducted by England's *Jazz Journal International*. Vache's style of playing, while not imitative of anyone, clearly has roots in the Swing Era.

And perhaps that is not surprising. For as a boy growing up in Rahway, New Jersey, Vache recalls, he listened exclusively to Dixieland and swing recordings from the extensive collection of his father, Warren Sr. In those days his father sold appliances and was a semi-professional musician, playing string bass when he could in traditional jazz groups. Today his father works strictly as a musician and also edits *Jersey Jazz* magazine.

"I discovered Clifford Brown and Fats Navarro at end of high school and began listening to some bebop—I still enjoy a lot," Vache says. He adds that he *hates* terms that compartmentalize music, such as Dixieland, swing, and bebop. But although one can hear the influence of Clifford Brown in a good deal of Vache's playing, his stylistic preferences had clearly begun forming before his discovery of bebop.

His playing varies somewhat, depending upon the context in which he is working. If he is in the company of older players, interpreting older tunes, he may work in more of a pure Swing Era style.[1] Improvising on his own, in a more modern group, Vache will incorporate more modern melodic and harmonic ideas. But his sense of drama—particularly in concert performances, he goes for broad statements and big climaxes—comes from Armstrong. And he opts for a nice, fat tone.

Asked to name his favorite trumpeter, Vache states Louis Armstrong, first and emphatically. Listen to Vache's solo on "Cadillac Taxi" on his album, "Skyscrapers," Concord 111. The phrasing may remind you a bit of the Armstrong from, say, the classic 1938 recording of "Struttin' With Some Barbecue." Vache borrows nothing here from the phrasing of any of his trumpet-playing contemporaries. Others Vache has enjoyed, he adds, include Bobby Hackett, Billy Butterfield (who he had just gone to see again in New York), Kenny Dorham, Blue Mitchell, Ruby Braff, Jack Sheldon (with whom he had worked at Benny Goodman's 40th Anniversary Carnegie Hall Concert, and at various jazz festivals), and Don Fagerquist (in addition to the previously-mentioned Brown and Navarro).

Vache started on piano at five or six. At nine or ten, he began studying trumpet with Jim Fitzpatrick of Plainfield, New Jersey. Today, his preferred instruments are cornet and flugelhorn.

He got his first paying jobs at age 15, playing stock charts in Walter Kross' Orchestra, a local dance band. "I knew I wanted to be a musician; I never wanted to do anything else. And I did casual engagements all through high school and at Montclair [New Jersey] State College." Vache's wife, Jill, chimes in: "He put himself through college, paid for his education with his horn." Vache explains that when his father got a job with Chuck Slate's Jazz Band, for example, he was invited to sit in, even though he was still in college. Vache also started taking lessons privately with trumpeter Pee Wee Erwin, who had played with Benny Goodman and Tommy Dorsey back in the '30s. "I studied with Pee Wee for 10 or 11 years before he died," Vache notes. "He had me play French etudes—very difficult." (Vache admits having "a mild passion

[1] Note how Armstrong-ish Vache sounds on the album, "The Great Freddie Moore" (New York Jazz, #J-001). Vache knows just what is appropriate in working with Moore, who was born in 1900.

for some classical." But as for rock, he says: "I'm afraid it speaks nothing to me. It's not a passing phase, but I find it musically valueless, almost.")

Vache worked in *Doctor Jazz*, a Broadway musical starring Bobby Van and Lola Falana. The show provided brief employment for a number of fine veteran jazz players. And it also provided exposure for younger players like Vache who were not only heard but seen on-stage in the production.

On the recommendation of Kenny Davern, Vache was chosen to re-create some of Bix Beiderbecke's famed solos in a concert by the New York Jazz Repertory Company at Carnegie Hall. Guitarist Bucky Pizzarelli, who also played in the Beiderbecke concert, then recommended Vache to Benny Goodman.

Vache worked with Goodman, off and on, for 10 years, from 1972-82. On most dates during this period, Goodman was working with his sextet. But occasionally, for major engagements, such as at Lincoln Center or Carnegie Hall, Goodman would assemble a big band. Vache enjoyed inheriting the solo spots in the famous big band arrangements that had once been handled by the likes of Bunny Berigan, Ziggy Elman, and Harry James. On the recording made of Goodman's 40th Anniversary Carnegie Hall Concert, for example, it is Vache's horn heard on "King Porter Stomp" and "And the Angels Sing." Trumpeter Jack Sheldon also got to solo on some numbers that night.

Vache was, in effect, Benny Goodman's trumpeter of choice during these years. And, considering that Goodman probably could have gotten just about his pick of players for any major engagements, his choice of Vache—who was just 20 when he began working with Goodman—said something. Clearly Goodman saw in Vache an outstanding player. Vache says he enjoyed working with Goodman, but adds Goodman could be "a weird egg. You never know what he wants. One time he had three of the best lead trumpet players in New York hired for a recording session—the kings. Now playing lead is one thing and playing jazz is another. Benny made the decision for whatever reason, and *I* played the lead that whole night." Vache groans, adding that he felt awkward about leading when his superiors were sitting beside him. He notes that particular Goodman album never has been released.

In the meantime, Vache became a member of the house band at Eddie Condon's for several years, playing with Vic Dickenson, Herb Hall, Connie Kay, Jimmy Andrews, and Red Balaban. He joined a distinguished roster of trumpeters who had played at Condon's in its various incarnations through the years, including Bobby Hackett, Wild Bill Davison, Jimmy McPartland, Max Kaminsky, Lee Castle, and Buck Clayton. And Vache cut his first album, for Monmouth Evergreen Records, half of it featuring duets with Bucky Pizzarelli, half of it with a band he had put together.

Vache got a chance to become a bandleader at the Crawdaddy Club in New York. "And then Scott Hamilton and I started working together. We signed with Concord records. We made several wonderful records and tours. Three or four times to Europe, twice to Japan, once to Australia," Vache says. Actually, by now Vache and Hamilton, an acclaimed 30-year-old swing tenor sax player, may be heard together on no less than 14 different Concord albums (including several vocal al-

Warren Vache Jr. (Courtesy Concord Records)

bums in which they play as members of the back-up jazz group). They're an unusually compatible team. Their most ambitious collaboration was the album "Skyscrapers," recorded with a nine-piece band, including George Masso, Harold Ashby, Joe Temperley, Norman Simmons, Chris Flory, Phil Flanigan, and Chuck Riggs. Hamilton commented recently that the album was Vache's conception from beginning to end. Vache selected the arrangers and the mix of old standards (including a particularly sensitive arrangement of Cole Porter's "Why Shouldn't I") and originals. For the album, for example, Vache got Buck Clayton to write and arrange fresh numbers. Concord flew Nat Pierce to New York from California to go over the arrangements *he* contributed, and onetime-Jimmy Dorseyite George Masso contributed the remainder.

Vache recorded with Woody Herman on an album for Concord, and has worked with Herman in a small band at New York's Rainbow Room and on cruises. He's also enjoyed working with Rosemary Clooney (recording, touring, and doing TV shows).

Vache served as music director for the last production in which Elizabeth Taylor and the late Richard Burton worked together, *Private Lives*. Throughout the play's run in Boston, Warren Vache and his trio played incidental music from a box in the theater. However, when the show arrived at Broadway's huge Lunt-Fontanne Theater, the producers nixed the idea of using live musicians, and opted to use Vache's group on tape instead.

Vache has done soundtrack work for a few motion picture and television productions. He has played horn back-up on some rock recordings which, he admits, he did not really have his heart in. "But I'd rather play the trumpet than make a living doing anything else," Vache says.

Vache was part of the lavish, off-again, on-again, production of *The Cotton Club*. In the movie, which cost something like $50 million to produce, star Richard Gere portrays a fellow from the late 1920s, who plays cornet. Vache was hired to coach Gere, who can play the cornet, in the hopes that Gere could do his own playing on the soundtrack. During the interview, just prior to the film's release, Vache comments that he still does not know whether his playing or Gere's playing will be used for the picture.

"I've recorded a track, but I'm hoping they'll use Richard's. He'd be the first actor in the history of movies to play his own cornet," Vache says. "He sounds very Bixian, believe it or not. He's a very talented guy, and very musical."

(When the film was released in December of 1984, Vache learned that Gere's track—which to this critic seemed adequate at best—had been used instead of his. He noted, too, that a lot of music recorded for the film had wound up on the cutting room floor.)

In what little spare time he has, Vache makes furniture. "Or I try to," he adds, joking about being a wood butcher. He's made such items as a blanket chest, a secretary desk, and a lowboy chair. And he likes to visit the clubs to listen to other musicians. Among younger players he enjoys are trombonist Dan Barrett, bassist Phil Flanigan, guitarists Howard Alden and Chris Flory, and drummer Chuck Riggs.

Touring the U.S. and foreign countries keeps Vache away from his wife, Jill, and their three-year-old son, Christopher, in Rahway, New Jersey, eight months out of the year. He's toured with George Wein's Newport All-Stars, and with the Concord All-Stars, including musicians such as Scott Hamilton, Cal Collins, Jake Hanna, Ross Tompkins and Monty Budwig.

Concord Jazz clearly views Vache as a major talent. The record company describes Vache's playing in a release as follows: "He possesses a rich, dark lower register and a bright, powerful upper tessitura, a smooth legato as well as a brilliant, crisp attack. His technique is remarkably facile, his muted playing displays pure intonation control and his vibrato is distinctive. The 'soul' of his style, however, lies in the fact that Warren Vache is absolutely fearless. He takes chances that would make any ordinary brass player blanch. His intervallic leaps are astounding. If these characteristics remind you of any other trumpet player, it could only be one of the 'greats.'" The boldness of Vache's playing is best sampled in his concert performances. His studio recordings, thus far, have been generally more restrained and inhibited. An enthusiastic audience really seems to bring out the best in him.

Carl Jefferson, President of Concord Jazz, which has featured Vache on eight albums to date, recalls that he met Vache about eight years ago through Jake Hanna and Scott Hamilton. "I was so taken with his playing, I signed him at once. I've been very proud to watch Warren's growth musically. His playing fills a really big gap. There's only one other younger lyric cornet player, Ruby Braff. And Ruby's a good bit older. Ruby and Warren are totally outstanding," Jefferson says. "Warren's got very good ears. I really enjoy listening to him. He's very flexible; he can almost play anything. I'm very proud to be associated with him. I think he'll be a real giant—if he isn't already."

Critics have not been shy about singing his praises, either. Thomas Willis of the *Chicago Tribune* wrote: "Trumpeter Warren Vache... jerked me up-right in my seat with 'Struttin' With Some Barbecue' early in the set. There may be cleaner and more accurate performers around, but they'd certainly have to go some."

John S. Wilson of the *New York Times* noted: "Vache has broken through the Dixieland curtain towards an identity of his own that builds from his traditional jazz roots and reaches out into a broad, middle area of jazz that is as searchingly contemporary as it is rooted in tradition."

Vache's brother Alan, 31, plays a traditional jazz clarinet with Jim Cullum's San Antonio-based "Happy Jazz Band," and has recorded for George Buck. The Vache brothers work together at least one week per year, besides running into each other occasionally at things such as the St. Louis Ragtime Festival.

More frequently, Warren Vache Jr. appears in concerts with groups that include his father, often with veteran players such as trumpeter Chris Griffin (alumnus of the original Benny Goodman Band), drummer Johnny Blowers (alumnus of the Bunny Berigan Band), pianist Lou Carter (alumnus of the Jimmy Dorsey Band), and so on.

Chris Griffin (trumpet), Warren Vache Sr. (bass), and Warren Vache Jr. (cornet), at a 1984 Ridgewood, New Jersey, jazz concert. (Chip Deffaa collection)

Vache has reached the stage where he can spend much of his time playing just the kind of music he likes. "You've got to do what you like," Vache says. "The rewards in the music business are more spiritual than they are real, so you better be doing something that you like. . . . I like what I'm doing. I've been very lucky. I hope to continue working."

Vache is currently studying theory and composition with Walt Levinsky, who went on from playing clarinet and sax with Tommy Dorsey to composing and orchestrating music for television and motion pictures. "Music's a fascinating thing. The more you know, the more you have to study, the more there is to find out. I've written a couple tunes—made a record of one. I'd like to write more songs and do some arranging," he says. "And I'd like to someday do an album of Ray Noble songs. Dad had a big collection of Noble records. I really do appreciate his songs now."

Vache says he's tired of critics asking how come he plays so many older numbers. He adds that in general, the fierceness with which partisans of traditional jazz, mainstream jazz, bebop, and other varieties defend their favorite sounds bothers him. "I've never understood why the hell there's so much warring-camp nonsense," he says. "It's one thing to like something; it's another to go around carrying a banner that says everyone who doesn't like something is a damn fool."

1984

SCOTT • HAMILTON

Expanding the Tradition

He even looks like a character out of the '40s," exclaims a woman filing into New York's West End Cafe. And indeed, Scott Hamilton can give that impression. He has a small, neatly trimmed mustache, brushed-back hair, and is wearing a loosely-fitting gray suit with a red tie. Once again, he's drawn a packed house, ranging from students from nearby Columbia University to white-haired couples. Many, no doubt, have been drawn by newspaper reviews suggesting he's a major jazz improviser, a Swing Era-style tenor saxophonist building upon the tradition of such figures as Coleman Hawkins, Ben Webster, and Illinois Jacquet.

He offers numbers such as "Shine," "Don't Get Around Much Anymore," "For All We Know," and "My Romance." Numbers first popularized in the '30s and '40s by the likes of Louis Armstrong, Duke Ellington, Isham Jones.

In his concert and club appearances throughout the U.S., Hamilton has garnered many rave notices. "A sound for sore ears," said Leonard Feather. "Big-toned, deep-swinging, melodic improvising that is the jazz equivalent of a prime steak dinner," said Nat Hentoff. Occasionally though, critics have asked why a player so young—for Hamilton is just 30—should be working in a tradition so old. Why, they ask, isn't he trying to stay on top of the latest trend?

One woman in the audience, Alexandra York, a former radio and TV commentator who today writes about art, offers a ready explanation. Re-discovering, re-appreciating past traditions *is* the latest trend throughout the arts, she insists between sets. "It's returning to representational painting and sculpture, and to plot in fiction." And there are musicians in New York, such as Bob Wilber, who insist that the next major development in jazz will be the re-discovery of older traditions by younger players, and the trend has begun to happen now.

What Hamilton offers might best be described as a contemporary *extension* of Swing Era playing, almost as if bebop and its successors had never happened. He is not trying to imitate anyone. And no one could mistake any Hamilton recording for one actually made back in the Swing Era. But his playing is clearly rooted in, and expanding upon, a tradition more than 40 years old. Hamilton has found a coterie of inspired players about his own age who have developed along the

Scott Hamilton. (Chip Deffaa collection)

same lines: guitarist Chris Flory, bassist Phil Flanigan, drummer Chuck Riggs, who work with him regularly, and lyrical cornetist Warren Vache Jr., who often teams up with him.

Is it anachronistic to offer Swing Era-inflected playing in 1985? Hamilton answers quietly: "Most tenor sax players today are influenced by Coltrane. That's been around for 25 years now. I don't see much difference in playing in a tradition carried on for 40 years rather than 25."

He muses between sips of iced herb tea: "If I could think of a good name for the type of music I play, I might use it."

* * *

Born in Providence, Rhode Island on September 12, 1954, Hamilton grew up listening to traditional jazz. His father had plenty of older records, he recalls, and he was buying plenty of his own as soon as he was able to. Boxes of records—all types of jazz, and big bands, and Sinatra and Bennett—seem on the verge of taking over Hamilton's West 55th Street, New York, apartment today. "My father got me listening to Louis Armstrong—Hot Fives, his big band from the '30s, the All-Stars. At age eight, I saw him with the All-Stars in Providence. That was very important to me. He was the first famous person I saw in the flesh. As a little kid, I loved Louis Armstrong, Count Basie's Band and the older (around 1940) Duke Ellington Band. I listened to rock when I was 12 and 13, then moved into blues singers. I began playing professionally at 14—harmonica, I didn't play sax until I was 16. I listened to Muddy Waters and B.B. King, and then came back to jazz with those ears.

"And then when I first heard Illinois Jacquet, I *flipped*; he turned me around. I listened to records night and day. The masters: Coleman and Don Byas and Ben and Lester Young and Gene Ammons and Ike Quebec. But the ones who had the biggest effect were the ones I saw live." He soaked up Paul Gonsalves, playing with Ellington, and Lockjaw Davis, playing with Basie, when he caught those bands on tour. "If you watch somebody play, you're taking lessons," he reflects. "I was never given much training at all except when I was a little kid—some clarinet and piano. I was always terrible about taking lessons."

As for avant garde jazz? "I tried very hard to like it when I was 15 or 16," he says. "It just wasn't me. I never felt it was something I should do."

He originally played strictly hard and fast. "I didn't even try to play a ballad for the first few years. But after I heard Illinois, I said, 'I got to learn a few ballads.'"

In the meantime, what was to eventually become the Scott Hamilton Quartet (and three quarters of today's Scott Hamilton Quintet) was coming together in Providence. Drummer Chuck Riggs, who came to Providence from Pawtucket, Connecticut, was just a few years older than Hamilton; they teamed up when Hamilton was 18. Guitarist Chris Flory, a year older than Hamilton, came to Providence from New York state. "I've known Chris since I was in high school, although he was in another band at first," Hamilton recalls. Bassist Phil Flanigan (also from New York state), two years younger than Hamilton, landed in Providence, and the four eventually wound up working together.

"We had to play mostly for dancing, mostly for younger audiences. We were playing things like we play now, but we'd disguise it a little—put a bigger beat to it, play it louder, play more blues (although I still like to play blues). We were fighting a lot of club owners and bookers. We tried to keep it a secret—what kind of a band we were, and just hoped we'd go over with the audience," Hamilton recalls.

Gigs were hard to come by. Bookers didn't see the merit in a band playing this older type of jazz. A rock band or a more conventional type of jazz group would have been easier to book. Work fizzled out. Hamilton's band split up.

When Hamilton struck off for New York in 1976, he had no inkling of what was about to happen. He didn't know if his band would ever again work as a band. He was hoping he could pick up a job on his own

Scott Hamilton (at left) still works with the same players he was working with in Rhode Island more than a dozen years ago: bassist Phil Flanigan, drummer Chuck Riggs, and guitarist Chris Flory (shown here relaxing between sets at Fat Tuesday's in New York). (Chip Deffaa collection)

maybe once a week.

He *had* to make it as a jazz musician, he felt. He hadn't had much interest in schooling. And he had never really learned to read music, and thus wasn't eligible for studio work. "I'm glad I never learned to read," he comments. "I don't have the temptation to do jingles or anything. I'm forced to do what I really like."

Almost immediately, Hamilton found top New York players who saw in him the gifts that had gone unrecognized by Rhode Island club owners and booking agents. Trumpeter Roy Eldridge was an important support, the man Hamilton would turn to if he needed someone to talk to. Veteran pianist John Bunch (today the fifth member of the Scott Hamilton Quintet) steered Hamilton to his first record date, and then to working with Benny Goodman. At Eddie Condon's, Hamilton first teamed up with Warren Vache Jr. Like Hamilton, Vache had discovered Louis Armstrong and the other giants in early boyhood via his father's old records; his stylistic roots too were in the Swing Era. And he also believed in expanding—not just preserving—that tradition. They found their playing complemented each other; their thinking was developing along similar lines. They have since worked together in the U.S. and Canada, in Europe, Japan and Australia, with Benny Goodman and Woody Herman, and on 14 Concord record albums. Says Vache of Hamilton: "He's one of the most complete musicians I know. He never stops listening or developing his ear. Working with him's a lot of fun." More recently, he has found another congenial partner in cornetist Ruby Braff.

Hamilton found steady work almost from the week he moved to New York. And it's never stopped since. Whenever he had a chance, he would get Flory, Flanigan, and Riggs to work with him. Soon all four were living near each other in New York and working again as a unit when they could.

"That first year was very fast, maybe a little too fast," Hamilton said. "I was still pretty young. You can handle pressure and heavy work schedules, and handle yourself better when you've had a few years experience." Musicians he had long idolized were now treating him like a peer. He couldn't quite believe it. He was thrilled, he said, to be listening to Benny Goodman, much less playing alongside of him.

When Hamilton appeared in 1977 with the Benny Goodman Orchestra at New York's Avery Fisher Hall, he recalls, he pantomimed all of the sax section parts. He was only really playing, he says, when he was called upon to solo. Why? Two reasons. "I don't really read at all," Hamilton admits. But surely he knew many of those Goodman classics by heart? He smiles and says something about the saxophone player sitting next to him not liking his tone. (He adds that his tone has improved a lot since then.) "So I just faked playing. That was the only concert that I pantomimed, though. When we did big band dates on the West Coast, I just sat there, rather than pretending to play, until it was time for me to solo."

He toured again with Goodman in '82 "with John Bunch and Chris Flory and Phil Flanigan and Mel Lewis and Warren—that was a hot band. And Benny—I love him; I'd go to work with Benny again immediately." There were dates at various times with Woody Herman and Buddy Tate and Zoot Sims. And festival pairings with real veterans such as Eddie Miller and Bud Freeman (who thinks Hamilton is wonderful), as well as—more commonly—somewhat younger mainstream artists. And since 1978, a steady flow of recording sessions for Concord.

Indeed, Hamilton and Vache have become the star younger members of the Concord stable. Concord President Carl Jefferson says of Hamilton's playing: "I just thrive on it. His playing is pretty and lyrical and musical—and great. He uses the full range, plays smoothly in the top range, almost into the alto range, then down to the bari range. If there are 10 tenors playing, I can pick him out. And he's very good as a leader, too. Men like Buddy Tate, Jake Hanna, Al Cohn, Dave McKenna, Cal Collins—all much older than him—will defer to him to set up a program. I've been all over the world with him for six years. He really wears well—both he as an individual and his music—with most everybody who isn't just green with envy."

What especially pleases Hamilton is the degree to which, in recent years, success has come to his group, not just to himself as a soloist. Hamilton is a believer in the value of organized groups in jazz.

Hamilton, Flory, Flanigan, and Riggs (with Norman Simmons, Mike Ledonne and John Bunch alternating as pianist over the years) have worked together often enough, long enough so that they can work separately for stretches without it affecting their rapport. Sometimes when Hamilton gets bookings on his own, the rhythm section will find a job as unit, which helps it maintain its cohesion until the whole group gets back together again.

Hamilton's most recent albums, "Close Up," "In Concert," and "The Second Set"—all recorded with his quintet rather than with thrown-together "all-star" bands—have given him the most satisfaction. "Being able to work together," he says, "means a lot to us."

And—especially important from a jazz critic's point of view—Hamilton has grown significantly since the start of his career. There's simply more substance to his work today. At his best, he plays with a deep relaxation; he makes what he is doing seem deceptively effortless. But he makes a satisfying addition to almost any ensemble. He is clearly someone to watch.

When he's not playing, Hamilton likes to read crime fiction or walk around New York. But given a choice, he adds, he prefers working to anything, even if it means living on the road and staying up late night after night in smoke-filled clubs. "I'm a night club player," he says. "I kind of like the worn-out feeling a little bit. What bothers me about vacations is I never get tired. I never do anything."

He holds his 36-year-old Selmer balanced-action tenor with pride. He insists the new saxes are not as comfortable, nor do they get as full a sound as his 1949 model. "Maybe the fact that I'm successful, doing what I like, might give some people the idea that they can play in that direction and make a living," he says. "I think there's room for a lot of different styles in jazz. When a music is good, it doesn't die."

1984-85

Scott Hamilton and Joe Wilder, 1985 Conneaut Lake, Pennsylvania, Jazz Festival. (Chip Deffaa collection)

W O O D Y • H E R M A N

50 Years of Leading the Herd

The Woody Herman Orchestra is soaring. "Oh yeah!" Herman shouts out, as the trumpets bite into the material. "—Hear ya, baby!" It's a fresh, uptempo original, and drummer Dave Miller's giving it a bit of a rock feel. Herman, standing in front of his 15 young musicians, is positively beaming.

You look out at the crowd. A lot of young faces there. Most are clearly loving it. It's some of the older people down front—the gray-haired men and women—who appear lost this afternoon. Some of them no doubt haven't seen Woody Herman, or bought one of his records, since the summer of '42, when they were young. He's *not*, for the most part, playing numbers in this concert that they remember from those years. And if he *does* play an occasional oldie, he *doesn't* play it just the way it was played way back when.

Maybe they're waiting for stuff that made the Hit Parade. But Herman offers instead Aaron Copland's "Fanfare for the Common Man," which hardly brings back romantic memories for them. And now, the musicians surge into Thelonious Monk's complex and intriguing "Epistrophy"—a new arrangement by a trombonist in the band, John Fedchock. This is music you have to *listen* to.

Woody Herman. (Courtesy Thomas Cassidy)

You can see the puzzlement on some of the older faces in the crowd. They don't understand why Woody Herman has to throw so much contemporary-sounding material at them. Why isn't he content to bring back sounds of the Swing Era? They had come to the concert, no doubt, seeking to recapture their lost youth. The thing is, Woody Herman never lost his.

* * *

Today, no less than when he started, Herman is a firm believer in the importance of letting his musicians express themselves, of offering new material, and of trying new approaches. Throughout the years, Herman has led one of the all-time great large jazz ensembles. And he has never sold out.

"Our band never really had a 'style,'" Herman notes. "I've changed midstream many times over the years, and when you do that, you lose your audience for a while. And then you desperately fight to get somebody to listen to you. I think it's healthy, though. There are too many bands that just got into one bag and stayed there because it was comfortable, I guess. But I was never comfortable doing that."

What brought down most of the big bands, Herman says, was "a culmination of sameness and lack of imagination. All of them relying on what worked for them before. By the '60s, Duke, Basie and our band were the only ones that could still get anything going. All the rest of them were nice ghost bands."

The Woody Herman Orchestra, with only minor interruptions, has basically been an ongoing concern since November, 1936.

Herman has no plans to retire. He's been on the road since boyhood, he says. At this point, settling down and actually *living* in a house, rather than mostly out of suitcases and hotel rooms, would seem foreign to him. And besides, it's simply too rewarding for him hearing the band night after night. Who knows, he adds, what sounds the next musician to join the band will have to contribute? The idea of sticking to one "style," of creating an orchestra—like, say, the Glenn Miller

Woody Herman and his Young Thundering Herd. (Chip Deffaa collection)

Orchestra—whose playing never varies from year to year, is anathema to him.

"I'm still struggling to find something that I feel will be better," Herman insists. "I'll probably go down swinging."

* * *

Herman was born May 16, 1913, in Milwaukee, Wisconsin. "I worked actively in vaudeville when I was a little kid. I did my first tour at nine; I was only a song and dance cat at that point," Herman recalls. "One of my big hits in vaudeville was a thing called, 'Oh Gee, Say Gee, You Ought to See My Gigi, from the Fiji Isles.' But then with the money I earned the first season, I got a saxophone and then later a clarinet." An early Milwaukee newspaper ad shows Herman, at age 10, holding his saxophone. The caption advises that in addition to the movies *You Never Know Women* and *Shell Shocked*, the theater will be presenting on stage: "WOODROW HERMAN, Wisconsin's only professional Juvenile in Songs, Dances and Saxophone Solos. After this engagement young Herman will play the entire Saxe Circuit of Theatres, after which he will play the Big Time Orpheum and Pantages Circuits."

Herman recalls: "My parents weren't in vaudeville but they were believers in it. They were great enthusiasts. However, when I announced, when I was about 11 or 12, that I was leaving show business and was going to be a hot jazz musician, I think they both went into a dead faint. It was pretty shocking to them."

By 14, he was working as a musician in a suburban roadhouse. He heard on records popular jazz of the mid-'20s such as that of Red Nichols and his Five Pennies, and the Indiana Five and other midwestern jazz groups. Herman was intrigued by one new stylist in music who was then not nearly so widely known, particularly to youths in the midwest, as Red Nichols: Duke Ellington.

"Right from the beginning, actually, I admired Ellington. I had records of his band when I was in high school. Yeah. It was then known as 'Duke Ellington and the Washingtonians,' and it was an eight-piece band. And I was already influenced by Ellington's approach," Herman says.

Who were some other influences, in the early years of Herman's musical career? "Some of the soloists who made big imprints on me, naturally were 'Pops'—Armstrong—and the great new force on the scene at that time was Coleman Hawkins. And I think every saxophone player in the world tried to sound like Coleman. In the late '20s, early '30s. He was the biggest new influence, as far as new sounds were concerned. I was mostly a saxophone player. First of all, alto, and then later on as I got older, to be a teenager, that's when I switched to tenor. And I, along with millions of other guys, thought we sounded just like

Hawk," Herman says.

"I was working professionally already, when I was in high school: first in a small band outside of town in a road-house, and then in my sophomore year I joined the most important band in the area: Joe Lichter's. It was a band made up of Chicago guys, and they were playing in Milwaukee, in the local ballroom. I was far and away younger than the rest of the guys. They were in their 20s and 30s, and I was 14 I guess. It was a ballroom band, but we were always jazz-oriented."

Herman says he owes a debt of gratitude to one nun who taught him at St. John's Cathedral High School. "She used to keep me out of

Woody Herman in his boyhood vaudeville days. (Frank Driggs collection)

trouble. And if I got kicked out of school for one reason or another, like falling asleep in class, she'd get me reinstated." Although Herman dropped out of high school to pursue his career in music, he never forgot Sister Fabian. Years later, he established a "Sister Fabian Scholarship" in her memory, which today helps promising Wisconsin student musicians to further their musical education.

"When I decided to leave school and leave home, I joined the Tom Gerun Band, which was a San Francisco band, playing the midwest at that point. It was a show-biz kind of band. But then all musicians had to be able to sing or do something else besides play their horn," Herman recalls. Herman sang on such Brunswick recordings by Gerun's Band as "Love Me" and "Sentimental Gentleman from Georgia." And he was soon joined in the reed section by another saxophonist who also doubled as a singer: Al Norris, who gained much greater fame as a singer after he changed his name to Tony Martin. Ginny Simms sang with the Gerun Band at the time, too.

Herman's success singing with the band brought him to the attention of Music Corporation of America (MCA), a major booking organization. "They put me in Gus Arnheim's Band just for a theater tour because I could entertain in the theaters. Bing Crosby had been with that band, and there were a lot of good musicians in it. And I worked with Harry Sosnik's Band for awhile. We're up to about '32, '33.

"And then I eventually joined Isham Jones, and that was the most important band I had played in until then. He was a great songwriter and he had very excellent players in the band. It was pretty much legitimate kind of dance music, but he also, for instance, had maybe a dozen arrangements in the book by Fletcher Henderson. He was not a narrow-minded musician. If a thing sounded good, he wanted to play it."

Herman sang on such Isham Jones Decca recordings as "There is No Greater Love" and "Darling." And Herman was among the younger, more jazz-interested members of the orchestra who cut a few small-band sides for Decca billed as the "Isham Jones Juniors."

Early in '36, Jones retired from bandleading. "He decided he had had enough. He was very, very wealthy and very successful by then—mostly as a songwriter. He received a great deal of money from ASCAP, and he just wanted to try other things to do. He bought a huge ranch in Colorado to raise turkeys, and the first season they had a big hailstorm. You know turkeys just stand there until they're stoned to death, and so he blew that one."

The Woody Herman Orchestra began with a nucleus of young, hot players from the disbanded Isham Jones Orchestra. "There were actually five of us from the Jones Band, and then we hired other people. Because that's all the people we could get that were interested in what we were interested in. We felt that we could play some blues probably better than anybody else, so we called our band, 'the Band that Plays the Blues.' Everybody in the band was a co-owner; the guys all were stockholders. But as the army took players away, then I bought up the stock and eventually became the sole owner."

Guitarist Chick Reeves wrote many of the early arrangements. Joe Bishop (who had played tuba for Jones but now switched to flugelhorn) and Gordon Jenkins also contributed arrangements (at no cost), to help create the initial "book." Initially, the band used "Blue Prelude" (which had been an Isham Jones specialty) as its theme, but shortly replaced that with a new composition, "Blue Flame" (which Herman continues to use to this day). Some of the band's early "hot" numbers were what would today be classified as Dixieland: "Weary Blues," "Muskrat Ramble," "Royal Garden Blues," etc. But these soon gave way to looser blues and swing originals.

Herman featured himself mostly on clarinet rather than on sax, he says, because the success of Benny Goodman had made the clarinet suddenly "the hot American boy's instrument."

It was rough going for the band at first. Some weeks they only got one or two jobs, and it was hard coming up with the funds to get to the bookings they did get.

Gradually, though, the band found an audience. It recorded some popular sides for Decca in the late '30s and early '40s. In those years, however, the band never really reached the top rung in terms of popularity. It was not up there with the bands of, say, Benny Goodman, Tommy and Jimmy Dorsey, Glenn Miller, Duke Ellington, Count Basie, Jimmie Lunceford, Artie Shaw, or Harry James. But Herman's easy-going personality helped him hold on to some musicians who could have earned more elsewhere. For example, Frankie Carlson, who was Herman's drummer from 1936-43, drummed on record dates with both Goodman and Miller. But he declined opportunities to join those bands, he told me, because he preferred the freedom Herman gave his musicians and the looser feeling of Herman's music.

"We had some small hits on the first band—stuff like 'Blues in the Night' and 'Woodchopper's Ball,'" Herman recalls. Among other recordings of this first band were "Blues on Parade," "Amen," "Bishop's Blues," "Who Dat Up Dere," "This Time the Dream's on Me," and "Golden Wedding." The band went through a number of female vocalists in these years, perhaps the best-remembered of whom was Mary Ann McCall. She was, in Herman's words: "a poor man's Billie Holiday. But she sang jazz; she could swing harder than anybody." And of course,

Woody Herman and "the Band that Plays the Blues." Setting the rhythm: Walter Yoder, bass; Frank Carlson, drums; Hy White, guitar; and Tommy Linehan, piano. (Institute of Jazz Studies)

Herman (who labels himself a "saloon singer") sang, too.

Herman began reorganizing his band during the recording strike of 1943-44. "We were getting all ready during the strike, working at it, developing ideas."

The music changed. The band sounded radically different by '44. "Well, mainly that was my doing. I started to hire a different breed of player, and certainly a different breed of arrangers. I was deeply influenced by Duke. Whether it shows or not, I was. I wasn't like a Charlie Barnet, who was going to be an imitator. But I was going to take all the good influences and try to apply them to something I was doing."

The draft caused tremendous personnel fluctuations in all of the big bands. While many of the top big bands (such as Benny Goodman's and Tommy Dorsey's) suffered in quality in '43 and '44 as the draft kept taking musicians, Herman managed to come up with players that collectively were *stronger* than the players he lost. And more than that, they had something new to say. Gone was "the Band that Plays the Blues." The new edition of the band, which music writer George T. Simon dubbed "the Herd," had a clean, modern sound.

"I did get my own direction. That was just, I guess luck. Having the right people on the scene at the right time. Ralph Burns (arranger/

Davey Tough. (Chip Deffaa collection)

Woody Herman's pace-setting First Herd, as seen in Earl Carroll's Vanities, *Hollywood, 1945. Left to right: Margie Hyams, vibes; Chubby Jackson, bass; Billy Bauer, guitar; Herman, clarinet; Neal Hefti, trumpet; Flip Phillips, tenor sax; Dave Tough, drums; Charles Frankhouser, trumpet; John LaPorta, alto sax; Ray Wetzel, trumpet; Pete Candoli, trumpet; Ralph Pfiffner, trombone; Sam Marowitz, alto sax; Carl Warwick, trumpet; Pete Mondello, tenor sax; Bill Harris, trombone; Skippy DeSair, baritone sax; Ed Kiefer, trombone.* (Frank Driggs collection)

pianist) was probably as much responsible for a lot of our sound as anyone, and then other people started to contribute. Bill Harris (on trombone) came into the band around that time. The transition period started in 1944. So about '45, we were ready. Billy Bauer was in as a guitar player. And trumpet players we were getting by the dozen. I already had Pete Candoli in the end of 'the Band that Plays the Blues.' I took him from Tommy Dorsey. Neal Hefti came in the same time, approximately, as Ralph Burns and Chubby did, from Charlie Barnet's Band, and so on. Chubby Jackson (bass) was particularly helpful in finding players." And at the heart of the First Herd was Davey Tough, who was, in Herman's opinion, easily the finest drummer in the country at the time. (*New Yorker* jazz critic Whitney Balliett has ranked Tough one of the three greatest jazz drummers of all time.) Tough was the oldest musician in the band, and when Herman hired him, some of the others wondered briefly if he'd fit in. But all doubts vanished when he played. As his successor, Don Lamond, told me: "He really had the secret of swinging a big band."

Ralph Burns was creating a wealth of new charts. Herman recalled: "Neal Hefti wasn't writing much then; he was just beginning. He wrote I think two tunes. . . . One was 'Good Earth' and the other one was 'Half Past Jumping Time.' Then he would contribute on a lot of stuff, like the trumpets would do—because a lot of our things were based on heads, and then the writers would bridge the gaps. In other words, when we ran out of gas, then they would write something and put it in the middle of a chart or something. And I was the editor. So our madness went together.

"The first big smash was in '45. That's when we switched to Columbia Records. And the whole band was completely different sounding. That's when we hit," Herman recalls. Numbers such as "Apple Honey," "Bijou," "Blowin' Up a Storm," "Northwest Passage," "Goosey Gander," "Caldonia," and "Wildroot" went over with both the critics and the public alike. And Frances Wayne proved an effective vocalist with the band in this period, too.

"We made a big dent," Herman recalls. "And even though the big band interest was beginning to wane, we got the good out of it." Herman's First Herd was *the* big band of '45-'46. Igor Stravinsky honored Herman's Herd by composing his "Ebony Concerto" for it.

"Isham Jones came in to hear the second band, the Herd, at the Palladium in Hollywood," Herman remembers. "And he said, 'I told you if you get some good guys it would be a great band.' Heh-heh. He didn't like the guys who had worked for him.

"Those were the two biggest years, incidentally, I ever had in my career: '45 and '46—and it's been all downhill since," Herman adds with a chuckle. The Herd was the nation's pace-setting band. It won the *Down Beat* readers' poll in 1945, the *Metronome* poll in 1946, a *Billboard* award in 1946, and *Esquire Magazine's* silver award in 1946-47.

Herman had his own radio show, his record sales were strong, and his future looked golden when he announced early in '47 that he was retiring from the music business. The retirement didn't last long.

"I was going to try to spend some time at home," he explains. Home was in California with his wife, Charlotte, and their infant daughter, Ingrid. "I lasted seven months, and then I reorganized the band. The first person I heard that impressed me enough to really get turned on to say, 'Hey, I got to put together another band,' was Ernie Royal, a trumpet player. I heard him playing in a little group in Hollywood one night, and I said, 'If we can get that guy, we'll be OK.'"

Herman spared no expense in putting together his Second Herd (which he refers to as his "bebop band"). "It was a hand-picked saxophone section, with three guys that could play tenor and maybe double

Few women played in big name bands, but Marjorie Hyams handled vibes in Herman's First Herd. (Chip Deffaa collection)

Woody Herman signing autographs for the bobby-soxers. (Chip Deffaa collection)

alto, so we could have a regular section, but still be able to pull on three tenors and a baritone—that's how that started, and then of course, Jimmy Giuffre wrote the original tune, 'Four Brothers.' Guys were working at it and blowing that way, out at the beach and different places in California, but it really didn't take a serious turn until Jimmy Giuffre actually wrote 'Four Brothers' for me."

On Herman's original, trend-setting recording of "Four Brothers," the four reeds were Zoot Sims, Stan Getz, and Herbie Steward on tenor, and Serge Chaloff on baritone. (Al Cohn eventually took Steward's chair in the band—the beginning of an association with Zoot Sims that would continue until Sims' death some 35 years later.) The unusual sax section produced a hip sound. Setting the beat for the band was Don Lamond, one of the very finest of modern drummers (heard prominently, for example, on Herman's 1947 recording of "The Goof and I"). Herman gave him total freedom, directing the others in the rhythm section to work with him, whatever he chose to do. This band made its mark at once. And the number "Four Brothers" remains a Herman staple.

Herman's Second Herd was a tremendous critical success. Herman's bands since the mid '40s have usually been critical successes.

But were they all financial successes? "No, we were losing money by the millions. In one year, I lost about $200,000—and in those days that was a lot of money. That was around the '47 band, the bebop band. That band was a complete loss as far as money was concerned. But we had great artistic success, so what the hell did we care? I could afford it because of what I had done in '45 and '46, but I was rapidly going in the hole already—and I've been in a hole ever since," Herman says.

By '49, the Second Herd (recording now for Capitol) included such players as Shelly Manne, Gene Ammons, Terry Gibbs, Milt Jackson, and Oscar Pettiford. Herman's repertoire of this period included "Lemon Drop" (an uptempo bebop song he still likes to sing), "That's Right," "Lollypop," and the pensive, laid-back "Early Autumn."

The economics proved unmanageable, though. He broke up the Second Herd, toured with a small group, which he built back into a big band in 1950. This became known as the Third Herd. Sonny Igoe was

Woody Herman's Band appeared in the 1943 motion picture, Winter Time, *with Cornell Wilde and Caesar Romero.* (Frank Driggs collection.)

on drums. Dave McKenna was at the keyboard. Then Nat Pierce came on board, as pianist/arranger. He would play a major role in Herman's bands, off-and-on, well into the '60s. Bill Harris was featured on trombone, initially. Urbie Green joined the section a bit later. Herman's Band won the *Metronome* readers' poll in 1953.

Herman came up with strong players throughout the '50s, but the audiences were not always there. He periodically was forced to cut back to smaller groups. For a spell (circa 1955), the Woody Herman Octet was working in Las Vegas, from 12:30 in the morning on.

By 1962, Herman was just about ready to give up on big bands for good. He was down to a sextet. He had pianist Nat Pierce put together a big band for one final month-long tour. But somehow, everything fell into place. The chemistry was just right. Herman's early '60s band was a particularly spectacular unit, with such players as Jake Hanna (drums), Nat Pierce (piano), Chuck Andrus (bass), Bill Chase (lead trumpet), and the supercharged Sal Nistico on tenor sax. Herman's band made a sensational comeback. It won its first Grammy Award in 1963. And basically, it's been working continuously since.

The quality has varied from time to time, due to the inevitable personnel changes. Key players will decide to give up life on the road, and their replacements don't always measure up. Occasionally Herman will call on old favorites to return to the band temporarily, to help him out for some important dates; they're usually glad to do it. Sometimes Herman will have to incorporate a number of new players into the band simultaneously, and the band will decline for a spell; a couple of years later, with a little luck, they'll still be together and sounding like a strong, tight band again.

In the 1970s, Herman explored fusion sounds. Arrangers Alan Broadbent and Tony Klatka brought influences from the world of rock into the band. For a time in the '70s, Herman's rhythm section included an electric bass and an electric piano. The band won frequent bookings at high schools and colleges, with Herman's musicians often giving clinics. The band won Grammy Awards in 1973 and '74. But Herman ultimately decided that that direction was not for him.

In recent years, Herman's pulled back more into the mainstream of jazz. He plays some rock-inflected charts. He can offer a little reggae, to boot. But primarily, this is a straight-ahead, big *jazz* band. He records frequently on the Concord Jazz label today.

In his 50 years as a bandleader, Herman has repeatedly altered his course. He's zigged and zagged, and tried new things as they've come along. And yet one can hear clear links between his current band and his bands of 40 or more years ago. Since 1947, Herman's reed sections have consisted of three tenors and a baritone, which gives his ensemble a different flavor from than that of most big bands, one well suited to the jazz originals he plays. His trumpet sections—whether you're listening to the First Herd of '45-'46 or the Swinging Herd of the early '60s or the Young Thundering Herd of today—seem to delight in showing off their technical prowess. As a section, they play tightly, they dart with finesse, and they attack hard. You feel an air of freedom in all of Herman's bands; he's never held the reins as tightly as, say, Benny Goodman has, and that communicates itself to the audience.

There's a certain overall excitement level that Herman has sought to maintain, since he began modernizing the band in the '40s. You sense it, whether you're listening to Herman's 1942 recording of "Down Under" (by a not-yet-famous Dizzy Gillespie) or to any of the First Herd's rousers, or to the current "Young Thundering Herd" doing "North Beach Breakdown." Exhilaration has been a defining characteristic of Herman's bands since almost the very beginning.

The band sometimes hits too relentlessly hard for this critic's tastes. (And musicians cannot blow that hard without sacrificing beauty of tone.) Greater interest in subtlety and nuance would be welcomed. But maintaining a high energy level has been part of the band's appeal for more than 40 years.

Jeff Hirshfield, one of Herman's drummers of the 1980s, told me: "Woody really liked you to play strong. He wanted the music to really be out front. We used to call it, 'playing in his face.'" Ed Soph, who occupied that drum chair a dozen years before, opined: "Woody's band had a small-group feel. It wasn't lugubrious and heavy, say, like Stan Kenton's band was. And it wasn't as orchestrated as, say, Duke's band was. It was just like an out-and-out screaming, hauling band."

* * *

Despite his world-wide fame, Woody Herman has rarely achieved the commercial success most of his fans would probably assume he's achieved. A big band is an expensive proposition. And Herman has played the music he and his musicians have wanted to play. He's never made making money his primary goal.

Herman says he's known for 30 years that he'll never be able to pay the back taxes, interest, and penalties which the government maintains he owes.

A manager in whom Herman had placed complete trust gambled away funds which should have been used for the band's payroll taxes. For three years, the manager filed no payroll taxes. Herman only found out what had been happening when the government presented him with a bill for back taxes, based on the band's gross earnings for those years. According to the tax law in effect at the time, Herman—not the manager—was held liable.

For a quarter of a century or more, Herman says, "I have had no credit, not a bank account, not anything. But that doesn't faze me, because I didn't care about that. That wasn't important. All I want is money to eat and sleep and live as well as I can. And I do live well. But I do not care about anything else—only music. So I've led my existence. The one that suffers is my daughter, but she's mentally about like I am, so she's still fighting city hall.

"The government's been on my butt for over 25 years. They've just never let me breathe, you know. If they see I'm still alive, they drop another one on me. The latest figure they gave me, sometime last year, I owed them a million, six hundred thousand dollars—right now.

"But it just rolls off of me like water off a duck's back because I refuse to believe what they're saying. They took whole years where they

Woody Herman. (Chip Deffaa collection)

would take the gross of what we earned and put that as my personal income; all the expenses were never allowed. As far as I'm concerned, we reached a Mexican standoff many years ago.

"Recently they did a very nasty thing. My wife and I, before she died, signed our house to our daughter and her children. And the government recently auctioned it off for a minimal part of what the property's worth. You know that's, that's heartbreaking. Something that I've fought to hold and keep all these years, 40 years.

"Now, what I have to do — my daughter and I and what's left — we have to put up the money, and take a tremendous loan, to pay back the money that this guy gave for the property. . . . The house is still in our possession, but every day it's breathing the last breath, you know.[1]

"The money I made in '45 and '46, that *went*. See, I never needed a bank account, ever. The money always was en route somewhere, to pay something. I have paid my share of taxes down through the years. But you can't put a dent when the figure is so high. If you pay everything you possibly can, every day — it still ain't going to make it. I knew approximately 30 years ago that I would never breathe another clear air breath, you know, as far as being independent at all.

"Now, if I work for George Wein or anything, I say, 'Don't worry about it. Just get me as much as you can, and you pay all my living and you pay all my transportation and you pay all my hotels, food — in other words, I don't want any of that responsibility. You just give me lots of money and it'll work out.'"

Herman's primary interest has been in maintaining the best possible bands, and he's never cared if he's shown a profit, so long as his bands have brought in enough income to keep going. And he intends to keep going, as long as possible.

"He's a truly amazing man," Ed Soph told me. "Coming from a vaudeville tradition, he truly believes that the show must go on, no matter what. I've seen this man when he's had food poisoning, come onstage, play a chorus of 'Woodchoppers,' then run backstage to the john and vomit, then come back and play another chorus. When I got a terrible ear infection and had to leave the band, Woody didn't dig it at all. The word was that unless you were on your deathbed, you made the gig! Just to see that sort of strength in the man, and that sort of drive, that sort of love for the music — because Lord knows, he wasn't

[1] Herman lost possession of the house, which he had purchased from Humphrey Bogart in 1946, but was permitted to stay on as a tenant. In August of 1987, Herman (who was by then seriously ill and incurring sizable medical bills) was nearly evicted from the house due to his inability to pay the rent. He was saved from eviction at the last minute, thanks to a donation from a Los Angeles radio station. Afterwards, a number of show business notables donated their services in benefits to help raise funds for him.

in it for the money. And the fact that, you know, that's history. That's the whole history of the thing right there. He's the living history."

"He's a tough guy, you know," 25-year-old Dave Miller observed. "He might not be in the best shape physically, but he's still going. It's great for music, because he finds younger players and gives them a place to go. And keeps jazz alive. That's a professional outlet to play jazz. There's just not that many left these days."

When Woody Herman dies, he says, the band will die with him. "My grandson's not interested [in taking over the band], and he's the only one I would allow to front it." There would be no point in authorizing a "ghost band" to continue after his death, Herman believes, a band which would only deteriorate from year to year.

* * *

When he looks back over all of the various editions he's led in the past, Herman says that he has no one favorite band. "I think every one of those bands had something to say. Right through the '70s, when we were into some form of fusion. Actually, we were more of a fusion band than people realized. But then when I reached a stone wall, I said, 'Nah, we found as much as we're going to find here. So let's just now analyze and take the best of what we got.'"

Herman has always been enthusiastic about playing original compositions and arrangements by members of his band. "In the band, now, I have three guys writing arrangements: John Fedchock, the lead trombone player, and Paul McKee, the second trombone player, who plays some of the jazz, and Brad Williams, the pianist. And I still have John Oddo on call, who was with the band a couple of years ago," he notes. He encourages his musicians to rehearse new pieces without him, which he may later edit.

"When they want to try something, they run it down and spend some time with it—and then present it to me on the gig. And I say, 'Well, you're going to have to fix, put B where C is,' and you know. We come back in a few days and it'll be all different," Herman notes. "Sometimes it works."

Herman doesn't play too many old arrangements. (This critic wishes the band would play more of them; a lot of good material has been permanently set aside.) "We don't like to go back too much," Herman says. "We will play things that people ask us to play because we feel it's part of my background, but it's usually a new version of it, or a somewhat changed version from the original. Because you go back too far and then it becomes hodge-podge. It was a great idea for the time, but when you try to apply that to now, it doesn't generally work out without some fixing."

Asked if he still enjoys doing a number like "Caldonia," which he's done countless times in 40 years, Herman responds: "What the hell wrong could there be to do it at all? It's a 12-bar blues, and if you can't think of anything to do for that thing, then you must be some sort of an idiot, right? So I say, 'If they want to hear that sucker . . .'

"I get frustrated because we had so many versions of 'Caldonia,' and we were controlled by soloists. In other words, when Sal Nistico was in the band, we played it so fast you couldn't make your foot work to it. And then we tried to do that now, and it's not the same, man. There ain't one Sal Nistico there. There's a lot of good players in the band, but there ain't one Sal Nistico, who used to play like a riveter. And he doesn't do that any more, either, which proves you change in life and get other ideas. He's happier with himself as he is. But he was a force, boy, in that '60s band. And Jake and the rhythm section was the only rhythm section that could play with him. When you're playing with different individuals, you have to do different things."

Herman's bands of the late '40s and early '50s included some very gifted musicians whose abuse of drugs and alcohol was known in the music world. But he dismisses the notion that there is any connection between using drugs or alcohol and being able to play good jazz. "Some of the best players I know in this day and age are the cleanest-living people I've ever known," he says. "But there was a time when the musicians were all crippled up, one way or another, and it was a sad time. It was no fun trying to run one of those bands, because when guys are out of their heads, it's very difficult to convince them of doing anything well. Their habit becomes more than they can handle. And so if they can't get whatever their habit is, they're almost like chained animals. Some great players I had were very sick. Some beat it and some didn't. And a lot of them died very young."

Herman says today's musicians are better, overall, than those during the big band era. "These guys are so accomplished. The other day, for instance, the second time they went through 'Ebony Concerto' they sounded like they owned the piece. When we originally did that back in '46, we spent weeks huffing and puffing, with the old man [Igor Stravinsky] counting and humming and whistling and clapping his hands, to try to get us to get through it." For an upcoming 50th anniversary concert, Herman plans to have Richard Stoltzman, a Grammy-winning classical clarinetist, play the clarinet part in "Ebony Concerto," which Stravinsky wrote for Herman in 1946.

Why isn't Herman doing the part himself? "Because I can't do it as well as I did it then," he answers truthfully. "And even then, I wasn't up to it. Nobody's up to that part. I once gave a copy of it, a mini-score, to Benny Goodman, because he said to me: 'I hear that part's hard.' I said: 'Is it hard? I've talked to everybody that might be able to advise me. It's impossible. You know, you can play it, but it's grotesque. Sounds ugly.' But Richard's one of the great artists of our time."[2]

Herman believes as many great jazz soloists are being produced today as in the heyday of the big bands, too, but that the public is not always getting a chance to hear them. It frustrates him the way the recording industry controls what the public hears, he says. "These record companies today dictate how you play, or what you play. They're doing it like they really know what they were talking about. That's sad. And the young guys, in an effort to make some money or maybe have a hit or some kind of a career, will listen to them like mad. . . . The record companies don't trust you at all. They 'know' what will work, by their standards."

He's pleased that he has been able to record with integrity. "Carl Jefferson [president of Concord Records] is very serious about his product. He doesn't stint on anything as far as quality is concerned," he says. But he notes that an independent label like Concord cannot get the distribution of a bigger outfit.

* * *

For relaxation, Herman may watch a ball game or a Grand Prix race. He listens to all-news radio stations, he says. He doesn't much listen to music "for pleasure." When he listens to music, he says, he's working; he's analyzing it. He rarely listens to old recordings by himself, or by other bandleaders.

"I was not too indebted to them, you know," he says of most of his onetime rivals in the band business. "I was pretty independent." He always enjoyed Ellington, he acknowledges. "Duke, I always felt, knew exactly what he was striving for.

"I was probably more friendly with Ellington than with any of the other bandleaders. He trusted me. And he sometimes thought very cagily about ofays [whites], and musicians particularly. He was very kind to me, always. I'm sure part of it was because he sensed my respect for his music, but also I think he felt that I would come up with a different

[2] Stoltzman toured with the Woody Herman Orchestra in 1986, '87, and '88. He commented in 1988: "I feel like I'm participating in a part of American history playing this music. Brahms and Beethoven are foreign. Woody was like a father to me. He gave me confidence, like he did with every musician he worked with."

Stoltzman unwittingly auditioned for Herman in 1984, when George T. Simon invited him to sit in with Simon's Twilight Jazz group at Eddie Condon's Club in New York. "It was a set-up. I played a couple of tunes, and George said, 'OK, Dick, that's enough.' I had this low feeling; I figured he was canceling me out. But then he said: 'There's somebody in the corner who wants to talk with you.'" A well-dressed older gentleman told Stoltzman: "I'm Woody Herman. Sit down. You're OK." Stoltzman asked for Herman's autograph. Herman refused, and began telling of his plan to have Stoltzman play his part in "Ebony Concerto."

Woody Herman, relaxing before the gig, in 1945 (above) and 40 years later (below).
(Chip Deffaa collection)

attitude on something, go off into a field that maybe he had escaped. He thought I had something to offer.

"Basie used to run me dry. I'd say, 'Geez, when are you going to move up a notch, you know, do something different?' But he wouldn't move, you know. Either the guys decided to play with him the way he wanted it, or he'd go home; he'd pout." Herman laughs a bit.

And what did he think of Glenn Miller, perhaps the most commercially successful of the leaders in the big band era?

"I thought he was a hell of a musician, who had the ability to be a very good arranger. But he never did it for himself. He did it for lots of other people. He did it for Benny Pollack's Band. For Ray Noble's Band. That shows you that he was an extremely fine musician. But as far as what he did for himself, he was so intent on making a success, he lost all reasoning about anything else. You know, cleanliness, even the way the uniforms of the musicians—you know, one of those things. He was building an erector set. And that's the way it sounded."

Herman has always adopted a looser attitude. You sense it in the informal way his musicians often appear: dressed not in blazers, but in pink, short-sleeve cotton sport shirts, with "Woody Herman's Thundering Herd" printed on the back. The morale of his musicians always seems to be good, as well.

"I'm not a taskmaster with them, except about the music," Herman says. "We get along well." His players, most of whom are graduates of the Eastman School of Music in Rochester, New York, are generally in their early '20s. Two exceptions are trumpeter/road manager Bill Byrne and tenor saxist Frank Tiberi, who have been with him since the 1960s. "For the last 50 years," he notes, "all my big bands have been made up of young people. It's just that the coach got very old in the interim."

Herman periodically reunites with past stars of his bands. Sal Nistico may join the big band for dates in Europe or at a jazz festival. Nat Pierce, John Bunch, Al Cohn, Carl Fontana, and Jake Hanna will occasionally get together with him for small-group dates, which may also feature gifted older soloists such as Buddy Tate or Harry "Sweets" Edison. "We always wind up doing things together, different times of the year, and we always look forward to it and have lots of fun. It's as much social as it is music," Herman says.

There's still a bit of the vaudevillian in Herman. He has a sense of showmanship which has rarely been noted in the many write-ups about his band. He might claim he hasn't danced professionally since his youth. But when the band gets cooking, even on a radically modern thing like "Pools," he'll do a kind of dance in place that makes you share in his enthusiasm. When he sings "Caldonia," he's got his own movements that have become part-and-parcel of his performance.

Drummer Dave Miller recalls that as Herman was finishing "Caldonia" on Miller's first night with the band, in 1983, Herman turned around and muttered, "Catch me!" An alarmed Miller got up from his drums and walked around in front, ready to catch the aging bandleader if he should fall. But Herman was in no danger of collapsing. He wanted Miller to "catch him" on the bass drum as he kicked, the way a vaudeville drummer instinctively would have. If the band is coming on strong, Herman will raise both arms skyward. It's a dramatic—and entirely characteristic—Herman pose. It's the way you'll see him on the cover of the recent Concord album, "Live at the Concord Jazz Festival"—and the way you'll see him in a photo from the early '30s, when he was singing with Gus Arnheim's Band.

Herman knows how to set up a number like "I've Got the World on a String," with evocative patter about 52nd Street in the '30s, and Billie Holiday, and Red McKenzie. And how to get extra applause with a thrown-away quip. As his concert comes to a close, the band digs into his theme, the lowdown "Blue Flame." Herman solos on clarinet, then suggests to the audience: "Maybe we can get together again sometime." The people begin to applaud. He adds as an afterthought: "Next time, let's make it at your place," and returns to his clarinet, as laughter joins the growing applause.

Although the big band is Herman's first love, he will periodically take a month or more off to do small group dates in the U.S. or abroad. With six or seven "all-stars," Herman can relax and do all the old tunes from the '30s and '40s he doesn't ordinarily play with the big band these days: "Embraceable You," "These Foolish Things," "Rose Room," and "Basin Street Blues," which his big band played in its very first performance, back in 1936. He gets more of a chance to play moving, low-register melodic stuff on his clarinet. The small groups may not produce sounds as *exciting* as the big band, but they're often more lyrical. It's Herman's chance to unwind, doing the old tunes with old colleagues.

"It gives you a little different feeling," he acknowledges. "It's *good* for me. It's good for my mental attitude. And it's good for me as a human being, you know. These guys are all friends of mine. And we have a joy—we just sit and laugh. A lot of times, we don't really say anything much, you know. There's a warmth there, that's all.

"I do the small group thing because I enjoy it, up to a point." He adds, though, that he doesn't allow himself to "go overboard" as a soloist. "I can't—I don't have enough attributes. I don't have teeth. I don't have that much control of my axe. So I will play as much as I can. But I'll rely then on the next cat, and the next cat, and the next cat. And then when I'm ready to be bailed out, I'll come back in."

In the past year, Herman figures he took off about six or eight weeks simply to relax. And he spent two stretches (each time for more than a month) doing small group work, in New York, and then again in Europe and Australia.

What do the 15 members of his "Thundering Herd" do, when he takes time off to rest or work with a small group?

"They do whatever they can do. I might lose one or two or three, but I don't think any more than that. They're all pretty dedicated, you know." He smiles a shy smile, like he's letting you in on a little secret. "They put up with my shenanigans."

1985-86

Postscript

Woody Herman gave his last public performance on March 24, 1987. On March 26th, complaining of side effects from medication he had taken for altitude sickness, he entered Sinai Hospital in Detroit. His condition deteriorated in the months that followed, due to what was ultimately determined to be congestive heart disease, complicated

Frank Tiberi. (Courtesy of Thomas Cassidy)

by emphysema.

The band continued filling engagements as usual, with reedman Frank Tiberi, a member of the band for 18 years, filling in for Herman. As Herman received reports from old friends that the band still sounded great, he changed his mind about letting the band continue after his death. Woody Herman's Thundering Herd was incorporated, with Herman's daughter at the helm, and Tiberi was officially named the new musical director.

Herman died of cardiopulmonary arrest on October 29, 1987. The Herd's first album recorded without Herman, "Ebony" (featuring Stoltzman on "Ebony Concerto"), was released by RCA in 1988. Their first New York appearance following Herman's death, "A Tribute to Woody" at Carnegie Hall on February 13, 1988, found them playing with their customary vigor. Tiberi, curiously, often evoked Herman physically, with the same slightly-stooped stance, gestures, and manner of speaking.

There is certainly a place for the Woody Herman Orchestra in today's music world. And Herman has structured the band in such a way that it should be able to maintain its musical identity without him. Whether it can be economically viable is another question.

And that is an important question for all lovers of big band sounds. For big bands are expensive to maintain. And in retrospect, the period in which big bands were economically viable—and, for some leaders, highly profitable—seems exceptionally brief.

The road bands that have been most frequently praised by critics in the past decade—the Count Basie Band, the Woody Herman Band, and the Buddy Rich Band—have all had financial problems. Rich died owing money to everyone from the IRS to the bus company his band had used. The Basie Band owes a sizable tax bill today. Herman's financial difficulties weighed upon him for 30 years.

Duke Ellington was able to lead his band for as long as he did because he was using his composer royalties to subsidize the band. The Ellington Band was praised world-wide, and played to packed houses as long as Ellington lived. But it was not, in its later years, economically self-sustaining.

Musicians have continued forming big bands, despite the near-insurmountable economic odds. Clark Terry's West Coast big band, for example, garnered a good deal of critical praise. Today, however, Terry has reluctantly returned to small-group work, now saddled with a sizable bill for back taxes on his big band. McCoy Tyner has put together occasional big bands, and hopes to do more work in the field. He adds that he's had instructive, and cautionary, talks about the difficulties of maintaining a big band, with bandleaders Woody Herman and Maynard

Ferguson. New bands continue to crop up.

There's no sound in the world to equal that of an organized big band. You can't put together a studio group and get them to play with the panache, cohesiveness, and collective sense of identity that a first-rate big band develops from night after night of playing together.

No one expects a symphony orchestra to be a money-making entity. And yet our culture finds ways of ensuring that our great symphonies continue to exist. To this critic, the suggestion offered by Artie Shaw in the beginning of this book makes sense: we should find ways to subsidize the best of the big bands, with government and/or corporate grants, just as we find ways to subsidize symphonies.

It's hard to imagine that happening anytime soon, however. So the future looks questionable. And this critic suspects that we, as a culture, are not going to fully appreciate just how great the big bands of the Count Basies and the Artie Shaws and the Woody Hermans really were, until one day we find that none of those bands are with us.

Bibliography

Balliett, Whitney, *American Musicians: Fifty-six Portraits in Jazz.* N.Y., Oxford University Press, 1986.

Balliett, Whitney, *Jelly Roll, Jabbo and Fats.* N.Y., Oxford University Press, 1983.

Basie, Count (as told to Albert Murray), *Good Morning Blues, The Autobiography of Count Basie.* N.Y., Random House, 1985.

Berger, Morroe, Edward Berger, and James Patrick, *Benny Carter: A Life in American Music.* Metuchen, N.J., The Scarecrow Press and the Institute of Jazz Studies, Rutgers University, 1982.

Bruyninckx, Walter, *Sixty Years of Recorded Jazz, 1917-1977.* Mechelen, Belgium, n.p., 1978.

Carmichael, Hoagy, *The Stardust Road.* N.Y., Greenwood Press, 1969.

Charters, Samuel B. and Leonard Kunstadt, *Jazz: A History of the New York Scene.* N.Y., Da Capo Press, 1981.

Chilton, John, *Who's Who of Jazz, fourth edition.* N.Y., Da Capo Press, 1985.

Clayton, Buck and Nancy Miller Elliott, *Buck Clayton's Jazz World.* N.Y., Oxford University Press, 1987.

Collier, James Lincoln, *Duke Ellington.* N.Y., Oxford University Press, 1987.

Condon, Eddie and Hank O'Neal, *The Eddie Condon Scrapbook of Jazz.* N.Y., St. Martin's Press, 1973.

Dance, Stanley, *The World of Count Basie.* N.Y., Charles Scribner's Sons, 1980.

Dance, Stanley, *The World of Duke Ellington.* N.Y., Charles Scribner's Sons, 1970.

Dance, Stanley, *The World of Earl Hines.* N.Y., Charles Scribner's Sons, 1977.

Dance, Stanley, *The World of Swing.* N.Y., Charles Scribner's Sons, 1974.

DeLong, Thomas A., *Pops: Paul Whiteman, King of Jazz.* Piscataway, N.J., New Century Publishers, 1983.

Driggs, Frank and Harris Lewine, *Black Beauty, White Heat: A Pictorial History of Classic Jazz, 1920-1950.* N.Y., William Morrow and Company, 1982.

Eberly, Philip K., *Music in the Air.* N.Y., Hastings House, 1982.

Ellington, Duke, *Music is My Mistress.* Garden City, N.Y., Doubleday, 1973.

Feather, Leonard, *The Encyclopedia of Jazz.* N.Y., Da Capo Press, 1985.

Feather, Leonard, *From Satchmo to Miles.* Briarcliff Manor, N.Y., Stein and Day, 1972.

Giddins, Gary, *Rhythm-a-ning: Jazz Tradition and Innovation in the '80s.* N.Y., Oxford University Press, 1985.

Giddins, Gary, *Riding on a Blue Note.* N.Y., Oxford University Press, 1981.

Gitler, Ira, *Swing to Bop.* N.Y., Oxford, 1985.

Goodman, Benny, and Irving Kolodin, *The Kingdom of Swing.* N.Y., Frederick Ungar Publishing Company, 1961.

Gourse, Leslie, *Every Day: The Story of Joe Williams.* London, Quartet Books, 1985.

Gourse, Leslie, *Louis' Children: American Jazz Singers.* N.Y., Quill, 1984.

Haskins, Jim, *The Cotton Club.* N.Y., New American Library, 1984.

Holiday, Billie, with William Dufty, *Lady Sings the Blues.* N.Y., Lancer Books, 1969.

Jewell, Derek, *A Portrait of Duke Ellington.* N.Y., W.W. Norton and Company, 1977.

Johnson, Grady, *The Five Pennies.* N.Y., Dell, 1959.

Kaminsky, Max with V.E. Hughes, *My Life in Jazz.* N.Y., Harper and Row, 1963

Keepnews, Orrin and Bill Grauer, Jr., *A Pictorial History of Jazz.* N.Y., Bonanza Books, 1966.

Kimball, Robert and William Bolcom, *Reminiscing with Sissle and Blake.* N.Y., The Viking Press, 1973.

Larkin, Philip, *All What Jazz.* N.Y., Farrar Straus Giroux, 1985.

Lax, Roger and Frederick Smith, *The Great Song Thesaurus.* N.Y., Oxford University Press, 1984.

McCarthy, Albert. *The Dance Band Era.* Radnor, Pennsylvania, Chilton Book Company, 1971.

McPartland, Marian. *All in Good Time.* N.Y., Oxford University Press, 1987.

Manone, Wingy and Paul Vandervoort II, *Trumpet on the Wing.* Garden City, Doubleday, 1948.

Mezzrow, Milton 'Mezz' and Bernard Wolfe, *Really the Blues.* N.Y., Random House, 1946.

Pleasants, Henry, *The Great American Popular Singers.* N.Y., Simon and Schuster, 1974.

Ramsey, Frederick, Jr. and Charles Edward Smith, editors, *Jazzmen.* N.Y., Limelight Editions, 1985.

Rust, Brian, *Jazz Records, 1897-1942.* Chigwell, England, Storyville Publications, 1982.

Sanford, Herb, *Tommy and Jimmy: The Dorsey Years.* N.Y., Da Capo Press, 1980.

Sanjek, Russell, *From Print to Plastic: Publishing and Promoting America's Popular Music (1900-1980).* N.Y., Institute for Studies in American Music, Conservatory of Music, Brooklyn College of the City University of New York, 1983.

Schuller, Gunther, *Early Jazz.* N.Y., Oxford University Press, 1968.

Schuller, Gunther, *Musing.* N.Y., Oxford University Press, 1986.

Shapiro, Nat and Nat Hentoff, editors, *Hear Me Talkin' to Ya.* N.Y., Dover Publications, 1966.

Shapiro, Nat and Nat Hentoff, editors, *The Jazz Makers.* N.Y., Rinehart, 1957.

Shaw, Arnold, *52nd Street: The Street of Jazz.* N.Y., Da Capo Press, 1977.

Shaw, Artie, *The Trouble with Cinderella.* N.Y., Da Capo Press, 1979.

Simon, George T., *The Big Bands.* N.Y., Schirmer Books, 1981.

Simon, George T., *Simon Says: The Sights and Sounds of the Swing Era, 1935-1955.* N.Y., Galahad Books, 1971.

Stearns, Marshall, *The Story of Jazz.* N.Y., Mentor Books, 1958.

Stewart, Rex, *Jazz Masters of the Thirties*. N.Y., Macmillan, 1972.

Stillman, Edmund and Marshall Davidson, *The American Heritage History of the 20's and 30's*. N.Y., American Heritage Publishing Co., Inc., 1970.

Sudhalter, Richard M. and Philip R. Evans, with William Dean-Myatt, *Bix, Man and Legend*. New Rochelle, N.Y., Arlington House, 1974.

Vache, Warren, Sr., *This Horn for Hire: Pee Wee Erwin Talks About His Life in Music*. Metuchen, N.J., The Scarecrow Press and the Institute of Jazz Studies, Rutgers University, 1987.

Walker, Stanley, *The Night Club Era*. N.Y., Blue Ribbon Books, 1933.

Williams, Martin, *Jazz Heritage*. N.Y., Oxford University Press, 1985.

Williams, Martin, *Jazz Masters of New Orleans*. N.Y., Macmillan, 1967.

Acknowledgments

I am greatly indebted to the Institute of Jazz Studies at Rutgers University, its director, Dan Morgenstern, and his associates, Ed Berger and Vincent Pelote. Their generous assistance has been invaluable, and I have drawn upon the Institute's collection of jazz clippings, books, oral histories, and photos. It's hard to imagine a research facility anywhere that is run on a more accessible basis.

I am grateful for the encouragement and advice that has been provided me by jazz authorities Richard Sudhalter and Frank Driggs. This book has been enhanced by rare photos from Driggs' unsurpassed collection, as well as by many sensitive shots taken by Nancy Miller Elliott.

My thanks to the editors of the various publications for which I originally wrote about the musicians in this book: Leslie Johnson of *The Mississippi Rag*, Ira and Glenn Sabin of *Jazz Times*, Art Lange of *Down Beat*, Rick Mattingly and Rick Van Horn of *Modern Drummer*, Ed Shanaphy of *Sheet Music*, Sue Byrom and Clarence Fanto of *The New York Post*, Larry Marscheck of *New Jersey Monthly*, Florence Kooistra of *The Ridgewood News*, Warren Vache Sr. of *Jersey Jazz*, Bill Smith and John Norris of *Coda* (Canada), and Laurie Wright of *Storyville* (Great Britain). Thanks, too, to Peter Levinson, Rebecca Reitz, Linda Yohn, Harriet Wasser, Thomas Cassidy, Abby Hoffer, and Bill Byrne for their aid in lining up interviews and securing photos.

I appreciate the assistance in various ways—clippings, leads on research, records, photos, background information, and more general help—provided by Vince Giordano, Rich Conaty, Stan Hester, Nathan Letts, Lloyd Rausch, Phil Schaap, P. R. Fajen, Alan Roberts, Marilyn Lipsius of RCA, Didier Deutsch of Atlantic Records, Clarence Tripp, Phil Evans, Robert Peller, Will Friedwald, Joe Boughton, and Rob Lindsay. Many thanks to Princeton's Ferris Professor of Journalism Emeritus Irving Dilliard, Lanny Jones, and Chuck Creasy. And to Chris Burchfield, Danny Scott, and Eric Orseck, for their help early on. My appreciation, also, to Joe Franklin—not just for his encouragement in recent years, but for long-ago broadcasts which helped teach a young boy that it was all right to like music that was different from what everybody else seemed to like.

Frank Reuter's copy-editing of this book is greatly appreciated. Frank Joliffe did the proofreading. Mia Ousley and Pioneer Graphics handled typesetting and design. Mark Joly was my agent.

Special thanks to George T. Simon, whose writings have set high standards for all of us who aspire to follow, for his kind preface. This book builds upon the foundation established by the likes of Simon, Stanley Dance, Whitney Balliett, John S. Wilson, Leonard Feather, Otis Ferguson, and Nat Hentoff.

And thanks to the musicians profiled in this book themselves. Some became real friends. I'll particularly miss the gutsy spirit of Maxine Sullivan. We spoke on numerous occasions, but one afternoon she shared recollections at length for the joint benefit of radio host Doug Hall and myself, and I'm grateful to Hall for asking her questions which prompted some recollections in this book. Other musicians, too numerous to list, helped me to set the stories in this book in context. I'll tell the stories of a few of them in *Voices of the Jazz Age*, to be published by University of Illinois Press, and hope to share additional stories in the future. And finally, thanks to my parents, and Art, Deb, and Fa, for many reasons.

"A Room With a View," 23
Aaronson, Irving, 21
"Ac-Cent-Tchu-Ate the Positive," 31
"Aces and Faces," 62
Adams, Pepper, 255, 257
"After You've Gone," 284
Alden, Howard, 68, 69, 70, 324
Alexander, Willard, 10, 245, 249, 265, 282
Ali's Alley, 281, 282
"All Right, OK, You Win," 274
"All the Things You Are," 23
"All Too Soon," 232, 299
Allen, Mose, 104
Allen, Red, 31, 64, 65, 111, 235
"Amapola," 156, 173
"Amen," 340
American Jazz Orchestra, 6
"American Patrol," 128
Ammons, Gene, 329, 347
Amoroso, Johnny, 160
"And the Angels Sing," 321
Anderson, Ernestine, 281
Andrews Sisters, 123
"Annie Laurie," 87, 96
"Any Old Time," 23, 27
Apollo Theater, 42, 59, 107, 127, 236, 237
"Apple Honey," 344
"April in Paris," 254, 271, 273, 274
Arcadia Ballroom, 135, 183
Armstrong, Louis, 4, 5, 6, 10, 11, 12, 21, 22, 47, 49, 53, 63, 64, 65, 71, 90, 92, 94, 103, 106, 111, 112, 114, 115, 129, 132, 133, 134, 139, 140, 146, 147, 153, 155, 163, 166, 172, 176, 180, 204, 252, 319, 320, 327, 329, 331, 337
Arnheim, Gus, 339, 357
"As Long as I Live," 100
"As the Tide was Flowing In," 96
Ashby, Harold, 13, 231-242, 290, 315, 323
Auld, Georgie, 23, 28, 224
Austin, Gene, 180
"Autumn in New York," 158
"Autumn Leaves," 228
Autrey, Herman, 116
"Avenue C," 52
Avery Fisher Hall, 331

"Baby Girl," 58
Bacharach, Burt, 160
"Back Bay Shuffle," 23
Bailey, Buster, 87, 88, 91, 104
Bailey, Mildred, 41, 90
Baker, Harold, 64
Baker, La Vern, 193, 194, 195
Baker, Mickey, 193, 195
Baker, Shorty, 116
Balliett, Whitney, 20, 344
Barker, Danny, 107
Barnet, Charlie, 42, 74, 212, 215, 216, 342, 344
Barrett, Dan, 68, 70, 324
Basie, Count, 3, 6, 7, 10, 12, 13, 33, 51, 52, 53, 55, 56, 57, 59, 60, 60, 61, 63, 68, 70, 72, 73, 94, 109, 116, 127, 141, 142, 153, 169, 176, 212, 215, 234, 243-250, 253-255, 257, 259-268, 270-276, 280-287, 299, 304, 329, 336, 340, 356, 359, 360
"Basin Street Blues," 357
Bauduc, Ray, 215
Bauer, Billy, 343, 344
"Beacon Hill Lavender," 19, 34, 37
"Beale Street Blues," 141
"Beale Street Boogie," 143
Beatles, 160
Bechet, Sidney, 64, 71, 80, 110, 176
Beiderbecke, Bix, 21, 34, 132, 166, 204, 321
"Begin the Beguine," 19, 23, 26, 38
Bell, Aaron, 80
"The Bells of St. Mary's," 158
Bellson, Louis, 9, 116, 127, 153, 161, 162, 313
Belton, C. S., 106
Beneke, Tex, 10, 48, 126, 127, 170
Benjamin Harrison Literary Club, 85, 94
Bennett, Tony, 21, 153, 195, 329
Benskin, Sammy, 176
Benson, Al, 196
Benson, George, 267, 284, 285
Berigan, Bunny, 10, 11, 12, 22, 43, 47, 65, 71, 72, 75, 76, 77, 143, 144, 146, 170, 321, 325
Berle, Milton, 41
Bernie, Ben, 71, 78
Bernstein, Artie, 42
Berry, Chu, 41, 108, 110, 111
"Between the Devil and the Deep Blue Sea," 99, 100
"Beyond the Blue Horizon," 31
"Bijou," 344
"Bill Bailey, Won't You Please Come Home," 302
Birdland, 193, 272, 275, 276, 281, 300
"Birmingham Breakdown," 293
Bishop, Joe, 340
"Bishop's Blues," 340
"Black, Brown, and Beige," 309, 310, 311
Blackhawk Cafe, 106, 121, 141, 213, 215
Blackwell, Otis, 194
Blakey, Art, 286
Blanchard, Terrence, 286
Blanton, Jimmy, 185
Bloom, Ken, 100
Blowers, Johnny, 12, 15, 71-82, 325
"Blowin' Up a Storm," 344
"Blue Balls," 59

"Blue Flame," 340, 357
Blue Note, 34, 35, 260, 261, 275, 276, 282
"Blue Prelude," 340
"Blue Rhythm Fantasy," 107
"The Blue Room," 44
"Blue Serge," 299, 300, 301
"Blue Skies," 42, 87, 91
"Blue Turning Grey Over You," 133
"Blueberry Hill," 71
Bluebird Club, 253
Bluebird Inn, 278
Blues Alley, 96
"Blues Backstage," 273, 283
"Blues in Hoss' Flat," 283
"Blues in the Night," 10, 31, 143, 340
"Blues on Parade," 340
"Body and Soul," 234
Bogart, Humphrey, 351
"Boogie Woogie," 119, 156, 172
Boswell, Connee, 90
"Bouncing with Bean," 111
Bower, Bugs, 160
Bowles, Russell, 104
Bowman, Dave, 75
"Boy Meets Horn," 44
Bradley, Will, 78, 125, 129
Braff, Ruby, 7, 49, 166, 320, 324, 331
Braud, Wellman, 106, 116
Brauner, Buzzy, 149, 153, 167
Brewer, Teresa, 314
Bricktop, 205,
Britton, Frank and Milt, 41
Broadbent, Alan, 348
Brown, Clifford, 64, 187, 320
Brown, Lawrence, 116, 237
Brown, Les, 50, 224
Brown, Ruth, 193
Brown, Walter, 235
Brummel, Al, 78
Brunis, George, 74, 75
Bryant, Willie, 56, 176, 189
"Bugle Call Rag," 44, 125, 146
Bunch, John, 4, 241, 331, 332, 356
Bundl, Rob, 39
Burns, Ralph, 342, 344
Bushkin, Joe, 63
Busse, Henry, 296
Butterfield, Billy, 11, 17, 30, 35, 49, 71, 79, 320
Byas, Don, 234, 329
Byrne, Bill, 356

"C Jam Blues," 232, 299
"Cadillac Taxi," 320
Cafe Society, 103, 108, 109, 115
"Caldonia," 344, 352, 353, 356, 357
"The Calloway Boogie," 189
Calloway, Cab, 12, 84, 166, 176, 189-193, 196, 200, 215
Calloway, Jean, 106
Camarata, Toots, 42
Candoli, Pete, 343, 344
Cantor, Eddie, 79, 180
Cantor, Joe, 21
Cantwell, Bob, 117
Capitol Theater, 126
Capp, Frankie, 68
"Caravan," 72, 76
Carlson, Frank, 340, 341
"The Carioca," 19, 34, 38
Carmichael, Hoagy, 92
Carnegie Hall, 44, 115, 193, 208, 212, 241, 309, 320, 321
Carney, Harry, 231, 232, 289, 291, 303
Carson, Tee, 261, 270
Carter, Benny, 4, 5, 6, 30, 41, 94, 103, 108, 109, 111, 186, 189, 206, 207, 277
Carter, Lou, 325
Casa Loma Band, 22, 24, 25, 182
Cassidy, Tom, 9
Castaldo, Charlie, 131, 145, 168
Castaldo, Lee—*see Castle, Lee*
Castle, Lee, 11, 13, 22, 119, 126, 127, 129-174, 321
Cat Club, 7, 8, 317
Catlett, Sid, 73, 76, 111, 116, 182, 183
Cavallaro, Johnny, 21
Center Theater, 94
Central Plaza, 196
Central Theater, 125
Chaloff, Serge, 346
"Changes," 44
Chaplin, Charles, 203
Chase, Bill, 348
Cheatham, Doc, 83, 84, 97, 103, 117, 319
"Cheatin' on Me," 84
Chester, Gary, 198
"China Boy," 141
"The Chinese Blues," 85
"Chinoiserie," 232, 240
Christian, Charlie, 185, 186
"The Christmas Song," 228
Clarke, Kenny, 186, 187, 188
Clayton, Buck, 7, 12, 51-70, 262, 271, 319, 321, 323
Clooney, Rosemary, 21, 64, 323
"Coasting with Panama," 191
Coates, Don, 83
Cohen, Paul, 53
Cohn, Al, 31, 34, 158, 332, 346, 356
Cohn, Joe, 34
Cohn, Sonny, 249, 255, 262, 263, 264, 265, 271
Cole, Cozy, 76, 191
Cole, Nat King, 92, 224, 252

Coleman, Bill, 63, 64
Coletrane, John, 116, 277, 329
Colombo, Lou, 35
"Concerto for Clarinet," 20
"Concerto for Cootie," 299, 315
Condon, Eddie, 62, 63, 71, 75, 94
"Confessin' the Blues," 235
Connell, Connie, 253
Conniff, Ray, 31, 198
Connors, Chuck, 316
"The Continental," 147
"Contrasts," 172
Coon-Sanders Band, 106, 213
Cooper, Al, 176, 178, 181, 184, 199
Cooper Union, 317
Copacabana, 224, 302
Copland, Aaron, 334
"Corner Pocket," 270
"Cornet Chop Suey," 133
Cosby, Bill, 268
Cotton Club, 92, 108, 296, 304
"Cottontail," 232, 314
Covington, Warren, 48, 156, 157, 158
Crawdaddy Club, 322
Crawford, Jimmy, 42, 104
Crescendo, 275, 276
Crosby, Bing, 10, 47, 153, 204, 215, 228, 339
Crosby, Bob, 10, 22, 47, 137, 170, 215, 219
"Crumbum," 147
Cugat, Xavier, 296
Culley, Wendell, 252
Curtis, Bob, 80
Curtis, King, 195

Dameron, Tadd, 277
Dancer, Earl, 54, 55
"Dancing in the Dark," 37
Daniels, Eddie, 313, 314
"Dark Eyes," 89, 92
"Darling," 339
"Darn That Dream," 94
Davern, Kenny, 71, 82, 321
David, Hal, 160
Davis, Eddie "Lockjaw," 272, 74, 329
Davis, Miles, 208, 252, 259, 266, 286
Davis, Spanky, 178
Davis, Wild Bill, 178, 231, 254
Davison, Wild Bill, 63, 321
"Deep Purple," 23, 172
DeLand, Fred, 74
Deppe, Lois, 85
Dickenson, Vic, 97, 319, 321
"Dinah," 206
"The Dipsy Doodle," 3
Dixon, Eric, 249, 251, 261, 262, 264, 265, 268, 271, 274
Dixon, Willie, 235, 236
"Djangology," 206
"Do Nothing Till You Hear From Me," 293, 299, 314, 315
"Do You Call That a Buddy?," 113
Donahue, Sam, 31, 157, 252
"Don't Be Cruel," 159, 194
"Don't Be That Way," 44
"Don't Get Around Much Anymore," 299, 327
"Don't Take Your Love From Me," 31
Dorham, Kenny, 320
Dorsey, Jane, 156, 157
Dorsey, Jimmy, 3, 10, 13, 41, 42, 47, 48, 53, 72, 74, 123, 129, 135, 136, 142, 146-153, 155-162, 165-167, 169, 172, 173, 204, 243, 296, 299, 325, 340
Dorsey, Julie, 159, 160
Dorsey, "Mom" (Mrs. Thomas F., Sr.), 140, 147, 156, 159
Dorsey, Tommy, 3, 10, 13, 22, 23, 24, 28, 33, 38, 41, 42, 47, 48, 53, 62, 72, 76, 87, 91, 118, 119, 120, 121, 123, 125, 127, 129, 135-139, 141, 142, 147-158, 160-162, 167-170, 172, 173, 204, 212, 219, 220, 221, 224, 225, 243, 277, 296, 299, 304, 320, 326, 340, 342, 344
Dorsey, Thomas F., Sr., 139, 140, 147
"Down Under," 349
Douglas, Tommy, 235
"Down for Double," 52, 60
"Down for the Count," 273
"Drink to Me Only with Thine Eyes," 89
"Drummer's Day," 78
Dunham, Katherine, 305
Dunham, Sonny, 134
Dunn, Johnny, 104
Durham, Eddie, 58, 60, 61

"Early Autumn," 347
"East of the Sun," 143
Eberle, Ray, 217
Eberly, Bob, 153, 158, 224
"Ebony Concerto," 344, 353, 359
Ecklund, Peter, 7
Eckstine, Billy, 272
Eddie Condon's Club, 321, 331, 354
Edison, Harry "Sweets," 61, 107, 252, 319, 356
Eldridge, Roy, 17, 31, 32, 64, 65, 73, 108, 110, 176, 183, 186, 187, 331
Ellington, Duke, 3, 6, 8, 10, 14, 33, 41, 44, 45, 55, 61, 70, 72, 106, 115, 116, 127, 153, 172, 185, 208, 212, 215, 216, 224, 231-241, 243, 244, 249, 252, 255, 256, 276, 288-318, 327, 329, 339, 337, 340, 342, 349, 354, 359
Ellington, Edward, 301
Ellington, Mercer, 14, 62, 176, 288-318

Ellington, Ruth, 289
Elliott, Nancy Miller, 70, 271
Elman, Ziggy, 39, 40, 44, 45, 47, 143, 146, 321
"Embraceable You," 357
"Epistrophy," 334
Erwin, Pee Wee, 44, 48, 49, 78, 81, 135, 138, 139, 163, 320
Etting, Ruth, 90
Evans, Gil, 277
Evans, Herschel, 57, 61, 245
"Everyday (I Have the Blues)," 101, 273, 274

Fagerquist, Don, 31
"Fanfare for the Common Man," 334
Farlow, Tal, 31
Fat Tuesday's, 330
Feather, Leonard, 5, 7, 288
Fedchock, John, 334, 352
Ferguson, Maynard, 11, 70, 360
Ferretti, Andy, 138
"Fiesta in Blue," 53
"Fine and Mellow," 110
Finnegan, Bill, 158, 225
Fisher, Eddie, 80
Fitzgerald, Ella, 41, 47, 71, 88, 89, 90, 91, 94, 97, 106, 109, 153, 186, 228
Fitzpatrick, Leo, 88
"Flamingo," 299
Flanagan, Tommy, 253, 278
Flanigan, Phil, 241, 323, 324, 329, 330, 331, 332
Flory, Chris, 241, 323, 324, 329, 330, 331, 332
"Flying Home," 190
"The Folks Who Live on the Hill," 94
Fontana, Carl, 356
"For All We Know," 327
Foster, Cecilia, 271
Foster, Frank, 13, 14, 251, 254, 255, 267-287
Foster, Pops, 106, 113
"Four Brothers," 346
Fowler, Billy, 106
Francis, Connie, 196
Francis, Panama, 12, 15, 68, 175-200
Freed, Alan, 196
Freeman, Bud, 49, 74, 135, 332
"Frenesi," 29
Fromm, Lou, 31
Frosk, John, 160
"Funky Willie," 178

Gabler, Milt, 110
Garber, Jan, 296
Garland, Joe, 111, 112
Gardner, Ava, 32
Garvey, Marcus, 181
Gastell, Carlos, 219, 224
Gere, Richard, 323
Gershwin, George, 204
Gerun, Tom, 339
"Get Down," 241
"Get Out of Town," 222
Getz, Stan, 346
Gibbs, Georgia, 194
Gibbs, Terry, 347
Gibeling, Howard, 160
Gibson, Dick, 66, 96
Gilford, Jack, 108, 109
Gillespie, Dizzy, 4, 35, 128, 176, 186, 187, 189, 252, 286, 298, 349
Ginsberg, Ben, 22
Giordano, Vince, 7, 36
"The Girl in My Dreams Tries to Look Like You," 298
Giuffre, Jimmy, 346
"Give Me a Kiss to Build a Dream On," 83
Glaser, Joe, 114, 183
Gleason, Jackie, 41, 48, 153
Glen Island Casino, 118, 121, 260, 265
"The Glider," 19
"Gloomy Sunday," 110
Golden Gate, 110, 111
"Golden Wedding," 340
Goldkette, Jean, 21, 41
"Gone with the Wind," 86, 91
Gonsalves, Paul, 231, 237, 239, 290, 329
"The Good Earth," 344
"Good Time Blues," 270
Goode, Mort, 163
Goodman, Benny, 3, 6, 10, 12, 13, 24, 25, 33, 39, 42-50, 59, 70, 72, 75, 76, 88, 90, 94, 115, 120, 125, 127, 129, 132, 137, 140, 144, 145, 146, 159, 161, 166, 169, 172, 182, 212, 215, 231, 234, 241, 319, 320, 321, 325, 331, 332, 340, 342, 349, 353
Goodman, Irving, 44
"The Goof and I," 346
Gordon, Dexter, 64, 277, 279
"Gradations," 37
Gramercy Five, 30, 31, 32
Grand Terrace, 57
Grappelli, Stephane, 13, 15, 201-209
Gray, Jerry, 27, 28, 225
Gray, Wardell, 278, 280
"Green Eyes," 165
Green, Freddie, 58, 59, 60, 61, 141, 249, 250, 264, 270, 283
Green, Jackie, 10
Green, Urbie, 157, 158, 241, 348
Greer, Sonny, 244
Grey, Al, 255
Griffin, Chris, 12, 39-50, 78, 135, 325

Grofe, Ferde, 180
Grusin, Dave, 313
Guarnieri, Johnny, 17, 30
Guillaume, Robert, 305
"Gulley Low Blues," 133
Guy, Joe, 111, 187

Hackett, Bobby, 49, 71, 74, 75, 96, 97, 252, 319, 320, 321
Haggart, Bob, 71, 81, 96, 97, 147
"Half Past Jumping Time," 344
Hall, Al, 107
Hall, Barry Lee, 314, 316
Hall, Edmond, 103, 115
Hall, Herb, 103, 117
Hamilton, Jimmy, 115, 116, 237, 239
Hamilton, Scott, 6, 13, 15, 70, 98, 322, 323, 324, 327-333
Hammond, John, 43, 57, 59, 63, 108, 109, 141, 245
Hampton, Lionel, 10, 47, 57, 70, 78, 79, 153, 199, 262
Hanna, Jake, 324, 332, 348, 353, 356, 356
Hanna, Sir Roland, 292, 293, 313
"Hard-to-Get Gertie," 53
Hardman, Glenn, 141
Harlem, 307, 309
Harlem Blues and Jazz Band, 12, 82, 117
Harlem Opera House, 42
Harris, Barry, 278
Harris, Bill, 343, 344, 348
Harrison, Donald, 284
Hartman, David, 271
"Hawaiian War Chant," 119
Hawkins, Coleman, 6, 12, 64, 65, 103, 110, 111, 206, 234, 327, 329, 337, 338
Hawkins, Erskine, 234, 252
Haymes, Dick, 47, 79, 212, 216, 224
Haymes, Joe, 42, 43, 135, 136, 141, 170
Hayton, Lennie, 27
Heard, J. C., 115
Hefti, Neal, 251, 274, 343, 344
Helbock, Joe, 86
Henderson, Fletcher, 25, 39, 41, 42, 106, 109, 182, 339
Herman, Charlotte, 345
Herman, Ingrid, 345, 359
Herman, Woody, 3, 10, 13, 15, 36, 48, 50, 51, 57, 67, 70, 71, 79, 169, 170, 172, 224, 246, 252, 260, 262, 299, 304, 323, 331, 332, 334-360
"Hey Lawdy Mama," 113
"The Hi De Ho Man (That's Me)," 189
Higginbotham, J. C., 30, 111, 235
"High Society," 183
Hill, Teddy, 176, 185, 187
Himber, Richard, 126, 144
Hines, Earl, 85, 97, 106, 116, 239
Hing, Kenny, 261, 268
Hinton, Milt, 82, 190, 191, 192, 193
Hirshfield, Jeff, 349
Hirt, Al, 314
Hodges, Johnny, 19, 20, 103, 116, 186, 232, 236, 237, 239, 262, 277, 290, 315
Holiday, Billie, 10, 12, 23, 27, 47, 52, 59, 71, 89, 90, 91, 103, 108, 109, 186, 340, 357
Holley, Major, 49
"Honeysuckle Rose," 208
Hopkins, Claude, 41, 182
Horne, Lena, 30, 64, 115, 307
"Hot and Bothered," 293
"Hot Lips," 204
Hotel Pennsylvania, 17, 44
House, Danny, 262, 263, 264
Hubbard, Freddie, 252, 259
Hughes, Bill, 249, 262, 264, 274
Humes, Helen, 94
Hunt, George, 57
Hunt, Pee Wee, 25
Hutchenrider, Clarence, 82
Hutton, Ina Ray, 85
Hyams, Margie, 343, 345

"I Can't Get Started," 232
"I Cover the Waterfront," 26, 110, 113
"I Cried for You," 178
"I Dream of Jeanie with the Light Brown Hair," 89
"I Got a Right to Sing the Blues," 110
"I Got Rhythm," 208
"I Got it Bad and That Ain't Good," 299
"I Hear a Rhapsody," 158, 172
"I Let a Song Go Out of My Heart," 19, 44
"I Never Knew," 138
"I Understand," 158
"If I Had a Ribbon Bow," 89
Igoe, Sonny, 49, 68, 347
"I'll Get By," 179
"I'll Get Mine Bye and Bye," 11, 113
"Ill Wind," 89, 99, 101
"I'm Coming, Virginia," 87, 91
"I'm Forever Blowing Bubbles," 85
"I'm Gonna Sit Right Down and Write Myself a Letter," 100
Imperial Theater, 21
"In a Mellotone," 280, 293, 299
"In the Hall of the Mountain King," 143
"In the Mood," 126
"Indian Love Call," 23
"Indiana," 167
Ingham, Keith, 97
"Interlude in B Flat," 22
"It Happened in Monterey," 172
"It Was a Lover and his Lass," 89
"It's Sand, Man," 60

"It's Wonderful," 89
"I've Got the World on a String," 84, 357

"Jackie Boy," 89
"Jackpot," 62
Jackson, Chubby, 343, 344
Jackson, Cliff, 94
Jackson, Duffy, 264
Jackson, Graham, 105, 106
Jackson, Milt, 28, 347
Jackson, Quentin "Butter," 190
Jacquet, Illinois, 327, 329
James, Harry, 11, 39, 40, 44, 45, 47, 62, 110, 125, 142, 144, 146, 165, 215, 216, 226, 321, 340
Janis, Conrad, 196
Jarvis, Jane, 49
"Jeepers Creepers," 92
Jefferson, Carl, 324, 332, 354
Jefferson, Hilton, 190
Jeffries, Herb, 199
Jenkins, Gordon, 340
Jenney, Jack, 17
"Jim," 110
Jimbo's Bop City, 279
"John Silver," 158, 173
Johnson, Dick, 19, 20, 34, 36, 37
Johnson, Gus, 158, 236
Johnson, Howard, 176
Johnson, Jack, 106, 107
Johnson, Keg, 190
Jolson, Al, 72, 73, 79, 82, 180, 203, 214
Jones, Elvin, 251, 253, 278
Jones, Hank, 31, 251
Jones, Isham, 327, 339, 340, 344
Jones, Jimmy, 239
Jones, Jo, 57, 59, 61, 73, 76, 141, 142, 215, 239
Jones, Jonah, 190, 191, 192, 193
Jones, Lis, 249, 259, 265
Jones, Quincy, 61, 262, 273, 285
Jones, Thad, 14, 15, 161, 247-259, 261, 262, 263, 265, 266, 267, 268, 274, 278, 280, 281, 282
Jones, Thad, Jr., 249, 266, 274, 275
Jordan, Taft, 63, 80, 117
"Josephine," 138
Josephson, Barney, 108, 109, 115
"Jumpin' at the Woodside," 3, 246, 268
"Jumpin' Pumpkins," 298, 300, 301
"June Night," 296
Jurgens, Dick, 296
"Just One of Those Things," 221
"Just Squeeze Me," 232

Kallen, Kitty, 31
Kaminsky, Max, 321
"Kansas City," 159
Kaye, Sammy, 166, 296
Kazebier, Nate, 44
"Keeping Out of Mischief Now," 83, 134
Kelly, George, 181, 182, 184
Kenton, Stan, 10, 219, 224, 349
Kessel, Barney, 31
Keyes, Evelyn, 32
Keyes, Joe, 57
"The Kid from Red Bank," 246
Kincaide, Dean, 147, 155
"Kinda Lonesome," 92
King, B. B., 329
"King Porter Stomp," 42, 146, 321
Kirby, John, 84, 87, 88, 91, 92, 93, 94, 106
Kirk, Andy, 252
Kirkland, Leroy, 193
Klatka, Tony, 348
Klein, Manny, 44
Klink, Al, 99
Kostelanetz, Andre, 86
Kress, Carl, 86
Krupa, Gene, 47, 73, 74, 75, 76, 123, 134, 135, 212, 215, 216, 219, 226
Kunzel, Eric, 311
Kyle, Billy, 89, 91, 107
Kyser, Kay, 125

La Moulin Rouge, 305
La Reuban Bleu, 94
"La Rosita," 146
"La Vie En Rose," 71
LaBelle, Patti, 305, 307
Laine, Frankie, 64
"Lament to Love," 216
Lamond, Don, 31, 344, 346
Lang, Eddie, 204, 205
Laushey, Tim, 173
Lawrence, Doug, 69
Lawson, Yank, 11, 49, 71, 79, 81, 96, 97, 142
Ledonne, Mike, 332
Lee, Barron, 106, 107
Lee, Peggy, 47, 64, 90, 224
Leeman, Cliff, 23, 167, 168
LeGrand, Michel, 208
"Lemon Drop," 347
Leonard, Jack, 47, 170
"Let's Get Together," 179
Levine, Bobby, 49
Levinsky, Walt, 49, 326
Levy, Lou, 313, 314
Lewis, Ed, 58
Lewis, John, 6
Lewis, Mel, 31, 249, 256, 258, 268, 281, 282, 332
Lewis, Ted, 74
Lichter, Joe, 338
Lincoln Center, 317, 321

Linehan, Tommy, 341
"Li'l Darlin'," 274
Lipman, Joe, 22
"Little Brown Jug," 122
"Little John Special," 187
"Little White Lies," 138
"Loch Lomond," 3, 83, 87, 88, 89, 91, 92, 96, 101
Lodice, Don, 170
Loew's State Theater, 107, 127
Logan, Ella, 88
"Lollypop," 347
Lombardo, Guy, 48, 296
"The Loud Minority," 282
"Love Jumped Out," 60
"Love Me a Little," 31
"Lover Man," 71
Lunceford, Jimmie, 6, 10, 42, 104, 212, 216, 225, 252, 276, 277, 340
"Lush Life," 301
Lymon, Frankie, 196
Lynn, Imogene, 31
Lyttelton, Humphrey, 68

McCall, Mary Ann, 340
McCaskell, George, 181
McDonough, Dick, 42
McEachern, Murray, 157
McGarity, Lou, 78, 147, 168
McKee, Paul, 352
McKenna, Dave, 332, 348
McKenzie, Red, 75, 76, 78, 357
McKiney's Cotton Pickers, 72, 106
McKinley, Ray, 10, 73, 76, 125, 126, 129, 143, 147, 173
McPartland, Jimmy, 321
McPhail, Jimmy, 294, 317
McRae, Carmen, 186, 299
McRae, Dave, 194
Mabley, Moms, 107
Mabon, Willie, 235
"Mack the Knife," 284
Mackrel, Dennis, 264, 270, 271
"Make Me a Pallet on the Floor," 180
Mandel, Johnny, 253
Manne, Shelly, 347
"Maria Elena," 156, 158, 172, 296
"Marie," 119, 137, 173
Marmarosa, Dodo, 17, 31, 32
Marsala, Joe, 80, 135
Marsalis, Branford, 313, 314
Marsalis, Ellis, 314
Marsalis, Wynton, 5, 165, 252, 285, 314
Marshall, John, 7
Martin, Freddy, 10
Martin, Tony, 339
Marx, Chico, 210, 218
Masso, George, 167, 323
Mastren, Carmen, 163, 167
May, Billy, 273
Meadowbrook, 121, 137, 148, 219
Meldonian, Dick, 68
Mel-Tones, 31, 219, 220, 221
Mercer, Johnny, 225, 226
Mercy College, 260
Metropole, 187
Michaels, Mike, 22
Michael's Pub, 208, 212, 230
Migliore, Mike, 69
Miller, Dave, 334
Miller, Eddie, 332
Miller, Glenn, 8, 9, 10, 12, 27, 36, 38, 48, 118-128, 129, 140, 141, 161, 169, 170, 172, 212, 217, 225, 289, 296, 312, 316, 336, 340, 356
Millinder, Lucky, 12, 91, 103, 107, 108, 114, 176, 183, 184, 185, 186, 187, 196, 197, 198
Mills Blue Rhythm Band, 106, 107
Mills, Irving, 106
Mince, Johnny, 82, 135, 170
"Minnie the Moocher," 191
Minor, Dan, 58
Minton's Playhouse, 185
"Misunderstood Blues," 283
Mitchell, Grover, 68, 257
Mitchell, Louis, 203
Modern Jazz Quartet, 6
Mole, Miff, 78, 145, 159, 168
Mondello, Toots, 153, 158
Monk, Thelonious, 186, 255, 280, 334
Monroe, Vaughn, 125
"The Mooche," 293
"Mood Indigo," 231, 295, 296
"Moon Mist," 299, 300
Mooney, Art, 48
Mooney, Joe, 42
"Moonglow," 19, 26, 29
"Moonlight Serenade," 122, 230
Moore, Anita, 294, 316
Moore, Bobby, 58
Moore, Freddie, 117, 188, 320
Moore, Gary, 41
Moore, Billy Jr., 225, 316
Morgan, Russ, 296
Morgenstern, Dan, 204
Morehouse, Chauncey, 159
Morrow, Buddy, 157, 166, 221
Morton, Benny, 58, 61, 115
Mosier, Gladys, 85, 86
Moten, Bennie, 245
"Moten Stomp," 58, 158
"Moten Swing," 59
"Muddy River Blues," 141
Mulligan, Gerry, 31, 255, 256, 257
Mundy, Jimmy, 39, 60, 88, 277

"Music, Maestro, Please," 119, 138
"Muskrat Ramble," 84, 183, 340
"Mutiny in the Nursery," 92
"My Blue Heaven," 89
"Mysterioso," 31

Nance, Ray, 315
Napoleon, Marty, 49, 134
Napoleon, Teddy, 134
Navarro, Fats, 187, 320
Nelson, Skip, 217, 218
Nestico, Sammy, 251
"Never No Lament," 299
Newman, Joe, 252, 255, 262, 274
Newton, Frankie, 108, 109
"Nice Work If You Can Get It," 91
Nichols, Red, 21, 22, 72, 337
Nick's, 74, 75, 76
"Night and Day," 89
Night Creature, 255, 307, 309
"Nightmare," 19, 25
Nistico, Sal, 348, 353
Noble, Ray, 326, 356
Noone, Jimmie, 21
Norman, Fred, 178
Norris, Al, 339
"North Beach Breakdown," 349
"Northwest Passage," 344
Norvo, Red, 41, 42, 71, 79, 118, 119, 127, 129

O'Brian, Helen, 43
O'Brien, Larry, 312
O'Connell, Helen, 153, 158, 173
Oddo, John, 352
"Oh Gee, Say Gee, You Ought to See My Gigi, From the Fiji Isles," 337
Oliver, Sy, 42, 62, 71, 80, 143, 199, 225, 277, 299
Olsen, George, 182
"On the Sunny Side of the Street," 173
"One Hundred Years from Today," 84
"One O'Clock Jump," 44, 59, 246, 264
"One to Another," 268
Onyx Club, 21, 86, 87, 91
"Opus One," 173
"Original Dixieland One-Step," 159
"Out of Nowhere," 115

Page, Oren "Hot Lips," 31, 56, 110, 143
Page, Walter, 57, 59, 61, 245
Paige, Patti, 64
Palace Theater, 41
Palladium, 219, 344
Palomar Ballroom, 28, 41, 42
Panassie, Hughes, 116, 205
"Parade of the Milk Bottle Caps," 76, 158
Paramount Theater, 107, 123, 127, 254
Park Central Hotel, 42
Parker, Charlie, 4, 64, 128, 153, 166, 186, 187, 193, 232, 235, 241, 272, 277, 278, 286
Parsons College, 69
Pastor, Tony, 22, 23, 28, 133, 136
"Patricia," 198
Paul, Les, 79
Payne, Sonny, 254, 274
Pearson, Billy, 105
Pennsylvania Hotel, 123
"Perdido," 298, 299, 315, 317
Peress, Maurice, 305, 306, 311
"Personality," 159
Perry, Dick, 160
Peterson, Ralph, Jr., 283
Pettiford, Oscar, 347
Phillips, Flip, 343
Pierce, Nat, 68, 246, 323, 348, 356
Pizzarelli, Bucky, 80, 102, 208, 321
Plaza Hotel, 198
"Please Don't Talk About Me When I'm Gone," 84
Pollack, Ben, 72, 215, 217, 218, 222, 356
Poole, Walter, 256
"Pools," 356
Pope, Bob, 73
"Potato Head Blues," 133
Powell, Bud, 186
Prado, Perez, 198
Pratt, Bobby, 168
"Prelude to a Kiss," 315
"Prelude to a Stomp," 107
Presley, Elvis, 150, 153, 154, 194, 226
"Pretty Peepers," 52
Procope, Russell, 89, 91, 231, 237, 290
Purdy, Bernard, 198
Purtill, Maurice "Moe," 12, 118-128, 163

Quebec, Ike, 329
Queenie Pie, 294, 295, 302, 305, 306, 307, 317
"Quiet Please," 143

Raft, George, 55
"Raggle-Taggle Gypsies," 96
Rainbow Room, 175, 176, 179, 199, 323
Ravinia, 9, 303
Rayman, Morris, 31, 32
"The Red Bank Boogie," 60, 246
Redman, Don, 41, 60, 72, 182, 185
Reese, Della, 302
Reeves, Chick, 341
Reig, Teddy, 193, 257
Reinhardt, Django, 13, 201, 205-208
Reno Club, 56, 68, 245

Rich, Buddy, 23, 51, 70, 76, 127, 141, 143, 146, 153, 167, 169, 170, 215, 220, 221, 222, 224, 228, 230, 304, 359
Richards, Chuck, 114
Richards, Red, 67, 116
Riddle, Nelson, 79
Riggs, Chuck, 323, 324, 329, 330, 331, 332
Riley, Herman, 316
Rivera, Dave, 192
Riverboat, 97
Roach, Max, 187, 188
Roberts, Caughey, 55, 58
"Rock Daniel," 185
Rockefeller Center, 170
"Rockin' Chair," 103, 115
"Rockin' in Rhythm," 310
Rogers, Buddy, 214
"Roll 'Em," 44
Rollini, Adrian, 135, 136
Romero, Caesar, 347
"Rose Room," 26, 37, 357
Roseland Ballroom, 56, 57, 58, 146, 148, 183
"Royal Garden Blues," 340
Royal, Ernie, 345
Royal, Marshall, 263, 274
Rudman, Bill, 100
"Runnin' Wild," 180
Rush, Otis, 235
Russell, Luis, 111
Russell, Pee Wee, 75, 78, 147
Russin, Babe, 170

"St. James Infirmary," 31, 143, 191, 219
"St. Louis Blues," 89, 92, 101, 112, 135
Salim, A. K., 253
"Salt Peanuts," 187
Sandke, Jordan, 7
Sandke, Randy, 7
"Satin Doll," 293
Sauter, Eddie, 31, 34, 42
Savitt, Jan, 71, 78, 125
Savoy Ballroom, 42, 59, 108, 116, 177, 182, 183, 184, 188, 198, 199, 200
"Savoy Blues," 135, 141
Schertzer, Hymie, 78
Schoenberg, Loren, 7, 51, 68, 70
Scott, Raymond, 118, 126
"Scuttlebut," 31
Seaton, Lynn, 270, 283
Selassie, Haile, 239, 240
"Sentimental Gentleman from Georgia," 339
"Sentimental Journey," 179
"Seven Come Eleven," 146
Severinsen, Doc, 9, 158
Shavers, Charlie, 89, 91, 92, 93, 107, 110, 153, 161, 162
Shaw, Artie, 3, 10, 11, 12, 13, 16-28, 46, 48, 71, 109, 120, 125, 133, 135, 136, 137, 138, 143, 144, 147, 166, 170, 172, 212, 215, 216, 222-224, 226, 340, 360
Shearing, George, 206
"The Shekomeko Shuffle," 147
Sheldon, Jack, 321
"Shine," 133, 327
"Shiny Stockings," 246, 250, 267, 273, 274
Shirley, Jimmy, 30
Shore, Dinah, 90, 198
"Shout, Sister, Shout," 185
Signorelli, Frank, 159
Simmons, Norman, 323, 332
Simms, Ginny, 339
Sims, Zoot, 31, 332, 346
Simon, George T., 24, 90, 91, 121, 137, 141, 144, 230, 342, 354
Sinatra, Frank, 41, 47, 49, 71, 79, 80, 82, 129, 142, 143, 153, 154, 155, 166, 210, 212, 219, 228, 267, 268, 284, 329
"Sing, Sing, Sing," 44, 76, 234
Singer, Lou, 91
Singleton, Zutty, 73
"Slammer on D Flat," 315
Slim, Memphis, 235, 236
Small's Paradise, 108
Smith, Bessie, 180
Smith, John
Smith, Mamie, 180
Smith, Stuff, 22, 86, 208
Smith, Tab, 107, 110, 116, 183
Smith, Tatti, 57
Smith, Willie, 21, 277
"Smoothie," 52
"So Rare," 155, 156, 172
"Softly, As in a Morning Sunrise," 19, 20, 34
"Solitude," 293, 294
Soloff, Lew, 314
"Song of India," 88, 119, 137, 173
Soph, Ed, 349, 351
"Sophisticated Lady," 293, 294, 295
Sophisticated Ladies, 303, 304, 305
"Sophisticated Swing," 155
Sosnik, Harry, 339
Spencer, O'Neill, 87, 89, 91, 107
Sperling, Jack, 170
Spivak, Charlie, 140, 144
Stabile, Dick, 123, 156, 252
Stacy, Jess, 47
Stafford, Jo, 79
"Stardust," 19, 20, 29, 30, 35, 36, 37, 165, 211, 228
Statler Hotel, 150, 151, 153, 156
Steele, Julia, 178
Steward, Herbie, 346
Stewart, Rex, 63

Stewart, Slam, 106
Still, William Grant, 29
Stitt, Sonny, 277, 278, 280
"Stolen Sweets," 178
Stoltzman, Richard, 353, 354, 359
Stone, Jesse, 193
"Stop! You're Breaking My Heart," 86
Stordahl, Axel, 79, 155
Storyville, 275, 276
Strand Theater, 127, 190, 192
"Strange Fruit," 103, 109, 110
Stravinsky, Igor, 344, 353
Strayhorn, Billy, 239, 298, 300, 301
"Street of Dreams," 160
"String of Pearls," 126
Stripling, Byron, 262, 263, 264
Struggle's, 83
"Struttin' With Some Barbecue," 320, 324
Stultz, Gene, 22
"Stumbling," 203
Sudhalter, Richard, 52, 53, 61, 81
"Sugarfoot Stomp," 44, 137, 146
Sullivan, Ed, 41, 48, 80
Sullivan, Maxine, 3, 10, 11, 12, 83-102, 199
"Summertime," 19, 26, 31, 34, 38
"Sunrise Serenade," 118, 122
"Sweet Georgia Brown," 167, 206
"Sweet Lorraine," 209
"Sweet Sue—Just You," 119
"Sweethearts on Parade," 112
"Swing That Music," 11
"S'Wonderful," 31

"Take the A Train," 293, 298, 299, 300, 315
"Tangerine," 165, 173
"Taps Miller," 60
Tate, Buddy, 61, 116, 319, 332, 356
Tatum, Art, 116, 204
Taylor, Billy, 106
Taylor, Jimmy, 105
Taylor, Sam "the Man," 190, 191, 194, 195
Teagarden, Jack, 13, 72, 129, 140, 141, 143, 168, 319
"Tears," 206
Terry, Clark, 96, 252, 262, 263, 264, 298, 313, 314, 359
"Thanks for the Beautiful Land on the Delta," 240
Tharpe, Sister Rosetta, 185
"That Old Black Magic," 217, 218
"That's My Home," 112
"That's Right," 347
"Them There Eyes," 110, 208
"There is No Greater Love," 339
"These Foolish Things," 357
"Things Ain't What They Used To Be," 298, 300
"This Love of Mine," 165, 172
"This Time the Dream's On Me," 340
Thornhill, Claude, 10, 31, 50, 86, 87, 88, 91
"Thou Swell," 204
Three Black Kings, 302, 303, 307
Three Deuces, 73
Tiberi, Frank, 356, 358, 359
Tilton, Martha, 88
"The Tin Roof Blues," 119
Tizol, Juan, 298
Torme, Mel, 13, 31, 97, 210-230
"The Touch of Your Hand," 150
Tough, Dave, 31, 73, 75, 76, 121, 342, 343, 344
Town Hall, 281, 309
Trafalgar Seven, 34
Tremaine, Paul, 134
"Trees," 87
Trotman, Lloyd, 194
Trumbauer, Frank, 21, 204
"Try a Little Tenderness," 71
Turner, Lana, 26, 31
Turney, Norris, 67, 117, 231, 290, 313, 315
"Twenty Two Cent Stomp," 315
Tyner, McCoy, 292, 359

"Upright Organ Blues," 141

Vache, Alan, 325
Vache, Jill, 320, 324
Vache, Warren, Jr., 6, 13, 49, 82, 241, 319-326, 329, 331, 332
Vache, Warren, Sr., 49, 319, 325
Valente, Caterina, 268
Vaughan, Sarah, 153, 195, 281, 303
Venuti, Joe, 201, 202, 204, 205, 207, 208
Village Vanguard, 96, 256, 257, 281, 282
Voorhees, Don, 94

Wade, J. D., 22
Waller, Fats, 53, 185, 245
Walters, Teddy, 31
"The Waltz You Saved For Me," 265
Waring, Fred, 41
"Warm Valley," 299
Warren, Earle, 58
Warwick, Carl, 107
Washington, Jack, 57
Waters, Ethel, 54, 90, 104, 180
Waters, Muddy, 329
Watts, Grady, 25
Wayne, Frances, 344
"We Just Couldn't Say Goodbye," 100
"Weary Blues," 340
Weatherford, Teddy, 55

Webb, Chick, 10, 88, 89, 106, 116, 176, 178, 179, 180, 188
Webster, Ben, 6, 232, 234, 235, 236, 241, 259, 280, 314, 327, 329
Webster, Freddy, 64
Wells, Dickie, 58, 61
Wein, George, 324, 351
Weiss, Sammy, 22
Wess, Frank, 251, 254, 255, 267, 274, 285
"West End Blues," 141
West End Cafe, 241, 327
Weston, Paul, 155
Wettling, George, 76, 147, 218
"What is This Thing Called Love?," 223
"What's New?," 158, 164
"What's Your Number?," 60
"When Day is Done," 41
"When My Sugar Walks Down the Street," 107
"When the Saints Go Marching In," 147
"When Your Lover Has Gone," 89
"Whirly Bird," 274
White, Rocky, 316
Whiteman, Paul, 34, 41 , 75, 204
Whiting, Margaret, 79
Whitman Sisters, 104
"Who?," 138
"Who Dat Up Dere?," 340
"Who is Sylvia?," 89
"Who Me?," 280
"Why Shouldn't I?," 323
"Why Was I Born?," 53, 59
Widespread Jazz Orchestra, 7
Wiggins, J. J., 314, 315
Wilber, Bob, 96, 97, 147, 328
Wilde, Cornell, 347
Wilder, Joe, 253, 333
"Wildroot," 344
Wilkins, Ernie, 161, 251, 253, 259, 272
Wilkins, Leroy, 245
Williams, Brad, 352
Williams, Cootie, 64, 262, 289, 290, 291, 299, 303, 314
Williams, Joe, 90, 97, 254, 273, 274
Williams, John, 271, 283
Williams, John, Jr., 11, 12, 67, 103-117
Williams, Midge, 88, 92
Wilson, Chuck, 69
Wilson, Dennis, 251, 264, 265, 271, 283
Wilson, Teddy, 10, 42, 59, 75, 96, 103, 109, 110, 115
Winding, Kai, 31
Witherspoon, Jimmy, 199, 235
Wolf Trap, 9, 311
Wood, Booty, 231, 241, 316
"Woodchopper's Ball," 340, 351
Woodman, Britt, 313, 316
Woods, Chris, 263, 264
Woodward, Aaron, 246, 249, 250, 266
Woodyard, Sam, 237, 241
Wylie, Austin, 21

"Yearning," 138
"Yellow Submarine," 160
"Yes Sir, That's My Baby," 107
"Yesterdays," 110
"You Been a Good Old Wagon, Daddy, But You Done Broke Down," 180
"You Gave Me Everything But Love," 101
"You Got It," 270
Yoder, Walter, 341
Young, Lester, 56, 57, 59, 61, 141, 234, 241, 245, 279, 329
Young, Snooky, 252, 254, 257, 262, 263, 274, 278
Young, Trummy, 66
"You're Driving Me Crazy," 213, 214
"You're a Sweet Little Headache," 27

Zarchy, Zeke, 44, 135, 170

About the Author

The late Maxine Sullivan called Chip Deffaa "the best thing that ever happened to *The New York Post*." TV talk-show host Joe Franklin calls him "our favorite jazz critic."

Deffaa's spunky jazz reviews and interviews are must reading for numerous buyers of *The Post*. British jazz fans know him from his critiques in *Crescendo*. He's also written for such publications as *Down Beat*, *Jazz Times*, *Modern Drummer*, *Sheet Music*, *New Woman*, *The Mississippi Rag*, *Avenue*, *New Jersey Monthly*, *The Princeton Alumni Weekly*, *Keyboard*, *The Philadelphia Inquirer*, England's *Storyville*, and Canada's *Coda*. He contributed to the landmark *New Grove Dictionary of Jazz*—and has even managed to sneak a few jazz references into non-jazz books to which he's contributed, such as *Roaring at 100* and *Fantasies Forever*.

At Princeton University, Deffaa was a student of the distinguished Ferris Professor of Journalism Irving Dilliard. He is a trustee of *The Princeton Tiger Magazine* today.